Techniques for Searching, Parsing, and Matching

Alberto Pettorossi

Techniques for Searching, Parsing, and Matching

 Springer

Alberto Pettorossi
DICII
University of Rome "Tor Vergata"
Rome, Italy

ISBN 978-3-030-63191-8   ISBN 978-3-030-63189-5   (eBook)
https://doi.org/10.1007/978-3-030-63189-5

This Springer imprint is published by the registered company Springer Nature Switzerland AG
The registered company address is: Gewerbestrasse 11, 6330 Cham, Switzerland

Preface

In this book we present some techniques for exploring trees and graphs. We illustrate the linear search technique and the backtracking technique, and as instances of tree exploration methods, we present various algorithms for parsing subclasses of context-free languages. They include: (i) the chop-and-expand parsers for $LL(k)$ languages, (ii) the shift-and-reduce parsers for $LR(k)$ languages and, among them, the $LR(0)$, the $SLR(1)$, the $LR(1)$, and the $LALR(1)$, and (iii) the operator-precedence parsers. We illustrate the use of the parser generators Bison and Yacc, and the lexical analyzer generator Flex.

We also illustrate some tree exploration and manipulation methods by presenting algorithms for visiting trees, evaluating boolean expressions, proving propositional formulas, and encoding trees. We consider the minimal spanning tree problem in undirected graphs and the shortest path problem in directed graphs. For the latter problem we present the solutions based on boolean matrix multiplication, semirings, and dynamic programming.

Finally, we consider the pattern-matching problem and we analyze the Knuth-Morris-Pratt algorithm. In Chapter 10 we present some parsing programs written in Prolog, and we briefly recall some decidability results concerning the $LL(k)$ languages and the $LR(k)$ languages.

This book was written for a course on Automata, Languages, and Translators, taught at the University of Rome "Tor Vergata". We assume that the reader is familiar with the basic notions of Automata Theory and Formal Languages.

Some of the algorithms we have presented are written in Java 1.5 and some others in Prolog. For the Java language the reader may refer to the Java Tutorial at `http://java.sun.com/docs/books/tutorial/`. All Java programs have been compiled using the Java compiler 1.8.0_25 running under Mac OS X 10.15.4 Darwin 19.4.0. For the Prolog language the reader may refer to `http://lpn.swi-prolog.org/`. The Prolog language incorporates a backtracking mechanism that can be used for exploring search spaces and solving parsing and matching problems.

I am grateful to Professor Leslie Valiant for teaching me some of the techniques presented in Chapter 8 while I was a student at the University of Edinburgh in 1979.

Many thanks to my colleagues of the Department of Civil Engineering and Informatics of the University of Rome "Tor Vergata" and the IASI Institute of the National Research Council of Italy. I am also grateful to all my students and co-workers, and in particular to Lorenzo Clemente, Emanuele De Angelis, Corrado Di Pietro, Fabio Fioravanti, Fulvio Forni, Fabio Lecca, Maurizio Proietti, and Valerio Senni for their support and encouragement.

My warmest thanks go also to my student Alessandro Cacciotti for building a tool for the manipulation of context-free grammars and the construction of $LR(1)$ and $LALR(1)$ parsers. That tool was very useful for checking many of the parsing examples presented in the book.

Thanks also to Mr. Ronan Nugent of Springer for his most appreciated cooperation and help.

Previous editions of this book were published by the Aracne Publishing Company, Ariccia (RM), Italy.

Roma, October 2021   Alberto Pettorossi

Contents

CHAPTER 1

Preliminary Definitions on Languages and Grammars

In this chapter we recall some preliminary definitions of formal languages. Let us consider a countable set V of elements, called *symbols*. The set V is also called the *alphabet*.

1.1. Free Monoids and Languages

The *free monoid over* (or *generated by*) the set V is the set V^* consisting of all finite sequences of symbols in V, that is,

$V^* = \{v_1 \ldots v_n \mid n \geq 0 \text{ and for each } 0 \leq i \leq n,\ v_i \in V\}$.

The unary operation $*$ (pronounced 'star') is called the *Kleene closure*, or the $*$ *closure* (pronounced 'the star closure'). Sequences of symbols are also called *words* or *strings*. The *length* of a sequence $w = v_1 \ldots v_n$, where for $i = 1, \ldots, n$, $v_i \in V$, is n. The length of w is also denoted $|w|$. The sequence of length 0 is called the *empty sequence* (or the *empty word*, or the *empty string*) and it is denoted by ε. For all $w \in V^*$, for all $a \in V$, the number of occurrences of the symbol a in the word w is denoted by $|w|_a$.

Given two sequences w_1 and w_2 in V^* their *concatenation*, denoted $w_1 \cdot w_2$ or $w_1 w_2$, is the sequence in V^* defined by recursion on the length of w_1 as follows:

$\begin{array}{ll} w_2 & \text{if } w_1 = \varepsilon \\ v_1((v_2 \ldots v_n) \cdot w_2) & \text{if } w_1 = v_1 v_2 \ldots v_n, \text{ for some symbols } v_1 v_2 \ldots v_n, \text{ with } n > 0. \end{array}$

We have that the length of $w_1 \cdot w_2$ is the length of w_1 plus the length of w_2. Concatenation is an associative binary operation on V^* whose neutral element is the empty sequence.

Any set of sequences which is a subset of V^* is called a *language* (or a *formal language*) over the alphabet V.

Given two languages A and B, their *concatenation*, denoted $A \cdot B$ or simply $A B$, is defined as follows:

$A \cdot B = \{w_1 \cdot w_2 \mid w_1 \in A \text{ and } w_2 \in B\}$.

Concatenation of languages is associative and its neutral element is the singleton $\{\varepsilon\}$ (recall that a set with one element only is called a singleton). For reasons of simplicity, when A is a singleton, say $\{w\}$, the concatenation $A \cdot B$ will also be written as $w \cdot B$ or simply $w B$. Analogously for B, instead of A.

We have that: $V^* = V^0 \cup V^1 \cup V^2 \cup \ldots \cup V^k \cup \ldots$, where for each $i \geq 0$, V^k is the set of all sequences of length k of symbols in V, that is, for each $k \geq 0$,

$V^k = \{v_1 \ldots v_k \mid \text{for } i = 1, \ldots, k,\ v_i \in V\}$.

Obviously, $V^0 = \{\varepsilon\}$, $V^1 = V$, and for $i, j \geq 0$, $V^i \cdot V^j = V^j \cdot V^i = V^{i+j}$. By V^+ we denote $V^* - \{\varepsilon\}$. The unary operation $^+$ (pronounced 'plus') is also called the *positive closure*, or the $^+$ *closure* (pronounced 'the plus closure').

© Springer Nature Switzerland AG 2021
A. Pettorossi, *Techniques for Searching, Parsing, and Matching*, https://doi.org/10.1007/978-3-030-63189-5_1

1

The set $V^0 \cup V^1$ is also denoted by $V^{0,1}$.

Given an element a in a set V,

(i) a^* denotes the set of all *finite* sequence of zero or more a's (thus, a^* is an abbreviation for $\{a\}^*$),

(ii) a^+ denotes the set of all *finite* sequence of one or more a's (thus, a^+ is an abbreviation for $\{a\}^+$),

(iii) $a^{0,1}$ denotes the set $\{\varepsilon, a\}$ (thus, $a^{0,1}$ is an abbreviation for $\{a\}^{0,1}$), and

(iv) a^ω denotes the *infinite* sequence made out of all a's.

Given a word w, for any $k \geq 0$, the *prefix of w of length k*, denoted $\underline{w}_k$, is defined as follows:

$$\underline{w}_k = \begin{cases} w & \text{if } 0 \leq |w| \leq k \\ u & \text{if } w = uv \text{ for some } u, v \in V^*, \text{ and } |u| = k. \end{cases}$$

In particular, for any w, we have that: $\underline{w}_0 = \varepsilon$ and $\underline{w}_{|w|} = w$.

From now on, unless otherwise specified, when referring to an alphabet, we will assume that it is a *finite* set of symbols.

1.2. Formal Grammars

Let us begin by recalling the following notions. For other notions of automata theory and formal language theory the reader may refer to [**10, 21**].

DEFINITION 1.2.1. [**Formal Grammar**] A *formal grammar* (or a *type 0 grammar*, or a *grammar*, for short) is a 4-tuple $\langle V_T, V_N, P, S \rangle$, where:

(i) V_T is a finite set of symbols, called *terminal symbols*,

(ii) V_N is a finite set of symbols, called *nonterminal symbols* or *variables*, such that $V_T \cap V_N = \emptyset$,

(iii) P is a *finite* set of pairs of strings, called *productions* (or *type 0 productions*), each pair $\langle \alpha, \beta \rangle$ being denoted by $\alpha \to \beta$, where $\alpha \in (V_T \cup V_N)^+$ and $\beta \in (V_T \cup V_N)^*$, and

(iv) S is an element of V_N, called *axiom* or *start symbol*.

The set V_T is called the *terminal alphabet*. The set V_N is called the *nonterminal alphabet*. The set $V = V_T \cup V_N$ is called the *alphabet* of the grammar. In a production $\alpha \to \beta$, α is called the *left hand side* (*lhs*, for short) and β is called the *right hand side* (*rhs*, for short).

Given a grammar $G = \langle V_T, V_N, P, S \rangle$ we may define a set of elements in V_T^*, called the *language generated by G*, as we now indicate.

Let us first introduce the binary relation $\to_G \subseteq V^* \times V^*$ which is defined as follows: for every sequence $\alpha \in V^+$ and every sequence β, γ, and δ in V^*,

$\gamma \alpha \delta \to_G \gamma \beta \delta$ iff there exists a production $\alpha \to \beta$ in P.

For any $k \geq 0$, the k-fold composition of the relation $\to_G$ is denoted $\to_G^k$. Thus, for instance, for every sequence $\sigma_0 \in V^+$ and every sequence $\sigma_2 \in V^*$, we have that:

$\sigma_0 \to_G^2 \sigma_2$ iff there exists $\sigma_1 \in V^+$ such that $\sigma_0 \to_G \sigma_1$ and $\sigma_1 \to_G \sigma_2$.

The transitive closure of $\to_G$ is denoted $\to_G^+$. The reflexive, transitive closure of $\to_G$ is denoted $\to_G^*$. When the grammar G is understood from the context, we will feel free to omit the subscript G, and instead of writing $\to_G$, $\to_G^k$, $\to_G^+$, and $\to_G^*$, we will simply write $\to$, $\to^k$, $\to^+$, and $\to^*$, respectively.

DEFINITION 1.2.2. [**Language Generated by a Grammar. Equivalence Between Grammars**] Given a grammar $G = \langle V_T, V_N, P, S \rangle$, the *language generated by G*, denoted $L(G)$, is the set

$$L(G) = \{w \mid w \in V_T^* \text{ and } S \to_G^* w\}.$$

The elements of the language $L(G)$ are said to be the *words* or the *strings* generated by the grammar G.

A grammar $G1$ is said to be *equivalent* to a grammar $G2$ iff $L(G1) = L(G2)$.

A language generated by a type 0 grammar is said to be a *type 0 language*. For productions, grammars, and languages, the term 'unrestricted' is often used instead of the term 'type 0'.

DEFINITION 1.2.3. [**Language Generated by a Nonterminal Symbol of a Grammar**] Given a grammar $G = \langle V_T, V_N, P, S \rangle$, the language generated by the nonterminal $A \in V_N$, denoted $L_G(A)$, is the set

$$L_G(A) = \{w \mid w \in V_T^* \text{ and } A \to_G^* w\}.$$

We will write $L(A)$, instead of $L_G(A)$, when the grammar G is understood from the context.

DEFINITION 1.2.4. [**Type 1, Context-Sensitive, Type 2, and Type 3 Production**] (1) Given a grammar $G = \langle V_T, V_N, P, S \rangle$ we say that a production is of *type 1* iff (1.1) *either* it is of the form $\alpha \to \beta$, where $\alpha \in (V_T \cup V_N)^+$, $\beta \in (V_T \cup V_N)^+$, and $|\alpha| \leq |\beta|$, *or* it is $S \to \varepsilon$, and (1.2) if the production $S \to \varepsilon$ is in P, then the axiom S does *not* occur on the right hand side of any production.

(cs) Given a grammar $\langle V_T, V_N, P, S \rangle$, we say that a production in P is *context-sensitive* iff (cs.1) *either* it is of the form $u A v \to u w v$, where $u, v \in V^*$, $A \in V_N$, and $w \in (V_T \cup V_N)^+$, *or* it is $S \to \varepsilon$, and (cs.2) if the production $S \to \varepsilon$ is in P, then the axiom S does *not* occur on the right hand side of any production.

(2) Given a grammar $G = \langle V_T, V_N, P, S \rangle$ we say that a production in P is of *type 2* (or *context-free*) iff it is of the form $\alpha \to \beta$, where $\alpha \in V_N$ and $\beta \in V^*$.

(3) Given a grammar $G = \langle V_T, V_N, P, S \rangle$ we say that a production in P is of *type 3* (or *regular*, or *right linear*) iff it is of the form $\alpha \to \beta$, where $\alpha \in V_N$ and $\beta \in V_T V_N \cup V_T \cup \{\varepsilon\}$.

DEFINITION 1.2.5. [**Type 1, Context-Sensitive, Type 2, and Type 3 Grammar and Language**] A grammar is of type 1, context-sensitive, of type 2 (or context-free), and of type 3 (or regular, or right linear) iff all its productions are of type 1, context-sensitive, of type 2, and of type 3, respectively.

A type 1, context-sensitive, type 2 (or context-free), and type 3 (or regular or right linear) language is the language generated by a type 1, context-sensitive, type 2, and type 3 grammar, respectively.

One can show that for each type 1 grammar there exists an equivalent context-sensitive grammar, and vice versa. Thus, the notions of type 1 and context-sensitive languages coincide. For this reason, instead of saying 'a language of type 1', we will also say 'a context-sensitive language' and vice versa.

One can also show that for each type 3 (or regular, or right linear) grammar there exists an equivalent grammar whose productions are all of the form $\alpha \to \beta$, where $\alpha \in V_N$ and $\beta \in V_N V_T \cup V_T \cup \{\varepsilon\}$. These grammars are said to be *left linear* grammars.

Given a grammar $G = \langle V_T, V_N, P, S \rangle$, an element of V^* is called a *sentential form* of G.

The following fact is an immediate consequence of the definitions.

FACT 1.2.6. Given a grammar $G = \langle V_T, V_N, P, S \rangle$ and a word $w \in V_T^*$, we have that w belongs to $L(G)$ iff there exists a sequence $\langle \alpha_1, \ldots, \alpha_n \rangle$ of $n \, (> 1)$ sentential forms such that:

(i) $\alpha_1 = S$,

(ii) for every $i = 1, \ldots, n-1$, there exist $\gamma, \delta \in V^*$ such that $\alpha_i = \gamma \alpha \delta$, $\alpha_{i+1} = \gamma \beta \delta$, and $\alpha \to \beta$ is a production in P, and

(iii) $\alpha_n = w$.

Let us now introduce the following concepts.

DEFINITION 1.2.7. [**Derivation of a Word and Derivation of a Sentential Form**] Given a grammar $G = \langle V_T, V_N, P, S \rangle$ and a word $w \in V_T^*$ in $L(G)$, any sequence $\langle \alpha_1, \alpha_2, \ldots, \alpha_{n-1}, \alpha_n \rangle$ of $n \, (> 1)$ sentential forms satisfying Conditions (i), (ii), and (iii) of Fact 1.2.6 above, is called a *derivation of the word* w from S in the grammar G. A derivation $\langle S, \alpha_2, \ldots, \alpha_{n-1}, w \rangle$ is also written as:

$$S \to \alpha_2 \to \ldots \to \alpha_{n-1} \to w.$$

If there is a derivation from S to w, we have that $S \to^+ w$ and $S \to^* w$.

A *derivation of a sentential form* $\varphi \in V^*$ from S in the grammar G is any sequence $\langle \alpha_1, \alpha_2, \ldots, \alpha_{n-1}, \alpha_n \rangle$ of $n \, (\geq 1)$ sentential forms such that Conditions (i) and (ii) of Fact 1.2.6 hold and $\alpha_n = \varphi$. That derivation is also written as:

$$S \to \alpha_2 \to \ldots \to \alpha_{n-1} \to \varphi.$$

If there is a derivation from S to φ, we have that $S \to^* \varphi$.

DEFINITION 1.2.8. [**Derivation Step**] Given a derivation $\langle \alpha_1, \ldots, \alpha_n \rangle$ of $n \, (\geq 1)$ sentential forms, for any $i = 1, \ldots, n-1$, the pair $\langle \alpha_i, \alpha_{i+1} \rangle$ is called a *derivation step* from α_i to α_{i+1} (or a *rewriting step* from α_i to α_{i+1}). A derivation step $\langle \alpha_i, \alpha_{i+1} \rangle$ is also denoted by $\alpha_i \to \alpha_{i+1}$.

Given a sentential form $\gamma \alpha \delta$ for some $\gamma, \delta \in V^*$ and $\alpha \in V^+$, if we apply the production $\alpha \to \beta$, we perform the derivation step $\gamma \alpha \delta \to \gamma \beta \delta$.

Given a context-free grammar G and a word w, a derivation $\alpha_0 \to \alpha_1 \to \ldots \to \alpha_n$ in G, where $\alpha_0 = S$ and $\alpha_n = w$, is said to be a *leftmost derivation* of w from S iff for $i = 0, \ldots, n-1$, in the derivation step $\alpha_i \to \alpha_{i+1}$ the sentential form α_{i+1} is obtained from the sentential form α_i by replacing the leftmost nonterminal symbol occurring in α_i. A derivation step $\alpha_i \to \alpha_{i+1}$ in which we get the sentential form α_{i+1} by replacing the leftmost nonterminal symbol in α_i, is also denoted by $\alpha_i \to_{lm} \alpha_{i+1}$ (the subscript *lm* stands for *leftmost*).

Analogous definitions are assumed by replacing the word 'leftmost' by the word 'rightmost'. In particular, a *rightmost derivation* is a derivation where at each step we replace the rightmost nonterminal symbol of the sentential form at hand. A rightmost derivation step is usually denoted by $\rightarrow_{rm}$ (the subscript rm stands for *rightmost*).

EXAMPLE 1.2.9. Let us consider the grammar with axiom E and whose productions are:

$$E \rightarrow E + T$$
$$E \rightarrow T$$
$$T \rightarrow T \times F$$
$$T \rightarrow F$$
$$F \rightarrow (E)$$
$$F \rightarrow a$$

Let us also consider the following three derivations $D1$, $D2$, and $D3$, where for each derivation step $\alpha_i \rightarrow \alpha_{i+1}$, we have underlined in the sentential form α_i the nonterminal symbol which is replaced in that step:

$D1: \underline{E} \rightarrow_{lm} \underline{E} + T \rightarrow_{lm} \underline{T} + T \rightarrow_{lm} \underline{F} + T \rightarrow_{lm} a + \underline{T} \rightarrow_{lm} a + \underline{F} \rightarrow_{lm} a + a$

$D2: \underline{E} \rightarrow_{rm} E + \underline{T} \rightarrow_{rm} E + \underline{F} \rightarrow_{rm} \underline{E} + a \rightarrow_{rm} \underline{T} + a \rightarrow_{rm} \underline{F} + a \rightarrow_{rm} a + a$

$D3: \underline{E} \rightarrow_{lm} E + \underline{T} \rightarrow_{rm} \underline{E} + F \rightarrow_{lm} T + \underline{F} \rightarrow_{rm} \underline{T} + a \rightarrow_{lm} \underline{F} + a \rightarrow_{lm} a + a$

We have that:
derivation $D1$ is a leftmost derivation,
derivation $D2$ is a rightmost derivation, and
derivation $D3$ is neither a rightmost nor a leftmost derivation. $\qquad\square$

THEOREM 1.2.10. Given a context-free grammar G, for every word $w \in L(G)$ there exists a leftmost derivation of w and a rightmost derivation of w.

PROOF. By structural induction on the derivation tree of w. $\qquad\square$

For context-free grammars we can associate a *derivation tree*, also called a *parse tree*, with every derivation of a word w from the axiom S.

Given a context-free grammar $G = \langle V_T, V_N, P, S \rangle$ and a derivation of a word w from the axiom S, that is, a sequence $\alpha_1 \rightarrow \alpha_2 \rightarrow \ldots \rightarrow \alpha_n$ of $n\,(> 1)$ sentential forms such that $\alpha_1 = S$ and $\alpha_n = w$ (see Definition 1.2.7 on page 4), the corresponding derivation tree T is constructed by applying the following two rules.

Derivation Tree Rule (1). The root of T is a node labeled by S.

Derivation Tree Rule (2). For $i = 1, \ldots, n-1$, we consider in the given derivation

$$\alpha_1 \rightarrow \alpha_2 \rightarrow \ldots \rightarrow \alpha_n$$

the i-th derivation step $\alpha_i \rightarrow \alpha_{i+1}$. Let us assume that in the i-th derivation step we have applied the production $A \rightarrow \beta$, where:

(i) $A \in V_N$,

(ii) $\beta = c_1 \ldots c_k$, for some $k \geq 0$, and

(iii) for $j = 1, \ldots, k$, we have that $c_j \in V_N \cup V_T$.

Thus, $\alpha_i = \gamma A \delta$ and $\alpha_{i+1} = \gamma \beta \delta$ for some γ and δ in $(V_T \cup V_N)^*$. In the derivation tree constructed so far, we consider the leaf node, say ℓ_i, labeled by the symbol A which is replaced by β in that derivation step. That node ℓ_i is identified by the fact that γ is the left-to-right concatenation of the labels of the leaves to the left of ℓ_i in the derivation tree constructed so far.

If $k \geq 1$, then we generate k son nodes of the node ℓ_i and they will be labeled, from left to right, by $c_1, \ldots, c_k$, respectively. (Obviously, after the generation of these k son nodes, the leaf node ℓ_i will no longer be a leaf node and will become an internal node of the new derivation tree.)

If $k=0$, then we generate one son node of the node ℓ_i. The label of that new node will be the empty word ε.

We have that at the end of the application of Rule 2 the left-to-right concatenation of the labels of all the leaves of the resulting derivation tree T is the word w.

The word w is said to be the *yield* of the derivation tree T.

EXAMPLE 1.2.11. Let us consider the grammar with axiom S and whose productions are:

$S \to a A S$

$S \to a$

$A \to S b A$

$A \to b a$

$A \to S S$

Let us also consider the following derivation D of the word $a\,a\,b\,b\,a\,a$:

$$D: \quad \underline{S} \to a \underline{A} S \to a \underline{S} b A S \to a a b \underline{A} S \to a a b b a \underline{S} \to a a b b a a$$
$$\quad (1) \qquad (2) \qquad (3) \qquad\qquad (4) \qquad\qquad (5)$$

where in each sentential form α_i we have underlined the nonterminal symbol which is replaced in the derivation step $\alpha_i \to \alpha_{i+1}$. The corresponding derivation tree is depicted in Figure 1.2.1 on the facing page. In the derivation D the numbers below the underlined nonterminal symbols denote the correspondence between the derivation steps and the nodes with the same number in the derivation tree of Figure 1.2.1. $\square$

Now let us introduce the following definitions.

DEFINITION 1.2.12. [**Unfold of a Context-Free Production**] Let us consider a context-free grammar $G = \langle V_T, V_N, P, S \rangle$. Let A and B be elements of V_N and $\alpha, \beta_1, \ldots, \beta_n, \gamma$ be elements of $(V_T \cup V_N)^*$. Let $A \to \alpha B \gamma$ be a production in P, and $B \to \beta_1 \mid \ldots \mid \beta_n$, for $n \geq 0$, be *all* the productions in P whose left hand side is B.

The *unfolding of B in $A \to \alpha B \gamma$ with respect to P* (or the *unfolding of B in $A \to \alpha B \gamma$ by using P*, or simply, the *unfolding of B in $A \to \alpha B \gamma$*) is the replacement of the production:

$A \to \alpha B \gamma$

by the n productions:

$A \to \alpha \beta_1 \gamma \qquad \cdots \qquad A \to \alpha \beta_n \gamma$

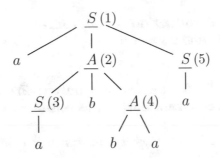

FIGURE 1.2.1. A derivation tree for the word $a\,a\,b\,b\,a\,a$ and the grammar given in Example 1.2.11 on the preceding page. This tree corresponds to the derivation $D:\ \underline{S} \to a\underline{A}S \to a\underline{S}bAS \to aab\underline{A}S \to aabba\underline{S} \to aabbaa$. The numbers, from (1) to (5), associated with the nonterminal symbols in the nodes of the tree, denote the correspondence between the nonterminal symbols and the five derivation steps of D.

DEFINITION 1.2.13. [**Fold of a Context-Free Production**] Let us consider a context-free grammar $G = \langle V_T, V_N, P, S\rangle$. Let A and B be elements of V_N and $\alpha, \beta_1, \ldots, \beta_n, \gamma$ be elements of $(V_T \cup V_N)^*$. Let $A \to \alpha\beta_1\gamma \mid \ldots \mid \alpha\beta_n\gamma$, for $n \geq 1$, be *some* productions in P whose left hand side is A, and $B \to \beta_1 \mid \ldots \mid \beta_n$ be *all* the productions in P whose left hand side is B.

The *folding of* $\beta_1, \ldots, \beta_n$ *in* $A \to \alpha\beta_1\gamma \mid \ldots \mid \alpha\beta_n\gamma$ *with respect to* P (or simply, the *folding of* $\beta_1, \ldots, \beta_n$ *in* $A \to \alpha\beta_1\gamma \mid \ldots \mid \alpha\beta_n\gamma$) is the replacement of the n productions: $A \to \alpha\beta_1\gamma \mid \ldots \mid \alpha\beta_n\gamma$ by the production: $A \to \alpha B\gamma$.

DEFINITION 1.2.14. [**Useful Symbol and Useless Symbol**] Given a context-free grammar $G = \langle V_T, V_N, P, S\rangle$ a symbol $X \in V_T \cup V_N$ is *useful* iff $S \to_G^* \alpha X\beta \to_G^* w$ for some $\alpha, \beta \in (V_T \cup V_N)^*$ and $w \in V_T^*$. A symbol is *useless* iff it is not useful.

DEFINITION 1.2.15. [**Reduced Grammar**] [**24**, page 130] A context-free grammar is said to be *reduced* if it has no useless symbols.

Hypothesis of Reduced Grammars and Absence of Trivial Unit Productions. In what follows, unless otherwise specified, we assume that:
(i) all grammars are *reduced* (that is, without useless symbols), and
(ii) in every production the right hand side is different from the left hand side.

In particular, for context-free grammars we assume that there are *no trivial unit productions*, that is, for all nonterminal symbols A, there is no production of the form $A \to A$.

DEFINITION 1.2.16. [**Epsilon Production**] A production $\alpha \to \beta$ is said to be an *epsilon production*, also written ε-production, iff β is the empty word ε.

DEFINITION 1.2.17. [**Nullable Symbol**] Given a context-free grammar G, we say that a nonterminal symbol A is *nullable* iff $A \to_G^* \varepsilon$.

DEFINITION 1.2.18. [**Production for a Nonterminal Symbol**] A production of the form $A \to \beta$, with $A \in V_N$ and $\beta \in (V_T \cup V_N)^*$, is said to be *a production for the nonterminal symbol* A.

DEFINITION 1.2.19. [**Left Recursive Context-Free Production and Left Recursive Context-Free Grammar**] Let us consider a context-free grammar $G = \langle V_T, V_N, P, S \rangle$.
(i) We say that a production in P is *left recursive* if it is the form $A \to A\alpha$, with $A \in V_N$ and $\alpha \in (V_T \cup V_N)^*$.
(ii) We say that a context-free grammar is *left recursive* if there exists a nonterminal symbol A such that for some $\alpha, \beta, \gamma \in (V_T \cup V_N)^*$ we have that:
$$S \to^* \alpha A \beta \quad \text{and} \quad A \to^+ A\gamma.$$

If we consider context-free grammars without trivial unit productions and, in general, context-free grammars where there are no derivations of the form: $A \to^+ A$, then in the above Definition 1.2.19 in $A\alpha$ we have that $\alpha \neq \varepsilon$, and in $A\gamma$ we have that $\gamma \neq \varepsilon$. If a reduced, context-free grammar G has a left recursive production, then G is left recursive.

We conclude this chapter by illustrating the following Figure 1.2.2 where we stratify the set N^N of the computable and non-computable functions from N to N (as usual, N denotes the set of the natural numbers). The reader may refer to other books for the definitions which are relevant here (see, for instance, [21]). The cardinality of N^N is $\aleph_1$. (Recall that $\aleph_1$ denotes the cardinality of the real numbers and $\aleph_0$ denotes the cardinality of the natural numbers.)

The subset of the computable functions from N to N, whose cardinality is $\aleph_0$, is stratified according to the Chomsky Hierarchy [21], that is, the types of languages associated with those functions. Obviously, for that stratification we require that a function from N to N is viewed as a language subset of V_T^*, for some given set V_T of terminal symbols.

The classes of languages: (i) type 0, (ii) type 1, (iii) type 2 (or context-free), (iv) deterministic context-free, and (v) type 3 are associated via a bijection, respectively, with the following classes of automata: (i) Turing Machines (TM), (ii) linear bounded automata, (iii) pushdown automata (pda), (iv) deterministic pushdown automata (dpda), and (v) finite automata.

The set *r.e.* is the set of all recursive enumerable languages over the set of V_T of terminal symbols. There is a bijection between the set *r.e.* and the set TM of the Turing Machines. There is a bijection also between the set *r.e.* and the set of functions from N to N definable in the λ-calculus.

The set *rec* is the set of all recursive languages over the set of V_T of terminal symbols. There is a bijection between the set *rec* and the set of the Turing Machines which halt for all input values.

NOTATION 1.2.20. [**Backus-Naur Form**] When presenting the syntax of a set of expressions, we will feel free to use the so called *Backus-Naur form* (which is actually a way of presenting languages generated by context-free grammars).

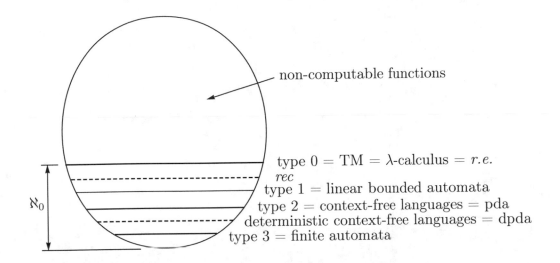

FIGURE 1.2.2. A stratification of the set N^N of all (computable and non-computable) functions from N to N. The computable functions from N to N are stratified according to the Chomsky Hierarchy [21].

For instance, given the set N of the natural numbers, the syntax of the set **Aexp** of the familiar arithmetic expressions with natural numbers ($n \in N$), sums ($+$), and products ($\times$), can be given as follows:

$e ::= n \mid e_1 + e_2 \mid e_1 \times e_2 \mid (e_1)$

Thus, in particular, $5 \times (4 + 2)$ is a legal expression in **Aexp**.

Sometimes, on the right hand side of the Backus-Naur forms we will drop the subscripts, and thus the syntax of the set **Aexp** can also be given as follows:

$e ::= n \mid e + e \mid e \times e \mid (e)$ $\square$

CHAPTER 2

Exploring Search Spaces

In this chapter we introduce the reader to some algorithms and techniques for exploring search spaces. In particular, we will consider:

(i) the technique for exploring *linear search spaces* represented as arrays (or linear lists),

(ii) the backtracking technique for exploring *general search spaces* represented as graphs, and

(iii) the depth first and breadth first algorithms for exploring *tree-like search spaces* with the objective of finding leaves satisfying a given property.

The presentation of these algorithms can be viewed as an introduction to the parsing algorithms which we will consider in the following chapters. Indeed, we will see that every parsing algorithm performs the exploration of a search space. (Actually, every algorithm performs the exploration of a suitably defined search space.)

2.1. Exploring Linear Search Spaces

In this section we will indicate how to explore a linear search space represented as an array. As a typical example of this technique, now we present the following elementary program *Sum* for summing up the elements of a given array A of length $n \geq 1$.

We assume that the elements of the array are all integers. The array A can also be viewed as a finite function from the set $\{1, \ldots, n\}$ to the set of integers.

Here is the Program *Sum*.

Program *Sum*

$\{n \geq 1\}$: *precondition*

$i := 0;\ sum := 0;$ establishing the invariant I.

$I \equiv \{sum = \sum_{j=1}^{i} A[j] \land i \leq n\}$: *invariant I*

while $i < n$ **do** $i := i + 1;$ working towards termination and
$\qquad\qquad sum := sum + A[i]$ re-establishing the invariant I.

od $(I \land \neg(i<n)) \rightarrow$ postcondition

$\{sum = \sum_{j=1}^{n} A[j]\}$: *postcondition*

Let us make the following comments on this program.

(i) The program is made out of two initialization statements followed by a while-loop. As stated by Kleene's Normal Form Theorem, the structure of this program is *universal*, in the sense that every Turing computable function can be computed via a unique while-loop (apart from a preliminary evaluation of a primitive recursive function and then, at the end of the while-loop, a subsequent evaluation of a primitive recursive function).

© Springer Nature Switzerland AG 2021
A. Pettorossi, *Techniques for Searching, Parsing, and Matching*, https://doi.org/10.1007/978-3-030-63189-5_2

(ii) The computation of the while-loop is characterized by the invariant I which holds before the execution of the while-loop, after every execution of the body of the while-loop, and at the end of the execution of the while-loop. The reader may easily check that, indeed, the initialization statements establish the invariant I and, in our case, they do so in a trivial way because if $n \geq 1$, we have that $(0 = \sum_{j=1}^{0} A[j]) \wedge 0 \leq n$.

In the body of the while-loop, once the value of i has been increased by 1, in order to re-establish the invariant we need to modify the value of the variable sum and to increase it by $A[i]$. Finally, when we exit from the while-loop and thus, it is no longer the case that $i < n$, the invariant should imply the postcondition $sum = \sum_{j=1}^{n} A[j]$, and indeed, this is the case.

(iii) Termination of the while-loop is guaranteed by the fact that at every execution of the body of the while-loop, i is increased by 1 and thus, sooner or later, it will be the case that $i < n$ does *not* hold and the execution of the while-loop terminates. Thus, as indicated by the usual approach to termination, there exists a function, namely $\lambda i.\, n{-}i$, which decreases at every execution of the body of the while-loop and it bounded from below by the value 0 because i cannot become larger than n.

Now, let us suppose that, instead of summing up all the elements of an array, we want to visit a given array A for finding out whether or not one of its elements satisfies a given property (or predicate) $prop : \Sigma \rightarrow \{true,\ false\}$, where Σ is the set from which the elements of the array A are taken. Thus, when viewing the array A of $n\,(\geq 1)$ elements as a finite function, we have that $A : \{1, \ldots, n\} \rightarrow \Sigma$. In order to perform the visit of the array A we can use the following *Linear Search* program which is a simple variant of the *Sum* program on page 11.

$\qquad\qquad \{n \geq 1\}$ $\qquad\qquad\qquad\qquad\qquad\qquad$ Program for *Linear Search*

$\quad i := 0;\ res := false;$

$\qquad\quad I = \{res = \bigvee_{j=1}^{i} prop(A[j]) \wedge i \leq n\}$

$\quad$**while** $i < n$ **do** $i := i + 1;$

$\qquad\qquad\qquad res := res \vee prop(A[i])$

$\qquad\qquad$**od**

$\qquad \{res = \bigvee_{j=1}^{n} prop(A[j])\}$

Starting from this program *Linear Search*, now we derive a more efficient *Linear Search* program by applying some simple transformations. In particular, we may use the following properties:

(i) $true \vee x = true$,

(ii) $false \vee x = x$, and

(iii) we may halt when we find an element $A[i]$ of A such that $prop(A[i])$ is *true*.

We derive the following program:

$\quad i := 0;\ res := false;$

$\qquad\quad \{false = \bigvee_{j=1}^{i-1} prop(A[j]) \wedge (\text{if } i \geq 1 \text{ then } res = prop(A[i])) \wedge i \leq n\}$

$\quad$**while** $i < n \wedge \neg res$ **do** $i := i + 1;$

$\qquad\qquad\qquad res := prop(A[i])$

$\qquad\qquad$**od**

By replacing i by a new identifier, also named i, which gets the value of the old i increased by 1, we derive the following program:

$i := 1$; $res := false$;
while $i \leq n \wedge \neg res$ **do** $i := i+1$; $res := prop(A[i-1])$ **od**

Now we can avoid the use of the index $i-1$ by anticipating, so to speak, the access to the array A. We swap the two instructions in the body of the while-loop and we get:

$i := 1$; $res := false$;
while $i \leq n \wedge \neg res$ **do** $res := prop(A[i])$; $i := i+1$ **od**

In order to avoid accessing the element $A[n+1]$ which is not defined, we may use the **cand** operator and we get the following Program $P1$. Recall that 'a **cand** b' is equivalent to '**if** a **then** b **else** $false$', and thus, b is not evaluated if a is $false$.

$$\{n \geq 1\}$$ Program $P1$
$i := 1$; $res := false$;
while $i \leq n$ **cand** $\neg prop(A[i])$ **do** $i := i+1$ **od**;
if $i \leq n$ **then** $res := true$
$$\{res = \bigvee_{j=1}^{n} prop(A[j])\}$$

We can transform Program $P1$ by using conditional rewrite rules and recursion, and we get the following Program $P2$:

$$\{n \geq 1\}$$ Program $P2$
$i := 1$;
$search(i):$ (1) $i \leq n \wedge \neg prop(A[i])$ $\rightarrow$ $search(i+1)$
          (2) $i \leq n \wedge prop(A[i])$ $\rightarrow$ $res := true$
          (3) $i > n$ $\rightarrow$ $res := false$
$$\{res = \bigvee_{j=1}^{n} prop(A[j])\}$$

We will not formally define here the operational semantics of the conditional rewrite rules which we have used in the above Program $P2$. It will suffice to say that, in order to perform $search(i)$, if it is the case that $i \leq n \wedge \neg prop(A[i])$ holds, then Rule (1) tells us to perform $search(i+1)$, that is, to apply again one of the three rules either (1), or (2), or (3), having increased the value of i by one unit.

The equivalence between Program $P1$ and Program $P2$ is shown in the following Exercise 2.1.1.

EXERCISE 2.1.1. (i) Show that $P1$ terminates iff $P2$ terminates.

Hint. Both programs terminate iff $i > n \vee (\exists i \ 1 \leq i \leq n \wedge A[i] = true)$.

(ii) Show that if $P1$ terminates, then ($P1$ sets res to the boolean value b iff $P2$ sets res to the same boolean value b).

Now we want to present a different kind of search of a linear search space. We call it *State Dependent Linear Search*. In this kind of search we want to visit an array, say A, whose elements are taken from a set Σ, for finding out whether or not one of its elements satisfies a given property (or predicate) *prop*, but this time the truth value of *prop* depends on both: (i) a *state q* belonging to a set Q of states, and (ii) the element of the array which is currently visited.

The visit of the array A begins in the initial state $q_0 \in Q$ and any time a new element of the array is visited, we get to a new state which is computed by the so called *next-state function* $\delta : Q \times \Sigma \to Q$. The function δ depends on the previous state and the element of the array which is currently visited. Thus, we have:

(i) an array A whose elements are taken from a set Σ,

(ii) an *initial state* $q_0 \in Q$,

(iii) a *next-state function* $\delta : Q \times \Sigma \to Q$, and

(iv) a property *prop* : $Q \times \Sigma \to \{true, false\}$.

We want a procedure which gives us the value *true* iff there exist a state q and an element a_i in the array A such that $prop(q, a_i) = true$.

Here is the program for the *State Dependent Linear Search*.

$$\begin{array}{ll}
\qquad \{n \geq 1\} & \text{Program for } State\ Dependent\ Linear\ Search \\
i := 1; & \\
q := q_0; & \\
st\text{-}search(q, i): & \left| \begin{array}{lll}
(1) & i \leq n \wedge \neg prop(q, A[i]) & \to\ st\text{-}search(\delta(q, A[i]),\ i{+}1) \\
(2) & i \leq n \wedge\ \ prop(q, A[i]) & \to\ res := true \\
(3) & i > n & \to\ res := false
\end{array} \right. \\
\quad \{res = \bigvee_{j=1}^{n} prop(\delta(\ldots \delta(\delta(q_0, A[1]), A[2])\ldots, A[j{-}1]), A[j])\} &
\end{array}$$

In the postcondition, instead of $prop(\delta(\ldots \delta(\delta(q_0, A[1]), A[2])\ldots, A[j{-}1]), A[j]))$, in order to avoid the use of the dots, we can write $prop(\delta^*(q_0, A, j))$, where δ^* is a function from $Q \times \Sigma^+ \times N^{>0}$ to Q (here Σ^+ denotes the set of the arrays whose elements are taken from Σ, and $N^{>0}$ denotes the set of the positive natural numbers), defined as follows:

$$\begin{aligned}
\delta^*(q_0, A, j) = &\ \textbf{if } j{=}1 \textbf{ then } \delta(q_0, A[1]) \\
&\ \textbf{else } \delta(\delta^*(q_0, A, j{-}1), A[j]).
\end{aligned}$$

By using the result of the above Exercise 2.1.1 on the preceding page which shows the equivalence between Program $P1$ and Program $P2$, we get the following program which is equivalent to the program for the *State Dependent Linear Search*:

$$\begin{array}{l}
i := 1;\ q := q_0;\ res :=\ false \\
\textbf{while } i \leq n \textbf{ cand } \neg prop(q, A[i]) \textbf{ do } q := \delta(q, A[i]);\ \ i := i{+}1 \textbf{ od}; \\
\textbf{if } i \leq n \textbf{ then } res := true
\end{array}$$

EXERCISE 2.1.2. Write a program to check whether or not in a given array there is an element which is equal to the sum of all the preceding elements.

Solution. Instantiating the above State Dependent Linear Search program, we get:

$$\begin{array}{l}
i := 1;\ sum := 0;\ res :=\ false \\
\textbf{while } i \leq n \textbf{ cand } \neg(sum = A[i]) \textbf{ do } sum := sum + A[i];\ \ i := i{+}1 \textbf{ od}; \\
\textbf{if } i \leq n \textbf{ then } res := true
\end{array}$$

$\square$

2.2. Backtracking Algorithms

Backtracking is a method for visiting all the nodes of a given finite tree starting from its root, when at each node we know:

(i) the list of all the son nodes which are assumed to be ordered in a *linear order*, which is the left-to-right order of the elements of the list,

(ii) a pointer p which identifies the node of that list which should be visited next, and

(iii) the father node, if any.

When reasoning about our programs and also in our pictures below, we assume that the head of every list of nodes is 'to the left' of all the other elements of the list. When we visit a list of nodes, we first visit its head and then, recursively, we visit the tail of the list. In what follows we will also use the following terminology. Given a list of son nodes, (i) the head of the list is said to be *oldest son node*, and (ii) the node, if any, which is immediately to the right of the given node m in the list, is said to be the *immediately younger brother node* of m, or the *next node after* m.

The general idea of the backtracking algorithms can be explained as follows [6].

When the visit of a given node n of a tree is completed (and thus also the visits of all the descendant nodes of that node n are completed), the visit of the tree continues by performing the visit of the subtree, if any, which is rooted at the node which is the immediately younger brother node of n. If that immediately younger brother node of n does not exist, then the visit of the father node of the node n is completed.

Thus, by applying the backtracking technique, the visit of the tree search space is the *preorder visit*, that is, at each node of the tree we first visit that node and then, recursively, we make the preorder visit of each node in the list of the son nodes of that node. The son nodes of that list are visited according to the left-to-right order of the elements of the list. The preorder visit realizes a depth first visit of the tree search space.

2.2.1. Dispositions.

The following program, called `Dispositions.java`, uses the backtracking technique, implemented as a recursion inside a do-while loop, for computing all the dispositions of length D whose elements are taken from the set $\{1, \ldots, B\}$ of B elements. In particular, if $B = 2$, that program computes in increasing order the following sequence of tuples each of which is made out of D elements (thus, for instance, the first tuple has D occurrences of 1's, the second tuple has $D-1$ occurrences of 1's and 1 occurrence of 2, and the last tuple has D occurrences of 2's):

$$\langle 1, 1, \ldots, 1, 1 \rangle, \quad \langle 1, 1, \ldots, 1, 2 \rangle, \quad \langle 1, 1, \ldots, 2, 1 \rangle, \quad \langle 1, 1, \ldots, 2, 2 \rangle, \quad \ldots,$$
$$\ldots,$$
$$\langle 1, 2, \ldots, 2, 2 \rangle, \quad \langle 2, 1, \ldots, 1, 1 \rangle, \quad \ldots, \quad \langle 2, 2, \ldots, 1, 1 \rangle \quad \ldots, \quad \langle 2, 2, \ldots, 2, 2 \rangle$$

The program `Dispositions.java` has the structure that we have indicate in Figure 2.2.1 on the next page (see also Figure 2.2.2 on page 17). In that program we have that:

(i) the first local choice identifies the oldest son node of the given initial node,

```
                                /* procedure generate() */
    void generate();
    begin
     select the first local choice;

     │  do   │ (α): make the local choice;      (β): down the tree (global value);
     │       │ if deepest level reached then do the leaf operation else generate()
     │       │ (β'): up the tree (global value)   (α'): remove local choice;
     │       │ select the next local choice;

     │  while  there is one more local choice to make;
    end
                                /* main program */
    id = 0;  generate();
```

FIGURE 2.2.1. Structure of a backtracking algorithm. The 'local choice' refers to the index of breadth **ib** and the 'global value' refers to the index of depth **id**. Note that **generate()** has no argument and this avoids the need of passing local data structures when making the recursive calls, thereby increasing efficiency. The data structures that are manipulated are all global data structures.

(ii) « to make the next local choice » is to increment the value of the *index of breadth* **ib**, that is, to move the pointer p one position to the right along the list of son nodes,

(iii) « to go *down the tree* » is to increment by 1 the value of the *index of depth* **id**, that is, to begin the visit of a son node,

(iv) « to go *up the tree* » is to decrement by 1 the value of **id**, that is, to go to the father node for beginning the visit of the immediately younger brother node, if any, and

(v) « to remove the local choice » is the step we have to make before making the next local choice (see the above Point (ii)).

By removing the local choice we complete the visit of the node, say n, which is our current local choice, and then, the next local choice, if any, can be made and the visit of the immediately younger brother node of n, if any, begins by executing one more time the body of the do-while loop.

For the index of breadth **ib** we have that: $1 \leq \text{ib} \leq \text{B}$, and for the index of depth **id** we have that: $0 \leq \text{id} \leq \text{D}$. The deepest level is reached when $\text{id} = \text{D}$.

We assume that « to make the local choice » does *not* increase the value of **ib**. The value of **ib** is increased when selecting the next local choice.

When the deepest level is reached, instead of going below a leaf node with $\text{id} = \text{D}$, we perform an operation associated with that leaf. That leaf operation, in general, depends on some global data structure which is manipulated while the visit of the tree progresses. In the case of the program **Dispositions.java** that global structure is the array **arrayDisp**.

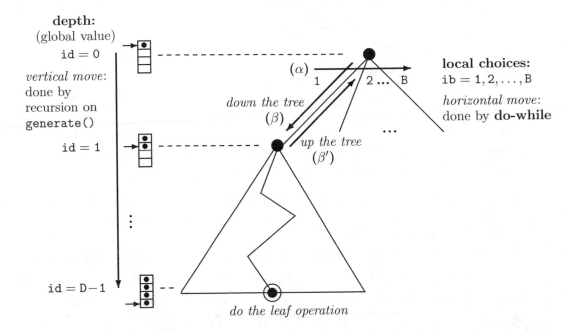

FIGURE 2.2.2. Visit of a tree of nodes by backtracking, starting from the topmost node. The dots (•) in the pictures of the array on the left represent the local choices which have been already made.

The removal of the local choice, denoted by (α'), may not be necessary if the action of making the next local choice is performed *destructively*.

This means that if the action of making a choice is done by assigning a value to a variable (as it is in our case, because we assign a value to the variable `ib`), then the action of making a new local choice automatically removes the old value of that variable (in our case the variable `ib`) and thus, automatically removes the local choice which was previously made. This is why in Figure 2.2.2 there is no reference to the action (α').

In the program `Dispositions.java` on this page we have that $D = 3$ and $B = 2$, and the dispositions of length 3 whose elements are taken from the set $\{1, \ldots, B\}$, that is, $\{1, 2\}$, are the following $8 \,(= B^D)$ sequences:

111, 112, 121, 122, 211, 212, 221, 222.

When computing these sequences we get the tree of nodes depicted in Figure 2.2.3 on the next page.

The nodes of that tree are visited using the program `Dispositions.java`, starting from the root node a, in the following depth first order (which realizes the so called *preorder traversal* of the tree):

$a, b, d, h, i, e, j, k, c, f, \ell, m, g, n$, and o

(these letters occur as labels of the nodes in Figure 2.2.3 on the following page).

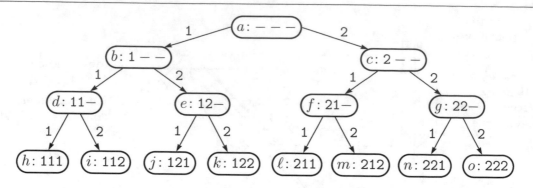

FIGURE 2.2.3. The tree of nodes when computing the 8 dispositions of length 3 of the elements 1 and 2, from 111 to 222. The dispositions are at the leaves.

```
/**
 * ============================================================================
 *                         Backtracking: DISPOSITIONS
 * Filename: "Dispositions.java"
 *
 * A disposition is a sequence of length D whose elements (not necessarily
 * distinct) are taken from a set of B elements.
 * ============================================================================
 */
public class Dispositions {
 private int id = 0;
 private final int   D = 3;
 private final int   B = 2;
 private int[] arrayDisp = new int[D];// by default: initially the elements
                                      //           of arrayDisp are all 0's
 private void printar(int[] array, int size) {
   for (int k=0; k<size; k++) {System.out.print(array[k]+" ");}
   System.out.println();
  }
 private void generate() {
    int ib=1;
    do {arrayDisp[id]=ib; id++;
        if (id==D) {printar(arrayDisp,D);} else generate();
        id--;
        ib++;}
    while (ib <= B);
  }
 public static void main(String[] args) {
   Dispositions disp = new Dispositions();
   disp.generate();
 }
}
/**
 * input:                    output:
 * ------------------------------------------------------------------------
 * javac Dispositions.java
 * java  Dispositions
 *                           1 1 1
 *                           1 1 2
 *                           1 2 1
```

```
*                              1 2 2
*                              2 1 1
*                              2 1 2
*                              2 2 1
*                              2 2 2
* -----------------------------------------------------------------------
*/
```

Now we present an algorithm that can be used, instead of the backtracking technique, for computing the 8 dispositions of length 3 whose elements are taken from the set $\{0, 1\}$, that is, the sequences: 000, 001, 010, 011, 100, 101, 110, 111.

This algorithm is based on the interpretation of those sequences as the binary expansions of the integers in $\{0, \ldots, 7\}$. Thus, if we start from the sequence 000 and we iteratively add 1 to the current sequence, we compute all those sequences. The operation of adding 1 is efficiently performed by: (i) moving from right to left over the current sequence until a 0 is encountered, and while making that move, (ii) replacing every 1, if any, by 0, and that 0 by 1. By doing so, for instance, from the sequence 001 we compute the next sequence 010, as desired.

A boolean version of this algorithm, with `false` instead of 0, and `true` instead of 1, has been used in the `main` method of Propositional Theorem Prover program starting on page 215.

2.2.2. Combinations.

Now we present a program, called `Combinations.java`, for computing all the combinations of B (≥ 1) elements taken in groups of cardinality D, with $1 \leq D \leq B$. They are also called the B-*over*-D *combinations*. The number of B-over-D combinations is the value of the binomial coefficient $\binom{B}{D}$, that is, $\dfrac{B!}{(B-D)!\,D!}$.

The program `Combinations.java` is a variant of the program `Dispositions.java` (see page 17) in the sense that in this case the local choices that can be made, depend on some global information. Indeed, the computation of the B-over-D combinations can be viewed as the computation of the dispositions of length D whose elements are taken from the set $\{1, \ldots, B\}$ with the following constraint:

« if an element has been already used for making a local choice at an ancestor node, then it cannot be used again for making a local choice at the current node. »

In order to recall all the choices made at the ancestor nodes, one can show that, since a combination of D elements is stored in the array `arrayComb` of D elements, it is enough to test whether or not `((id == 0) || (ib > arrayComb[id-1]))` holds. (We leave to the reader the proof of this simple fact.) The identifier `ib`, with $1 \leq$ `ib` $\leq$ B, is the index of breadth and `id`, with $0 \leq$ `id` $\leq$ D-1, is the index of depth (see also Figure 2.2.2 on page 17). In our case, in order to recall all the choices made at the ancestor nodes, we could have also used a boolean vector.

```
/**
 * ================================================================
 *                      Backtracking: COMBINATIONS
 * Filename: "Combinations.java"
 *
 * Combinations are dispositions, where the order of the elements
```

```
 * is NOT significant. In the dispositions the order is significant.
 *
 * The combinations of 'B over D' are the different SETS (not sequences) of
 * the B elements taken in groups of cardinality D.
 * The B elements are assumed to be: 1,...,B.
 * The combinations will be presented in lexicographic order, that is,
 * X_1,...,X_D comes before Y_1,...,Y_D iff there exists k, with 0<=k<D,
 * such that X_1 = Y_1, ..., X_k = Y_k, X_{k+1} < Y_{k+1}.
 *
 * In order to compute the combinations of 'B over D' we use a backtraking
 * algorithm which takes into account some global information to know
 * whether or not a given element can be used for making the current
 * local choice. That global information depends on previous local choices
 * made at the nodes which are ancestors of the node where the current
 * local choice is made.
 * ============================================================================
 */

public class Combinations {
 private int id = 0;
 private final int  B = 4;              // B should be positive
 private final int  D = 2;              // D should be positive and D <= B
 private int[] arrayComb = new int[D];// by default: initially the elements
                                      //             of arrayComb are all 0's

 private void printar(int[] array, int size) {
     for (int k=0; k<size; k++) {System.out.print(array[k]+" ");}
     System.out.println();
 }

 private void generate() {
     int ib=1;
     do {// ------ For id == 0 the first element is always ok.
         // ------ Combinations are generated in 'increasing order':
         //        this is due to the test (ib > arrayComb[id-1]) below.
         if ((id == 0) || (ib > arrayComb[id-1]))
             {arrayComb[id] = ib; id++;
             if (id == D) {printar(arrayComb,D);} else generate();
             id--;};
         ib++;}
     while (ib <= B);
 }
 public static void main(String[] args) {
   Combinations comb = new Combinations();
   comb.generate();
 }
}
/**
 * input:                 output:
 * ------------------------------------------------------------------------
 * javac Combinations.java
 * java  Combinations
 *                        1 2
 *                        1 3
 *                        1 4
 *                        2 3
 *                        2 4
 *                        3 4
 * ------------------------------------------------------------------------
 */
```

2.2.3. n-Queens.

Finally, we present a program, called `Queens.java`, for solving the n-queens problem [6]. This program implements a backtracking algorithm which can easily be understood because it is a variant of the algorithm we have presented in the program `Combinations.java` (see page 19).

This variant is based on the fact that when making the local choices, we have to comply with the following constraint:

« when making any local choice, we have to determine whether or not the candidate local choice is *available*, that is, we have to determine whether or not the following global condition holds: the new queen to be placed on the board, is *not* under attack of any other queen already placed on the board. »

Attacks to a queen can come from a queen which is either in the same *column*, or in the same *up-diagonal*, or in the same *down-diagonal*. No attack to a queen can come from a queen on the same *row* simply because, by construction, every queen is placed on a different row (see Figure 2.2.4 on page 23). The columns taken by the queens on the board are identified by the value `false` in the array $col[0, \ldots, m-1]$. Analogously for the up-diagonals and the down-diagonals for which we use the boolean arrays $up[0, \ldots, 2(m-1)]$ and $down[0, \ldots, 2(m-1)]$, respectively.

A new queen can be placed in column `k`, up-diagonal `u`, and down-diagonal `d` iff the corresponding elements of the arrays `col`, `up`, and `down`, that is, `col[k]`, `up[u]`, and `down[d]`, are all `true`. Once a queen is placed in that position, all those elements are set to `false`, meaning that that position is no longer available for a subsequent queen to be placed on the board. All the elements of the arrays `col`, `up`, and `down` are initialized to `true` meaning that all positions are available for the first queen.

In our program `Queens.java` which we now present, the number of queens is stored in the variables `nqueens` and `m`.

```
/**
 * ======================================================================
 *                       Backtracking: n QUEENS
 * Filename: "Queens.java"
 *
 * From: E.W. Dijkstra: 'A Short Introduction to the Art of Programming'.
 * EWD 316 August 1971. The command line for executing this program is:
 * java Queens n (n should be at least 1).
 *
 * The queens are placed from top to bottom, one for each row.
 * ======================================================================
 */

public class Queens {
  int nq = 0;        // index of queen to be placed in the current solution.
                     // See generate().
  int nqueens, nqueens1;     // number of queens, number of queens minus one
  int[] arrayQ;
  boolean[] col, up, down;
                                             // constructor of the class Queens
  Queens(int[] arrayQ, boolean[] col, boolean[] up,
         boolean[] down, int nqueens) {
    this.nqueens  = nqueens;
    this.nqueens1 = nqueens-1;
    this.arrayQ   = arrayQ;
```

```
        this.col     = col;
        this.up      = up;
        this.down    = down;
        }
/**
 * ---------------------------------------------------------------
 * Dijkstra uses different 'up' and 'down' boolean arrays corresponding to
 * different notions of the up-diagonal and down-diagonal.
 * ---------------------------------------------------------------
 */
private void printar(int[] arrayA, int size) {
    for (int k=0; k<size; k++) {System.out.print(arrayA[k]+" ");}
                              System.out.println();}

private void generate()
    {int h=0;
    do {if (col[h] && up[nq+h] && down[nq-h+nqueens1])
            {arrayQ[nq]=h; col[h]=false; up[nq+h]=false;
             down[nq-h+nqueens1]=false; nq=nq+1;
             if (nq==nqueens) {printar(arrayQ,nqueens);} else generate();
             nq=nq-1;col[h]=true; up[nq+h]=true;
             down[nq-h+nqueens1]=true;};
          h=h+1;}
    while (h < nqueens);}
//---------------------------------------------------------------
public static void main(String[] args) {

    int m=0;        // m is the number of queens. See the field nqueens.
    try {m = Integer.parseInt(args[0]);
         if (m <= 0) {throw new Exception();}
    } catch (Exception e) {
         System.out.print("The number of queens should be >= 1.");
         System.out.println(" By default we assume 1 queen only.");
         m=1;
    };
System.out.println("Number of queens = "+m);
int[]     arrayQ = new int[m];          // integer array [0..m-1]
boolean[] col    = new boolean[m];      // boolean array [0..m-1]
boolean[] up     = new boolean[2*m-1];  // boolean array [0..2(m-1)]
boolean[] down   = new boolean[2*m-1];  // boolean array [0..2(m-1)]
//------------ initialization of the arrays to 'true' values ------------
int k=0; do {col[k]=true; k=k+1;} while (k<m);
    k=0; do {up[k]=true; down[k]=true; k=k+1;} while (k<2*m-1);
//---------------------------------------------------------------
Queens queens = new Queens(arrayQ, col, up, down, m);
queens.generate();
}
}
/**
 * input:              output:
 * ---------------------------------------------------------------
 * javac Queens.java
 * Java  Queens 6
 *
 *                Number of queens = 6
 *                1  3  5  0  2  4
 *                2  5  1  4  0  3
 *                3  0  4  1  5  2
 *                4  2  0  5  3  1
 * ---------------------------------------------------------------
 */
```

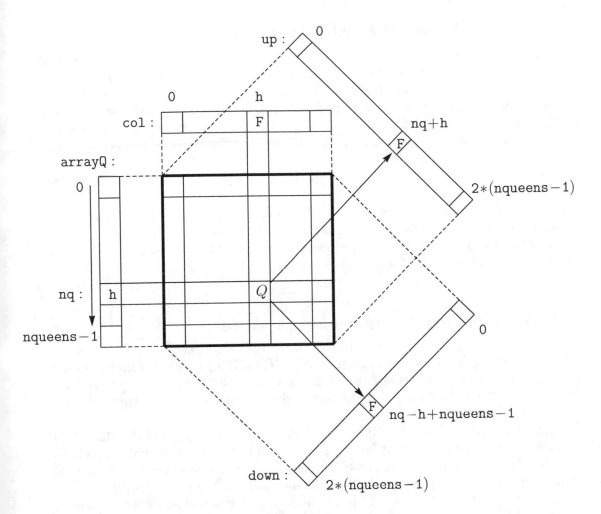

FIGURE 2.2.4. The queen Q in position [nq,h], that is, in row nq and column h, forces the following values, where F stands for false: col[h] = F, up[nq+h] = F, and down[nq-h+nqueens-1] = F. These false values tell us the column, the up-diagonal, and the down-diagonal which are taken by that queen. These positions are not available for a different queen. The array col is from col[0] to col[nqueens-1].

2.3. Visiting Trees While Looking for Good Nodes

In this section we will present some algorithms for visiting trees with the objective of finding 'good' nodes, that is, nodes which satisfy a given property (or predicate) p. We assume that the trees are generated in a dynamic fashion, in the sense that any given tree is specified by: (i) its root node, and (ii) a function f which for each node of the tree, returns the list of its son nodes. Any such function f will be called a *tree-generating function*. We assume that the nodes of the trees we will consider, are of type α. We also assume that:

(i) the predicate p is a function whose type is: $\alpha \rightarrow bool$, where $bool = \{true, false\}$, and

(ii) the tree-generating function f is a function whose type is: $\alpha \rightarrow \alpha list$, where $\alpha\ list$ denotes the type of the lists whose elements are of type α.

In what follows the infix *append* function between two lists is denoted by $<>$. Thus, $<>$ has type: $(\alpha\ list) \times (\alpha\ list) \rightarrow (\alpha\ list)$.

2.3.1. Depth First Visit of Trees: Basic Version.

Now we present a function, called *existsev* (short for *exists eventually*), which given: (i) a predicate p, (ii) a tree-generating function f, and (iii) a list L of nodes, returns *true* if there exists a node n in L which is the root of the tree, say t_n, generated by the function f such that in t_n there exists a node m such that $p(m) = true$, otherwise it returns *false*.

The correctness of the algorithm we will give for evaluating the function *existsev* is based on the assumption that for any node n, the tree which is rooted in n is finite. This finiteness assumption is required because given any node n, the tree rooted in n is generated and visited in a *depth first* manner (see the line marked with (†)).

If a node is the root of an infinite tree (because of the particular tree-generating function f which is given), then the evaluation of *existsev* may not terminate even if in that infinite tree there exists a node which satisfies p.

The *existsev* function is defined as follows. (In the first line we have given its *type* and in the other lines we have given its *definition*.)

$existsev : (\alpha \rightarrow bool) \times (\alpha \rightarrow \alpha\ list) \times (\alpha\ list) \rightarrow bool$

$existsev\ p\ f\ L =$ **if** $L=[\ ]$ **then** *false*

      else if $p(hd(L))$ **then** *true*

      else $existsev\ p\ f\ (f(hd(L)) <> tl(L))$ (†)

Let us consider a predicate p, a tree-generating function f, and a node n. Suppose that f generates a finite tree rooted in n. Then we have that there exists a node m in the tree rooted in n generated by f such that $p(m) = true$ iff $existsev(p, f, [n]) = true$. The inductive proof of this statement is left to the reader.

The following example illustrates the behaviour of the function *existsev* while performing the depth first visit of a tree of natural numbers (thus, in this example the type α is the type of the natural numbers.)

EXAMPLE 2.3.1. Let N denote the set of natural numbers. Let us consider the predicates $p : N \to bool$ and $odd : N \to bool$, and the tree-generating function f defined as follows:

$$
\begin{aligned}
p(x) &= x = 25 \\
odd(0) &= false \\
odd(n+1) &= not(odd(n)) \\
f(x) &= [x+4, x+5] \quad \text{if } x < 25 \text{ and } odd(x) \\
f(x) &= [x+5] \quad \text{if } x < 25 \text{ and } not(odd(x)) \\
f(x) &= [] \quad \text{otherwise}
\end{aligned}
$$

where $not(false) = true$ and $not(true) = false$. The search space is the tree of natural numbers depicted in Figure 2.3.1. In that figure we have also depicted the first six frontiers which are determined by the depth first visit of the tree, as we will explain below. The other frontiers are depicted on Figure 2.3.2 on the next page.

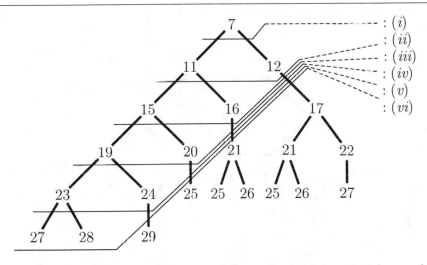

FIGURE 2.3.1. The tree generated from the initial node 7 by applying the tree-generating function f of Example 2.3.1. We have also depicted the first six frontiers of the depth first visit of the tree.

Every recursive call of the function $existsev$ is of the form: $existsev \; p \; f \; l$, where the predicate p and the function f do not change, while the list l of natural numbers which is initially $[7]$ (because 7 is the root of the tree), changes as follows for each new recursive call (see also the frontiers depicted on Figure 2.3.1 and Figure 2.3.2 on the following page):

$$
\begin{aligned}
(i) &: \quad [7] \\
(ii) &: \quad [11, 12] \\
(iii) &: \quad [15, 16, 12] \\
(iv) &: \quad [19, 20, 16, 12] \\
(v) &: \quad [23, 24, 20, 16, 12] \\
(vi) &: \quad [27, 28, 24, 20, 16, 12]
\end{aligned}
$$

$$(vii): \qquad [28, 24, 20, 16, 12]$$
$$(viii): \qquad [24, 20, 16, 12]$$
$$(ix): \qquad [29, 20, 16, 12]$$
$$(x): \qquad [20, 16, 12]$$
$$(xi): \qquad [25, 16, 12]$$

Note that the head of the last list $[25, 16, 12]$ is 25 and, since $p(25)$ is *true*, the execution of the function *existsev* stops. As the reader may verify, this sequence of eleven lists of nodes is the sequence of the *frontiers of the tree*, which are determined by the depth first visit of the tree with root 7. Indeed, in each successive call of the function *existsev*, the leftmost element of the list is replaced by its son nodes. In Figure 2.3.1 on the previous page we have depicted the first frontier $[7]$ (the node 7 is the initial node), the second frontier $[11, 12]$, the third frontier $[15, 16, 12]$, ..., until the sixth frontier which is $[27, 28, 24, 20, 16, 12]$. The other frontiers, from the seventh frontier which is $[28, 24, 20, 16, 12]$, until the eleventh one which is $[25, 16, 12]$, are shown in Figure 2.3.2. □

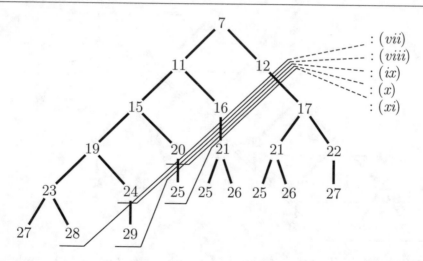

FIGURE 2.3.2. The frontiers, from the seventh one to the eleventh one, of the depth first visit of the tree generated from the initial node 7 by applying the tree-generating function f of Example 2.3.1 on the previous page.

2.3.2. Depth First Visit of Trees: Burstall's Version.

In this section we present a different algorithm for visiting trees in a depth first manner. It has been suggested to us by R. M. Burstall.

As in the previous Section 2.3.1, we are given a predicate p, a tree-generating function f, and a node n. Suppose that f generates a finite tree rooted in n. The following function $existsev1(p, f, n)$ returns *true* iff in the tree rooted in n and generated from n by the function f there exists a node m such that $p(m) = true$, otherwise it returns *false*.

As for the function *existsev* which is defined on page 24, the correctness of the *existsev1* function is based on the assumption that for any node n, the tree rooted in n, is finite. This assumption is necessary because the tree rooted in n is generated and visited in a *depth first* manner (see the line marked with (††)).

Given a predicate p and a list L of nodes, the function $exists(p, L)$ returns *true* if in the list L there exists a node m such that $p(m)$ is *true*, otherwise it returns *false*.

The functions $existsev1$ and $exists$ are defined as follows.

$existsev1 : (\alpha \to bool) \times (\alpha \to \alpha \ list) \times \alpha \to bool$

$existsev1 \ p \ f \ x = $ **if** $p(x)$ **then** *true*

$\qquad\qquad\qquad$ **clse** $exists \ (existsev1 \ p \ f) \ f(x)$ $\qquad$ (††)

$exists : (\alpha \to bool) \times (\alpha \ list) \to bool$

$exists \ p \ L = $ **if** $L=[\ ]$ **then** *false*

$\qquad\qquad$ **else if** $p(hd(L))$ **then** *true*

$\qquad\qquad$ **else** $exists \ p \ tl(L)$

Note that in the above function we use the partial application technique: the predicate which is the first argument of the function $exists$ in the line marked with (††), is the result of the application of the function $existsev1$ (which is of arity 3) to the predicate p and the function f. Thus, at line (††) the type of $existsev1 \ p \ f$ is $\alpha \to bool$, which is the type of a predicate on nodes, and the type of $f(x)$ is $\alpha \ list$, which is the type of a list of α's.

NOTE 2.3.2. The functions $existsev$ and $existsev1$ are equivalent in the sense that for any given predicate p of type $\alpha \to bool$, any tree generating function f of type $\alpha \to \alpha list$, and any given initial node n of type α, we have that:

$existsev \ p \ f \ [n] = existsev1 \ p \ f \ n$. $\qquad\qquad\qquad\qquad\qquad$ □

As we will see in more detail in Chapter 3, one can use this depth first visit algorithm for parsing strings (or words) generated by formal grammars. Here is an example where we consider the regular grammar G with axiom P and whose productions are:

$\qquad P \to b \qquad\qquad\qquad P \to bQ \qquad\qquad Q \to a \qquad\qquad Q \to aQ$

We want to check whether or not the string ba belongs to the language $L(G)$ generated by G. We can do so by constructing a tree whose root node is the pair $\langle P, ba \rangle$ made out of the axiom P and the *string-to-parse ba*. The nodes of that tree are constructed by applying to any node $\langle \sigma_1, \sigma_2 \rangle$, where σ_1 is a *sentential form* and σ_2 is a string of terminal symbols, either (i) the *chop* operation, or (ii) the *expand* operation, which we will describe below.

The construction of the tree finishes when a node of the form $\langle \varepsilon, \varepsilon \rangle$ is constructed, and this fact indicates that the string ba belongs to the language generated by G. Indeed, one can show that, in general, given a grammar H with axiom S, and a string σ, we have that $\sigma \in L(H)$ iff the node $\langle \varepsilon, \varepsilon \rangle$ belongs to the tree constructed from the root node $\langle S, \sigma \rangle$. Here is the description of the *chop* and *expand* operations.

(i) The *chop* operation is applied to a node of the form $\langle a\sigma_1, a\sigma_2 \rangle$, where a is a terminal symbol, $\sigma_1 \in \{a, b, P, Q\}^*$, and $\sigma_2 \in \{a, b\}^*$, and it constructs the single son node $\langle \sigma_1, \sigma_2 \rangle$. Thus, the *chop* operation consists in deleting the leftmost terminal

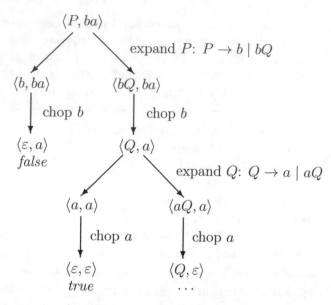

FIGURE 2.3.3. The tree of nodes which shows that the string ba is generated by the grammar G with axiom P and whose productions are: $P \to b \mid bQ$, $Q \to a \mid aQ$.

symbol of both components of the pair in the node, if they are the same terminal symbol.

We assume that the *chop* operation cannot be applied to a node which is *not* of the form $\langle a\sigma_1, a\sigma_2 \rangle$ specified above.

(ii) The *expand* operation is applied to a node of the form $\langle A\sigma_1, \sigma_2 \rangle$, where A is a nonterminal symbol, $\sigma_1 \in \{a, b, P, Q\}^*$, and $\sigma_2 \in \{a, b\}^*$, and it constructs the list of the son nodes of that node which is $[\langle \alpha_1\sigma_1, \sigma_2 \rangle, \ldots, \langle \alpha_n\sigma_1, \sigma_2 \rangle]$, if $\alpha_1, \ldots, \alpha_n$ are the right hand sides of all the productions of the given grammar whose left hand side is A. Thus, the *expand* operation is based on the replacement in all possible ways of the leftmost nonterminal symbol of the sentential form of the node. For instance, given the node $\langle P, ba \rangle$, the *expand* operation constructs the list $[\langle b, ba \rangle, \langle bQ, ba \rangle]$ of son nodes, because for the symbol P in the grammar G we have the two productions $P \to b$ and $P \to bQ$.

We assume that the *expand* operation cannot be applied to a node which is *not* of the form $\langle A\sigma_1, \sigma_2 \rangle$ specified above.

Figure 2.3.3 shows the tree with root $\langle P, ba \rangle$ which is generated by the *chop* and *expand* operations. The fact that in that tree there is the node $\langle \varepsilon, \varepsilon \rangle$ indicates that the string ba belongs to the language generated by G.

The construction of the tree which we have described above in terms of the *chop* and *expand* operations, can also be described in terms of a suitable tree-generating function f. We leave the definition of that tree-generating function to the reader. The predicate p which tells us when we have found the node $\langle \varepsilon, \varepsilon \rangle$, may be defined as follows: for any given node $\langle \sigma_1, \sigma_2 \rangle$, we have that $p(\langle \sigma_1, \sigma_2 \rangle) = true$ iff $\sigma_1 = \sigma_2 = \varepsilon$.

2.3.3. Breadth First Visit of Trees.

In this section we present a third algorithm for visiting trees. The visit is performed in a *breadth first* manner and thus, in order to ensure the correctness of this algorithm, we do not need the hypothesis that the tree generated from any given node by the given tree-generating function, is finite.

Given a function f with type $\alpha \rightarrow \alpha list$ and a list L of elements of type α, the function $flatmap(f, L)$ returns the concatenation of the lists produced by applying the function f to every element of L.

The function *exists* is the one we have presented on page 27.

The function *bf-existsev* (short for *breadth first exists eventually*) is very similar to the function *existsev* presented on page 24. They have the same type. However, in the case of the function *bf-existsev*, the tree is generated and visited in a breadth first manner (see the line marked with (†††)). Indeed, at each recursive call of the function *bf-existsev*, we construct the list of the son nodes of *all* nodes occurring in the list of the previous call of *bf-existsev*. Thus, the tree is generated level-by-level, by generating the nodes at distance $k+1$ from the root, only after the generation of all nodes at distance k, for any $k \geq 0$.

The functions *flatmap*, *exists*, and *bf-existsev* are defined as follows.

$bf\text{-}existsev : (\alpha \rightarrow bool) \times (\alpha \rightarrow \alpha\ list) \times (\alpha\ list) \rightarrow bool$
$bf\text{-}existsev\ p\ f\ L = $ **if** $L = [\,]$ **then** *false*
          else if *exists* $p\ L$ **then** *true*
          else $bf\text{-}existsev\ p\ f\ (flatmap\ f\ L)$ (†††)

$exists : (\alpha \rightarrow bool) \times (\alpha\ list) \rightarrow bool$
$exists\ p\ L = $ **if** $L = [\,]$ **then** *false*
        else if $p(hd(L))$ **then** *true*
        else *exists* $p\ tl(L)$

$flatmap : (\alpha \rightarrow \alpha\ list) \times (\alpha\ list) \rightarrow (\alpha\ list)$
$flatmap\ f\ L = $ **if** $L = [\,]$ **then** $[\,]$
        else $(f(hd(L)) <> (flatmap\ f\ tl(L))$

Note that the functions *existsev* and *bf-existsev* may not terminate if starting from a given node, the iterated application of the function f generates an infinite tree.

EXERCISE 2.3.3. Show that the following function definition of *existsev* is *not* correct:
$existsev\ p\ f\ L = $ **if** *exists* $p\ L$ **then** *true*
        else *existsev* $p\ f\ (f(hd(L)) <> tl(L))$
Hint: Consider the case when $L = [\,]$.   □

EXERCISE 2.3.4. Show that the following function definition for *bf-existsev* is *not* correct:
$bf\text{-}existsev\ p\ f\ L = $ **if** $L = [\,]$ **then** *false*
        else if $p(hd(L))$ **then** *true*
        else $bf\text{-}existsev\ p\ f\ (flatmap\ f\ L)$

Hint: Some nodes are used for generating their son nodes, but for them we never test whether or not p holds.   □

EXERCISE 2.3.5. Show that the following function definition for *bf-existsev* is *not* correct:

$$bf\text{-}existsev\ p\ f\ L = \textbf{if}\ exists\ p\ L\ \textbf{then}\ true$$
$$\textbf{else}\ bf\text{-}existsev\ p\ f\ (flatmap\ f\ L)$$

Hint: Consider the case when $L = [\,]$.   □

CHAPTER 3

Chop-and-Expand Parsers for Context-Free Languages

In this chapter we illustrate the Chop-and-Expand parser for context-free languages in a functional language (similar to Standard ML [17]), an imperative language (Java 1.5), and a logic language (Prolog [5]). The idea of this parser is to perform a depth first visit of tree-like search space as indicated in Chapter 2. This parser works for context-free grammars which are *not left recursive*, that is, grammars in which no nonterminal symbol A exists such that: (i) $S \to^* \alpha A \beta$ for some $\alpha, \beta \in (V_T \cup V_N)^*$, and (ii) $A \to^+ A\gamma$ for some $\gamma \in (V_T \cup V_N)^*$ (see Definition 1.2.19 on page 8). If the given grammar is left recursive, the Chop-and Expand parser may not be able to explore via the depth first search the whole search space, and thus parsing may not terminate.

The reader will find in the companion book [21] the description of two general algorithms which work for *any* context-free grammar (left recursive or not left recursive): (i) the Cocke-Younger-Kasami parser, and (ii) the Earley parser. We will not describe these algorithms here.

3.1. Chop-and-Expand Context-Free Parser in a Functional Language

As indicated in Section 2.3.2 on page 26, in order to solve a parsing problem in the case of context-free grammars, we have to explore a search space which is a tree, whose root node is made out of the pair $\langle S, \textit{string-to-parse} \rangle$, where S is the axiom of the grammar and *string-to-parse* holds the input string to be parsed.

Below we present a program written in a functional language which performs the chop-and-expand parsing of a string generated by a context-free grammar $G = \langle V_T, V_N, P, S \rangle$. We use the recursive function *exists* which takes two arguments: (i) a list of *states*, also called *nodes*, and (ii) a context-free grammar which is not left recursive.

The list of states represents the current frontier of the tree which must be visited with the objective of finding in the tree a state of the form $\langle \varepsilon, \varepsilon \rangle$ (where ε is the empty string). The context-free grammar tells us how to construct the tree to be visited starting from its root, and indeed, by using that grammar we can construct, as we will see below, the son states of any given state by applying the function *expand*.

The portion of the tree which is strictly above the current frontier, has been already visited and no state of the form $\langle \varepsilon, \varepsilon \rangle$ exists in that portion of the tree.

Contrary to the function shown on page 27, the function *exists* presented here is a first order function (and *not* a higher-order function, because none of its arguments is a function or a predicate). This first order function *exists* has the advantage of allowing us to derive a chop-and-expand parser written in Java (see page 38) by a straightforward translation.

Now we indicate: (i) the conventions, (ii) the variables, and (iii) the data structures which are used in our first order function *exists*.

Any list of characters is written as a list and also as a string. For instance, [b,c,c] is also written as bcc. Given a list ℓ, the head function $hd(\ell)$ and the tail function $tl(\ell)$ are defined as usual. Thus, we have that $hd(\text{bcc}) = \text{b}$ and $tl(\text{bcc}) = \text{cc}$. In particular, for any character c, the list [c] made out of that character only, is also written as the string c. The empty string is denoted by ε. The type of the list of characters is called *char list*. It is also called *string*.

In what follows, when we write lists we will separate their members by either commas or blanks.

Pairs are denoted by using the angle brackets '$\langle$' and '$\rangle$'. For instance, the pair of the strings b and cb is denoted by $\langle \text{b,cb} \rangle$.

The type of the lists of states is also called *state list*. The type of the lists of strings is also called *string list*. This type is also called *right-hand-sides* when the elements of the lists denote the right hand sides of all the productions for a given nonterminal symbol. For instance, given a context-free grammar whose productions for the nonterminal symbol P are P $\rightarrow$ b and P $\rightarrow$ aQQ, the list [b, aQQ] has type *right-hand-sides*.

Given a nonterminal symbol, say P, and the productions for it, say P $\rightarrow$ b and P $\rightarrow$ aQQ, these productions can be grouped together and represented as the pair $\langle$P, [b, aQQ]$\rangle$ whose type is *symbol* $\times$ *right-hand-sides*.

The type of the lists of *symbol* $\times$ *right-hand-sides* pairs is called (*symbol* $\times$ *right-hand-sides*) *list*. This type is also called *grammar* when the first components of the pairs of the list are all distinct symbols. For instance, given the context-free grammar whose productions are:

P $\rightarrow$ b   P $\rightarrow$ aQQ   Q $\rightarrow \varepsilon$ Q $\rightarrow$ b   Q $\rightarrow$ bP

it can be represented as the list of pairs [$\langle$P, [b, aQQ]$\rangle$, $\langle$Q, [ε, b, bP]$\rangle$] which has type *grammar*. Each element in that list is a pair of a nonterminal symbol and the list of the right hand sides of all the productions for that nonterminal symbol.

In Table 3.1 on page 33 we show the syntactic categories of the identifiers occurring in the function *exists* and some examples of these syntactic categories. As usual, we write the terminal symbols and the nonterminal symbols using lower case and upper case letters, respectively.

The variable *sf* whose type is *char list* (also called *sentform* in Table 3.1), stores the value of a sentential form. A state, that is, a node of the tree, is a pair of a sentential form and a string of terminal symbols. We have that a descendant of a state $\langle \sigma_1, \sigma_2 \rangle$ is the state $\langle \varepsilon, \varepsilon \rangle$ iff the sentential form σ_1 generates the string σ_2 of terminal symbols.

The function *rhs* (short for *right hand sides*) takes in input a nonterminal symbol, that is, an element of type *char*, and produces in output the list of the right hand sides of the productions in the given grammar whose left hand side is the given nonterminal symbol. The type of the function *rhs* is: *char* $\rightarrow$ ((*char list*) *list*), which can also be written as: *char* $\rightarrow$ (*string list*) or as: *char* $\rightarrow$ *right-hand-sides*.

Types of identifiers.	Examples. (a and b are terminals. P, Q, and R are nonterminals.)
• Sentential form (with terminal and nonterminal symbols). *sentform sf* : *char list*	PRb
• String (with terminal symbols only). *string s* : *char list*	bb
• State. ⟨*sentform sf, string s*⟩ : *state*	⟨PRb, bb⟩
• List of states. *stl* : *state list*	[⟨PRb, bb⟩ ⟨bPQ, ab⟩]
• The right hand sides of the productions for the same nonterminal symbol. *rhs* : *char* → (*char list*) *list*	Given the productions P → b | aQQ we have that: *rhs*(P) = [b, aQQ]
• Grammar as a list of pairs. Each pair is made out of a nonterminal symbol and the list of all the right hand sides of the productions for that symbol. *gr* : (*symbol* × *right-hand-sides*) *list*	The grammar with the productions P → b | aQQ and Q → ε | b | bP is represented as: [⟨P, [b, aQQ]⟩ ⟨Q, [ε, b, bP]⟩]

TABLE 3.1. Types and examples of the identifiers occurring in the function *exists*. The members of the lists of states and the members of the lists of productions are separated by blanks (not by commas).

Note that our representation of a context-free grammar as a list of ⟨*symbol, right-hand-sides*⟩ pairs makes it easy to evaluate the function *rhs*. Indeed, (i) no two pairs in the list which represents a grammar have the same nonterminal symbol as their first component, and (ii) for each element of the form ⟨A, Rs⟩ in the list which represents a grammar, we have that: $rhs(A) = Rs$.

Given a list of states which is the frontier of a tree to be visited, the function *expand* allows us to produce the new frontier of the expanded tree to be visited. This new frontier is obtained by replacing the *leftmost state* in the given list of states (that is, the head of the list of states) by its son states. These son states are generated according to the given context-free grammar by using the function *expand*, as we now indicate.

Let the frontier of the given tree be the state list $h : T$, where the state h is the pair of the form ⟨$A\sigma, s$⟩, for some nonterminal $A \in V_N$, string $\sigma \in (V_T \cup V_N)^*$, and string $s \in V_T^*$. Then the frontier of the new tree is:

$$[⟨\alpha_1\sigma, s⟩, \ldots, ⟨\alpha_n\sigma, s⟩] <> T$$

where $A \to \alpha_1 \mid \ldots \mid \alpha_n$ are *all* the productions of the given context-free grammar whose left hand side is A, and $<>$ denotes the infix *append* operation on lists. The function *expand* has the following type:

$$expand : (char\ list)\ list \times char\ list \times char\ list \to state\ list$$

that is, $expand : right\text{-}hand\text{-}sides \times sentform \times string \to state\ list$, and it is defined as follows

$$expand(rhs(A),\ \sigma,\ s) = [\langle \alpha_1\sigma,\ s\rangle,\ \ldots,\langle \alpha_n\sigma,\ s\rangle].$$

For instance, given the two productions $P \to b \mid aQQ$ and the state list *stl* which is $[\langle PRb,\ bb\rangle\quad \langle bPQ,\ ab\rangle]$, after the execution of the statement

$$new\text{-}stl = expand(rhs(P),\ Rb,\ bb) <> tl(stl)$$

we get that a new value for *new-stl* which is

$$[\langle bRb,\ bb\rangle\quad \langle aQQRb,\ bb\rangle\quad \langle bPQ,\ ab\rangle]$$

Here is the code of the function *exists* for the Chop-and-Expand parser for a context-free grammar which is not left recursive. $terminal(x)$ and $nonterminal(x)$ are predicates which return *true* iff x is a terminal or a nonterminal symbol, respectively. The function *exists* has the following type:

$$exists : state\ list \times grammar \to bool$$

where, as already mentioned, the type *grammar* is $(symbol \times right\text{-}hand\text{-}sides)\ list$.

Chop-and-Expand Parser

```
exists stl gr =
if stl=[ ] then false
else let hd(stl)=⟨sf, s⟩ in
    if sf = ε and s = ε then true
    else if sf ≠ ε and nonterminal(hd(sf)) then                    (†)
        begin                                              // EXPAND
        new-stl = expand(rhs(hd(sf)), tl(sf), s) <> tl(stl);
        exists new-stl gr
        end
    else if sf ≠ ε and s ≠ ε and terminal(hd(sf)) and hd(sf)=hd(s) then (††)
        exists (⟨tl(sf),tl(s)⟩ : tl(stl)) gr                // CHOP
    else exists tl(stl) gr
```

Note that in line (††) above, the condition 'and $terminal(hd(sf))$' is not necessary. We have added it for reasons of symmetry with respect to the above line (†).

The initial call of the function *exists* is of the form:

$$exists\ [\langle S,\ string\text{-}to\text{-}parse\rangle]\ given\text{-}grammar$$

where S is the axiom of the *given-grammar* and the first argument of the function *exists* is a list of states which consists of one state only, and that state is the pair $\langle S,\ string\text{-}to\text{-}parse\rangle$.

3.2. Chop-and-Expand Context-Free Parser in Java

In this section we present the two Java programs: List.java and CFParser.java, which realize the context-free parsing using the Chop-and-Expand algorithm illustrated in Section 2.3.2 on page 26 and Section 3.1 on page 31. In those sections that algorithm is presented using a functional language.

The C++ versions of those programs can be found in [19, page 69]. A similar version of the program List.java can be found (with the same name) in Section 7.4 on page 232.

```
/**
 * ============================================================================
 *                     Generic Class List <T>      (class used for parsing)
 * Filename: "List.java"
 *
 * Every object of the class List<T> is a list of elements of type T.
 * The following methods are available:
 *
 *    cons(T d), head(), tail(), isSingleton(), isEmpty(),
 *    append(List<T> list2), makeEmpty(), copy(), and listPrint().
 *
 * Also cloneCopy() is available if we uncomment line (***) below and
 * comment the previous line.
 *
 * The head of the list is to the right, not to the left.
 *
 * Note that tail() is destructive.
 * After a tail operation, if we need the original value of the list, we
 * should reconstruct it by 'consing' the head of the list.
 * ============================================================================
 */

import java.util.*;         // needed for using ArrayList<T> and Iterator

public class List<T> {      // it is ok if we do not use cloneCopy()

// public class List<T> implements Cloneable { // (***) In order to use
//          // cloneCopy(), uncomment this line and comment the previous one.

    private ArrayList<T> list;

    public List() {                     // constructor
        list = new ArrayList<T>();
    }

    public void cons(T datum) {   // the head of the list is to the right,
        list.add(datum);          // not to the left.
    }                             // add(_) is a method of ArrayList<T>


    public T head() {                  // the head of the list is to the right.
        if (list.isEmpty())            // It is the last element: >------------+
            {System.out.println("Error: head of empty list!");};//            |
            T obj = list.get(list.size() - 1); // <------------------------+
        return obj;                    // isEmpty(), size(), and get(int i)
    }                                  // are methods of ArrayList<T>
```

```
    public void tail() {              // destructive tail() method
       if (list.isEmpty())
          {System.out.println("Error: tail of empty list!");};
       list.remove(list.size() - 1); // isEmpty(), size(), and remove(int i)
    }                                 // are methods of ArrayList<T>

    public boolean isSingleton() {
       return list.size() == 1;       // size() is a method of ArrayList<T>
    }

    public boolean isEmpty() {
       return list.isEmpty();         // isEmpty() is a method of ArrayList<T>
    }

    // As usual, the head of the list 'this.append(list2)', after appending
    // the 'list2' to the list 'this', is the head of the list 'this', before
    // the append operation. Thus, 'this' = 'this' <> 'list2'.
    //                              --- append(12) is not destructive!
    public List<T> append(List<T> list2) {
    List<T> 12 = list2.copy();        // 12 is an argument to a recursive call
                                      // to append. list2 should be copied!
    if (this.isEmpty()) {return 12;}
    else {T a = this.head(); this.tail();
        List<T> l = this.append(12); l.cons(a);
        this.cons(a);                 // reconstructing the list 'this'
        return l;}
    }
/**
 * ---------------- Examples of isEmpty() ----------------------------------
 * System.out.println(new List<Integer>().isEmpty());   prints true
 * System.out.println(new List().isEmpty());            prints true
 * List <Integer> v = new List();
 * System.out.println(v.isEmpty());                     prints true
 * System.out.println(v == null);                       prints false
 * -------------------------------------------------------------------------
 */
    public void makeEmpty() {
       list.clear();                  // clear() is a method of ArrayList<T>
    }
    // ------------------------- Printing a list ---------------------------
    // We assume that an element of the list has a toString() method.
    public void listPrint() {
       System.out.print("[ ");
       for (Iterator iter = list.iterator(); iter.hasNext(); ) {
          System.out.print((iter.next()).toString() + " ");
          };
       System.out.print("]");
    }

    // ------------------------ Making a copy of a list without clone() ----
    public List<T> copy() {
       List<T> copyList = new List<T>();
       for (Iterator<T> iter = list.iterator(); iter.hasNext(); ) {
          copyList.list.add(iter.next());
       };
       return copyList;
    }
```

```
// ------------------------ Making a copy of a list with clone() -------
  public List<T> cloneCopy() {                      // see (***) above
      try { List<T> copyList = (List<T>)super.clone();
            copyList.list = (ArrayList<T>)list.clone();
            return copyList;
      } catch (CloneNotSupportedException e) {
        throw new InternalError();
      }
  }
}
/** -------------------------------------------------------------------
 * Let us consider the following class to test List.java:
 * public class ListTest { public static void main(String[] args) {
 * Integer k = new Integer(6); List<Integer> la = new List<Integer>();
 * la.cons(k); System.out.print("\nla: "); la.listPrint();
 * la.cons(new Integer(4));    la.cons(new Integer(9));
 *               // in Java 1.5: we can write: 9, instead of: new Integer(9)
 * System.out.print("\nla: "); la.listPrint();
 * List<Integer> lb = new List<Integer>(); lb = la.copy();
 * System.out.print("\nlb: "); lb.listPrint();
 * lb.tail(); System.out.print("\nlb.tail(): ");
 * lb.listPrint();            // tail() is destructive!
 * la.append(lb);             // append(12) is not destructive!
 * System.out.print("\nla: ");la.listPrint();lb=la.append(lb.append(lb));
 * System.out.print("\nlb: ");lb.listPrint();
 *  } }                       // end of "main" and end of "class ListTest"
 * --- After compilation and execution: javac ListTest.java; java ListTest
 * we get some warnings and the output (the list head is to the right):
 * la: [ 6 ]
 * la: [ 6 4 9 ]
 * lb: [ 6 4 9 ]
 * lb.tail(): [ 6 4 ]
 * la: [ 6 4 9 ]
 * lb: [ 6 4 6 4 6 4 9 ]
 * -----------------------------------------------------------------------
 */
```

Now we will present the program CFParser.java. The method exists, which is listed immediately above the main method, implements in Java the *exists* function (see the Chop-and-Expand parser presented on page 34).

The program CFParser.java takes as input a context-free grammar as a string gg of characters and a string stp of characters, and produces as output a boolean value which tells us whether or not stp belongs to the language generated by gg. The details of the external and internal representations of the grammar gg are indicated in the initial comments. For instance, the grammar with axiom P and productions: $P \to b \mid a\,Q\,Q$, $Q \to \varepsilon \mid b \mid b\,P$, is externally represented as the string P>b|aQQ;Q>e|b|bP and internally represented as the list $[\langle 'P', ["b", "a\,Q\,Q"]\rangle, \langle 'Q', ["", "b", "b\,P"]\rangle]$, where "" denotes the empty string ε. The internal representation of gg is obtained from its external representation by applying a recursive descent parsing technique, that we do not explain in this book. The reader may refer to [2, pages 181–182]. Other examples of application of that technique can be found in Section 7.1 on page 193, Section 7.2 on page 203, Section 7.3 on page 214, and Section 7.4 on page 227.

```
/**
 * ==============================================================================
 *                  CHOP-AND-EXPAND PARSER FOR CONTEXT FREE GRAMMARS
 * Filename:"CFParser.java". Thanks to R. M. Burstall and E. W. Dijkstra.
 *
 * ------------------------------------------------------------------------------
 *                              --- TYPES ---
 *   List<char>   = String
 *   State        = <sentential_form, string>
 *   List<State>  = list of states
 *   Rsides       = list of String : list of right hand sides
 *   SyRs         = <Sy,Rs> = <char:symbol, Rsides:Rs = its right hand sides>
 *   Gram         = List<SyRs> : list of SyRs pairs (type of a grammar)
 * ------------------------------------------------------------------------------
 * We use GENERIC TYPES to avoid the redefinition of the functions head(),
 * tail(), cons(), isEmpty(), makeEmpty(), and append(List<String> l2) for:
 *
 * - list of String (type: List<String>). It is the type of the list of all
 *      right hand sides of a nonterminal. This type is also called: Rsides.
 * - list of States (type: List<State>)
 * - list of SyRs   (type: List<SyRs>). It is the type of a grammar. It is
 *      the type of the list of <nonterminal, list of its right hand sides>.
 *      This type is also called: Gram.
 * Redefinition of functions is necessary for printing lists of different
 * types.
 * ------------------------------------------------------------------------------
 * The input grammar is given as a string, named 'gg', generated from Gram
 * according to the following productions:
 *
 * character ::= 'a'..'d'  |  'f'..'z'  |  'A'..'Z'
 *               ('e' is reserved: see below)
 * charlist  ::= character | character charlist  (that is, String)
 * Rsides    ::= 'e'  |  charlist  |  charlist '|' Rsides
 * SyRs      ::= char '>' Rsides
 * Gram      ::= SyRs | SyRs ';' Gram
 *
 * The empty productions, also called epsilon-rules, are allowed.
 * The character 'e' is reserved for denoting the right hand side of
 * an empty production, that is, 'e' denotes the empty charlist.
 * For instance:
 * gg="P>b|aQQ;Q>e|b|bP" stands for: P->b, P->aQQ, Q->e, Q->b, Q->bP
 * In P>b|aQQ;Q>e|b|bP  we have that:
 *     \_/      aQQ is a string: "aQQ"
 *     \___/    b|aQQ is a list of elements of type String, i.e., an Rsides.
 *                 It is: ["b", "aQQ"]
 *   \_____/ P>b|aQQ is a SyRs, i.e., a pair of a symbol and its
 *                         right hand sides. It is: <'P', ["b", "aQQ"]>
 * The axiom of the grammar is the nonterminal of the left hand side
 * of the first production of the grammar.
 *
 * The string to parse, named 'stp', is either a non-empty sequence of
 * characters from the set {'a',...,'d','f',...,'z'} or is the empty
 * sequence denoted by 'e'.
 * -------------------- ASSUMPTIONS ON THE INPUT --------------------------
 * (1) The input grammar is given as a string generated from Gram according
 *     to the rules stated above. Actually, we can add a final dot because of
 *     the getCh() method of the IndexString class (see below). For instance,
 *     we can write "P>b|aQQ;Q>e|b|bP.", instead of "P>b|aQQ;Q>e|b|bP".
```

```
 * (2) When writing the input grammar, the productions relative to the same
 *     nonterminal should be grouped together. For instance, we should write
 *     "P>a|aQQ;Q>e|b|bP", instead of "P>a;Q>e;P>aQQ;Q>b;Q>bP".
 * ------------------------------------------------------------------------
 * The grammar should not be left recursive, that is, it should not be the
 * case that a nonterminal A exists such that A r ->* A s, for some strings
 * r and s of terminal and/or nonterminal symbols of the grammar.
 * ------------------------------------------------------------------------
 * This context-free parser works by exploring in a depth first fashion all
 * possible words generated by the grammar and consistent with the
 * character at hand in the string to parse 'stp'.
 * ------------------------------------------------------------------------
 * There is a global variable 'traceon'. If it is set to 'true' then we
 * can see the various steps through the execution of the program, and in
 * particular, the sequence of the lists of states which are generated
 * during the depth first visit of search space.
 * ------------------------------------------------------------------------
 * After performing a tail() operation on a list we need to reconstruct
 * the list which, otherwise, is modified (see statements marked by (***)).
 * ========================================================================
 */
import java.util.*;
// ------------------------------------------------------------------------
// string with an index pointing at the next available character.
 class IndexString {
   public String string;
   public int index;

   public IndexString(String string) {  // constructor
      this.string = string;
      this.index  = 0;       // index points to the next character to be read
   }
   public void back(){
      index--;
   }
   public char getCh() {
      char x;
      if (index < string.length()) { x = string.charAt(index); }
      else x = '.';
      index++; return x;   // index is incremented by one unit.
   }                       // If index==string.length(), then char x is '.'
 }
//-------------------------------------------------------------------------
// state : <String:sentential_form,  String:input_string>
 class State {
   public String sentForm;
   public String inString;

   public State() {
      this.sentForm = "";
      this.inString = "";           // -----------------------------------------
   }                                // state : printing function
   // for reasons of readability the empty string is printed as "e"
   public void statePrint() {
      String sentForm1 = sentForm.equals("") ? "e" : sentForm;
      String inString1 = inString.equals("") ? "e" : inString;
      System.out.print("(" + sentForm1 + ", " + inString1 + ")");
   }
```

```
                                      // -----------------------------------------
                                      // List<State> : printing functions
    public static void stlPrintNE(List<State> L) {
      if (!L.isEmpty())
        {State h = L.head(); h.statePrint();  L.tail();
         if (!L.isEmpty()) {System.out.print("    ");}; stlPrintNE(L);
         L.cons(h);                      //reconstructing the list L of states (***)
        };
    }
    public static void stlPrint(List<State> L) {
      if (L.isEmpty()){System.out.print("  []");}
      else {System.out.print("  ["); stlPrintNE(L); System.out.print("]");}
    }
 }

// --------------------------------------------------------------------------------
//           (left hand side),     (right hand sides)
// SyRs: <    char: symb,       List<String>: rhss >
 class SyRs {
   public char symb;
   public List<String> rhss;

   public SyRs() {
     this.symb = '-';
     this.rhss = null;
   }                                   // -----------------------------------------
                                       // List<String> = Rsides:printing functions
    public static void rPrintNE(List<String> L) {
      if (!L.isEmpty()) {
              String h = L.head();
              if (h.equals("")) {System.out.print("e");}
              else {System.out.print(h);};
              L.tail();
              if (!L.isEmpty()) {System.out.print(" |  ");};
              rPrintNE(L);
              L.cons(h);               // reconstructing the list L          (***)
                        }
    }

    public static void rPrint(List<String> L) {
      if (L.isEmpty()) {System.out.print("<>");}
      else {System.out.print(" "); rPrintNE(L); System.out.print(" ");}
    }
                                       // -----------------------------------------
                                       // SyRs : printing function
    public static void SyRsPrint(SyRs r) {
    System.out.print(r.symb + " -> "); rPrint(r.rhss);
    }
 }
// --------------------------------------------------------------------------------
// Gram : List<SyRs>   (it is the type of a grammar)

 class Gram {
   public List<SyRs> gg;

   public Gram() {
     this.gg = new List<SyRs>();
   }
```

```
                              // ------------------------------------------
                              // List<SyRs> = Gram: printing functions
    public static void printGramNE(List<SyRs> L) {
      if (!L.isEmpty())
         {SyRs h = L.head(); SyRs.SyRsPrint(h);
          System.out.print("\n"); L.tail();
          if (!L.isEmpty()) {System.out.print("  ");}; printGramNE(L);
          L.cons(h);
         }
    }

    public static void printGram(List<SyRs> L) {
      if (L.isEmpty()) {System.out.print("{ }");}
      else {System.out.print("{ "); printGramNE(L); System.out.print("}");}
    }
}
// ---------------------------------------------------------------------
public class CFParser {
//---------------------------------------------------------------------
/*                    RECURSIVE DESCENT PARSING
 * for making the grammar from the string gg.
 * The function 'parseString' gets one of the alternatives (as a list of
 * characters) of the right hand sides of the productions of a nonterminal.
 */
public static String parseString(IndexString f) {
  char x = f.getCh();
  String chl;
  if (('a'<=x && x<='z')||('A'<=x && x<='Z'))
       { chl = x + parseString(f); }
  else { chl = "";
         f.back(); };
  return chl;
} // At the end, the 'index' of the class IndexString points to either '>'
  // or '|' or ';' or is equal to the length of the string of the
  // IndexString f, thus, returning '.'
                              // ------------------------------------------
public static List<String> parseRsides(IndexString f) {
  List<String> rs = new List<String>();
  String chl2 = parseString(f);
                         //this is the case of the epsilon production
  if (chl2.equals("e")) {chl2 = "";};
  char x = f.getCh();
  if (x=='|') { rs = parseRsides(f); rs.cons(chl2); return rs; }
  else {//Here x can be either ';' or '.'. No other characters are possible.
        f.back();   // ready to get again either ';' or '.'.
        rs.cons(chl2); return rs; }
        // At the end, in rs we have all the productions of a nonterminal.
}
                              // ------------------------------------------
public static SyRs parseProds(IndexString f)
                                    throws RuntimeException {
  SyRs sRs1 = new SyRs(); sRs1.symb = f.getCh();
  char x = f.getCh();
  if (x=='>') { List<String> rs1 = new List<String>();
               rs1 = parseRsides(f); sRs1.rhss=rs1; return sRs1; }
  else { // x should have been '>'. If it is not '>' we throw an exception.
        throw new RuntimeException("Error in production!\n"); }
}
```

```java
                              // -------------------------------------------
public static List<SyRs> parseGram(IndexString f)
                                        throws RuntimeException {
  SyRs sRs1 = parseProds(f);
  char x = f.getCh();
  // Here x can be either ';' or '.'.  No other characters are possible.
  if (x==';') { List<SyRs> gram2 = new List<SyRs>();
                gram2 = parseGram(f); gram2.cons(sRs1);
                return gram2; }
  else if (x=='.') { List<SyRs> gram1 = new List<SyRs>(); gram1.cons(sRs1);
                return gram1; }
  else { throw new RuntimeException("Error parseGram!"); }
  }


//-------------------------------------------------------------------
//                      trace function

public static void trace(boolean traceon, String s, List<State> stl) {
  if (traceon)
    {System.out.print("\n" + s +":\n"); State.stlPrint(stl);};
  }
//-------------------------------------------------------------------
//  visiting the search space: constructing new lists of states

public static List<String> rightSides(char s, List<SyRs> gr)
                                throws RuntimeException {
  if (gr.isEmpty())
    { throw new RuntimeException ("No production for "+ s +
                              " in the grammar.\n");}
  else {SyRs sR = new SyRs(); sR = gr.head();
        if (sR.symb == s) { return sR.rhss; }
        else { List<String> rs = new List<String>();
             gr.tail(); rs = rightSides(s,gr);
             gr.cons(sR);             // reconstructing the grammar gr (***)
             return rs; }
     }
  }
//-------------------------------------------------------------------
//                      final function

public static boolean isFinal(State st) {
  return (st.sentForm.equals("")) && (st.inString.equals(""));
  }
//-------------------------------------------------------------------
//                      chop function

public static void chop(State st) {// The state st is modified. The first
                               // characters of the strings are chopped
  st.sentForm = st.sentForm.substring(1, st.sentForm.length());
  st.inString = st.inString.substring(1, st.inString.length());
  }
//-------------------------------------------------------------------
//                      expand function

public static List<State> expand(List<String> rs, String v, String w) {
  State st = new State();
  List<State> stl = new List<State>();
  if (rs.isEmpty()) { stl.makeEmpty(); return stl; }
```

```java
   else {String cs = rs.head();
         rs.tail();   stl = expand(rs,v,w);
         rs.cons(cs);                    // reconstructing the list rs (***)
         st.sentForm = cs.concat(v);
         st.inString = w;
         stl.cons(st); return stl; }
 }
//-----------------------------------------------------------------------
//                    exists function
//
// This code is directly derived from the code of the exists function
// in functional style. The search space is visited in a depth first manner.
//
 private static boolean exists (boolean traceon, List<State> stl1,
                                List<SyRs> gr) {
   if (stl1.isEmpty()) { return false; }
   else
   { State st1 = new State(); st1 = stl1.head();
     String st1sentForm = st1.sentForm;
     String st1inString = st1.inString;
   if (isFinal(st1)) { return true; }
   else if (!(st1sentForm.equals("")) &&
            ('A'<=st1sentForm.charAt(0)) && (st1sentForm.charAt(0)<='Z'))
       { List<State> stl2 = new List<State>();
         List<String> rs  = new List<String>();
         stl1.tail();                    // rs : rhs's of the nonterminal symbol
         rs = rightSides(st1sentForm.charAt(0),gr);
                                         // delete the nonterminal symbol
         st1sentForm = st1sentForm.substring(1, st1sentForm.length());
                                         // EXPAND the nonterminal symbol
         stl2 = expand(rs,st1sentForm,st1inString);
         stl1 = stl2.append(stl1);       // stl1 = stl2 <> stl1
         trace(traceon,"expand",stl1);   // tracing ---
         return exists(traceon,stl1,gr); }
     else if (!(st1sentForm.equals("")) && !(st1inString.equals(""))
         && ((('a'<=st1sentForm.charAt(0)) && (st1sentForm.charAt(0)<='d')) ||
            (('f'<=st1sentForm.charAt(0)) && (st1sentForm.charAt(0)<='z')))
         && (st1sentForm.charAt(0) == st1inString.charAt(0)))
         { chop(st1); stl1.tail(); stl1.cons(st1); // CHOP the terminal symbol
           trace(traceon,"chop",stl1);      // tracing ---
           return exists(traceon,stl1,gr); }
     else { stl1.tail();
            trace(traceon,"fail",stl1);     // tracing ---
            return exists(traceon,stl1,gr); }
   }
 }
//-----------------------------------------------------------------------
//                     main program

public static void main(String[] args) {
/** -------------------------------------------------------------------
 *  gg  : given-grammar
 *  stp : string-to-parse
 *  -------------------------------------------------------------------
 */
  String gg ="P>b|aQQ;Q>e|b|bP";   // Example 0 (with an empty production)
  String stp="ab";                 // true
  boolean traceon = true;          // variable for tracing the execution
```

```
//------------------------------------------------------------------------
// From the string gg to the List<SyRs> gr0.
// We first construct the IndexString f from the String gg.
// gr0 is the grammar encoded by the given string gg.
//------------------------------------------------------------------------
 IndexString f  = new IndexString(gg);
 List<SyRs> gr0 = new List<SyRs>();

 char axiom = gg.charAt(0);
 if (('A'<=axiom) && (axiom<='Z'))
   { System.out.print("\nThe input grammar is ");
     System.out.print("(\"e\" denotes the empty string in the rhs):\n");
     gr0 = parseGram(f);
/**
 * ------------------------------------------------------------------------
 * In order to avoid parsing, the above statement 'gr0 = parseGram(f);' can
 * be replaced by the following statements (erase the *'s, please):
 *
 * SyRs Prs = new SyRs(); Prs.symb='P';                    // P
 * String ch1P = "b";                                      //    b
 * String ch2P = "aQQ";                                    //     |aQQ
 * List<String> rsP = new List<String>();
 *           rsP.cons(ch2P); rsP.cons(ch1P);               //    b|aQQ
 * Prs.rhss = rsP;                                         // P>b|aQQ
 * SyRs Qrs = new SyRs(); Qrs.symb='Q';                    // Q
 * String ch1Q = "";                                       //    e
 * String ch2Q = "b";                                      //    |b
 * String ch3Q = "bP";                                     //     |bP
 * List<String> rsQ = new List<String>();
 *           rsQ.cons(ch3Q); rsQ.cons(ch2Q); rsQ.cons(ch1Q);// e|b|bP
 * Qrs.rhss = rsQ;
 * --------------------------- gr0 corresponding to gg="P>b|aQQ;Q>e|b|bP"
 * gr0.cons(Qrs); gr0.cons(Prs);
 *                         [<symb,     rhss>      <symb,     rhss>     ]
 *                           |      /  \           |      /  |  \
 * gr0 is the list of pairs: [<'P', ["b", "aQQ"]>, <'Q', ["", "b", "bP"]>]
 * "" is the empty string.
 * ------------------------------------------------------------------------
 */
     Gram.printGram(gr0); }
 else System.out.print("Not a grammar in input.");

 System.out.print("\n\nThe axiom is " + axiom + ".\n");
 State st = new State();
 st.sentForm = axiom + "";              // from char to String (of length 1).
 st.inString = stp;
 List<State> stl = new List<State>();
 stl.cons(st);
 System.out.print("The initial list of states is:\n");
 State.stlPrint(stl);

 boolean ans = exists(traceon,stl,gr0);
 System.out.print("\n\nThe following string of characters:\n  ");
 System.out.print(stp + "\nis ");
 if (!ans) {System.out.print("NOT ");};
 System.out.print("generated by the given grammar.\n");
 } // end of main
}
```

```
/**
 * When printing the statelist, the head is to the left.
 * input:   output:
 * -----------------------------------------------------------------------
 * javac CFParser.java
 * java  CFParser
 *
 *         The input grammar is ("e" denotes the empty string in the rhs):
 *         { P -> b | aQQ
 *           Q -> e | b | bP
 *         }
 *
 *         The axiom is P.
 *         The initial statelist is:
 *           [(P, ab)]
 *         expand:
 *           [(b, ab)   (aQQ, ab)]
 *         fail:
 *           [(aQQ, ab)]
 *         chop:
 *           [(QQ, b)
 *         expand:
 *           [(Q, b)   (bQ, b)    (bPQ, b)]
 *         expand:
 *           [(e, b)   (b, b)    (bP, b)    (bQ, b)   (bPQ, b)]
 *         fail:
 *           [(b, b)    (bP, b)    (bQ, b)    (bPQ, b)]
 *         chop:
 *           [(e, e)    (bP, b)    (bQ, b)    (bPQ, b)]
 *
 *         The following string of characters:
 *           ab
 *         is generated by the given grammar.
 * -----------------------------------------------------------------------
 *                            Various Examples
 *
 * String gg="P>b|aQQ;Q>e|b|bP";        // Example 0 (empty production in gg)
 * String stp="a";                       // true
 * String stp="abaa";                    // false
 * String stp="aba";                     // true
 * String gg="P>a|aQ;Q>b|bP";            // Example 1 -----------------------
 * String stp="ab";                      // true
 * String stp="ababa";                   // true
 * String stp="aaba";                    // false
 * String gg="P>a|bQ;Q>b|aQ";            // Example 2 -----------------------
 * String stp="baab";                    // true
 * String stp="bbaaba";                  // false
 * String gg="S>a|aAS;A>SbA|ba|SS";      // Example 2.7 of Hopcroft-Ullman ---
 * String stp="aabaaa";                  // true
 * String stp="aabba";                   // false
 * String stp="aabbaa";                  // true
 * String gg="S>aB|bA;A>bAA|a|aS;B>aBB|b|bS";// same numbers of a's and b's
 * String stp="bbabaaab";                // true
 * String stp="babaaab";                 // false
 * -----------------------------------------------------------------------
 */
```

3.3. Chop-and-Expand Context-Free Parser in a Logic Language

Here is a logic program which realizes a Chop-and-Expand Parser.

Chop-and-Expand Parser

1. $parse(G, [\,], [\,]) \leftarrow$
2. $parse(G, [A|X], [A|Y]) \leftarrow terminal(A), parse(G, X, Y)$ % CHOP
3. $parse(G, [A|X], Y) \leftarrow nonterminal(A), member(A \rightarrow B, G),$ % EXPAND
   $\qquad\qquad\qquad append(B, X, Z), parse(G, Z, Y)$
4. $member(A, [A|X]) \leftarrow$
5. $member(A, [B|X]) \leftarrow member(A, X)$
6. $append([\,], L, L) \leftarrow$
7. $append([A|X], Y, [A|Z]) \leftarrow append(X, Y, Z)$

Together with these seven clauses we also need the clauses which define the terminal symbols and the nonterminal symbols. Recall that in logic programming $[A|X]$ represents the list whose head is the element A and whose tail is the list X. In particular, if $[A|X] = [2, 3, 1, 1]$, then $A = 2$ and $X = [3, 1, 1]$. All constants in Prolog should begin with lower case letters, so that, in particular, the axiom S is represented by the character s.

The first argument of $parse$ is a context-free grammar, the second argument is a list of terminal symbols and nonterminal symbols (that is, a sentential form), and the third argument is a word represented as a list of terminal symbols. We assume that context-free grammars are represented as lists of productions of the form $x \rightarrow y$, where x is a nonterminal symbol and y is a list of terminal and nonterminal symbols.

We have that $parse(G, [s], W)$ holds iff from the symbol s we can derive the word W using the grammar G, that is, W is a word of the language generated by G.

EXAMPLE 3.3.1. Let us consider the context-free grammar $G = \langle \{a, b\}, \{S\}, \{S \rightarrow aSb, S \rightarrow ab\}, S \rangle$. It is represented by the clauses:

$terminal(a) \leftarrow$
$terminal(b) \leftarrow$
$nonterminal(s) \leftarrow$

together with the list $[s \rightarrow [a, s, b], s \rightarrow [a, b]]$ which represents the productions of G. The left hand side of the first production is assumed to be the start symbol. For this grammar G the query $\leftarrow parse([s \rightarrow [a, s, b], s \rightarrow [a, b]], [s], [a, a, b, b])$ evaluates to true, and this means that the word $aabb$ belongs to the language generated by G.

Note that in the clause $member(A, [B|X]) \leftarrow member(A, X)$, we do not require that A is different from B. Indeed with this clause, the query of the form $\leftarrow member(A, \ell)$, where A is a variable and ℓ is a ground list, generates by backtracking all members of the list ℓ with their multiplicity. $\qquad\square$

More examples of Prolog programs for parsing words generated by grammars can be found in Section 10.1 on page 293.

CHAPTER 4

Parsers for Deterministic Context-Free Languages: *LL(k)* Parsers

In this chapter we will present the so called $LL(k)$ parsers for deterministic context-free languages. We assume that the reader is familiar with the basic notions of context-free languages and context-free grammars which can be found in classical books such as [**9, 10**]. In particular, we assume that the reader knows the notions of *unfolding* and *folding* of context-free productions we have given in Definitions 1.2.12 (on page 6) and 1.2.13 (on page 6).

Unless otherwise specified, V_T, V_N, and S denote respectively, the set of terminal symbols, the set of nonterminal symbols, and the start symbol of the grammars we will consider. By V we denote the set $V_T \cup V_N$.

Before studying the $LL(k)$ parsers, let us recall that [**22**, Theorem 13]:

(i) it is *undecidable* whether or not given a context-free grammar G, there exists $k \geq 0$ such that G is equivalent an $LL(k)$ grammar,

(ii) it is *undecidable* whether or not given a context-free grammar G and a number $k \geq 0$, that grammar is equivalent an $LL(k)$ grammar, and

(iii) it is *undecidable* whether or not given a context-free grammar G, that grammar is equivalent to an $LL(1)$ grammar.

In Theorem 4.1.5 on page 48 we will see that it is *decidable* whether or not given a context-free grammar G, there exists an $LL(0)$ grammar which is equivalent to G.

4.1. Introduction to *LL(k)* Parsing

The $LL(k)$ *parsers* are algorithms for parsing the languages which are generated by the $LL(k)$ grammars (see Definition 4.1.1 below). In those grammars we assume the following hypotheses.

Hypotheses for $LL(k)$ Parsing, for $k \geq 0$.

(i) No useless symbols occur in the productions.
(ii) No trivial unit productions occur in the productions.
(iii) ε-productions may be present for the start symbol or other symbols of V_N.
(iv) The symbol \$ does not belong to $V_T \cup V_N$.
(v) The input string in V_T^* to be parsed is terminated by \$.

We begin by giving the formal definition of an $LL(k)$ grammar, for any $k \geq 0$. Recall that, as indicated on page 2, given a string w and a natural number $k \geq 0$, the prefix $\underline{w}_k$ of length k of the string w is defined as follows:

$$\underline{w}_k = \begin{cases} w & \text{if } |w| \leq k \\ u & \text{if } w = uv \text{ for some } u, v \in V^* \text{ and } |u| = k. \end{cases}$$

A. Pettorossi, *Techniques for Searching, Parsing, and Matching*, https://doi.org/10.1007/978-3-030-63189-5_4

Obviously, for every string w, $|w|_0 = \varepsilon$.

DEFINITION 4.1.1. [**$LL(k)$ Grammar**] [**3**, page 336] For any $k \geq 0$, a context-free grammar (possibly with ε-productions) is an $LL(k)$ grammar if for any $x, y, z \in V_T^*$ and for any $\alpha, \beta, \gamma \in (V_N \cup V_T)^*$, we have that:

if   (1) $S \to_{lm}^* xA\alpha \to_{lm} x\beta\alpha \to_{lm}^* xy$ and

(2) $S \to_{lm}^* xA\alpha \to_{lm} x\gamma\alpha \to_{lm}^* xz$ and

(3) $\underline{y}_k = \underline{z}_k$

then $\beta = \gamma$.

Note that (1) and (2) are two leftmost derivations of two (possibly different) words xy and xz.

DEFINITION 4.1.2. [**$LL(k)$ Language**] For any $k \geq 0$, an $LL(k)$ language is a language such that there exists an $LL(k)$ grammar which generates it.

In what follows we will also need the following definition of a strong $LL(k)$ grammar (see, in particular, Fact 4.1.4, Theorem 4.2.12 on page 55, Fact 4.2.13 on page 55, Theorem 4.3.6 on page 71, and Fact 4.3.9 on page 72).

DEFINITION 4.1.3. [**Strong $LL(k)$ Grammar**] For any $k \geq 0$, a context-free grammar (possibly with ε-productions) is a *strong $LL(k)$* grammar if for any x_1, x_2, $y, z \in V_T^*$ and for any $\alpha_1, \alpha_2, \beta, \gamma \in (V_N \cup V_T)^*$ we have that:

if   (1) $S \to_{lm}^* x_1A\alpha_1 \to_{lm} x_1\beta\alpha_1 \to_{lm}^* x_1y$ and

(2) $S \to_{lm}^* x_2A\alpha_2 \to_{lm} x_2\gamma\alpha_2 \to_{lm}^* x_2z$ and

(3) $\underline{y}_k = \underline{z}_k$

then $\beta = \gamma$.

Note that (1) and (2) are two leftmost derivations of two (possibly different) words x_1y and x_2z.

One can easily show the following fact (see also Fact 4.3.17 on page 77).

FACT 4.1.4. [**$LL(0)$ Grammar and $LL(0)$ Language**] Any $LL(0)$ grammar or strong $LL(0)$ grammar generates a language $L \subseteq V_T^*$ which is either the empty set of words or it consists of one word only. If one assumes, as we do, that for any $k \geq 0$, there are no useless symbols in the $LL(k)$ grammars, then L is consists of one word only.

THEOREM 4.1.5. [**Decidability of Equivalence of a Context-Free Grammar to an $LL(0)$ Grammar**] Given a context-free grammar G, it is *decidable* whether or not there G is equivalent to an $LL(0)$ grammar.

PROOF. First, recall that a language L is $LL(0)$ iff $L = \emptyset$ or L is a singleton (see Fact 4.1.4). Then, (α) it is decidable whether or not $L(G)$ is empty, because $L(G)$ is empty iff the axiom of G is useless, and (β) it is decidable whether or not if $L(G)$ is not empty, then $L(G)$ is a singleton. The proof of Point (α) can be found in [**21**].

We show Point (β) as follows. It is decidable whether or not $L(G)$ is finite. If $L(G)$ is infinite, then $L(G)$ is not a singleton. If $L(G)$ is finite and not empty, then, by exploring breadth-first all the derivations from the axiom of G, after a finite number of steps, we get a word, say w, of $L(G)$. Then, consider the language $L' = L(G) \cap (\Sigma^* - \{w\})$. We have that L' is context-free because it is the intersection of a context-free language with a regular language. Now, $L(G)$ is a singleton iff L' is empty, and emptiness of L' is decidable, because L' is context-free.   □

As a consequence of Fact 4.1.4 on the preceding page, Fact 4.2.13 on page 55, and Theorem 4.3.18 on page 77, we have that the parsing problem when we deal with $LL(0)$ grammars, or strong $LL(0)$ grammars, or $LL(0)$ languages, is trivial.

Thus, we make the following assumption.

Unless otherwise specified, when referring to $LL(k)$ grammars (or languages) or strong $LL(k)$ grammars (or languages), we will assume that $k \geq 1$.

An $LL(k)$ *parser*, also called a *k-predictive parsing algorithm*, is a deterministic pushdown automaton (see Figure 4.1.1) which once initialized, performs its moves according to a table T, called a *parsing table*, as we will indicate.

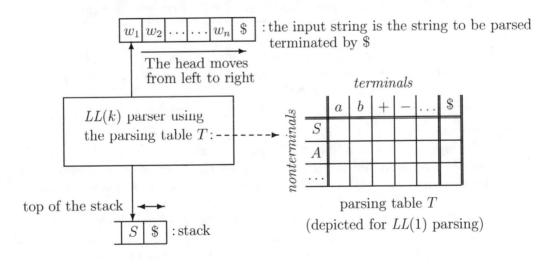

FIGURE 4.1.1. A deterministic pushdown automaton for $LL(k)$ parsing, with $k \geq 1$. The string to be parsed is $w_1 w_2 \ldots w_n$. Initially, the stack has two symbols only: (i) S on top of the stack, and (ii) $\$$ at the bottom of the stack. The input string is the string to be parsed with the extra rightmost symbol $\$$. We have depicted the parsing table T for the $LL(1)$ parsers. For the $LL(k)$ parsers, with $k > 1$, different tables should be used.

If the string to parse is the string w, the string given in input to the parsing pushdown automaton is $w\,\$$. The initial configuration of the stack is the string: $S\,\$$ and S is at the top of the stack. Recall that, unless otherwise specified, we assume that the stack is represented as a string with the top symbol on the left.

DEFINITION 4.1.6. [**Words Accepted by $LL(k)$ Parsers**] A word w is accepted by an $LL(k)$ parser, for $k \geq 1$, if the parser, starting from the configuration in which: (i) the input tape holds the word $w\,\$$, (ii) the head of the input tape (or input head) points at the leftmost symbol of w, and (iii) the stack holds $S\,\$$, being S the top of the stack, eventually reaches the configuration where: (i) the head of the input tape points at $\$$, and (ii) the top of the stack is $\$$ and no other symbols are on the stack.

Note that when presenting the $LL(k)$ parsers, some textbooks use different conventions. For instance, some authors do *not* use the symbol $\$$ at the bottom of the stack and do *not* add the symbol $\$$ at the right end of the input string.

4.2. $LL(1)$ Parsers

In this section we will study the $LL(1)$ parsers and the $LL(1)$ grammars. In these parsers the parsing automaton depicted in Figure 4.1.1 on the previous page makes its moves according to a table T, called the *parsing table*, which is a matrix whose rows are labeled by the nonterminal symbols in V_N, and whose columns are labeled by the terminal symbols in V_T. In the table T there is also one extra column which is labeled by the symbol $\$$.

A move of the parsing automaton is either a *chop move* or an *expand move*. These moves are specified as follows (see also Figure 4.2.1 on the facing page).

---

chop move:

> if the input head is pointing at a terminal symbol, say a, and the same symbol a is at the top of the stack, then the input head is moved one cell to the right and the stack is popped;

---

expand move:

> if the input head is pointing at a terminal symbol, say a, and the top of the stack is a nonterminal symbol, say A, then the stack is popped and a new string $\alpha_1\alpha_2 \ldots \alpha_n$, with $\alpha_i \in V_T \cup V_N$, for $i = 1, \ldots, n$, is pushed onto the stack if the production $A \to \alpha_1\alpha_2 \ldots \alpha_n$ is at the entry (A, a) of the parsing table T (thus, after this move the new top symbol of the stack will be α_1).

In order to explain how to construct the parsing table T of the parsing automaton for the language generated by an $LL(1)$ grammar, we need the following notions of $First_1$ and $Follow_1$ [**2**].

We first introduce the notion of $First_1(x)$, for any $x \in V_T \cup V_N$.

DEFINITION 4.2.1. [**The Set $First_1(x)$ for Symbols**] Let us consider a context-free grammar $\langle V_T, V_N, P, S \rangle$, possibly with ε-productions, without useless symbols. Let V be $V_T \cup V_N$. For every $x \in V$, $First_1(x)$ is the set of the terminal symbols in V_T beginning any string β such that $S \to^* \lambda x \rho \to^* \lambda \beta \rho$, with $\lambda, \rho \in V^*$, with the stipulation that $First_1(x)$ should have the extra element ε iff x is a nullable nonterminal symbol (see Definition 1.2.17 on page 7).

We can compute the value of $First_1(x)$, for any $x \in V$, as indicated by the following algorithm. Note that for every $x \in V$, the value of $First_1(x)$ depends, in general, on the value of $First_1(y)$, for all $y \in V$.

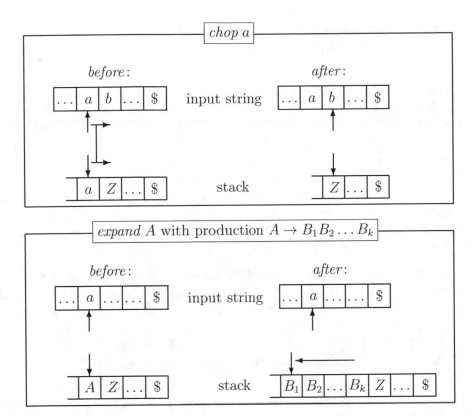

FIGURE 4.2.1. The *chop* move and the *expand* move of an *LL*(1) parser. a and b are symbols in V_T and Z is a symbol in $V_T \cup V_N \cup \{\$\}$.

ALGORITHM 4.2.2. [**Computing the Set $First_1(x)$ for Symbols**] Let us consider a context-free grammar $\langle V_T, V_N, P, S \rangle$, possibly with ε-productions, without useless symbols. Let V be $V_T \cup V_N$. $First_1$ is a function from $V \cup \{\varepsilon\}$ to the set of all subsets of $V_T \cup \{\varepsilon\}$, that is, $First_1 : V \cup \{\varepsilon\} \to 2^{V_T \cup \{\varepsilon\}}$. For every $x \in V \cup \{\varepsilon\}$, $First_1(x)$ is the *smallest* subset of $V_T \cup \{\varepsilon\}$ defined as follows:

(i) $\qquad\qquad\qquad\qquad First_1(\varepsilon) = \{\varepsilon\}$.

(ii) For $a \in V_T$, $\quad First_1(a) = \{a\}$.

(iii) For $A \in V_N$, $First_1(A)$ is a set of terminal symbols which is initialized to $\emptyset$ and is modified according to the following rule.

For each production $A \to B_1 B_2 \ldots B_{k-1} B_k$,
where: (1) $k \geq 0$, and (2) for $i = 1, \ldots, k$, $B_i \in V_T \cup V_N$,

$\qquad\qquad\qquad\qquad\qquad$ add the elements of $First_1(B_1) - \{\varepsilon\}$ and
if $B_1 \to^* \varepsilon$ $\qquad\qquad$ *then* $\quad$ add the elements of $First_1(B_2) - \{\varepsilon\}$ and
if $B_1 B_2 \to^* \varepsilon$ $\qquad$ *then* $\quad$ add the elements of $First_1(B_3) - \{\varepsilon\}$ and
$\qquad \ldots$
if $B_1 B_2 \ldots B_{k-1} \to^* \varepsilon$ $\quad$ *then* $\quad$ add the elements of $First_1(B_k) - \{\varepsilon\}$ and
if $B_1 B_2 \ldots B_{k-1} B_k \to^* \varepsilon$ *then* $\quad$ add ε.

Note that if $B_1 B_2 \ldots B_k \to^* \varepsilon$, then $A \to^* \varepsilon$ and $\varepsilon \in First_1(A)$. The following fact is a straightforward consequence of the definition of the function $First_1$.

FACT 4.2.3. [**The Nonterminal A is Nullable iff $\varepsilon \in First_1(A)$**] For any $A \in V_N$, $A \to^* \varepsilon$ iff the empty string $\varepsilon \in First_1(A)$. In particular, if $A \to \varepsilon$, then $\varepsilon \in First_1(A)$.

In Algorithm 4.2.2 we have stipulated that $First_1(x)$ is the *smallest* subset of $V_T \cup \{\varepsilon\}$ satisfying Conditions (i), (ii), and (iii). The reason for that stipulation is that, since $First_1(x)$ may depend on itself (and, this happens, for instance, when in the given grammar there is a production of the form $A \to AB$), there could be more than one subset of $V_T \cup \{\varepsilon\}$ satisfying Conditions (i), (ii), and (iii).

We can extend the above definition of the function $First_1$ from elements in $V \cup \{\varepsilon\}$ to strings in V^*, by defining a new function, also called $First_1$, from V^* to the set of all subsets of $V_T \cup \{\varepsilon\}$, as follows. In particular, when given a string made out of one symbol only, the function $First_1$ for strings returns to same value returned by the function $First_1$ for symbols.

DEFINITION 4.2.4. [**The Set $First_1(\alpha)$ for Strings**] Let us consider a context-free grammar $\langle V_T, V_N, P, S \rangle$, possibly with ε-productions, without useless symbols. Let V be $V_T \cup V_N$. $First_1$ is a function from V^* to the set of all subsets of $V_T \cup \{\varepsilon\}$, that is, $First_1 : V^* \cup \{\varepsilon\} \to 2^{V_T \cup \{\varepsilon\}}$, such that for all $x \in V$ and $\alpha \in V^*$,

(i) $First_1(\varepsilon) = \{\varepsilon\}$

(ii) $First_1(x\alpha) = $ if $x \to^* \varepsilon$ then $(First_1(x) - \{\varepsilon\}) \cup First_1(\alpha)$
      else $First_1(x)$

where $First_1(x)$ on the right hand side is constructed as specified by Algorithm 4.2.2, while $First_1(\alpha)$ is a recursive call to the function $First_1$ for strings being defined.

Note that in Equation (ii) of Definition 4.2.4, the string α may also be ε, and yet the recursive definition of $First_1$ for strings is well-founded.

The following fact is a straightforward consequence of the definitions of the function $First_1$ for symbols and strings.

FACT 4.2.5. [**Properties of the Set $First_1(\alpha)$ for Strings**] For any string $\alpha \in V^*$, we have that:

(i) $\varepsilon \in First_1(\alpha)$ iff $\alpha \to^* \varepsilon$, and (ii) if $\alpha \not\to^* \varepsilon$, then $\emptyset \neq First_1(\alpha) \subseteq V_T$.
We also have that, for any $A \in V_N$,

if $A \to \beta_1 \mid \ldots \mid \beta_n$ are all the productions for A,

then $First_1(A) = \bigcup_{i=1}^{n} First_1(\beta_i)$, and thus, for $i = 1, \ldots, n$, $First_1(\beta_i) \subseteq First_1(A)$.

Now we define the set $Follow_1(A)$ for any nonterminal A. $Follow_1$ is a function from V_N to the set of all subsets of $V_T \cup \{\$\}$, that is, $Follow_1 : V_N \to 2^{V_T \cup \{\$\}}$.

DEFINITION 4.2.6. [**The Set $Follow_1(A)$ for Nonterminals**] Let us consider a context-free grammar $\langle V_T, V_N, P, S \rangle$, possibly with ε-productions, without useless symbols. Let V be $V_T \cup V_N$. For any nonterminal $A \in V_N$, $Follow_1(A)$ is the *smallest* subset of $V_T \cup \{\$\}$ which includes every symbol occurring in a sentential form derived from $S\$$ immediately to the right of A, that is, for all $\alpha, \beta \in V^*$ and $b \in V_T \cup \{\$\}$,

if $S\$ \to^* \alpha A b \beta$ then $b \in Follow_1(A)$.

We can compute the value of $Follow_1(A)$, for every nonterminal symbol A, as indicated by the following algorithm.

ALGORITHM 4.2.7. [**Computing the Set *Follow*$_1$(A) for Nonterminals**] Let us consider a context-free grammar $\langle V_T, V_N, P, S \rangle$, possibly with ε-productions, without useless symbols. *Follow*$_1$ is a function from V_N to the set of all subsets of $V_T \cup \{\$\}$ such that for each nonterminal $A \in V_N$, *Follow*$_1$(A) is the *smallest* subset of $V_T \cup \{\$\}$ which satisfies the following rules.

Rule (i). *If the nonterminal A is the axiom S then $\$ \in$ Follow$_1$(A),*
that is, $\$ \in$ *Follow*$_1$(S).

Rule (ii). *If there is a production $B \to \alpha A \beta$ with $\alpha, \beta \in V^*$ and $\beta \to^* \varepsilon$*
then *Follow*$_1$(B) $\subseteq$ *Follow*$_1$(A).

Rule (iii). *If there is a production $B \to \alpha A \beta$ with $\alpha, \beta \in V^*$,*
then $(First_1(\beta) - \{\varepsilon\}) \subseteq$ *Follow*$_1$(A).

Note that for every $A \in V_N$, the definition of *Follow*$_1$(A) depends, in general, on the definition of *Follow*$_1$(B) for all $B \in V_N$, and the definition of *First*$_1$(x) for all $x \in V$.

Note also that the premises of Rules (ii) and (iii) are *not* mutually exclusive, because the premise of Rule (iii) may hold independently of the fact that $\beta \to^* \varepsilon$ or $\beta \not\to^* \varepsilon$. If $\beta = \varepsilon$, then Rule (iii) is superfluous because its conclusion says that $\emptyset \subseteq$ *Follow*$_1$(A). Note that in Rule (iii) we take away $\{\varepsilon\}$ from *First*$_1$(β), and this means that we do not consider the case where $\beta \to^* \varepsilon$, but this case is taken into account by Rule (ii).

In Algorithm 4.2.7 we have stipulated that *Follow*$_1$(x) is the *smallest* subset (and not *any* subset) of $V_T \cup \{\$\}$ satisfying Rules (i), (ii), and (iii). The reason for that stipulation is that, since *Follow*$_1$(x) may depend on itself (and, this happens, for instance, when in the given grammar there is a production of the form $A \to BA$), there could be more than one subset of $V_T \cup \{\$\}$ satisfying Rules (i), (ii), and (iii).

Rule (i) of Algorithm 4.2.7 is motivated by the fact that we have stipulated that the string given in input to the parsing automaton, is the string to be parsed followed by the symbol $\$$. We have that *Follow*$_1$(S) = $\{\$\}$ if S does *not* occur on the right hand side of any production.

In order to motivate Rule (ii) and, in particular, the inclusion *Follow*$_1$(B) $\subseteq$ *Follow*$_1$(A), let us consider the grammar G with axiom S and the following productions:

$$S \to A\,a \mid B\,b$$
$$B \to A$$
$$A \to c$$

This grammar generates the language $L(G) = \{ca, cb\}$. Due to the production $B \to A$, we have that *Follow*$_1$(B) = $\{b\}$ and *Follow*$_1$(A) = $\{a, b\}$, as one can see from the following two derivations depicted in Figure 4.2.2 (we have underlined the relevant sentential forms): (i) $S \to \underline{A\,a} \to c\,a$, and (ii) $S \to \underline{B\,b} \to \underline{A\,b} \to c\,b$.

As a particular instance of Rule (iii), by Fact 4.2.5 on the preceding page, we have that if there is a production $B \to \alpha A x \beta$ with $\alpha, \beta \in V^*$, $x \in V$, and $x \not\to^* \varepsilon$, then $First_1(x) \subseteq$ *Follow*$_1$(A).

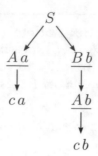

FIGURE 4.2.2. Derivations of the words ca and cb generated by the grammar G with axiom S and productions: $S \to Aa \mid Bb, \quad B \to A,$ $A \to c$.

The following fact is a straightforward consequence of the definition of the function $Follow_1$.

FACT 4.2.8. [**Properties of the Set** $Follow_1(A)$ **for Nonterminals**] For every nonterminal A, we have that:
(i) the empty string $\varepsilon \notin Follow_1(A)$, and (ii) $\emptyset \neq Follow_1(A) \subseteq V_T \cup \{\$\}$.

Note that in the theory of $LL(k)$ parsing we do *not* consider augmented grammars (see Definition 5.1.4 on page 86) and thus, in particular, we consider neither the new start symbol S' nor the extra production $S' \to S\$$.

In the case of an $LL(1)$ parser the table T is constructed as follows.

ALGORITHM 4.2.9. [**Constructing the** $LL(1)$ **Parsing Table for a Given** $LL(1)$ **Grammar** G]

For each production $A \to \alpha$ of G with $A \in V_N$ and $\alpha \in (V_T \cup V_N)^*$,
Rule (1): if $a \in First_1(\alpha)$, then we place $A \to \alpha$ in row A and column a of the table T, and
Rule (2): if $\varepsilon \in First_1(\alpha)$ (that is, $\alpha \to^* \varepsilon$), then for each $b \in Follow_1(A)$ we place $A \to \alpha$ in row A and column b of the table T. Note that, in particular, Rule (2) is applied if $\alpha = \varepsilon$, because in that case $\varepsilon \in First_1(\alpha)$.

One of the columns of the $LL(1)$ parsing table is labeled by $\$$ because we stipulate that $\$ \in Follow_1(S)$, where as usual, S is the axiom of the grammar.

Note that given *any* context-free grammar G, we can construct a parsing table T by using this Algorithm 4.2.9. One can show that if an entry of the parsing table T is multiply defined (that is, more than one production must be placed in the same entry of the table T), then the given grammar G is *not* an $LL(1)$ grammar.

Once the parsing table T has been constructed, it can be used by the deterministic pushdown automaton of Figure 4.1.1 on page 49 for parsing any given input string $w\$$. We have the following fact which we state without proof.

FACT 4.2.10. Let us consider the parsing automaton of Figure 4.1.1 on page 49 and let us assume that it is working using the table T. Initially, the stack of the automaton has the string $S\,\$$ (with S as top symbol and $\$$ on the bottom of the stack) and the input string is $w\,\$$.

(i) If that automaton should use an entry of T without any production, then the input string w *does not belong* to the language generated by the given grammar G.

(ii) If the input head of that automaton points at the symbol $\$$ in the input string and the top of the stack is $\$$ (in this case it could make a chop move of $\$$), then the input string w is accepted by the parsing automaton and w *belongs* to the language generated by the given grammar G.

We have the following theorem which we state without proof.

THEOREM 4.2.11. [**LL(1) Grammars and LL(1) Languages**] The LL(1) grammars are those which generate languages whose words are accepted by the deterministic pushdown automaton of Figure 4.1.1 on page 49, with the parsing table constructed as indicated by Algorithm 4.2.9 on the facing page.

The following theorem, also stated without proof, characterizes the LL(1) grammars and the strong LL(1) grammars [**3**, page 343].

THEOREM 4.2.12. [**LL(1) Grammars and Strong LL(1) Grammars**] (i) A context-free grammar G is an LL(1) grammar iff for every pair of distinct productions $A \rightarrow \alpha$ and $A \rightarrow \beta$ with $\alpha \neq \beta$ (recall that α or β may be ε), and for every string $w\,A\,\sigma$ such that $S \rightarrow^*_{lm} w\,A\,\sigma$ with $w \in V_T^*$ and $\sigma \in V^*$, we have that:

$$First_1(\alpha\,\sigma) \cap First_1(\beta\,\sigma) = \emptyset.$$

(ii) A context-free grammar G is a *strong LL(1)* grammar iff for every pair of distinct productions $A \rightarrow \alpha$ and $A \rightarrow \beta$ with $\alpha \neq \beta$ (recall that α or β may be ε), we have that:

$$First_1(\alpha\,Follow_1(A)) \cap First_1(\beta\,Follow_1(A)) = \emptyset.$$

As a consequence of this theorem we have the following fact [**3**, page 344].

FACT 4.2.13. [**Equivalence of LL(1) Grammars and Strong LL(1) Grammars**] The notions of an LL(1) grammar and a strong LL(1) grammar coincide.

We also have the following result.

FACT 4.2.14. [**Every LL(1) Grammar has no Left Recursive Productions**] Consider any context-free grammar G (recall that we allow productions of the form $B \rightarrow \varepsilon$, for any $B \in V_N$) with neither useless symbols nor trivial unit productions, such that there exists a production of the form $A \rightarrow A\alpha$ with $\alpha \in (V_T \cup V_N)^+$. Then the grammar G is not LL(1).

PROOF. The proof is based on the fact that if we construct the LL(1) parsing table for the grammar G, then in that table there is an entry with more than one production.

By hypothesis, in the production $A \rightarrow A\alpha$ we have that $\alpha \neq \varepsilon$. We also have that there exists $w \in V_T^*$ such that $\alpha \rightarrow^* w$ because otherwise any nonterminal B occurring in w for which there is no w' such that $B \rightarrow^+ w'$ with $w' \in V_T^*$, would be a useless symbol.

Now let us observe that, since A is not useless, there should be at least one more production for A. Let it be of the form: $A \rightarrow \beta$ with $\beta \in (V_T \cup V_N)^*$. From the two productions $A \to A\alpha$ and $A \to \beta$, by the definition of the function $First_1$, we have that:

(1) $First_1(A\alpha) \cup First_1(\beta) \subseteq First_1(A)$

(Note that, in general, it is not the case that $First_1(A\alpha) \cup First_1(\beta) = First_1(A)$, because, besides $A \to A\alpha$ and $A \to \beta$, there may be some more productions for A).

From (1) we get:

(2.1) $First_1(\beta) \subseteq First_1(A)$

From (2.1) we get:

(2.2) $(First_1(\beta) - \{\varepsilon\}) \subseteq (First_1(A) - \{\varepsilon\})$

By the definition of $First_1(A\alpha)$, we also have that:

(3) $First_1(A\alpha) =$ if $A \to^* \varepsilon$ then $(First_1(A) - \{\varepsilon\}) \cup First_1(\alpha)$ else $First_1(A)$

From (2.1) and (3) we get:

(4.1) if $A \not\to^* \varepsilon$ then $First_1(\beta) \subseteq First_1(A\alpha)$

From (2.2) and (3) we get:

(4.2) if $A \to^* \varepsilon$ then $(First_1(\beta) - \{\varepsilon\}) \subseteq First_1(A\alpha)$

From (4.1) and (4.2) we get:

(4) if $A \to^* \varepsilon$ then $(First_1(\beta) - \{\varepsilon\}) \subseteq First_1(A\alpha)$ else $First_1(\beta) \subseteq First_1(A\alpha)$

Now let us consider the following two cases: (i) $\beta \not\to^* \varepsilon$, and (ii) $\beta \to^* \varepsilon$.

Case (i): $\beta \not\to^* \varepsilon$. In this case $\varepsilon \notin First_1(\beta)$ and for all $x \in First_1(\beta)$, we have that $x \in V_T$. Since $\varepsilon \notin First_1(\beta)$, from (4) we get that $First_1(\beta) \subseteq First_1(A\alpha)$. Thus we have the following portion of the $LL(1)$ parsing table for any $x \in First_1(\beta)$:

	$\ldots$	x	$\ldots$
A		$A \to A\alpha$ $A \to \beta$	

Case (ii): $\beta \to^* \varepsilon$. Since $A \to^* \varepsilon$, by (3) we have that $First_1(\alpha) \subseteq First_1(A\alpha)$. Now let us consider the two subcases: (ii.1) $\alpha \not\to^* \varepsilon$, and (ii.2) $\alpha \to^* \varepsilon$.

Subcase (ii.1): $\beta \to^* \varepsilon$ and $\alpha \not\to^* \varepsilon$.

Since $\alpha \not\to^* \varepsilon$, there exists $y \in First_1(\alpha) \cap V_T$, and since $First_1(\alpha) \subseteq First_1(A\alpha)$ (because $A \to \beta \to^* \varepsilon$), we have that $y \in First_1(A\alpha)$. Thus, we have to place the production $A \to A\alpha$ in the $LL(1)$ parsing table in row A and column y. Also the production $A \to \beta$ should be placed in that position because $\beta \to^* \varepsilon$ and $y \in Follow_1(A)$ (because of the production $A \to A\alpha$).

Thus, we have the following portion of the $LL(1)$ parsing table:

	$\ldots$	y	$\ldots$
A		$A \to A\alpha$ $A \to \beta$	

Subcase (ii.2): $\beta \to^* \varepsilon$ and $\alpha \to^* \varepsilon$.

In this subcase we have that: $A\alpha \to^* A$ (because $\alpha \to^* \varepsilon$) and $A \to \beta \to^* \varepsilon$. Thus, $A\alpha \to^* \varepsilon$. Now, $Follow_1(A) \neq \emptyset$ (because of Fact 4.2.8 on page 54), and for every $y \in Follow_1(A)$, we have to place in the $LL(1)$ parsing table in row A and column y both productions $A \to A\alpha$ and $A \to \beta$.

Hence, having examined the two cases: (i) $\beta \not\to^* \varepsilon$ and (ii) $\beta \to^* \varepsilon$, we conclude that the given grammar G is not $LL(1)$, because in both cases there are the multiple entries in the $LL(1)$ parsing table. $\square$

The result of the above Fact 4.2.14 can be extended as follows. Recall from Definition 1.2.19 on page 8 that a context-free grammar is said to be left recursive if there exists a nonterminal symbol A such that for some $\alpha, \beta, \gamma \in (V_T \cup V_N)^*$ we have that: $S \to^* \alpha A \beta$ and $A \to^+ A\gamma$.

FACT 4.2.15. [**Every** *LL(k)* **Grammar is not Left Recursive**] For all $k \geq 0$, every context-free grammar with neither useless symbols nor trivial unit productions, if it is left recursive, then it is not an $LL(k)$ grammar.

PROOF. An informal proof of this Fact 4.2.15 is as follows. Let us consider the grammar G_1 with axiom S and productions $S \to S\,b\,|\,a$. In order to parse the word $a\,b^n$, for some $n \geq 0$, given the initial stack configuration $S\,\$$ with top symbol S, we have to perform n expand moves using the production $S \to S\,b$ and one expand move using the production $S \to a$. Since the number n can only be known by having a lookahead of n input symbols (that is, by knowing n symbols to the right of the one at which the input head is pointing) and n is unbounded, we have that it does not exist any $k \geq 0$ such that the grammar G_1 is an $LL(k)$ grammar.

A formal proof of this Fact 4.2.15 can be given as follows. We restrict ourselves to the case of $LL(1)$ grammars and we leave to the reader the case of $LL(k)$ grammars, for $k > 1$. Without loss of generality, we will consider the case of a grammar $G = \langle V_T, V_N, P, S \rangle$, whose set P of productions includes the following two productions:

$$A_0 \to \beta_0\, A_1\, \gamma_0 \qquad \text{with } \beta_0 \to^* \varepsilon$$
$$A_1 \to \beta_1\, A_0\, \gamma_1 \qquad \text{with } \beta_1 \to^* \varepsilon$$

whereby we may get $A_0 \to^+ A_0\,\gamma$ (with $\gamma = \gamma_1 \gamma_0$) via, so to speak, 'a loop' of length 2. We leave it to the reader to consider the more general case in which the productions form 'a loop' of length $n > 2$ such as, for instance, the productions of the following form:

$$A_0 \quad \to \quad \beta_0\, A_1\, \gamma_0 \qquad \text{with } \beta_0 \to^* \varepsilon$$
$$A_1 \quad \to \quad \beta_1\, A_2\, \gamma_1 \qquad \text{with } \beta_1 \to^* \varepsilon$$
$$\cdots$$
$$A_{n-1} \to \quad \beta_{n-1}\, A_n\, \gamma_{n-1} \qquad \text{with } \beta_{n-1} \to^* \varepsilon$$
$$A_n \quad \to \quad \beta_n\, A_0\, \gamma_n \qquad \text{with } \beta_n \to^* \varepsilon$$

Since in the given grammar G there are no useless symbols, either A_0 or A_1 should have at least one more production. By symmetry between A_0 and A_1, we will assume, without loss of generality, that A_0 has one or more extra productions.

Let V be $V_T \cup V_N$. Recall that, by the definition of $First_1$, for any $\alpha, \beta \in V^*$,

$$First_1(\alpha\,\beta) = \text{if } \alpha \to^* \varepsilon \text{ then } \big((First_1(\alpha) - \{\varepsilon\}) \cup First_1(\beta)\big) \text{ else } First_1(\alpha).$$

Thus, since $A_0 \to \beta_0 \, A_1 \, \gamma_0$ and $\beta_0 \to^* \varepsilon$, we have that:

$First_1(A_0) \supseteq First_1(\beta_0 \, A_1 \, \gamma_0) =$

$\qquad = (First_1(\beta_0) - \{\varepsilon\})$

$\qquad\qquad \cup \big(\text{if } A_1 \to^* \varepsilon \text{ then } (First_1(A_1) - \{\varepsilon\}) \cup First_1(\gamma_0)$

$\qquad\qquad\quad \text{else } First_1(A_1)\big)$

Hence, $First_1(A_0) \supseteq First_1(A_1) - \{\varepsilon\}$. $\hfill (\dagger 1)$

Since $A_1 \to \beta_1 \, A_0 \, \gamma_1$ and $\beta_1 \to^* \varepsilon$, symmetrically from ($\dagger$1) we get:

$First_1(A_1) \supseteq First_1(A_0) - \{\varepsilon\}$. $\hfill (\dagger 2)$

Thus, from ($\dagger$1) and ($\dagger$2) we get: $First_1(A_0) - \{\varepsilon\} = First_1(A_1) - \{\varepsilon\}$. $\hfill (\dagger 3)$

We also have that $L(A_0) \neq \emptyset$, because A_0 is not useless.

Now let us consider the following two cases:

Case (1): $\varepsilon \notin L(A_0)$.

Case (2): $\varepsilon \in L(A_0)$.

In Case (1) we have that $\varepsilon \notin First_1(A_0)$, and among the extra productions for A_0 there is a production of the form: $A_0 \to \delta_0$, with $\delta_0 \in V^+$ and $\delta_0 \not\to^* \varepsilon$. Since $L(A_0) \neq \emptyset$, we have that $A_0 \to \delta_0 \to^* w$ and $w \in V_T^+$. Thus, there exists a terminal symbol x in the set $First_1(\delta_0)$. Now, for any $x \in V_T$,

(i) $x \in First_1(\delta_0)$ implies $x \in First_1(A_0)$, because $First_1(\delta_0) \subseteq First_1(A_0)$ (recall that $A_0 \to \delta_0$ and $\delta_0 \not\to^* \varepsilon$), and

(ii) $x \in First_1(A_0)$ implies $x \in First_1(A_1)$, because of ($\dagger$3), and

(iii) $x \in First_1(A_1)$ implies $x \in First_1(\beta_0 \, A_1 \, \gamma_0)$, because $\beta_0 \to^* \varepsilon$.

Therefore, when constructing the $LL(1)$ parsing table, we have to insert in row A_0 and column x:

(i) the production $A_0 \to \delta_0$, because $x \in First_1(\delta_0)$, and

(ii) the production $A_0 \to \beta_0 \, A_1 \, \gamma_0$, because $x \in First_1(\beta_0 \, A_1 \, \gamma_0)$.

In Case (2) among the productions for A_0 we have a production of the form: $A_0 \to \delta_0'$, with $\delta_0' \in V^*$ such that $\delta_0' \to^* \varepsilon$.

Now, when constructing the $LL(1)$ parsing table, the production $A_0 \to \delta_0'$ should be inserted in row A_0 and column x, for every symbol x in $Follow_1(A_0)$, because $\delta_0' \to^* \varepsilon$.

In the rest of the proof it is important to recall that by Fact 4.2.8 on page 54, for every nonterminal symbol A, $\emptyset \neq Follow_1(A) \subseteq (V_T \cup \{\$\})$.

Now we will show that in the $LL(1)$ parsing table in row A_0 and column x, for *some* symbol x in $Follow_1(A_0)$, we will also insert the production $A_0 \to \beta_0 \, A_1 \, \gamma_0$, thereby showing that the grammar G is not an $LL(1)$ grammar.

Let us consider two subcases:

Subcase (2.1): $\beta_0 \, A_1 \, \gamma_0 \to^* \varepsilon$.

Subcase (2.2): $\beta_0 \, A_1 \, \gamma_0 \not\to^* \varepsilon$.

In Subcase (2.1) it is immediate that the production $A_0 \to \beta_0 \, A_1 \, \gamma_0$ should be inserted in row A_0 and column x for every symbol x in $Follow_1(A_0)$.

In Subcase (2.2), since $\beta_0 \, A_1 \, \gamma_0 \not\to^* \varepsilon$, we have that $\varepsilon \notin First_1(\beta_0 \, A_1 \, \gamma_0)$.

We also have that:

$$First_1(\beta_0 \, A_1 \, \gamma_0) = (First_1(\beta_0) - \{\varepsilon\}) \cup First_1(A_1 \, \gamma_0) \tag{†4}$$

and, since $A_1 \, \gamma_0 \to \beta_1 \, A_0 \, \gamma_1 \, \gamma_0$ and $\beta_1 \to^* \varepsilon$,

$$First_1(A_1 \, \gamma_0) = (First_1(\beta_1) - \{\varepsilon\}) \cup First_1(A_0 \, \gamma_1 \, \gamma_0) \tag{†5}$$

and

$$First_1(A_0 \, \gamma_1 \, \gamma_0) \supseteq First_1(\gamma_1 \, \gamma_0). \tag{†6}$$

From (†4), (†5), and (†6), we have that: $First_1(\beta_0 \, A_1 \, \gamma_0) \supseteq First_1(\gamma_1 \, \gamma_0).$ (†7)

Since $\varepsilon \notin First_1(\beta_0 \, A_1 \, \gamma_0)$, from (†7) we get that $\varepsilon \notin First_1(\gamma_1 \, \gamma_0)$. Thus, by Fact 4.2.5 on page 52, we also get that:

(i) $\gamma_1 \, \gamma_0 \not\to^* \varepsilon$ and (†8)

(ii) $\emptyset \neq First_1(\gamma_1 \, \gamma_0) \subseteq V_T$. (†9)

From (†9) and $A_0 \to^* \beta_0 \, \beta_1 \, A_0 \, \gamma_1 \, \gamma_0$, we get that:

$$Follow_1(A_0) \supseteq First_1(\gamma_1 \, \gamma_0) \neq \emptyset. \tag{†10}$$

Thus, there exists $x \in V_T$ such that $x \in Follow_1(A_0) \cap First_1(\gamma_1 \, \gamma_0)$.

Since in the *LL*(1) parsing table we should insert the production $A_0 \to \beta_0 \, A_1 \, \gamma_0$ in row A_0 and column x, for *every* symbol x in $First_1(\beta_0 \, A_1 \, \gamma_0)$, by (†7) we will insert that production in column y, for *every* symbol y in $First_1(\gamma_1 \, \gamma_0)$, and by (†10) we will insert it in column z, for *some* symbol z in $Follow_1(A_0)$.

This concludes the proof of Subcase (2.2) and also the proof of Case (2).

Thus, both in Case (1) and Case (2) there is one entry of the *LL*(1) parsing table with two productions in row A_0, and this shows that the grammar G is not an *LL*(1) grammar. $\qquad\square$

The following example illustrates Case (1) and Subcases (2.1) and (2.2) of the proof of Theorem 4.2.15 on page 57.

EXAMPLE 4.2.16. (1) The grammar with axiom A_0 and productions:

$$A_0 \to B \, A_1 \, b \mid f, \qquad A_1 \to C \, A_0 \, d, \qquad B \to a \mid \varepsilon, \qquad C \to c \mid \varepsilon$$

is an instance of Case (1) of the proof of Theorem 4.2.15.

We have that $L(A_0) = \{(a+c+a\,c)^m \, f \, (d\,b)^n \mid n \geq m \geq 0\}$. The *LL*(1) parsing table for this grammar has the two productions for A_0 in row A_0 and column f, because: (i) $First_1(B \, A_1 \, b) = \{a, c, f\}$, and (ii) $First_1(f) = \{f\}$. The following derivation:

$$B \, A_1 \, b \to A_1 \, b \to C \, A_0 \, d\,b \to A_0 \, d\,b \to f \, d\,b$$

shows that $f \in First_1(B \, A_1 \, b)$. We leave it as an exercise to the reader to verify that $First_1(A_0) = \{a, c, f\}$.

(2.1) The grammar with axiom A_0 and productions:

$$A_0 \to B \, A_1 \mid \varepsilon, \qquad A_1 \to A_0, \qquad B \to a \mid \varepsilon$$

is an instance of Subcase (2.1) of the proof of Theorem 4.2.15.

We have that $L(A_0) = a^*$. The *LL*(1) parsing table for this grammar has the two productions for A_0 in row A_0 and column \$, because: (i) $B \, A_1 \to^* \varepsilon$, (ii) $A_0 \to \varepsilon$, and (iii) $Follow_1(A_0) = \{\$\}$.

We leave it as an exercise to the reader to verify that $First_1(A_0) = \{\varepsilon, a\}$.

(2.2) The grammar with axiom A_0 and productions:

$$A_0 \to B\, A_1\, b \mid \varepsilon, \qquad A_1 \to C\, A_0\, d, \qquad B \to a \mid \varepsilon, \qquad C \to c \mid \varepsilon$$

is an instance of Subcase (2.2) of the proof of Theorem 4.2.15.

We have that $L(A_0) = \{(a+c+a\,c)^m (d\,b)^n \mid n \geq m \geq 0\}$. The $LL(1)$ parsing table for this grammar has the two productions for A_0 in row A_0 and column d, because: (i) $First_1(B\, A_1\, b) = \{a, c, d\}$, and (ii) $Follow_1(A_0) = \{d\}$. The following derivation:

$$B\, A_1\, b \to A_1\, b \to C\, A_0\, d\, b \to A_0\, d\, b \to d\, b$$

shows that $d \in First_1(B\, A_1\, b)$. We leave it as an exercise to the reader to verify that $First_1(A_0) = \{\varepsilon, a, c, d\}$. □

EXAMPLE 4.2.17. [**An $LL(1)$ Grammar and Its $LL(1)$ Parsing Table**] Let us consider the grammar G with axiom S and whose productions are:

$S \to aAb \mid b$
$A \to a \quad \mid bSA$

We have that:

$$First_1(aAb) = \{a\}, \quad First_1(b) = \{b\}, \quad First_1(a) = \{a\}, \quad First_1(bSA) = \{b\}.$$

The parsing table is:

	a	b	$\$$
S	$S \to aAb$	$S \to b$	
A	$A \to a$	$A \to bSA$	

In Figure 4.2.3 on the next page we have depicted the sequence of the input string and stack configurations while parsing the string $a\,b\,b\,a\,b\,\$$. (That sequence from configuration (1) to configuration (10) is divided into three subsequences, each of them to be read from left to right.) The black triangle ▲ indicates the symbols at hand in the input string and the top of the stack (as usual in our pictures of this section, in every stack configuration the top of the stack is the leftmost symbol).

In the last configuration of Figure 4.2.3 we have that both the top of the stack and the input head are pointing at the symbol $\$$. Thus, the given string $a\,b\,b\,a\,b$ belongs to the language generated by the grammar G. □

EXAMPLE 4.2.18. [**$LL(1)$ Parsing of Arithmetic Expressions**] Let us consider the context-free grammar G with axiom E and the following productions:

$E \to E + T \mid T$
$T \to T \times F \mid F$ $\qquad\qquad\qquad\qquad (G)$
$F \to (E) \quad \mid a$

This grammar is left recursive and thus, for all $k \geq 0$ it is not $LL(k)$ (see Fact 4.2.15 on page 57). If we want to use an $LL(k)$ parsing algorithm we have to look for an

input string:	$a\,b\,b\,a\,b\,\$$ ▲		$a\,b\,b\,a\,b\,\$$ ▲		$a\,b\,b\,a\,b\,\$$ ▲		$a\,b\,b\,a\,b\,\$$ ▲
	(1)	$\xrightarrow{\text{expand } S}$	(2)	$\xrightarrow{\text{chop } a}$	(3)	$\xrightarrow{\text{expand } A}$	(4)
stack:	$S\,\$$ ▲		$a\,A\,b\,\$$ ▲		$A\,b\,\$$ ▲		$b\,S\,A\,b\,\$$ ▲

	$a\,b\,b\,a\,b\$$ ▲		$a\,b\,b\,a\,b\$$ ▲		$a\,b\,b\,a\,b\$$ ▲
$\xrightarrow{\text{chop } b}$	(5)	$\xrightarrow{\text{expand } S}$	(6)	$\xrightarrow{\text{chop } b}$	(7)
	$S\,A\,b\,\$$ ▲		$b\,A\,b\,\$$ ▲		$A\,b\,\$$ ▲

	$a\,b\,b\,a\,b\$$ ▲		$a\,b\,b\,a\,b\$$ ▲		$a\,b\,b\,a\,b\$$ ▲
$\xrightarrow{\text{expand } A}$	(8)	$\xrightarrow{\text{chop } a}$	(9)	$\xrightarrow{\text{chop } b}$	(10)
	$a\,b\,\$$ ▲		$b\,\$$ ▲		$\$$ ▲

FIGURE 4.2.3. *LL(1)* parsing of the string $a\,b\,b\,a\,b\,\$$. The given grammar has axiom S and the following productions: $S \to a\,A\,b \mid b$, $A \to a \mid b\,S\,A$. The black triangle ▲ indicates the symbol at hand in the input string and the top of the stack (which is the leftmost symbol of the stack).

---

equivalent grammar which is *not* left recursive. One such context-free grammar is the following grammar $\widetilde{G}$ (with ε-productions):

$$
\begin{array}{lll}
E \to T\,\widetilde{E} & \widetilde{E} \to \varepsilon \mid +\,T\,\widetilde{E} & \\
T \to F\,\widetilde{T} & \widetilde{T} \to \varepsilon \mid \times\,F\,\widetilde{T} & (\widetilde{G}) \\
F \to (E) \mid a & &
\end{array}
$$

The grammar $\widetilde{G}$ can be obtained from the grammar G by avoiding the left recursion and using ε-productions. (The derivation of the grammar $\widetilde{G}$ from G is based on the fact that, for instance, the language $a\,b^*$ is generated from the axiom S by the productions $S \to a\,Z$ and $Z \to \varepsilon \mid b\,Z$.) The grammar $\widetilde{G}$ is an *LL(1)* grammar as shown by the *LL(1)* parsing table depicted in Figure 4.2.4 on the next page.

	a	$($	$)$	$+$	$\times$	$\$$
E	$E \to T\widetilde{E}$	$E \to T\widetilde{E}$				
$\widetilde{E}$			$\widetilde{E} \to \varepsilon$	$\widetilde{E} \to +T\widetilde{E}$		$\widetilde{E} \to \varepsilon$
T	$T \to F\widetilde{T}$	$T \to F\widetilde{T}$				
$\widetilde{T}$			$\widetilde{T} \to \varepsilon$	$\widetilde{T} \to \varepsilon$	$\widetilde{T} \to \times F\widetilde{T}$	$\widetilde{T} \to \varepsilon$
F	$F \to a$	$F \to (E)$				

FIGURE 4.2.4. $LL(1)$ parsing table for the grammar with axiom E and productions: $E \to T\widetilde{E}$, $\widetilde{E} \to \varepsilon \mid +T\widetilde{E}$, $T \to F\widetilde{T}$, $\widetilde{T} \to \varepsilon \mid \times F\widetilde{T}$, $F \to (E) \mid a$.

In order to construct that parsing table, we have first to compute the $First_1$ sets and the $Follow_1$ sets. They are:

$First_1(\varepsilon) = \{\varepsilon\}$

$First_1(T\widetilde{E}) = \{(, a\}$ $\qquad$ $First_1(+T\widetilde{E}) = \{+\}$ $\qquad$ $First_1(\widetilde{E}) = \{\varepsilon, +\}$

$First_1(F\widetilde{T}) = \{(, a\}$ $\qquad$ $First_1(\times F\widetilde{T}) = \{\times\}$ $\qquad$ $First_1(\widetilde{T}) = \{\varepsilon, \times\}$

$First_1((E)) = \{(\}$ $\qquad$ $First_1(a) = \{a\}$ $\qquad$ $First_1(F) = \{(, a\}$

$Follow_1(E) = \{), \$\}$ $\qquad$ $Follow_1(\widetilde{E}) = \{), \$\}$ $\qquad$ $Follow_1(F) = \{\times, +,), \$\}$

$Follow_1(T) = \{+,), \$\}$ $\qquad$ $Follow_1(\widetilde{T}) = \{+,), \$\}$

(Recall that for constructing the $LL(1)$ parsing table we need to compute the $Follow_1$ set for every nullable symbol.) In particular, the fact that $Follow_1(\widetilde{E}) = \{), \$\}$ and $Follow_1(\widetilde{T}) = \{+,), \$\}$ is shown by following derivations (see the underlined sentential forms, of which the first two show the presence of $\$$ in these $Follow_1$ sets):

$$E \to \underline{T\widetilde{E}} \to T \to \underline{F\widetilde{T}} \to F \to (E) \to \underline{(T\widetilde{E})} \to (T) \to \underline{(F\widetilde{T})} \to^* (a)$$
$$\downarrow$$
$$(T + T\widetilde{E}) \to \underline{(F\widetilde{T} + T\widetilde{E})} \to^* (a + a)$$

Figure 4.2.5 on the facing page shows the sequence of input string and stack configurations while parsing the arithmetic expression a (thus, the input string is $a\,\$$) according to the grammar $\widetilde{G}$. $\qquad\qquad$ □

With reference to Example 4.2.18 above, note that the following grammar H, which is not left recursive and has no ε-productions, is *not* $LL(1)$:

$$E \to T \quad \mid T\widetilde{E} \qquad\qquad \widetilde{E} \to +T \mid +T\widetilde{E}$$
$$T \to F \quad \mid F\widetilde{T} \qquad\qquad \widetilde{T} \to \times F \mid \times F\widetilde{T} \qquad\qquad (H)$$
$$F \to (E) \mid a$$

input string:	$a\,\$$ ▲		$a\,\$$ ▲		$a\,\$$ ▲		$a\,\$$ ▲
	(1)	$\xrightarrow{\text{expand } E}$	(2)	$\xrightarrow{\text{expand } T}$	(3)	$\xrightarrow{\text{expand } F}$	(4)
stack:	$E\,\$$ ▲		$T\widetilde{E}\,\$$ ▲		$F T\widetilde{E}\,\$$ ▲		$a\widetilde{T}\widetilde{E}\,\$$ ▲

		$a\,\$$ ▲		$a\,\$$ ▲		$a\,\$$ ▲
	$\xrightarrow{\text{chop } a}$	(5)	$\xrightarrow{\text{expand } \widetilde{T}}$	(6)	$\xrightarrow{\text{expand } \widetilde{E}}$	(7)
		$\widetilde{T}\widetilde{E}\,\$$ ▲		$\widetilde{E}\,\$$ ▲		$\$$ ▲

FIGURE 4.2.5. *LL(1)* parsing of the string $a\,\$$ according to the grammar $\widetilde{G}$ with axiom E and productions: $E \to T\widetilde{E}, \quad \widetilde{E} \to \varepsilon \mid +T\widetilde{E},$ $T \to F\widetilde{T}, \quad \widetilde{T} \to \varepsilon \mid \times F\widetilde{T}, \quad F \to (E) \mid a$. The black triangle ▲ indicates the symbol at hand in the input string and the top of the stack (which is the leftmost symbol of the stack).

This grammar H can be obtained from the given grammar G by eliminating the left recursion *without* using ε-productions, and thus grammar H is equivalent to grammars G and $\widetilde{G}$.

(The derivation of the grammar H from the grammar G is based on the fact that, for instance, the language $a\,b^*$ is generated from the axiom S by the productions $S \to a \mid a\,Z$ and $Z \to b \mid b\,Z$.)

To show that grammar H is not *LL(1)*, let us consider the following grammar which is a simplified version of H.

This grammar has axiom T and the productions:

$$T \to F \quad \mid F\widetilde{T}$$
$$\widetilde{T} \to \times F \mid \times F\widetilde{T}$$
$$F \to (T) \mid a$$

We have that:

$First_1(F) = First_1(F\widetilde{T}) = \{(, a\}$ $\qquad First_1(\times F) = First_1(\times F\widetilde{T}) = \{\times\}$

$First_1((T)) = \{(\}$ $\qquad\qquad\qquad\qquad First_1(a) = \{a\}$

We get the following parsing table (there is no need to compute the $Follow_1$ sets because ε does not occur in any of the $First_1$ sets, that is, no symbol is nullable):

	a	$($	$)$	$\times$	$\$$
T	$T \to F$ $T \to F\widetilde{T}$	$T \to F$ $T \to F\widetilde{T}$			
$\widetilde{T}$				$\widetilde{T} \to \times F$ $\widetilde{T} \to \times F \widetilde{T}$	
F	$F \to a$	$F \to (T)$			

We have that grammar H is not $LL(1)$ because in this table there exists an entry which has more than one production (actually, there are three such entries). □

EXAMPLE 4.2.19. [**A Grammar Which is Not an $LL(1)$ Grammar**] Let us consider the grammar G whose axiom is S and whose productions are:

$$S \to \varepsilon \quad | \ ab\,A$$
$$A \to S\,a\,a \ | \ b$$

We have that:

$First_1(\varepsilon) = \{\varepsilon\}$ $\qquad First_1(ab\,A) = \{a\}$ $\qquad First_1(S) = \{\varepsilon, a\}$

$First_1(S\,a\,a) = \{a\}$ $\qquad First_1(b) = \{b\}$

$Follow_1(S) = \{\$, a\}$ $\qquad Follow_1(A) = \{\$, a\}$

The parsing table is:

	a	b	$\$$
S	$S \to ab\,A$ $S \to \varepsilon$		$S \to \varepsilon$
A	$A \to S\,a\,a$	$A \to b$	$A \to S\,a\,a$

The given grammar is *not* $LL(1)$ because in this parsing table for the symbol S on the top of the stack and the input symbol a, there are two productions. □

4.3. $LL(k)$ Parsers (for $k \geq 1$)

In this section we consider the general case of $LL(k)$ parsers and $LL(k)$ grammars, with $k \geq 1$.

We first need the following definition which is a generalization of Definition 4.2.1 on page 50.

DEFINITION 4.3.1. [**The Set $First_k(\alpha)$**] Let us consider a context-free grammar, possibly with ε-productions. For $k \geq 0$, $First_k$ is a function from V^* to the set of all subsets of $V_T^0 \cup V_T^1 \cup V_T^2 \cup \ldots \cup V_T^k$, that is, $\{\varepsilon\} \cup V_T \cup V_T^2 \cup \ldots \cup V_T^k$. Given a string $\alpha \in V^*$, we have that:

$$First_k(\alpha) =_{def} \{w \mid (\alpha \to^* w\,\beta \text{ and } w \in V_T^k \text{ and } \beta \in V_T^*) \text{ or }$$
$$(\alpha \to^* w \text{ and } w \in V_T^i \text{ for some } 0 \leq i < k)\}.$$

For any $\alpha \in V^*$ and $\beta \in V_T^*$, we have that: (i) if $\alpha \to^* \beta$, then $First_0(\alpha) = \{\varepsilon\}$, and (ii) for any $k \geq 1$, $\varepsilon \in First_k(\alpha)$ iff $\alpha \to^* \varepsilon$.

We will also need the following binary operation on languages.

DEFINITION 4.3.2. [**k-bounded Concatenation**] Given two languages L_1 and L_2, their *k-bounded concatenation*, denoted $\odot_k$, for any $k \geq 1$, is defined as follows:

$$L_1 \odot_k L_2 = \{w \mid (|w| \leq k \text{ and } w \in L_1 \cdot L_2) \text{ or } (|w| = k \text{ and } \exists z, \ wz \in L_1 \cdot L_2)\}.$$

where the concatenation operation '$\cdot$' on languages is defined as usual (see Chapter 1).

For instance, given the languages $L_1 = \{\varepsilon, abb\}$ and $L_2 = \{b, bab\}$, we have that:

$L_1 \cdot L_2 = \{b, bab, abbb, abbbab\}$ and

$L_1 \odot_2 L_2 = \{b, ba, ab\}$.

Note that in $L_1 \odot_k L_2$ with $k \geq 1$, there may be words whose length is less than k.

Now we will describe how the $LL(k)$ parsing is performed, for any $k \geq 1$.

Supposed we are given a string v to be parsed and an $LL(k)$ grammar G. Suppose also that we have parsed a proper prefix p of the given string v, that is, $v = p\,u$ for some $u \in V_T^+$ and the input head is pointing at the leftmost symbol of u. We assume that the sentential form we have generated so far is: $p\,A\,z$, for some $z \in V^*$, that is, all symbols in p have been chopped and the stack is holding $A\,z\,\$$ with the top of the stack pointing at A.

In order to determine the production for expanding A, the parser uses a parsing table which is constructed as we will indicate, after the construction of some other tables, each of which is parameterized by: (i) a nonterminal symbol, and (ii) a language subset of $V_T^* \$^{0,1}$. A table named T and whose parameters are the nonterminal B and the language L, will be denoted by $T[B, L]$.

The table $T[B, L]$ can be represented as a matrix whose rows have three components (or columns):

(i) the first one is a word w in $V_T^* \$^{0,1}$,

(ii) the second one is a production for B, and

(iii) the third one is a *list of sets of words* which depends on: (iii.1) the production for B which is the second component, and (iii.2) the language L. Each set in this list of sets of words is called a *local follow sets* for B.

The rows of table $T[B, L]$ are constructed by considering the productions for B. For each one of these productions, say $B \to \alpha$, we first compute the set of words:

$First_k(\alpha) \odot_k L$

and we then construct a row of the table $T[B, L]$ of the form:

w	$B \to \alpha$	M

for each word w in $First_k(\alpha) \odot_k L$. In each of these rows M is a list of set of words such that:

(i) *if* $\alpha \in V_T^*$, *then* $M = [\,]$, and

(ii) *if* α is of the form: $x_0 B_1 x_1 \ldots B_m x_m$, with $m \geq 0$, and for $h = 0, \ldots, m$, $x_h \in V_T^*$, and for $i = 1, \ldots, m$, $B_i \in V_N$, then $M = [Y_1, \ldots, Y_m]$, where, for $i = 1, \ldots, m$, $Y_i = First_k(x_i B_{i+1} x_{i+1} \ldots B_m x_m) \odot_k L$.

The first table to be constructed is $T[S, \{\$\}]$.

When constructing the various tables, we maintain a set of tables to be constructed. Thus, initially, that set of tables to be constructed has exactly one element which is the table $T[S, \{\$\}]$.

At the end of the construction of a table, say $T[B, L]$, we update that set of tables to be constructed as follows. For each row of the table $T[B, L]$ of the form:

w	$B \to x_0 B_1 x_1 \ldots B_m x_m$	$[Y_1, \ldots, Y_m]$

where: (i) $w \in V_T^*$, (ii) $m \geq 1$, (iii) for $h = 0, \ldots, m$, $x_h \in V_T^*$, and (iv) for $i = 1, \ldots, m$, $B_i \in V_N$, we add to the set of tables to be constructed the m tables $T[B_i, Y_i]$, for $i = 1, \ldots, m$.

The process of constructing tables terminates when we have constructed all the tables which occur in the set of tables to be constructed.

At that point we can construct the parsing table for the $LL(k)$ parsing for $k \geq 1$. In that parsing table the rows are indexed by the parameters of the tables we have constructed (thus, the rows are as many as those tables), and the columns are indexed by the words in $V_T^0 \$ \cup V_T^1 \$ \cup \ldots \cup V_T^{k-1} \$ \cup V_T^k$ (recall that $V_T^0 \$$ is equal to $\{\$\}$). The entry of the parsing table in row $[B_i, Y_i]$ and column w is the production which is the second component of the row of table $T[B_i, Y_i]$ whose first component is w.

Thus,

(i) the index $[B_i, Y_i]$ of each row of the parsing table consists of the symbol B_i on the top of the stack and the string Y_i which is equal to $First_k(\sigma_i)$, where σ_i is the string of the symbols *below the top* of the stack, and

(ii) the index w of each column of the parsing table is the string of at most $k \, (\geq 1)$ symbols to the right of the input head (which is pointing at the leftmost symbol of w).

Now we will give an example of the construction of the tables in the case of an $LL(2)$ context-free grammar G. This example will clarify the rules we have given above for the general case of the $LL(k)$ parsing, for any $k \geq 1$.

EXAMPLE 4.3.3. Let us consider the following grammar G with axiom S and whose productions are:

$$S \to aAaa \mid bAba$$
$$A \to b \mid \varepsilon$$

This grammar is not $LL(1)$ because the $LL(1)$ parsing table is as follows (indeed, $Follow_1(A) = \{a, b\}$).

	a	b	$\$$
S	$S \rightarrow aAaa$	$S \rightarrow bAba$	
A	$A \rightarrow \varepsilon$	$A \rightarrow b$ $A \rightarrow \varepsilon$	

The construction of the $LL(2)$ parsing table will show that this grammar is an $LL(2)$ grammar.

> *Construction of the initial table $T[S, \{\$\}]$.*

For S we have the two productions: $S \rightarrow aAaa$ and $S \rightarrow bAba$. For each of them, say $S \rightarrow \alpha$, we have to compute the set of words:

$First_2(\alpha) \odot_2 \{\$\}$.

Thus, we have:

$First_2(aAaa) \odot_2 \{\$\} = \{ab, aa\} \odot_2 \{\$\} = \{ab, aa\}$

$First_2(bAba) \odot_2 \{\$\} = \{bb\} \odot_2 \{\$\} = \{bb\}$

From these values we get the three rows of the table $T[S, \{\$\}]$. We have that:

$T[S, \{\$\}]$:

ab	$S \rightarrow aAaa$	$L1$
aa	$S \rightarrow aAaa$	$L2$
bb	$S \rightarrow bAba$	$L3$

where the lists $L1$, $L2$, and $L3$ of set of words are defined as follows:

$L1 = [First_2(aa) \odot_2 \{\$\}] = [\{aa\}]$

(Note that aa is the word in V_T^* which follows A in the right hand side of the production $S \rightarrow aAaa$, and there is only the nonterminal symbol A in $aAaa$).

$L2 = [First_2(aa) \odot_2 \{\$\}] = [\{aa\}]$

$L3 = [First_2(ba) \odot_2 \{\$\}] = [\{ba\}]$

(Note that ba is the word in V_T^* which follows A in the right hand side of the production $S \rightarrow bAba$ and there is only the nonterminal symbol A in $bAba$.)

Thus, we get the following table $T[S, \{\$\}]$:

$T[S, \{\$\}]$:

ab	$S \rightarrow aAaa$	$[\{aa\}]$
aa	$S \rightarrow aAaa$	$[\{aa\}]$
bb	$S \rightarrow bAba$	$[\{ba\}]$

Having constructed this table, we insert in the set of tables to be constructed the following two tables:

$T[A, \{aa\}]$ and $T[A, \{ba\}]$.

Note that either the first row or the second row of table $T[S, \{\$\}]$ forces us to insert table $T[A, \{aa\}]$ in the set of tables to be constructed.

Construction of the table $T[A, \{aa\}]$.

For A we have the two productions: $A \to b$ and $A \to \varepsilon$. Thus, we have that:

$First_2(b) \odot_2 \{aa\} = \{ba\}$

$First_2(\varepsilon) \odot_2 \{aa\} = \{aa\}$

From these values we get the two rows of the table $T[A, \{aa\}]$. We have that:

$T[A, \{aa\}]$:

ba	$A \to b$	M1
aa	$A \to \varepsilon$	M2

where the lists $M1$ and $M2$ of sets of words are both empty because in the right hand sides of the productions $A \to b$ and $A \to \varepsilon$ there are no nonterminal symbols. Thus, we get the following table $T[A, \{aa\}]$:

$T[A, \{aa\}]$:

ba	$A \to b$	[]
aa	$A \to \varepsilon$	[]

After the construction of this table we do *not* add any new table to the set of tables to be constructed because in the right hand sides of the productions $A \to b$ and $A \to \varepsilon$ there are no nonterminal symbols.

Construction of the table $T[A, \{ba\}]$.

For A we have the two productions: $A \to b$ and $A \to \varepsilon$. Thus, we have that:

$First_2(b) \odot_2 \{ba\} = \{bb\}$

$First_2(\varepsilon) \odot_2 \{ba\} = \{ba\}$

From these values we get the two rows of the table $T[A, \{ba\}]$. We have that:

$T[A, \{ba\}]$:

bb	$A \to b$	N1
ba	$A \to \varepsilon$	N2

where the lists $N1$ and $N2$ of sets of words are both empty because in the right hand sides of the productions $A \to b$ and $A \to \varepsilon$ there are no nonterminal symbols. Thus, we get the following table $T[A, \{ba\}]$:

$T[A, \{ba\}]$:

bb	$A \to b$	[]
ba	$A \to \varepsilon$	[]

After the construction of this table we do *not* add any new table to the set of tables to be constructed because in the right hand sides of the productions $A \to b$ and $A \to \varepsilon$ there are no nonterminal symbols.

Construction of the parsing table.

Having constructed the three tables $T[S, \{\$\}]$, $T[A, \{aa\}]$, and $T[A, \{ba\}]$, we can construct the $LL(2)$ parsing table. We have depicted it in Figure 4.3.1 on the facing page.

	aa	ab	ba	bb	$a\$$	$b\$$	$\$$
$[S, \{\$\}]$	$S \to aAaa$	$S \to aAaa$		$S \to bAba$			
$[A, \{aa\}]$	$A \to \varepsilon$		$A \to b$				
$[A, \{ba\}]$			$A \to \varepsilon$	$A \to b$			

FIGURE 4.3.1. The $LL(2)$ parsing table for the grammar with axiom S and productions: $S \to aAaa \mid bAba, \ A \to b \mid \varepsilon$.

In Figure 4.3.2 we have shown the sequence of the input string and stack configurations when parsing the string $bba\$$. The symbol ▲ indicates the symbol at hand in the input string (that is, the position of the input head) and the top of the stack (as usual in this section, in every stack configuration the top of the stack is the leftmost symbol).

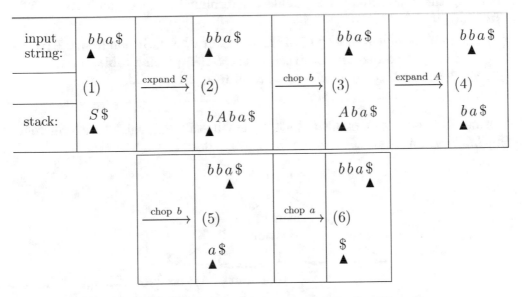

FIGURE 4.3.2. $LL(2)$ parsing of the string $bba\$$. The given grammar with axiom S has the following productions: $S \to aAaa \mid bAba$, $A \to b \mid \varepsilon$. The symbol ▲ indicates the symbol at hand in the input string and the top of the stack (which is the leftmost symbol).

Note that the expansion of S (see configurations (1) and (2) of Figure 4.3.2) is done using the production $S \to bAba$ (see the entry at row $[S, \{\$\}]$ and column bb of the parsing table depicted in Figure 4.3.1) because:

(i) below S on the stack there is $\$$ (and $[S, \{\$\}]$ identifies the row), and

(ii) the symbols in the position of the input head and at its right are bb (and bb identifies the column).

Analogously, the expansion of A is done using the production $A \to \varepsilon$ (see the entry at row $[A, \{ba\}]$ and column ba of the parsing table depicted in Figure 4.3.1) because:

(i) below A on the stack there are the symbols ba (and $[A, \{ba\}]$ identifies the row), and

(ii) the symbols in the position of the input head and at its right are ba (and ba identifies the column).

In the final configuration (6) of Figure 4.3.2 on the previous page we have that both the input head and the top of the stack are pointing at the symbol \$.

Thus, the given string bba belongs to the language generated by the grammar G. $\qquad\square$

We have the following property of the $LL(k)$ parsing, for any $k \geq 1$.

$LL(k)$ Parsing, for $k \geq 1$.

The production which has to be applied by the Chop-and-Expand parser for expanding the nonterminal A is uniquely determined by (see also Figure 4.3.3):

 (i) A itself,

 (ii) the prefixes of length k (≥ 0) of the words in $V_T^* \$$ derivable from $z\$$ (these prefixes are needed for constructing the $LL(k)$ parsing table), and

 (iii) the leftmost k symbols of u (or u itself if $|u| < k$).

The reader may want to look also at what we will state on page 72 with reference to strong $LL(k)$ grammars.

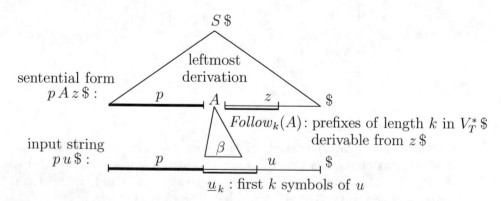

$\underline{u}_k$: first k symbols of u

FIGURE 4.3.3. $LL(k)$ parsing, for $k \geq 1$. The derivation from S to pAz is a leftmost derivation. $Follow_k(A)$ depends on the given grammar only. Recall that, as stated in Fact 4.2.13 on page 55, every $LL(1)$ grammar is also a strong $LL(1)$ grammar and vice versa. Thus, for $k = 1$, the string $Follow_k(A)$ need not be considered.

Now in order to state Theorem 4.3.6 on page 71, we define for any nonterminal A and for any $k \geq 1$, the set $Follow_k(A)$.

DEFINITION 4.3.4. [**The Set $Follow_k(A)$**] Let us consider a context-free grammar $\langle V_T, V_N, P, S \rangle$, possibly with ε-productions, without useless symbols. Let V be $V_T \cup V_N$. For any $k \geq 1$, $Follow_k$ is a function from V_N to the set of all subsets of $V_T^* \$^{0,1}$. For any $A \in V_N$, $Follow_k(A)$ is the *smallest* set such that for any string $w \in (V_T^0 \$ \cup V_T^1 \$ \cup V_T^2 \$ \cup \ldots \cup V_T^{k-1} \$ \cup V_T^k)$,

> if $S \$ \to^* \alpha A \beta$ for some $\alpha \in V^*$ and $\beta \in V^* \$$ and $w \in First_k(\beta)$
>
> then $w \in Follow_k(A)$.

Thus, by definition, for every nonterminal $A \in V_N$, $Follow_k(A)$ is a set of words w in $V_T^0 \$ \cup V_T^1 \$ \cup V_T^2 \$ \cup \ldots \cup V_T^{k-1} \$ \cup V_T^k$ which occur in a sentential form derived from $S \$$ immediately to the right of A.

We have that for any $k \geq 1$ and $A \in V_N$, the empty string ε is *not* an element of $Follow_k(A)$.

NOTE 4.3.5. On page 158 the reader will find an extension of this Definition 4.3.4 where the $Follow_k$ set is defined also for terminal symbols. In that extended definition the symbol $\$$ is not considered. $\qquad \square$

Note that the above Definition 4.3.4 does *not* provide an algorithm that, for any $k \geq 1$, given the productions of an $LL(k)$ grammar, constructs the set $Follow_k(A)$ for any nonterminal A. However, for $k=1$, we did provide an algorithm for constructing the set $Follow_1(A)$ (see Algorithm 4.2.7 on page 53).

The following result which we state without proof, characterizes the $LL(k)$ grammars and the strong $LL(k)$ grammars for any $k \geq 1$ [**3**, pages 342–344].

THEOREM 4.3.6. [**$LL(k)$ Grammars and Strong $LL(k)$ Grammars**] (i) A context-free grammar G is an $LL(k)$ grammar iff for every pair of distinct productions $A \to \alpha$ and $A \to \beta$ with $\alpha \neq \beta$, and for every string $w A \sigma$ such that $S \to^*_{lm} w A \sigma$, we have that:

> $First_k(\alpha \sigma) \cap First_k(\beta \sigma) = \emptyset$.

(ii) A context-free grammar G is a *strong $LL(k)$* grammar iff for every pair of distinct productions $A \to \alpha$ and $A \to \beta$ with $\alpha \neq \beta$, we have that:

> $First_k(\alpha \, Follow_k(A)) \cap First_k(\beta \, Follow_k(A)) = \emptyset$.

EXAMPLE 4.3.7. The grammar G with axiom S and the following productions:

> $S \to aAaa \mid bAba$
>
> $A \to b \mid \varepsilon$

is an $LL(2)$ grammar as the above Example 4.3.3 shows, but it is *not* a strong $LL(2)$ grammar.

Indeed, we have that:

> $Follow_2(A)) = \{aa, ba\}$ and
>
> $First_2(b \, Follow_2(A)) \cap First_2(\varepsilon \, Follow_2(A)) = \{ba, bb\} \cap \{aa, ba\} = \{ba\} \neq \emptyset$.

We leave it to the reader to check the following facts which we state without proofs.

FACT 4.3.8. The rules we have given above for constructing the parsing table for $LL(1)$ parsing, can be obtained by instantiating for $k = 1$ the rules for $LL(k)$ parsing for $k \geq 1$.

FACT 4.3.9. [**$LL(k)$ Languages Can Be Generated by Strong $LL(k)$ Grammars**] For any $k \geq 0$, if a language L can be generated by an $LL(k)$ grammar, then L can be generated by a strong $LL(k)$ grammar.

In view of this fact, if we consider the strong $LL(k)$ grammar which generates a given $LL(k)$ language L, then the language L can parsed by using a Chop-and-Expand parser whose expansion steps satisfy the following property.

Strong $LL(k)$ Parsing, for $k \geq 1$.

The production which has to be applied by the Chop-and-Expand parser for expanding the nonterminal A is uniquely determined by:

(i) A itself, and

(ii) the first k symbols of the input string which are to the right of the last symbol which has been chopped (or the whole string to the right of that symbol, if there are less than k symbols to the the right of it).

The reader may want to look also at what we stated on page 70, where the Chop-and-Expand $LL(k)$ parsing process has been described with respect to $LL(k)$ grammars, rather than strong $LL(k)$ grammars.

Now we recall the notions of the Chomsky normal form and Greibach normal form for extended context-free grammars, that is, context-free grammars where every nonterminal symbol may have an ε-production (see, for instance, [**21**]).

DEFINITION 4.3.10. [**Chomsky Normal Form. Version with Epsilon Productions**] An extended context-free grammar $G = \langle V_T, V_N, P, S \rangle$ is said to be in *Chomsky normal form* if its productions are of the form:

$A \to B\,C$ for $A, B, C \in V_N$ or

$A \to a$ for $A \in V_N$ and $a \in V_T$.

If $\varepsilon \in L(G)$, then (i) the set of productions of G includes also the production $S \to \varepsilon$, and (ii) S does not occur on the right hand side of any production [**2**].

DEFINITION 4.3.11. [**Greibach Normal Form. Version with Epsilon Productions**] An extended context-free grammar $G = \langle V_T, V_N, P, S \rangle$ is said to be in *Greibach normal form* if its productions are of the form:

$A \to a\,\alpha$ for $A \in V_N$, $a \in V_T$, $\alpha \in V_N^*$.

If $\varepsilon \in L(G)$, then the set of productions of G includes also the production $S \to \varepsilon$.

FACT 4.3.12. [**From $LL(k)$ Grammars to $LL(k+1)$ Grammars in Greibach Normal Form**] [**3**, page 362] Let L be a language that can be generated by an $LL(k)$ grammar for some $k \geq 0$. Then: (i) $L - \{\varepsilon\}$ can be generated by an $LL(k+1)$ grammar in Greibach normal form without ε-productions, and (ii) L can be generated by an $LL(k+1)$ grammar G in Greibach normal form without ε-productions and we have to add to that grammar the production $S \to \varepsilon$ iff $\varepsilon \in L$ [**22**, Theorems 3, Theorem 4, and Corollary 3].

In the following two examples the reader may see in action the techniques for producing from an $LL(1)$ grammar an equivalent $LL(2)$ grammar in Greibach normal form. These techniques constitute the basis for the proof of the above Fact 4.3.12. Without loss of generality, we assume that the given $LL(1)$ grammar has no unit productions, that is, productions of the form $A \to B$, for some $A, B \in V_N$ [**21**].

EXAMPLE 4.3.13. [**From *LL(1)* Grammars to *LL(2)* Grammars in Greibach Normal Form: Example 1**] Let us consider the $LL(1)$ grammar G with axiom S and the following productions:

$$S \to AB \qquad\qquad A \to aA \mid \varepsilon \qquad\qquad B \to bA \mid \varepsilon$$

This grammar G is, indeed, an $LL(1)$ grammar, as the reader may verify, because the $LL(1)$ parsing table is as follows:

	a	b	$\$$
S	$S \to AB$	$S \to AB$	$S \to AB$
A	$A \to aA$	$A \to \varepsilon$	$A \to \varepsilon$
B		$B \to bA$	$B \to \varepsilon$

This table is constructed after computing the following sets: $First_1(S) = \{a, b, \varepsilon\}$, $First_1(A) = \{a, \varepsilon\}$, $First_1(B) = \{b, \varepsilon\}$, $First_1(AB) = \{a, b, \varepsilon\}$, $Follow_1(S) = \{\$\}$, $Follow_1(A) = \{b, \$\}$, and $Follow_1(B) = \{\$\}$.

We want to derive a grammar in Greibach normal form which is equivalent to G. In that equivalent grammar we allow also the production $S \to \varepsilon$ if $\varepsilon \in L(G)$. In our case, indeed, we have the production $S \to \varepsilon$ because $\varepsilon \in L(G)$.

We start from the axiom S and we perform *leftmost unfolding* steps (that is, we unfold the leftmost nonterminals of the sentential forms), thereby producing new sentential forms from old ones. We stop these unfolding steps when we get: either

(H1) ε, or

(H2) a terminal symbol $a \in V_T$, or

(H3) a string of the form $a\sigma_1 \ldots \sigma_n$, for some $n \geq 1$, where $a \in V_T$, and
for $i = 1, \ldots, n$, we have that $\sigma_i \in V_T V_N^* \cup \{S\}$.

One can show that by doing so, we always construct a *finite* tree of sentential forms (see Figure 4.3.4 on the next page for the case of our grammar G). Every leaf of that tree allows us to generate, as we will indicate, a production of a grammar in Greibach normal form equivalent to G.

Note that, since we perform only leftmost unfolding steps, the decomposition of the sentential form into a sequence of the form $a\sigma_1 \ldots \sigma_n$ satisfying the Condition (H3) above, may not be unique. For instance, $abAS$ can be decomposed either into the two substrings: a and bAS, or into the three substrings: a, bA, and S.

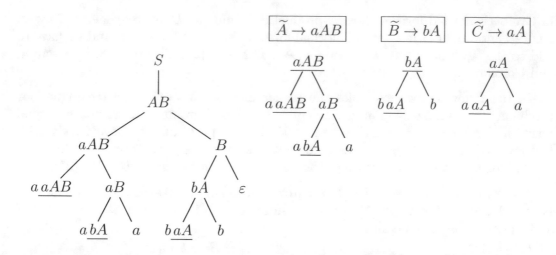

FIGURE 4.3.4. Trees of sentential forms obtained by unfolding the left-most nonterminals. The given grammar has axiom S and productions: $S \to AB$, $A \to aA \mid \varepsilon$, $B \to bA \mid \varepsilon$. The nullable symbols are S, A, and B. We have indicated within boxes the productions which are generated by the roots of the trees of sentential forms whose root is *not* the axiom S.

Then we apply as long as possible the following Tree Closure Rule.

Tree Closure Rule.
For each leaf where Condition (H3) holds, for $i = 1, \ldots, n$, with $n \geq 1$, and for every σ_i which is *not* a terminal symbol and is different from S, we construct a new tree of sentential forms whose root is σ_i and whose nodes are obtained from the root by performing leftmost unfolding steps until at each leaf one of the above two Conditions (H2) or (H3) becomes true.
(Note that Condition (H1) can never become true because $\sigma_i \in V_T V_N^*$.)

The leaves of these new trees we will construct, may determine the construction of more trees of sentential forms, because we have to apply the above *Tree Closure Rule* until all leaves of all trees of sentential forms are either:

(i) ε, or
(ii) a terminal symbol, or
(iii) a string of the form $a\sigma_1 \ldots \sigma_n$, for some $n \geq 1$, where $a \in V_T$, and
      for $i = 1, \ldots, n$, each substring σ_i is the label of the root of a tree.

Having terminated the constructions of all these trees, we consider for each tree with root σ different from S, a new nonterminal A_σ and we introduce a production of the form $A_\sigma \to \sigma$. We also introduce a production of the form $A_a \to a$, where A_a is a new nonterminal symbol, for each leaf of a tree which is made out of the terminal symbol a only.

We then perform all possible folding steps, both at the roots and at the leaves of the trees we have constructed, by using the productions of the form $A_\sigma \to \sigma$ or $A_a \to a$ we have introduced. In particular, a leaf with the sentential form $a\sigma_1 \ldots \sigma_n$, with $n \geq 0$, is replaced by the leaf with the sentential form $aA_{\sigma_1} \ldots A_{\sigma_n}$.

Finally, we get the desired productions of the grammar in Greibach normal form by considering for every root-to-leaf path in every tree, a production of the form $A \to \gamma$, where A is the label of the root and γ is the label of the leaf.

In the case of our grammar G above, starting from the trees of sentential forms depicted in Figure 4.3.4 on the facing page, we first introduce the following three productions (see the roots, different from S, of the trees of Figure 4.3.4):

$$\widetilde{A} \to aAB$$
$$\widetilde{B} \to bA$$
$$\widetilde{C} \to aA$$

Then, by using these productions, we perform the folding steps at the leaves and at the roots of those trees (see the underlined substrings in Figure 4.3.4 on the preceding page). Finally, from the root-to-leaf paths of those trees, after the folding steps, we get the following productions in Greibach normal form (see also Figure 4.3.5):

$$S \to a\widetilde{A} \mid a\widetilde{B} \mid a \mid b\widetilde{C} \mid b \mid \varepsilon$$
$$\widetilde{A} \to a\widetilde{A} \mid a\widetilde{B} \mid a$$
$$\widetilde{B} \to b\widetilde{C} \mid b$$
$$\widetilde{C} \to a\widetilde{C} \mid a$$

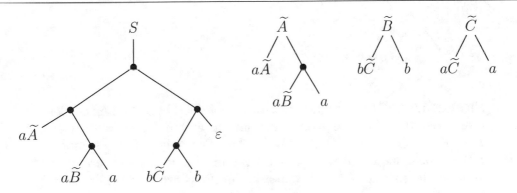

FIGURE 4.3.5. Root-to-leaf paths of the trees of Figure 4.3.4 on the preceding page after performing the folding steps.

Note that no unit productions are generated. We leave it to the reader to check that these productions belong to an *LL(2)* grammar. □

The following example is a bit more complex than the above Example 4.3.13 on page 73, in the sense that the sentential forms of some of the leaves will be viewed as concatenations of the form $a\sigma_1 \ldots \sigma_n$ with $n > 1$, while in Example 4.3.13 we always had $n = 1$.

EXAMPLE 4.3.14. [**From $LL(1)$ Grammars to $LL(2)$ Grammars in Greibach Normal Form: Example 2**] Let us consider the $LL(1)$ grammar G_1 with axiom T and the following productions:

$$T \to FT'$$
$$T' \to \varepsilon \quad | \times FT' \qquad\qquad (G_1)$$
$$F \to (T) \mid a$$

This grammar G_1 is an $LL(1)$ grammar which can be derived from the following left recursive grammar G_2 (which is *not* an $LL(1)$ grammar) with productions:

$$T \to F \quad | T \times F$$
$$F \to (T) \mid a \qquad\qquad (G_2)$$

Starting from the axiom T of the grammar G_1, by performing some unfolding steps by using the productions of the grammar G_1 itself, according to the rules described in the above Example 4.3.13 on page 73, we get the three trees of sentential forms depicted in Figure 4.3.6.

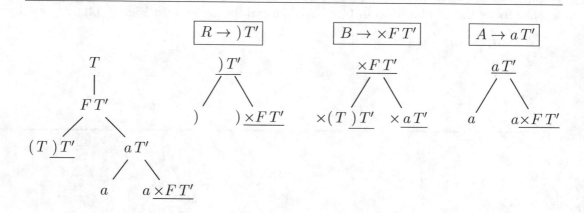

FIGURE 4.3.6. Trees of sentential forms obtained by unfolding the leftmost nonterminals. The given grammar has axiom T and productions: $T \to FT'$, $T' \to \varepsilon \mid \times FT'$, $F \to (T) \mid a$. The only nullable symbol is T'. We have indicated within boxes the productions which are generated by the roots of trees of sentential forms whose root is not the axiom T.

Note that: (i) the string $\times(T)T'$ has been viewed as the concatenation $\times \sigma_1 \sigma_2 \sigma_3$ where $\sigma_1 = ($, $\sigma_2 = T$, and $\sigma_3 =)T'$, and (ii) the string $\times aT'$ has been viewed as the concatenation $\times \sigma_1$ where $\sigma_1 = aT'$.

Then we introduce the four productions:

$$R \to)T'$$
$$B \to \times FT'$$
$$P \to ($$
$$A \to aT'$$

In particular, (i) the production $P \to ($ comes from $\sigma_1 = ($ in $\times (T)T' = \times\sigma_1\sigma_2\sigma_3$, and (ii) the production $A \to aT'$ comes from $\sigma_1 = aT'$ in $\times aT' = \times\sigma_1$.

Then if we perform the folding steps by using these productions, we get from the root-to-leaf paths of the trees of Figure 4.3.6 on the preceding page, the grammar G_3 which has the following productions in Greibach normal form:

$$
\begin{array}{ll}
T \to (T\,R & | \, a \quad | \, a\,B \\
R \to) & | \,)\,B \\
B \to \times P\,T\,R & | \, \times A \qquad\qquad\qquad\qquad (G_3) \\
P \to (& \\
A \to a & | \, a\,B
\end{array}
$$

No unit productions are generated, and since the axiom T is not nullable, we do not have the production $T \to \varepsilon$. We leave it to the reader to check that the grammar G_3 is an $LL(2)$ grammar (see, in particular, the productions for B). $\qquad\square$

FACT 4.3.15. [**Grammars in Greibach Normal Form and $LL(1)$ Grammars and Languages**] If a grammar G is in Greibach normal form and for each nonterminal A and terminal a, there exists at most one production of the form $A \to a\,\alpha$ for some $\alpha \in V_N^*$ and the only ε-production allowed is $S \to \varepsilon$, then G is $LL(1)$.

Recall that in any $LL(1)$ grammar we allow ε-productions for *each* nonterminal symbol, and thus the class of such grammars properly includes the class of the grammars in Greibach normal form mentioned in the above Fact 4.3.15.

FACT 4.3.16. [**Grammars in Chomsky Normal Form and $LL(k)$ Grammars and Languages**] [4, page 689] For any $k \geq 0$, every $LL(k)$ language has an $LL(k+1)$ grammar in Chomsky normal form.

As already mentioned, we have the following result.

FACT 4.3.17. [**$LL(0)$ Languages**] A language $L \in LL(0)$ iff $L = \emptyset$ or L is a singleton. If one assume, as we do, that there are no useless symbols in the $LL(k)$ grammars, for any $k \geq 0$ (see the hypotheses listed on page 47), then L is a singleton.

THEOREM 4.3.18. [**Hierarchy of $LL(k)$ Grammars and Languages**] For every $k \geq 0$, (i) the class of the $LL(k)$ grammars is properly contained in the class of the $LL(k+1)$ grammars, and (ii) the class of the $LL(k)$ languages is properly contained in the class of the $LL(k+1)$ languages.

The proof of this Theorem 4.3.18 is obvious for $k = 0$. The proof for all $k \geq 1$ is based on the fact that the language:

$$
L_k = \{a^n w \mid n \geq 1 \text{ and } w \in \{b, c, b^k d\}^n\} \qquad\qquad (L_k)
$$

is an $LL(k)$ language and it is not an $LL(k-1)$ language [4, page 686]. The $LL(k)$ grammar G_k which generates L_k, has axiom S and the following productions:

$$
\begin{array}{ll}
S \to a\,T & A \to b\,B \quad | \, c \qquad\qquad\qquad (G_k) \\
T \to S\,A \, | A & B \to b^{k-1}\,d \, | \varepsilon
\end{array}
$$

Moreover, every $LL(k)$ grammar which generates L_k should have an epsilon production, that is, a production whose right hand side is the empty word ε. [4, page 687].

FACT 4.3.19. [**$LL(k)$ Grammars and Epsilon Productions**] For all $k \geq 1$, if a language is generated by an $LL(k+1)$ grammar without epsilon productions, then it is generated by an $LL(k)$ grammar (possibly with epsilon productions) [**4**, page 688].

The grammar G_{k+1} with axiom S and the following productions (none of which is an epsilon production):

$$S \to a\,S\,A \quad | \, a\,A$$
$$A \to b^{k-1}\,d \,\, | \, b \quad | \, c \qquad\qquad (G_{k+1})$$

is an $LL(k+1)$ grammar which generates the $LL(k)$ language L_k (see above on the previous page). Recall that the language L_k is generated by the $LL(k)$ grammar G_k, and thus it is an $LL(k)$ language.

We have the following result due to D. J. Rosenkrantz and R. E. Stearns [**22**]. It refers to the class of the $LR(1)$ languages (see Definition 5.4.8 on page 113).

FACT 4.3.20. [**$LL(k)$ Languages Contained in $LR(1)$ Languages**] For every $k \geq 0$, the class of the $LL(k)$ languages is *properly* contained in the class of the $LR(1)$ languages. Thus, $\bigcup_{k \geq 0} LL(k) \subset LR(1)$.

Since, as we will state in Fact 5.8.12 on page 154, the class of the $LR(1)$ languages coincides with the class of the deterministic context-free languages (see Definition 5.2.13 on page 97), we have the following consequences of Fact 4.3.20:

(i) *every language which is generated by an $LL(k)$ grammar, for some $k \geq 0$, is a deterministic context-free language,* and

(ii) there exists a proper subclass $\mathcal{C}$ of the deterministic context-free languages such that for every language L in $\mathcal{C}$ there is no $k \geq 0$ such that L is generated by an $LL(k)$ grammar.

Concerning the relationship between $LL(k)$ grammars and $LR(k)$ grammars (these classes of grammars will be introduced in Definition 5.1.1 on page 85), we anticipate here two results that will be presented later on.

(i) For any $k \geq 0$, the class of strongly reduced $LL(k)$ grammars (the notion of strongly reduced grammar is introduced in Definition 5.4.18 on page 124) is properly contained in the class of strongly reduced $LR(k)$ grammars (see Theorem 5.4.19 on page 124 [**25**, page 248]).

(ii) Since by Theorem 5.8.13 on page 154 strongly reduced $LR(k)$ grammars are unambiguous (the notion of unambiguous grammar is introduced in Definition 5.8.1 on page 149), we have that also *strongly reduced $LL(k)$ grammars are unambiguous.*

FACT 4.3.21. [**$LL(k)$ Languages Contained in $LR(1)$ Languages: an Example**] The language $L = \{a^n b^n \mid n \geq 1\} \cup \{a^n c^n \mid n \geq 1\}$ is a deterministic context-free language (and thus an $LR(1)$ language) and there is no $k \geq 0$ such that L is an $LL(k)$ language [**4**, page 689].

One can show that the language $L = \{a^n b^n \mid n \geq 1\} \cup \{a^n c^n \mid n \geq 1\}$ is actually an $LR(0)$ language (and thus, it is an $LR(1)$ language) by using the techniques we will present in the following Chapter 5.

The following fact is an immediate consequence of the Kleene Theorem (see, for instance, [21, Section 2.5]).

FACT 4.3.22. [**Regular Languages and $LL(1)$ Grammars**] Every regular language has an $LL(1)$ grammar.

FACT 4.3.23. [**Avoiding the Occurrence of the Axiom on the Right Hand Sides of the Productions of $LL(k)$ Grammars**] For any $k \geq 1$, for any $LL(k)$ grammar $G = \langle V_T, V_N, P, S \rangle$, the grammar $G' = \langle V_T, V_N, P \cup \{S' \to S\}, S' \rangle$, where S' is a new nonterminal symbol, is an $LL(k)$ grammar such that: (i) $L(G') = L(G)$, and (ii) the axiom S' does not occur on the right hand side of any production.

Note that if we unfold S in the production $S' \to S$ of G', we also get a grammar which is an $LL(k)$ grammar such that Conditions (i) and (ii) hold.

The following exercise shows that by eliminating ε-productions from an $LL(1)$ grammar we may get an $LL(2)$ grammar.

EXERCISE 4.3.24. (i) Show that the grammar G_1 with axiom S and the productions:

$$S \to a\,A$$
$$A \to \varepsilon \mid a\,S$$

is $LL(1)$. (ii) Show that the grammar G_2 with axiom S and the productions:

$$S \to a\,A \mid a$$
$$A \to a\,S$$

is not $LL(1)$ and it is $LL(2)$. Note that: (i) grammar G_2 is obtained from grammar G_1 by eliminating the ε-production $A \to \varepsilon$, and (ii) both grammars G_1 and G_2 generate the regular language $(a\,a)^* a$.

Solution. (i) Here is the $LL(1)$ parsing table for the grammar G_1:

	a	$\$$
S	$S \to a\,A$	
A	$A \to a\,S$	$A \to \varepsilon$

Note that $Follow_1(S) = Follow_1(A) = \{\$\}$.

(ii) Here is the $LL(1)$ parsing table for the grammar G_2:

	a	$\$$
S	$S \to a$ $S \to a\,A$	
A	$A \to a\,S$	

Since there are two productions for the symbol S on the top of the stack and the input symbol a, the grammar G_2 is not $LL(1)$. Here is the $LL(2)$ parsing table for the grammar G_2:

	$a\,a$	$a\,\$$	$\$$
$[S, \{\$\}]$	$S \to a\,A$	$S \to a$	
$[A, \{\$\}]$	$A \to a\,S$		

$\square$

EXERCISE 4.3.25. Show that the grammar G with axiom S and the productions:

$$S \to a\,S \mid \varepsilon$$

is $LL(1)$.

Solution. Here is the $LL(1)$ parsing table for the grammar G:

	a	$\$$
S	$S \to a\,S$	$S \to \varepsilon$

Note that $Follow_1(S) = \{\$\}$. $\square$

We have the following decidability result which is a consequence of the result stated in [23].

FACT 4.3.26. [**Decidability of Equivalence for $LL(k)$ Grammars**] There exists an algorithm which always terminates and for all $h, k \geq 0$, given an $LL(h)$ grammar $G1$ and an $LL(k)$ grammar $G2$, tells us whether or not they are equivalent, that is, $L(G1) = L(G2)$.

More decidability results are listed in Section 10.2 on page 296.

4.4. Time Complexity of $LL(k)$ Parsing

We have the following complexity result.

FACT 4.4.1. [**Parsing of $LL(k)$ Languages in Linear Time**] Any $LL(k)$ language can be parsed in $O(n)$ time, where n is the length of the input word to be parsed. We assume that the time complexity is measured by the number of *chop* and *expand* actions performed on the stack.

PROOF. We will consider the case of $k = 1$ (for $k > 1$ the proof is similar and we leave it to the reader). We have to show that the number of *expand* actions between any two *chop* actions is bounded by a constant (independent of the length of the input word to be parsed).

Let us consider a given $LL(1)$ grammar $\langle V_T, V_N, P, S \rangle$ and its $LL(1)$ parsing table T. We have the following two cases.

Case (i): in P there are no ε-productions, and

Case (ii): in P there is at least one ε-production.

Case (i). In this case between any two *chop* actions it is impossible to perform more than $|V_N|$ *expand* actions. This bound on the number of *expand* actions is shown as follows. First note that by construction, in the $LL(1)$ parsing table T there are $|V_N|$ rows, and in any of the columns of table T there are at most $|V_N|$ entries with one production (recall that any entry of T is either empty or it has exactly one production).

Now, during $LL(1)$ parsing, we cannot perform more than $|V_N|$ consecutive *expand* actions after a *chop* action, because otherwise the given $LL(1)$ grammar would be left recursive, as we now show.

Suppose that, during $LL(1)$ parsing, immediately after a *chop* action, we look at a given occurrence of an input symbol, say c, and we perform an *expand* action of a nonterminal, say A, using a production of the form $A \rightarrow B\gamma$, for some nonterminal B and string $\gamma \in (V_T \cup V_N)^*$. That production occurs in row A and column c of table T. Then, this *expand* action is immediately followed by one more *expand* action of the nonterminal B using the production for B which is in row B and column c of table T. Thus, if we perform more than $|V_N|$ consecutive *expand* actions, it is the case that there exists a nonterminal A such that $A \rightarrow^+ A\delta$, for some string $\delta \in (V_T \cup V_N)^*$, that is, the given $LL(1)$ grammar is left recursive.

Case (ii). Let us begin the analysis of this case by looking first at a particular example of an $LL(1)$ parsing table. Let us consider the table for the grammar G with axiom S and productions: $S \rightarrow AAAa$, $A \rightarrow BBB$, and $B \rightarrow \varepsilon$ (see Figure 4.4.1).

Note that $First_1(S) = \{a\}$ and $Follow_1(A) = Follow_1(B) = \{a\}$.

	a	$\$$
S	$S \rightarrow AAAa$	
A	$A \rightarrow BBB$	
B	$B \rightarrow \varepsilon$	

FIGURE 4.4.1. The $LL(1)$ parsing table for the grammar G with axiom S and productions $S \rightarrow AAAa$, $A \rightarrow BBB$, and $B \rightarrow \varepsilon$.

From the stack configuration $S\$$ (with top to the left) we can generate, by performing an *expand* action, the configuration $AAAa\$$ and then by one more *expand* action, the configuration $BBBAAa\$$. Then, by performing an *expand* action that uses an ε-production, we get the configuration $BBAAa\$$. Eventually, after some more *expand* actions, we get the configuration $a\$$, where a *chop* action should be performed.

We may rearrange this expansion process, by postponing as long as possible the expansions that use ε-productions, by performing first: (i) the expansions of nonterminals that are *not* on the top of the stack, and (ii) the expansions that do *not* use ε-productions. This rearranged expansion process has the same length of the non-rearranged one, and produces the same final stack configuration.

By performing this rearranged expansion process, starting from the stack configuration $S\$$ we get, before making any *expand* action that uses an ε-production, the configuration $BBBBBBBBBa\$$ with 9 B's produced from the configuration $S\$$ after 4 *expand* actions of nonterminals which are not all on the top of the stack. The first of these *expand* actions is the expansion of the nonterminal S and the three remaining expansions are those of the nonterminal A.

Now let us compute an upper bound, call it M, of the maximum number of *expand* actions we can make, in the general case, starting from a stack configuration of the form $S\,\$$, where S is a nonterminal symbol, before being forced to make a *chop* action. Note that, since the *expand* actions never shorten the initial stack configuration $S\,\$$, there is no loss of generality in considering the initial configuration $S\,\$$.

For the computation of the upper bound M, we assume that the expansion process is rearranged as we have indicated above, that is:

(i) the *expand* actions can be made anywhere on the stack configuration, and not only on the top symbol (which is the leftmost one), and

(ii) the *expand* actions that use ε-productions are postponed as long as possible.

We leave to the reader to show that the assumption of considering only expansion processes which are rearranged, does not invalidate our argument for computing the upper bound M.

Let ℓ be the length of the longest nullable prefix of the right hand side of a production of the given $LL(1)$ grammar. In more formal terms, let ℓ be the maximum k such that in the given grammar there is a production of the form *either*

(i) $A \to \gamma$, where $\gamma \in (V_N)^k$ and $\gamma \to^* \varepsilon$, *or*

(ii) $A \to B_1 \dots B_k\, a\, \delta$, where $B_1 \dots B_k \to^* \varepsilon$, $a \in V_T$, and $\delta \in (V_T \cup V_N)^*$.

For instance, given the productions $S \to A\,A\,A\,a$, $A \to B\,B\,B$, and $B \to \varepsilon$ (see the grammar G of Figure 4.4.1 on the preceding page), we have that $\ell = 3$.

Starting from the stack configuration $S\,\$$, if we perform at most $\sum_{i=0}^{|V_N|-2} \ell^i$ $(= \dfrac{1 - \ell^{|V_N|-1}}{1 - \ell})$ *expand* actions (this summation will be explained below), we get, by a rearranged expansion process, before performing any *expand* action which uses an ε-production, a stack configuration, call it $\widetilde{\sigma}$, which has at most $\ell^{|V_N|-1}$ nonterminals to the left of a terminal symbol. To see an example of this expansion process the reader may look at lines 1–3 of Figure 4.4.2 on the next page, where from line 1 to line 2 we have performed one expansion using $S \to A\,A\,A\,a$, and from line 2 to line 3 we have performed three expansions using $A \to B\,B\,B$.

Now we explain the limits $i = 0$ and $i = |V_N| - 2$ of the summation $\sum_{i=0}^{|V_N|-2} \ell^i$.

Given an $LL(1)$ grammar, let us first introduce a binary relation, denoted $>$, on the set of the nonterminal symbols of that grammar.

For any production of the form $A \to \gamma B \delta$, where: (i) $\gamma \in (V_N)^*$, (ii) $(\gamma B) \to^* \varepsilon$, (iii) $\delta \in (V_T \cup V_N)^*$, and (iv) $A \neq B$, we define A *greater than* B, denoted $A > B$.

We have that the length of the longest chain $A_0 > A_1 > \dots > A_p$ of distinct nonterminals that can be defined for any given $LL(1)$ grammar such that $A_1, \dots, A_p$ are all nullable, is at most $|V_N|$, that is, $p \leq |V_N| - 1$. Indeed, by Fact 4.2.15 on page 57, any $LL(1)$ grammar is not left recursive, and if $p > |V_N| - 1$, then the grammar is left recursive (because $A_1, \dots, A_p$ are nullable).

The summation is from $i = 0$ to $i = |V_N| - 2$ because, in order to make sure that we replace the nonterminal A_0 by the last nullable nonterminal A_p in the chain $A_0 > A_1 > \dots > A_p$, we need to make at most $|V_N| - 1$ subsequences of *expand* actions, one subsequence for each value of i, from $i = 0$ to $i = |V_N| - 2$ (recall that $p \leq |V_N| - 1$).

	stack configuration (top to the left)	# of *expand* actions to get the next configuration	upper bound of the length of the prefix of nullable symbols	index i of $\sum_{i=0}^{\|V_N\|-2} \ell^i$
1	$S\,\$$	$1\ (=3^0)$	ℓ^0	$i=0$
2	$A\,A\,A\,a\,\$$	$3\ (=3^1)$	$\ell^1(=\ell^{\|V_N\|-2})$	$i=1$
3	$B\,B\,B\ B\,B\,B\ B\,B\,B\ a\,\$$	$9\ (=3^2)$	$\ell^{\|V_N\|-1}$	
4	$a\,\$$			

FIGURE 4.4.2. Analysis of the rearranged expansion process for the grammar G with axiom S and productions $S \to A\,A\,A\,a$, $A \to B\,B\,B$, and $B \to \varepsilon$ (this ε-production is used nine times at the end of the expansion process from line 3 to line 4). We have that $\ell=3$ and $\|V_N\|=3$.

By the first subsequence of *expand* actions (which is the one for $i=0$, consisting of one *expand* action only) we replace A_0 by smaller nonterminals in the chain, possibly, by A_1's only. By the $(\|V_N\|-1)$-th subsequence of *expand* actions (which is the one for $i=\|V_N\|-2$) we replace A_{p-1}, if any, by A_p.

In the case of the above grammar G with axiom S and productions

$$S \to A\,A\,A \qquad A \to B\,B\,B \qquad B \to \varepsilon$$

(see Figure 4.4.2) we have that:

(i) $S \succ A \succ B$,

(ii) the first subsequence of *expand* actions is made out one *expand* action only, that is, the expansion of S using the production $S \to A\,A\,A$ (that subsequence produces the stack configuration $A\,A\,A\,a\,\$$), and

(iii) the second subsequence is made out of the three *expand* actions, that is, the expansions of the three A's using the production $A \to B\,B\,B$ (that subsequence produces the stack configuration $B\,B\,B\ B\,B\,B\ B\,B\,B\,a\,\$$).

Then, starting from the stack configuration $\widetilde{\sigma}$ we have derived above (recall that $\widetilde{\sigma}$ has at most $\ell^{\|V_N\|-1}$ nonterminal symbols to the left of a terminal symbol), we can perform *expand* actions using ε-productions. In Figure 4.4.2, from line 3 to line 4, we have applied to the nine B's the *expand* action using the production $B \to \varepsilon$.

Thus, we conclude that between any two *chop* actions, we can perform at most

$$M = \frac{1 - \ell^{\|V_N\|-1}}{1 - \ell} + \ell^{\|V_N\|-1}$$ *expand* actions, that is, $O(\ell^{\|V_N\|})$ *expand* actions. Since the value of M does not depend on the length n of the input word to be parsed, we get that also in Case (ii) the $LL(1)$ parsing can be done in $O(n)$ steps. $\qquad\square$

CHAPTER 5

Parsers for Deterministic Context-Free Languages: $LR(k)$ Parsers

In this chapter we will present the so called $LR(k)$ parsers for deterministic context-free languages.

Before studying the $LR(k)$ parsers, let us recall that, as a consequence of Theorem 10.2.2 on page 297:

(i) it is *undecidable* whether or not given a context-free grammar G, there exists a number $k \geq 0$ such that the grammar G is equivalent an $LR(k)$ grammar, and

(ii) it is *undecidable* whether or not given a context-free grammar G and a number $k \geq 0$, that grammar G is equivalent an $LR(k)$ grammar.

We also recall the following two undecidability results (see [10] and also Section 10.2 on page 296):

(iii) it is *undecidable* whether or not given a context-free grammar G, that grammar G is equivalent to an $LR(0)$ grammar, that is, it is undecidable whether or not $L(G)$ is a prefix-free, deterministic context-free language (see Definition 5.2.11 on page 97), and

(iv) it is *undecidable* whether or not given a context-free grammar G, that grammar G is equivalent to an $LR(1)$ grammar, that is, it is undecidable whether or not $L(G)$ is a deterministic context-free language.

Note that it is *decidable* whether or not given a deterministic context-free language by an $LR(1)$ grammar G, that grammar G is equivalent to an $LR(0)$ grammar (that is, G generates a prefix-free, deterministic context-free language (see [9, page 355])).

5.1. Introduction to $LR(k)$ Parsing

The $LR(k)$ *parsers*, for any $k \geq 0$, are algorithms for parsing the languages which are generated by the $LR(k)$ grammars which are defined as follows [3, pages 372-373].

DEFINITION 5.1.1. **[$LR(k)$ Grammar. Version 1]** For any $k \geq 0$, a context-free grammar $G = \langle V_T, V_N, P, S \rangle$, possibly with ε-productions and without any occurrence of the start symbol S on the right hand side of any production, is an $LR(k)$ grammar if for $\$ \notin V_T$, for every sentential form $\alpha\beta\gamma \in (V_T \cup V_N)^*$, there exists a rightmost derivation of the form:

$$S\,\$^k \to^*_{rm} \alpha\,A\,\gamma\,\$^k \to_{rm} \alpha\,\beta\,\gamma\,\$^k$$

where: (i) the symbol $\$$ occurs only on the rightmost positions of every sentential form, (ii) $A \in V_N$, and (iii) the substring β which replaces A, can be determined by knowing the leftmost k symbols of $\gamma\,\$^k$ (see also Figure 5.4.21 on page 131).

Here is an equivalent definition of the $LR(k)$ grammars [3, page 372].

© Springer Nature Switzerland AG 2021
A. Pettorossi, *Techniques for Searching, Parsing, and Matching*, https://doi.org/10.1007/978-3-030-63189-5_5

DEFINITION 5.1.2. [**$LR(k)$ Grammar. Version 2**] For any $k \geq 0$, a context-free grammar $G = \langle V_T, V_N, P, S \rangle$, possibly with ε-productions and without any occurrence of the start symbol S on the right hand side of any production, is an $LR(k)$ grammar if for $\$ \notin V_T$, for any $w, x, y \in V_T^*$, for any $\alpha, \beta, \gamma \in (V_T \cup V_N)^*$, and for any $A, B \in V_N$,

> *if*   (1) $S \to_{rm}^* \alpha A w \to_{rm} \alpha \beta w$ *and*
>
>   (2) $S \to_{rm}^* \gamma B x \to_{rm} \alpha \beta y$ *and*
>
>   (3) $\underline{w}_k = \underline{y}_k$
>
> *then* $\alpha = \gamma$, $A = B$, and $x = y$.   □

Note that in the case of the rightmost derivations in Conditions (1) and (2) of the above definition, if Conditions (1)–(3) do hold, then the production which is applied in the last step is $A \to \beta$.

DEFINITION 5.1.3. [**$LR(k)$ Language**] For any $k \geq 0$, a language is an $LR(k)$ language if it is generated by an $LR(k)$ grammar.

Note also that given a context-free grammar $G = \langle V_T, V_N, P, S \rangle$, we can avoid every occurrence of the start symbol S on the right hand side of the productions, by considering the new, equivalent grammar $G' = \langle V_T, V_N \cup \{S'\}, P \cup \{S' \to S\}, S' \rangle$, where S' is a new start symbol. It is easy to see that $L(G) = L(G')$ because the language generated by the symbol S in G is equal to the language generated by the symbol S' in G'.

In what follows we will introduce some algorithms for parsing various subclasses of context-free languages. In particular, we will introduce algorithms for parsing:
(i) $LR(0)$ languages (see page 88),
(ii) $SLR(1)$ languages (see page 104),
(iii) $LR(1)$ languages (see page 108), and
(iv) $LALR(1)$ languages (see page 132).

Unless otherwise specified, in this section we assume that V_T, V_N, and S denote, respectively, the set of the terminal symbols, the set of nonterminal symbols, and the start symbol. As usual, we will use the symbol V to denote the set $V_T \cup V_N$.

When presenting the $LR(k)$ parsers, for any given context-free grammar $G = \langle V_T, V_N, P, S \rangle$, we consider its augmented version which is defined as follows.

DEFINITION 5.1.4. [**Augmented Context-Free Grammars**] Given a context-free grammar $G = \langle V_T, V_N, P, S \rangle$ with start symbol S, its *augmented grammar*, call it $G' = \langle V_T \cup \{\$\}, V_N \cup \{S'\}, P', S' \rangle$, is the grammar obtained by considering:
(i) the new start symbol $S' \notin V_N$,
(ii) a new terminal symbol $\$ \notin V_T$, and
(iii) the extra production $S' \to S\,\$$, that is, $P' = P \cup \{S' \to S\,\$\}$.
In some cases we will assume that the extra production is $S' \to S$, instead of $S' \to S\,\$$. We will always indicate whether in the augmented grammar the extra production is $S' \to S\,\$$ or $S' \to S$ (see also Table 5.2 on page 162).

We have the following fact.

FACT 5.1.5. [**Languages Generated by Grammars and Augmented Grammars**] The language $L(G)$ generated by a context-free grammar G is equal to the language $L(G')$ generated by the augmented grammar G' if G' has the extra production $S' \to S$, while if G' has the extra production $S' \to S\,\$$, then $L(G') = L(G)\,\$$.

For the grammars we consider when presenting the $LR(k)$ parsers we assume the following hypotheses.

Hypotheses for $LR(k)$ Parsing, for $k \geq 0$.

(i) No useless symbols occur in the productions.

(ii) No trivial unit productions occur in the productions.

(iii) ε-productions may be present for the start symbol S or any other symbols of V_N.

(iv) The symbol $\$$ does not belong to $V_T \cup V_N$, where $V_T \cup V_N$ is the alphabet of the non-augmented grammar.

(v) The input string to be parsed is terminated by the symbol $\$$ that can occur only at the right end of the input string.

(vi) The start symbol S (or S' in case of augmented grammars) does *not* occur on the right hand side of any production.

(vii) The symbol $\$$ does not occur on the right hand side of any production with the exception that $\$$ may occur in the production $S' \to S\,\$$ for the new start symbol S' of the augmented grammar.

On Section 5.2.2 on page 101 and Section 5.4.2 on page 127 we will comment on Hypothesis (i) that the start symbol S (or S' in case of augmented grammars) does *not* occur on the right hand side of any production. We will also comment on a condition based on the number of productions for start symbol S.

5.2. *LR(0)* Parsers

In this section we will study the $LR(0)$ parsers and the $LR(0)$ grammars. Given a context-free grammar $G = \langle V_T, V_N, S, P \rangle$, an $LR(0)$ parser for G, if any, uses a parsing automaton (see Figure 5.2.1 on page 89) which makes its moves according to a table, called the $LR(0)$ *parsing table*. This table is a matrix whose rows are labeled by the states of a finite automaton M we will define, and whose columns are labeled by the terminal symbols in V_T and the nonterminal symbols in V_N. In this table there is one extra column labeled by the symbol $\$$ which is a new terminal symbol not belonging to V_T. The columns of the table labeled by the elements in $V_T \cup \{\$\}$ constitute the so called *action part* of the table, while the columns labeled by the elements in V_N constitute the so called *goto part* of the table.

One can show that, for any given context-free grammar G, if the $LR(0)$ parsing table for G has at most one action in every entry (we will clarify this condition later), then the grammar G generates a language L such that $L\$$ is an $LR(0)$ language.

In the sequel we need the following definition.

DEFINITION 5.2.1. [**Item and Complete Item**] Given a context-free grammar $G = \langle V_T, V_N, P, S \rangle$, a production of G with one extra symbol '$.$' (pronounced 'dot') in any position on the right hand side, is called an *item* of G. Thus, for a production whose right hand side has length n we have $n+1$ items. In particular, for a production of the form $A \to \varepsilon$, where A is a nonterminal symbol and ε is the empty string, we have the following item only: $A \to .$ (whose right hand side consists of the dot only). Instead of $A \to .$, we will feel free to write $A \to \varepsilon.$ or $A \to .\varepsilon$.

An item is said to be *complete* if it is of the form $A \to \beta.$, where $\beta \in (V_T \cup V_N)^*$, that is, the dot is at the rightmost position.

EXAMPLE 5.2.2. Let us consider the context-free grammar G with axiom S and whose productions are:

> 1. $S \to SA$ 2. $S \to A$ 3. $A \to aSb$ 4. $A \to ab$

We have the following twelve items:

$$
\begin{array}{llll}
S \to .SA & S \to .A & A \to .aSb & A \to .ab \\
S \to S.A & \boxed{S \to A.} & A \to a.Sb & A \to a.b \\
\boxed{S \to SA.} & & A \to aS.b & \boxed{A \to ab.} \\
& & \boxed{A \to aSb.} &
\end{array}
$$

Among those items we have four complete items which are those within rectangles.

Now we present a five step algorithm which given a context-free grammar, constructs the $LR(0)$ parsing table, call it T, which is required by the parsing automaton of Figure 5.2.1 on the facing page. Then, we will explain how, once the table T has been constructed and there is at most one action in each of its entries, we can use the automaton of Figure 5.2.1 with table T for performing the $LR(0)$ parsing of the language $L\$$. Indeed, we can use that automaton for checking whether or not any given word belongs to the language $L\$$.

In order to fix our ideas, each step of the algorithm will be illustrated using a running example which refers to the context-free grammar G of the above Example 5.2.2.

ALGORITHM 5.2.3. **Constructing the $LR(0)$ Parsing Table.**

We are given a context-free grammar $G = \langle V_T, V_N, P, S \rangle$ and we want to construct the $LR(0)$ parsing table for the automaton of Figure 5.2.1 on the facing page.
Step (1). First we consider the augmented grammar $G' = \langle V_T \cup \{\$\}, V_N \cup \{S'\}, P', S' \rangle$, where the set P' of productions is $P \cup \{S' \to S\$\}$. As usual, we assume that $\$ \notin V_T$ and $S' \notin V_N$. For example, in the case of the grammar G with axiom S and whose productions are:

> 1. $S \to SA$ 2. $S \to A$ 3. $A \to aSb$ 4. $A \to ab$

we consider the augmented grammar $G' = \langle V_T \cup \{\$\}, V_N \cup \{S'\}, P', S' \rangle$ with axiom S' and whose productions are:

> 0. $S' \to S\$$ 1. $S \to SA$ 2. $S \to A$ 3. $A \to aSb$ 4. $A \to ab$

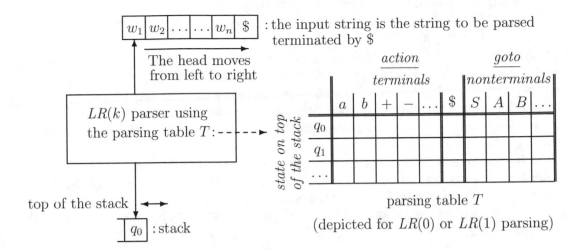

FIGURE 5.2.1. A deterministic pushdown automaton for $LR(k)$ parsing, with $k \geq 0$. The string to be parsed is $w_1 w_2 \ldots w_n$. Initially, the stack has one symbol only: the initial state q_0 at the bottom of the stack. The input string is the string to be parsed with the extra rightmost symbol $. We have depicted the parsing table T for $LR(0)$ or $LR(1)$ parsers. For the $LR(k)$ parsers, with $k \geq 2$, different parsing tables should be used.

REMARK 5.2.4. [**Avoiding a New Start Symbol in the Augmented Grammar for $LR(0)$ Parsing**] If the start symbol S of a given grammar H does *not* occur on the right hand side of any production of H, then we can take the augmented grammar H' to be H itself, where in every production for S we have added $ as the rightmost symbol. □

Step (2). For each production in G' of the form $A \to \alpha_1 \alpha_2 \ldots \alpha_n$, where $n \geq 0$ and for $i = 1, \ldots, n$, $\alpha_i \in V_T \cup V_N \cup \{\$\}$ (obviously, only α_n can be $), we construct the associated *big production* as the following linear graph made out of $n+1$ nodes and n arcs:

$$\boxed{A \to \ .\alpha_1\alpha_2 \ldots \alpha_n} \xrightarrow{\alpha_1} \boxed{A \to \alpha_1 \ . \ \alpha_2 \ldots \alpha_n} \xrightarrow{\alpha_2} \ldots \xrightarrow{\alpha_n} \boxed{A \to \alpha_1 \alpha_2 \ldots \alpha_n \ .}$$

In particular, if the production is $A \to \varepsilon$ (in this case $n = 0$), then the associated big production is the following graph with one node only (recall that $.\varepsilon = \varepsilon. \ = \ .$):

$$\boxed{A \to \ .}$$

Note also that in a big production: (i) the *leftmost node* is an item of the grammar G' of the form $A \to \ .\alpha_1 \ldots \alpha_n$ with $A \in V_N$ and for $i = 1, \ldots, n$, we have that $\alpha_i \in V_T \cup V_N \cup \{\$\}$, and (ii) any other node is an item of the grammar G' with the dot in a different position, and (iii) the *rightmost node* is a complete item of the grammar G'.

In a big production the arc from a node m to a node n is labeled by the symbol in $V_T \cup V_N \cup \{\$\}$ which in the node m occurs on the right of the dot and in the node n occurs on the left of the dot.

Step (3). We consider the graph made out of all the big productions of the grammar G' we have constructed at Step (2). Then, for all nonterminals $A, B \in V_N \cup \{S'\}$ and strings $\alpha, \beta, \gamma \in (V_T \cup V_N \cup \{\$\})^*$, we add an arc labeled by ε from every node whose label is an item of the form $A \to \alpha \,.\, B\beta$ to every node whose label is the item $B \to .\gamma$. These ε-arcs may relate either nodes into two different big productions or nodes of the same big production.

• If the augmented grammar G' is the grammar G itself, then we also add an ε-arc between any two nodes whose label has an item of the form $S \to .\alpha \,\$$, for some production $S \to \alpha$, where S is the start symbol of G.

In the case of our augmented grammar G', at the end of Step (3) we get the graph of Figure 5.2.2.

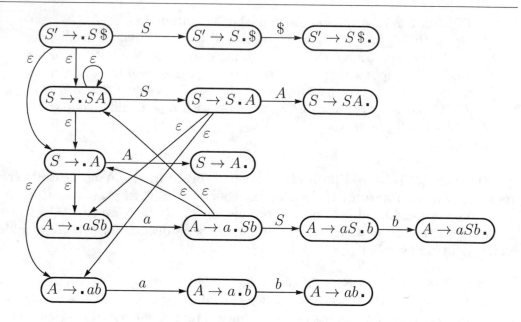

FIGURE 5.2.2. The graph of the big productions with the ε-arcs for the grammar G' with axiom S' and productions: 0. $S' \to S\,\$$, 1. $S \to SA$, 2. $S \to A$, 3. $A \to aSb$, 4. $A \to ab$. Each big production is depicted as a sequence of nodes which are horizontally aligned.

Step (4). By applying the Powerset Construction Procedure (see, for instance, [21]) to the graph of the big productions obtained at the end of Step (3), we get a finite automaton. Let that finite automaton be called M.

In the case of our augmented grammar G', at the end of Step (4) we get the finite automaton of Figure 5.2.3 on the facing page.

As a result of the Powerset Construction, each state of M is labeled by a set of items of the grammar G'.

The initial state of M is the one whose label has the item of the leftmost node of the big production associated with $S' \to S\,\$$, that is, the item $S' \to .\,S\,\$$. The items in the states of the automaton M include those of the grammar G and the three extra items $S' \to .\,S\,\$$, $S' \to S\,.\,\$$, and $S' \to S\,\$\,.$, which are generated by the production $S' \to S\,\$$ of the augmented grammar G'.

The final state of M is the one whose label has the item $S' \to S\,\$\,..$ (As usual we write double lines around the final states.)

• If the augmented grammar G' is equal to the given grammar G with axiom S (and thus, as indicated in Remark 5.2.4 on page 89, we have that S does not occur on the right hand side of any production of G), then:
(i) the initial state of M is the one whose label has the set of items $\{S \to .\,\alpha\,\$ \mid S \to \alpha$ where $\alpha \in V^*\}$, and
(ii) a final state of M is every state whose label has an item of the form: $S \to \alpha\,\$\,.$, for some production $S \to \alpha$, with $\alpha \in V^*$.

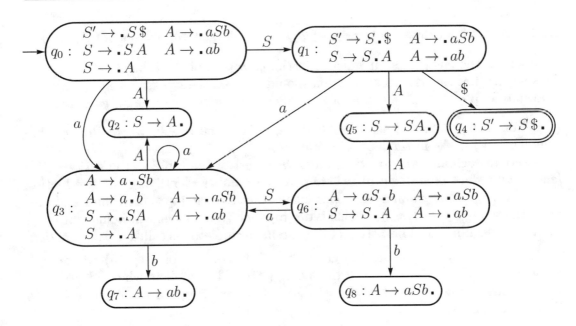

FIGURE 5.2.3. The finite automaton M for the $LR(0)$ parsing of the grammar G' with axiom S' and productions: 0. $S' \to S\,\$$, 1. $S \to SA$, 2. $S \to A$, 3. $A \to aSb$, 4. $A \to ab$. The label of each state is a set of items which is computed by the Powerset Construction Procedure from the graph of Figure 5.2.2 on the facing page.

Step (5). The $LR(0)$ parsing table T is then constructed from the automaton M as follows. The meaning of the various entries of that table will be clarified when we will describe the behaviour of the parsing automaton of Figure 5.2.1 on page 89 which uses that parsing table.

(5.1) For each transition $(q_i) \xrightarrow{\;a\;} (q_j)$, where a is terminal symbol different from $\$$,

we insert in the entry $T[q_i, a]$ which is in the *action* part of the table T, the action *sh* q_j (short for *shift* q_j). This means that the parsing automaton should take the input symbol a at hand, push it on the stack, and push the state q_j on the stack. Then the new input symbol at hand is the one to the right of the previous symbol a at hand. This action of the parsing automaton is called a *shift action*.

(5.2) For each transition $(q_i) \xrightarrow{\;\$\;} ((q_j))$

we insert in the entry $T[q_i, \$]$ which is in the *action* part of the table T, the action *acc* (short for *accept*). This means that the parsing automaton should accept the given input string. This action of the parsing automaton is called the *accept action*. (Note that, in the case where we take the augmented grammar G' to be the given grammar G, the number of the final states of the automaton M is equal to the number of the productions for S.)

(5.3) For each transition $(q_i) \xrightarrow{\;A\;} (q_j)$ with the nonterminal symbol A,

we insert in the entry $T[q_i, A]$ which is in the *goto* part of the table T, the state q_j. This means that the parsing automaton should push on the stack the state q_j (see the following Step (5.4)). This action of the parsing automaton is called a *goto action*.

(5.4) For each complete item $A \to \alpha_1 \ldots \alpha_n \bullet$ for some $n \geq 0$, where the α_i's are symbols in $V_T \cup V_N$, in the label of a state q_i,
we insert in each entry of row q_i in the *action* part of the table T, the action *red p* (short for *reduce production p*), where p is the number identifying the production $A \to \alpha_1 \ldots \alpha_n$ of the grammar G'. This means that the parsing automaton should replace the string $\alpha_1 q_{\alpha_1} \ldots \alpha_n q_{\alpha_n}$ which is on the stack (the top element being state q_{α_n}) by the nonterminal A. This action of the parsing automaton is called a *reduce action*.

In the case of our augmented grammar G' at the end of Step (5) we get the parsing table T of Figure 5.2.4 on the facing page. The numbers which identify the productions of the grammar G' are necessary for specifying the *reduce* actions, and they are as follows:

$$0.\ S' \to S\,\$ \qquad 1.\ S \to SA \qquad 2.\ S \to A \qquad 3.\ A \to a\,S\,b \qquad 4.\ A \to a\,b$$

This conclude the presentation of the algorithm for constructing the $LR(0)$ parsing table.

Now let us explain how the parsing table T is used by the parsing automaton of Figure 5.2.1 on page 89 for performing the $LR(0)$ parsing. Initially, the stack has the initial state q_0 only. Then the parsing automaton reads the input string (which is terminated by the symbol $\$$), one symbol at a time from left to right, and it performs the actions as indicated by the table T. If the top of the stack is the state q and the input symbol is a, for any $a \in V_T \cup \{\$\}$, then the parsing automaton considers the entry $T[q, a]$. There are three cases.

	action				*goto*	
	a	b	$\$$		S	A
q_0	sh q_3				q_1	q_2
q_1	sh q_3		acc			q_5
q_2	red 2	red 2	red 2			
q_3	sh q_3	sh q_7			q_6	q_2
q_4	red 0	red 0	red 0			
q_5	red 1	red 1	red 1			
q_6	sh q_3	sh q_8				q_5
q_7	red 4	red 4	red 4			
q_8	red 3	red 3	red 3			

where:

0. $S' \to S\,\$$
1. $S \to SA$
2. $S \to A$
3. $A \to aSb$
4. $A \to ab$

FIGURE 5.2.4. $LR(0)$ parsing table T for the grammar G' with axiom S' and productions: 0. $S' \to S\,\$$,   1. $S \to SA$,   2. $S \to A$, 3. $A \to aSb$,   4. $A \to ab$. It has been derived from the finite automaton of Figure 5.2.3 on page 91. The row for state q_4 can be eliminated, because in state q_1, when $\$$ is read, the input string is accepted.

Case (1): *shift and goto.* If $T[q, a] = sh\ q'$, then the parsing automaton pushes the symbol a from the input string on the stack, and then it pushes the state q' on the stack.

Case (2): *accept.* If $T[q, a] = acc$, then the parsing automaton accepts the whole input string.

Case (3): *reduce and goto.* If $T[q, a] = red\ p$, where p is the number identifying the production $A \to \alpha_1 \ldots \alpha_n$ (with $\alpha_i \in V_T \cup V_N \cup \{\$\}$, for $i = 1, \ldots, n$) of the grammar G', then the parsing automaton pops from the stack the whole string $\alpha_1 q_{\alpha_1} \ldots \alpha_n q_{\alpha_n}$ (the top of the stack being the state q_{α_n}). This leaves a state, say $\widetilde{q}$, on the top of the stack. Then the parsing automaton pushes A on the stack and then pushes also the state $T[\widetilde{q}, A]$. Thus, after every *reduce* action the parsing automaton performs a *goto* action. In the *reduce* and *goto* actions no symbol is read on the input, that is, an ε-move is made on the input.

The behaviour of the parsing automaton we have described, satisfies the following property: every symbol α in $V_T \cup V_N \cup \{\$\}$ on the stack has above itself a state of the automaton M. We call that state the *cover state of the symbol* α.

Figure 5.2.5 on page 95 shows the behaviour of the automaton of Figure 5.2.1 on page 89 using the $LR(0)$ parsing table of Figure 5.2.4 on this page, while parsing the input string $a\,a\,b\,a\,b\,b\,\$$ which is read from left to right. The symbol ▲ points at the input character at hand. The stack grows and shrinks at the right end, and the symbol ▲ points at the top of the stack. In that figure time flows, so to speak, from top to bottom in the sense that, for any $i \geq 0$, the ⟨stack, input⟩ configuration at time $i+1$ is generated by the ⟨stack, input⟩ configuration at time i according to the actions described in the rightmost column, which we named the *shift/reduce-goto* column.

In the literature, for every state q of the automaton M and for every symbol $a \in V_T \cup \{\$\}$, the entry $T[q, a]$ is also called '*action*(q, a)', and for every $A \in V_N$, the entry $T[q, A]$ is also called '*goto*(q, A)' (see also Figure 5.2.5 on the next page).

With reference to Figure 5.2.5, the reader should note that the sequence of stack configurations shows *in reverse order* the rightmost derivation of the input string when it is accepted. The *accept* action stands for the *reduce* action: *red* 0 $(S' \to S\,\$)$. In our case, in fact, by looking at the *reduce* action, we get the following rightmost derivation of $a\,a\,b\,a\,b\,b\,\$$ from the axiom S':

$$S' \to_{rm} \quad (12)\ S\,\$ \qquad \to_{rm} \quad (11)\ A\,\$ \qquad \to_{rm}$$

$$\to_{rm} \quad (10)\ a\,S\,b\,\$ \qquad \to_{rm} \quad (8)\ a\,S\,A\,b\,\$ \qquad \to_{rm}$$

$$\to_{rm} \quad (7)\ a\,S\,a\,b\,b\,\$ \qquad \to_{rm} \quad (4)\ a\,A\,a\,b\,b\,\$ \qquad \to_{rm}$$

$$\to_{rm} \quad (3)\ a\,a\,b\,a\,b\,b\,\$.$$

Since, according to our conventions production 0 of the grammar G' is $S' \to S\,\$$, and the symbol $\$$ occurs in this production only, we have that the action *red* 0 is never present in the sequence of configurations of the parsing automaton of Figure 5.2.1 on page 89, such as those we have depicted in Figure 5.2.5 on the next page.

Moreover, in the $LR(0)$ parsing table we can always eliminate the row corresponding to the final state, because in that state, when $\$$ is read, the input string is accepted (see Step (5.2) of Algorithm 5.2.3 on page 88).

For example, the row for state q_4 in Figure 5.2.4 on the previous page can be eliminated. Therefore, in Step (5.4) of Algorithm 5.2.3 (see page 92) we could require that the state q_i be *not final* and we could eliminate from the $LR(0)$ parsing table the row corresponding to the final state.

Now let us make a few remarks on Algorithm 5.2.3 for constructing the $LR(0)$ parsing table.

REMARK 5.2.5. [*Reduce action is independent of the input symbol*] The *reduce* action does *not* depend on the input symbol at hand. For instance, in table T of Figure 5.2.4 on the preceding page for the state q_2 we have that: $T[q_2, a] = T[q_2, b] = T[q_2, \$] = red\ 2$. Analogously, for the states q_4, q_5, q_7, and q_8. $\square$

REMARK 5.2.6. [*Multiple actions*] One can show that if during the construction of the table T we have to place more than one action in a given entry or, in particular, more than one complete item occurs as the label of a state of the finite automaton M, then the augmented grammar G' which has been derived from the given grammar G, is *not* an $LR(0)$ grammar [**10**]. This means that the language $L(G') = L(G)\,\$$ which is generated by the grammar G' cannot be parsed using the $LR(0)$ parsing algorithm for G'.

If we have to place more than one action in a given entry of the table T, we say that there is a *conflict*. Depending on the actions simultaneously present in the same entry, a conflict can be either a *shift-reduce conflict*, or *reduce-reduce conflict*. Note that, by construction of the parsing table, a conflict cannot be a *shift-shift conflict*. $\square$

time	stack (the top is marked by ▲)	input (the symbol at hand is marked by ▲)	*shift/reduce-goto*
0	q_0 ▲	$a\,a\,b\,a\,b\,b\,\$$ ▲	$action(q_0, a) = sh\ q_3$
1	$q_0\,a\,q_3$ ▲	$a\,a\,b\,a\,b\,b\,\$$ ▲	$action(q_3, a) = sh\ q_3$
2	$q_0\,a\,q_3\,a\,q_3$ ▲	$a\,a\,b\,a\,b\,b\,\$$ ▲	$action(q_3, b) = sh\ q_7$
3	$q_0\,a\,q_3\,a\,q_3\,b\,q_7$ ▲	$a\,a\,b\,a\,b\,b\,\$$ ▲	$action(q_7, a) = red\ 4\ (A \to ab)$ $goto(q_3, A) = q_2$
4	$q_0\,a\,q_3\,A\,q_2$ ▲	$a\,a\,b\,a\,b\,b\,\$$ ▲	$action(q_2, a) = red\ 2\ (S \to A)$ $goto(q_3, S) = q_6$
5	$q_0\,a\,q_3\,S\,q_6$ ▲	$a\,a\,b\,a\,b\,b\,\$$ ▲	$action(q_6, a) = sh\ q_3$
6	$q_0\,a\,q_3\,S\,q_6\,a\,q_3$ ▲	$a\,a\,b\,a\,b\,b\,\$$ ▲	$action(q_3, b) = sh\ q_7$
7	$q_0\,a\,q_3\,S\,q_6\,a\,q_3\,b\,q_7$ ▲	$a\,a\,b\,a\,b\,b\,\$$ ▲	$action(q_7, b) = red\ 4\ (A \to ab)$ $goto(q_6, A) = q_5$
8	$q_0\,a\,q_3\,S\,q_6\,A\,q_5$ ▲	$a\,a\,b\,a\,b\,b\,\$$ ▲	$action(q_5, b) = red\ 1\ (S \to SA)$ $goto(q_3, S) = q_6$
9	$q_0\,a\,q_3\,S\,q_6$ ▲	$a\,a\,b\,a\,b\,b\,\$$ ▲	$action(q_6, b) = sh\ q_8$
10	$q_0\,a\,q_3\,S\,q_6\,b\,q_8$ ▲	$a\,a\,b\,a\,b\,b\,\$$ ▲	$action(q_8, \$) = red\ 3\ (A \to aSb)$ $goto(q_0, A) = q_2$
11	$q_0\,A\,q_2$ ▲	$a\,a\,b\,a\,b\,b\,\$$ ▲	$action(q_2, \$) = red\ 2\ (S \to A)$ $goto(q_0, S) = q_1$
12	$q_0\,S\,q_1$ ▲	$a\,a\,b\,a\,b\,b\,\$$ ▲	$action(q_1, \$) = accept$

FIGURE 5.2.5. The sequence of configurations of the parsing automaton of Figure 5.2.1 on page 89 while parsing the string $a\,a\,b\,a\,b\,b\,\$$ using the *LR(0)* parsing table of Figure 5.2.4 on page 93 for the grammar G' with axiom S' and productions: 0. $S' \to S\,\$$, 1. $S \to SA$, 2. $S \to A$, 3. $A \to aSb$, 4. $A \to ab$.

REMARK 5.2.7. [*Undefined entry*] If during the parsing process of the input word $w\,\$$, the pushdown automaton of Figure 5.2.1 on page 89 when using the table T, finds an undefined entry, then $w\,\$$ is *not* in the $LR(0)$ language $L(G')$ generated by the augmented grammar G', and thus the word w is *not* in the language generated by the given grammar G. □

One can show that the following is an alternative definition of $LR(0)$ grammars. This definition is based on the construction of the finite automaton M of Step (4) of Algorithm 5.2.3 on page 88 [**10**, page 252].

DEFINITION 5.2.8. [$LR(0)$ **Grammar and** $LR(0)$ **Language**] A context-free grammar G is an $LR(0)$ grammar if

(i) the start symbol does *not* occur in the right hand side of any production, and

(ii) in every state of the automaton M of Step (4) of Algorithm 5.2.3 on page 88 if there is a complete item of G, then in that state no other complete item occurs nor any item with a terminal symbol immediately to the right of the dot.

A language is an $LR(0)$ language if it is generated by an $LR(0)$ grammar.

Note that when constructing the finite automaton M of Step (4) of Algorithm 5.2.3, it never happens that in a state with a complete item: (i) there is an item with a nonterminal symbol immediately to the right of the dot, and (ii) there is no item with a terminal symbol immediately to the right of the dot. In that case, in fact, one can show that in the given grammar there would be a useless symbol, contrary to our hypotheses.

Note also that the grammar G of Example 5.2.2 on page 88 is not an $LR(0)$ grammar, but as shown in the parsing table depicted in Figure 5.2.4 on page 93, the language $L(G)\,\$$ is an $LR(0)$ language. This language is generated by the $LR(0)$ grammar G' which is the augmented version of the grammar G.

REMARK 5.2.9. [**On Context-Free Grammars and the Associated Augmented Grammars**] If the axiom of a context-free grammar G occurs on the right hand side of a production, then, by definition, G *is not an* $LR(0)$ *grammar*. In that case, by using Algorithm 5.2.3 on page 88 for constructing the $LR(0)$ parsing table starting from the grammar G, we first introduce the associated *augmented grammar* G'. If the constructed $LR(0)$ parsing table of the grammar G' is free from conflicts (either shift-reduce conflicts or reduce-reduce conflicts), then the *augmented grammar* G' *is an* $LR(0)$ *grammar*.

This remark holds for the class of the $LR(0)$ grammars, but also for the classes of the $SLR(1)$ grammars, the $LR(1)$ grammars, and the $LALR(1)$ grammars, which we will introduce in the following sections.

Now we give an example of a grammar which is an $LR(0)$ grammar and it is *not* $LL(k)$ for any $k \ge 0$.

EXAMPLE 5.2.10. [**An *LR(0)* Grammar**] Let us consider the grammar G with axiom S and whose productions are:

$$S \to A \mid B \qquad A \to aAb \mid 0 \qquad B \to aBbb \mid 1$$

The language generated by this grammar is:

$$L = \{a^n\, 0\, b^n \mid n \geq 0\} \cup \{a^n\, 1\, b^{2n} \mid n \geq 0\}.$$

The grammar G is $LR(0)$ and it is *not* $LL(k)$ for any $k \geq 0$.

Now we will present a few results which we state without proof. First, we recall the following definitions (see [**21**, Section 3.3]).

DEFINITION 5.2.11. [**Prefix-Free Language**] A language L is said to be *prefix-free* (or to enjoy the *prefix property*) iff *no* word in L is a proper prefix of another word in L, that is, for every word $u \in L$, the word uv for $v \neq \varepsilon$ is *not* in L.

DEFINITION 5.2.12. [**Deterministic Pushdown Automaton**] A pushdown automaton $\langle Q, \Sigma, \Gamma, q_0, Z_0, F, \delta \rangle$ is said to be a *deterministic pushdown automaton* (or a *dpda*, for short) iff
(i) $\forall q \in Q$, $\forall Z \in \Gamma$, if $\delta(q, \varepsilon, Z) \neq \{\}$ then $\forall a \in \Sigma$, $\delta(q, a, Z) = \{\}$ (that is, no other moves are allowed when an ε-move is allowed), and
(ii) $\forall q \in Q$, $\forall Z \in \Gamma$, $\forall x \in \Sigma \cup \{\varepsilon\}$, $\delta(q, x, Z)$ is *either* $\{\}$ *or* a singleton (that is, if a move is allowed, then that move can be made in one way only, that is, there exists only one next configuration for the dpda).

DEFINITION 5.2.13. [**Deterministic Context-Free Language**] A context-free language L is said to be a *deterministic context-free language* iff it is accepted by a deterministic pushdown automaton *by final state*, that is, for each word $w \in L$, the deterministic pushdown automaton, starting from the input string $w\,\$$ and the initial state q_0, eventually reaches a final state, having read all the symbols of $w\,\$$.

DEFINITION 5.2.14. [**Language Accepted by a Parsing Pushdown Automaton**] Let us consider the parsing automaton A of Figure 5.2.1 on page 89, with its parsing table T. That table specifies the moves of A for each symbol in input and each symbol on the top of the stack.

An input word w is accepted by the automaton A if starting from the configuration where:
(i) w is the string to be read with the extra symbol $\$$ at the right end (that is, initially the input head points at the leftmost symbol of w), and
(ii) the initial state q_0 is on the stack, then A eventually performs the *accept* action.

The *language accepted by a parsing pushdown automaton* A with table T is the set of input words accepted by A.

Let us consider an algorithm P which given a context-free grammar G, constructs its augmented grammar G' and the parsing table $T_{G'}$ for the parsing automaton A of Figure 5.2.1 on page 89. Depending on the augmented grammar G', the algorithm P may or may not generate a parsing table $T_{G'}$ such that the language accepted by the parsing automaton A using that table, is equal to $L(G')$.

In particular, if the parsing table $T_{G'}$ has conflicts, then the language accepted by the parsing automaton A using that table, is *not* equal to $L(G')$.

One can show that the augmented grammar G' is an $LR(0)$ grammar iff Algorithm 5.2.3 on page 88 produces a parsing table $T_{G'}$ such that the language accepted by the parsing automaton A using that table, is equal to $L(G')$ [**10**].

Now we define the language which is accepted by an algorithm for constructing parsing tables.

DEFINITION 5.2.15. [**Language Accepted by an Algorithm for Constructing Parsing Tables**] Let us consider an algorithm P that, given a context-free grammar G, constructs the augmented grammar G' and the parsing table $T_{G'}$ for the parsing automaton A of Figure 5.2.1 on page 89.

We say that the *algorithm P accepts the language L* if L is the language accepted by the parsing automaton A when it uses the parsing table $T_{G'}$.

The following Theorems 5.2.16 and 5.2.17, which we state without proof, provide two alternative definitions of the class of the $LR(0)$ languages and relate the class of deterministic context-free languages to the class of the $LR(0)$ languages.

THEOREM 5.2.16. The class of the $LR(0)$ languages is the class of the context-free languages which are accepted by Algorithm 5.2.3 on page 88. (Thus, it is appropriate to call Algorithm 5.2.3 an algorithm for constructing $LR(0)$ parsing tables.)

THEOREM 5.2.17. [**$LR(0)$ Languages and Deterministic Context-Free Languages**] (i) The class of the $LR(0)$ languages is the class of deterministic context-free languages which enjoy the prefix property [**10**, pages 121 and 260].

(ii) A language $L \subseteq V_T^*$ is a deterministic context-free language iff the language $L\,\$$, with $\$$ not in V_T, can be generated by an $LR(0)$ grammar [**10**, page 260].

For any deterministic context-free language L, for any $LR(0)$ grammar G' which generates $L\,\$$, we have that the axiom S' of G' does not occur on the right hand side of any production (indeed, this is true for the axiom of any $LR(0)$ grammar). However, we do not insist that the grammar G' be the result of adding the production $S' \to S\,\$$ to a grammar which generates the language L and whose axiom is S.

This Theorem 5.2.17 is important because it relates the class of the $LR(0)$ languages to the class of the deterministic context-free languages, and as we will see in Theorem 5.4.16 on page 123, the class of the deterministic context-free languages coincides with the class of the $LR(1)$ languages (see Section 5.4 starting on page 108).

Note that, given a language L which is generated by an $LR(1)$ grammar G with axiom S (see Section 5.4 starting on page 108), an $LR(0)$ grammar which generates the language $L\,\$$ cannot, in general, be derived from the grammar G by adding the production $S' \to S\,\$$, where S' is the new axiom, as the following example shows.

EXAMPLE 5.2.18. Let us consider the grammar G with axiom S and productions:

$$S \to E \qquad E \to E + T \qquad E \to T \qquad T \to T \times a \qquad T \to a$$

It is an $LR(1)$ grammar as the reader may easily check, after learning about the $LR(1)$ grammars on Section 5.4.

Let L be the language generated by G. (Note that the grammar with axiom E and productions:

$$E \to E + T \qquad E \to T \qquad T \to T \times a \qquad T \to a$$

which also generates L, is *not* an $LR(1)$ grammar simply because the axiom E occurs on the right hand side of a production.)

Now, let us consider the augmented grammar G' obtained from G by adding the production $S' \to S\,\$$. Thus, the grammar G' has the axiom S' and the following productions:

$$S' \to S\,\$$$

$$S \to E \qquad E \to E + T \qquad E \to T \qquad T \to T \times a \qquad T \to a$$

Grammar G' generates the language $L\,\$$, but it is *not* an $LR(0)$ grammar as the reader may verify (it is an $LR(1)$ grammar). An $LR(0)$ grammar which generates $L\,\$$ is the following one with axiom S' and productions:

$$S' \to E \qquad E \to T + E \qquad E \to T\,\$ \qquad T \to T \times a \qquad T \to a$$

Note the productions $E \to T+E$ and $E \to T\,\$$, instead of the productions $E \to E+T$ and $E \to T$ of the grammar G'. $\qquad\qquad\square$

5.2.1. Avoiding the Powerset Construction for *LR*(0) Parsing.

Algorithm 5.2.3 on page 88 for constructing the $LR(0)$ parsing tables, can be replaced by the following algorithm which, given a context-free grammar, first constructs the corresponding augmented grammar G', then constructs the deterministic finite automaton M, and finally constructs the $LR(0)$ parsing table.

After the construction of the augmented grammar G', the construction of the automaton M is done by applying the five rules in the boxes below:

(i) the Initialization Rule,

(ii)–(iv) the Closure Rules (1), (2), and (3), and

(v) the Final State Rule.

These rules construct the automaton M by generating:

(i) states,

(ii) sets of items in the label of every state, and

(iii) arcs between states.

The Closure Rules (1), (2), and (3) should be applied *as long as possible*, that is, until neither new items nor new states nor new arcs can be added to the finite automaton M under construction.

When constructing the automaton M, *priority should be given to the application of the Closure Rule (1) with respect to the Closure rules (2) and (3)*.

This means that the Closure Rules (2) and (3) should *not* be applied, if by applying the Closure Rule (1), we add a new item to the label of a state of the automaton.

The Closure Rule (1) should have priority because, before applying the Closure Rules (2) and (3), we should already know the closures of all sets of items considered so far.

Initialization Rule. The initial state q_0 of the finite automaton M has its set of items initialized by the item $S' \to \,.\,S\,\$$.

If the axiom S does *not* occur on the right hand side of any production, and we take the augmented grammar G' to be G itself, where in every production for S we have added a rightmost symbol $\$$, *then* the label of the initial state q_0 of the finite automaton M has an item of the form $S \to \,.\,\alpha_1 \ldots \alpha_n \$$, for each production of the form $S \to \alpha_1 \ldots \alpha_n$, where $n \geq 0$ and for $i = 1, \ldots, n$, $\alpha_i \in V_T \cup V_N$.

Closure Rule (1). For all $A, B \in V_N$, for all $\alpha, \beta, \gamma \in V^*$, for all states p of the finite automaton M,

if in the label of state p there is an item of the form $A \to \alpha \,.\, B\beta$, *then* we add to that label *all* items of the grammar G' of the form: $B \to \,.\,\gamma$.

In order to present the Closure Rules (2) and (3), we need the following definitions.

DEFINITION 5.2.19. [**Closure of a Set of Items**] Given a set I of items, its *closure*, denoted $\overline{I}$, is the set of items which is obtained from I by applying as long as possible the Closure Rule (1).

Obviously, we have that any set I of items is a subset of its closure $\overline{I}$.

DEFINITION 5.2.20. [*use/make* **Operation**] Given a finite automaton M and the closure $\overline{I}$ of a set I of items, the *use/make* operation on the automaton M and the set $\overline{I}$, denoted $use/make(M, \overline{I})$, behaves as follows:

if in M there exists a state q with label $\overline{I}$

   then (Case *use*)   it returns this state q

   else (Case *make*) it returns a new state with label $\overline{I}$.

We leave it to the reader to check that, when constructing the finite automaton M, for all closures $\overline{I}$, the state q with label $\overline{I}$ in M, if any, is unique.

Closure Rule (2). For all $A_1, \ldots, A_n, B \in V_N$, for all $\alpha_1, \beta_1, \ldots, \alpha_n, \beta_n \in V^*$, for all states p of the finite automaton M,

if in the label of state p all the items with the dot immediately to the left of the nonterminal B are: $A_1 \to \alpha_1 \,.\, B\beta_1, \ldots, A_n \to \alpha_n \,.\, B\beta_n$, for some $n > 0$,

then, let q be the state (which may be p itself) returned by $use/make(M, \overline{I})$, where $\overline{I}$ is the closure of the set $\{A_1 \to \alpha_1 B \,.\, \beta_1, \ldots, A_n \to \alpha_n B \,.\, \beta_n\}$ of items,

   (2.1) we add to M the new state q, if q is returned in the Case *make*, and

   (2.2) we add to M a new arc with label B from state p to state q.

Closure Rule (3). For all $a \in V_T$, $A_1, \ldots, A_n \in V_N$, for all $\alpha_1, \beta_1, \ldots, \alpha_n, \beta_n \in V^*$, for all states p of the finite automaton M,

if in the label of state p all the items with the dot immediately to the left of the terminal a are: $A_1 \to \alpha_1 \cdot a\beta_1, \ldots, A_n \to \alpha_n \cdot a\beta_n$, for some $n > 0$,

then, let q be the state (which may be p itself) returned by $use/make(M, \overline{I})$, where $\overline{I}$ is the closure of the set $\{A_1 \to \alpha_1 a \cdot \beta_1, \ldots, A_n \to \alpha_n a \cdot \beta_n\}$ of items,

(3.1) we add to M the new state q, if q is returned in the Case *make*, and

(3.2) we add to M a new arc with label a from state p to state q.

Final State Rule. The final state of the finite automaton M is the one whose label has the item $S' \to S\,\$\cdot$.

If the axiom S does *not* occur on the right hand side of any production, and we take the augmented grammar G' to be G itself where in every production for S we have added a rightmost symbol $\$$, *then* every state of the finite automaton M whose label has the item $S \to \alpha_1 \ldots \alpha_n \$ \cdot$, for some production of the form $S \to \alpha_1 \ldots \alpha_n$, where $n \geq 0$ and for $i = 1, \ldots, n$, $\alpha_i \in V_T \cup V_N$, is a final state.

The correctness of these five boxed rules is a consequence of the correctness of the application of the Powerset Construction Procedure.

These rules allow us to construct the deterministic finite automaton M without constructing the so called big productions and without applying the Powerset Construction Procedure.

From M we then construct the $LR(0)$ parsing table T as indicated in Step (5) of Algorithm 5.2.3 on page 91.

NOTE 5.2.21. The finite automaton M we construct by using the above boxed rules, is minimal, because when applying the Closure Rules (2) and (3), we do not add to M a new state with label $\overline{I}$, if a state with that same label exists in M. □

5.2.2. Remarks on the Hypotheses for *LR(k)* Parsing.

In this section we will make a few remarks on the hypotheses we made on page 87 for the $LR(k)$ parsing algorithms, for $k \geq 0$. More remarks will be made on Section 5.4.2 on page 127.

On page 87 we have assumed that the start symbol S (or S' in case of augmented grammars) does *not* occur on the right hand side of any production. Indeed, if the start symbol occurs on the right hand side of a production, then we may get an $LR(0)$ parsing table which *does not* allow a correct parsing as the following example shows.

EXAMPLE 5.2.22. Let us consider the grammar G with axiom S and the following productions:

$$1.\ S \to A\,a\,\$ \qquad 2.\ A \to S\,a \qquad 3.\ A \to a$$

The language generated by this grammar is the regular language denoted by the regular expression $(a\,a)^+\$$. The finite automaton M to be constructed for generating the $LR(0)$ parsing table, is shown in Figure 5.2.6 on the next page.

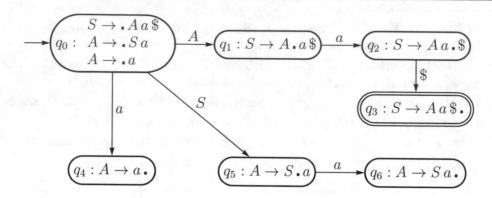

FIGURE 5.2.6. The finite automaton M for the $LR(0)$ parsing of the grammar G with axiom S and productions: 1. $S \to A\,a\,\$$, 2. $A \to S\,a$, 3. $A \to a$.

The corresponding parsing table is depicted in Figure 5.2.7.

	action		goto	
	a	$\$$	S	A
q_0	sh q_4		q_5	q_1
q_1	sh q_2			
q_2		acc		
q_3	red 1	red 1		
q_4	red 3	red 3		
q_5	sh q_6			
q_6	red 2	red 2		

where:
1. $S \to A\,a\,\$$
2. $A \to S\,a$
3. $A \to a$

FIGURE 5.2.7. $LR(0)$ parsing table for the grammar G with axiom S and productions: 1. $S' \to S\,\$$, 2. $S \to SA$, 3. $S \to A$. It has been derived from the finite automaton of Figure 5.2.6.

This parsing table does *not* allow a correct parsing. Indeed, if we parse the word $a\,a\,a\,a\,\$$ which belongs to $(a\,a)^+\$$ (and thus it should be accepted), we get, instead, an error as indicated by the sequence of stack configurations depicted in Figure 5.2.8 on the facing page (indeed, there is no transition for the state q_2 and the input symbol a).

We leave it to the reader to check that, on the contrary, the grammar G' with axiom S' and productions:

0. $S' \to S\,\$$ 1. $S \to A\,a$ 2. $A \to S\,a$ 3. $A \to a$

is an $LR(0)$ grammar, and we get a correct $LR(0)$ parsing table.

time	stack (the top is marked by ▲)	input (the symbol at hand is marked by ▲)	*shift/reduce-goto*
0	q_0 ▲	$a\,a\,a\,a\,\$$ ▲	$action(q_0, a) = sh\ q_4$
1	$q_0\,a\,q_4$ ▲	$a\,a\,a\,a\,\$$ ▲	$action(q_4, a) = red\ 3\ (A \to a)$ $goto(q_0, A) = q_1$
2	$q_0\,A\,q_1$ ▲	$a\,a\,a\,a\,\$$ ▲	$action(q_1, a) = sh\ q_2$
3	$q_0\,A\,q_1\,a\,q_2$ ▲	$a\,a\,a\,a\,\$$ ▲	no action is defined

FIGURE 5.2.8. The sequence of configurations of the parsing automaton of Figure 5.2.6 on the preceding page while parsing the string $a\,a\,a\,a\,\$$ using the $LR(0)$ parsing table of Figure 5.2.7 on the facing page for the grammar G with axiom S and productions: 1. $S \to A\,a\,\$$, 2. $A \to S\,a$, 3. $A \to a$.

This grammar G' that also generates the language $(a\,a)^+\$$, is obtained from the grammar G by: (i) erasing the rightmost symbol $\$$ of the production $S \to A\,a\,\$$, and (ii) adding the production $S' \to S\,\$$ so that the axiom S' does not occur on the right hand side of any production. □

5.3. *SLR*(1) Parsers

In this section we will describe a new algorithm for constructing the parsing table of the automaton of Figure 5.2.1 on page 89.

This algorithm is a variant of Algorithm 5.2.3 on page 88 for constructing $LR(0)$ parsing tables. It provides the definition of a class of the deterministic context-free languages, called $SLR(1)$ languages (short for *Simple LR*(1) languages), as specified by the following definition.

Actually, as it is stated in Theorem 5.8.12 on page 154, any deterministic context-free language can be generated by an $SLR(1)$ grammar, and thus the class of the deterministic context-free languages coincides with the class of languages that can be generated by an $SLR(1)$ grammar.

DEFINITION 5.3.1. [*SLR*(1) **Languages**] A language is an $SLR(1)$ language iff it is accepted by the following Algorithm 5.3.2 (this notion of acceptance is given in Definition 5.2.15 on page 98).

Here is the algorithm for constructing $SLR(1)$ parsing tables.

ALGORITHM 5.3.2. **Constructing the $SLR(1)$ Parsing Table.**

Given a context-free grammar G, we first consider its augmented grammar G'. Then, in order to fill the entries of the $SLR(1)$ parsing table T for the parsing automaton of Figure 5.2.1 on page 89, we use the Algorithm 5.2.3 on page 88 for constructing $LR(0)$ parsing tables, with the following rule (5.4*), instead of rule (5.4) on page 92:

(5.4*) for every state q of the deterministic finite automaton M,

> *if* there exists in q a complete item $A \to \alpha \,\bullet\,$, for some $A \in V_N$ and $\alpha \in V^*$,
>
> *then* for every terminal symbol a of the set $Follow_1(A)$, we insert in the entry $T[q, a]$ of the parsing table the *reduce* action *red p*, where p identifies the production $A \to \alpha$ of the augmented grammar G'.

If by using this algorithm we fill some entries of the table T by either:
  (i) *shift* actions (in the *action* columns), or
 (ii) *reduce* actions (in the *action* columns), or
(iii) *goto* actions (in the *goto* columns), and no more than one action is placed in every entry of that table,
then the augmented grammar G' is said to be an $SLR(1)$ grammar.

Note that the parameter 1 in the name '$SLR(1)$' is due to the fact that in our algorithm we have used the set $Follow_1(A)$, rather than the set $Follow_k(A)$, for some $k > 1$.

Here is an example of an $SLR(1)$ grammar and the construction of corresponding parsing table according to Algorithm 5.3.2.

EXAMPLE 5.3.3. [**$SLR(1)$ Parsing: An Example**] Let us consider the following augmented grammar:

  0. $E' \to E\,\$$
  1. $E \to E + T$
  2. $E \to T$
  3. $T \to T \times F$
  4. $T \to F$
  5. $F \to (E)$
  6. $F \to a$

The finite automaton constructed at the end of Step (4) by Algorithm 5.2.3 on page 88 is shown in Figure 5.3.1 on the next page.

The parsing table constructed from the finite automaton of Figure 5.3.1, is shown in Figure 5.3.2 on page 106. To construct that table we have first to compute the following $Follow_1$ sets:

$Follow_1(E) = \{+,), \$\}$,

$Follow_1(T) = \{+, \times,), \$\}$,   and

$Follow_1(F) = \{+, \times,), \$\}$

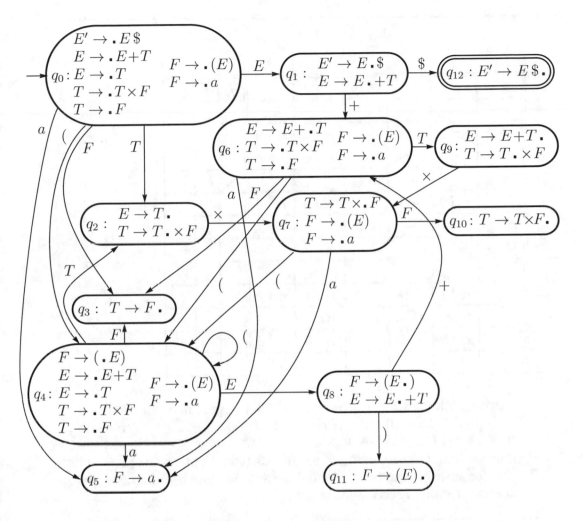

FIGURE 5.3.1. The finite automaton for the $SLR(1)$ parsing of the grammar with axiom E' and productions: 0. $E' \to E\,\$$, 1. $E \to E{+}T$, 2. $E \to T$, 3. $T \to T{\times}F$, 4. $T \to F$, 5. $F \to (E)$, 6. $F \to a$. The label of each state is a set of items and it is generated by the Powerset Construction Procedure starting from the graph of the big productions whose construction is left to the reader (see Algorithm 5.2.3 on page 88 for constructing the $LR(0)$ parsing tables).

Note that, contrary to the $LR(0)$ parsing tables, in the $SLR(1)$ parsing tables we may have in the same row both a *reduce* action and a *shift* action (which, obviously, are placed in different columns).

In particular, state q_9 shows that the given grammar is not an $LR(0)$ grammar. In state q_9, by using one symbol of lookahead on the input string, we do the following actions:

| | *action* | | | | | | *goto* | | |
	a	$+$	$\times$	$($	$)$	$\$$	E	T	F
q_0	$sh\ q_5$			$sh\ q_4$			q_1	q_2	q_3
q_1		$sh\ q_6$				acc			
q_2		$red\ 2$	$sh\ q_7$		$red\ 2$	$red\ 2$			
q_3		$red\ 4$	$red\ 4$		$red\ 4$	$red\ 4$			
q_4	$sh\ q_5$			$sh\ q_4$			q_8	q_2	q_3
q_5		$red\ 6$	$red\ 6$		$red\ 6$	$red\ 6$			
q_6	$sh\ q_5$			$sh\ q_4$				q_9	q_3
q_7	$sh\ q_5$			$sh\ q_4$					q_{10}
q_8		$sh\ q_6$			$sh\ q_{11}$				
q_9		$red\ 1$	$sh\ q_7$		$red\ 1$	$red\ 1$			
q_{10}		$red\ 3$	$red\ 3$		$red\ 3$	$red\ 3$			
q_{11}		$red\ 5$	$red\ 5$		$red\ 5$	$red\ 5$			
q_{12}						$red\ 0$			

where:
0. $E' \rightarrow E\,\$$
1. $E \rightarrow E+T$
2. $E \rightarrow T$
3. $T \rightarrow T \times F$
4. $T \rightarrow F$
5. $F \rightarrow (E)$
6. $F \rightarrow a$

FIGURE 5.3.2. $SLR(1)$ parsing table for the grammar with axiom E' and productions: 0. $E' \rightarrow E\,\$$, 1. $E \rightarrow E+T$, 2. $E \rightarrow T$, 3. $T \rightarrow T \times F$, 4. $T \rightarrow F$, 5. $F \rightarrow (E)$, 6. $F \rightarrow a$. It has been derived from the automaton of Figure 5.3.1 on the preceding page. The row for state q_{12} can be eliminated because in state q_1, when $\$$ is read, the input string is accepted.

(i) if the lookahead symbol is $\times$, then we perform a *shift* action by placing $\times$ on the top of the stack, and we look for an F, because of the item $T \rightarrow T \,.\, \times F$ in which the symbol $\times$ is followed by F, and otherwise,

(ii) if the lookahead symbol is different from $\times$ and belongs to $Follow_1(E)$, then we perform a *reduce* action by reducing production 1 which is: $E \rightarrow E+T$. Indeed, in state q_9 we have only the complete item $E \rightarrow E+T\,.$, besides the item $T \rightarrow T\,.\, \times F$.

The action $red\,0$ has been inserted in the row for state q_{12} in the $SLR(1)$ parsing table of Figure 5.3.2 in the hypothesis that $\$$ belongs to the $Follow_1$ set of the axiom of every augmented grammar (as it is the case for the axiom of every grammar).

Thus, in our case, for the axiom E' of the augmented grammar we have assumed that $\$ \in Follow_1(E')$. On the contrary, if we assume that $Follow_1(E') = \emptyset$, then the action $red\,0$ should have not been inserted.

Note, however, that the way in which we fill the row for state q_{12} does not make any difference during parsing, because in state q_1, when the symbol $\$$ is read, the input string is accepted, and thus state q_{12} is never reached. As a consequence, the row for state q_{12} can be eliminated.

Now we give an example of a grammar which is *not SLR*(1).

EXAMPLE 5.3.4. [**A Grammar which is not an *SLR*(1) Grammar**] Let us consider the grammar with axiom S and the following productions:

1. $S \to L = R$ 2. $S \to R$ 3. $L \to *R$ 4. $L \to a$ 5. $R \to L$

Its augmented grammar has axiom S' and the extra production $S' \to S\,\$$. The language generated by this grammar is the language of the so called *left-values* and *right-values* of assignments. In this language the string $*R$ denotes the content of the location R.

If we apply Algorithm 5.2.3 on page 88 for constructing the $LR(0)$ parsing table, we get a state with items: $S \to L\,.=R$ and $R \to L\,.$ (see state q_3 in Figure 5.3.3). We also have that $Follow_1(L) = \{=\}$ and $Follow_1(R) = \{=\}$.

Thus, in the $SLR(1)$ parsing table for that state q_3 and terminal symbol '=', we should insert according to Algorithm 5.3.2 on page 104, both a *shift* action (because of the symbol '=') and a *reduce* action (because $R \to L\,.$ is a complete item and the symbol '=' is an element of $Follow_1(R)$). Then we would have a so called *shift-reduce conflict*, and thus the given grammar is *not SLR*(1).

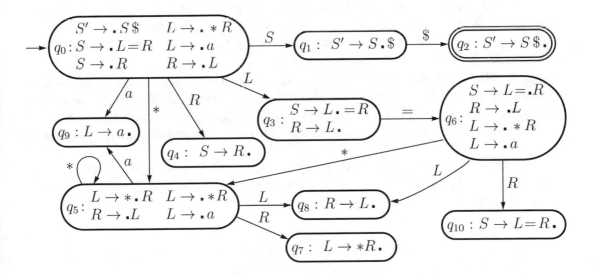

FIGURE 5.3.3. The finite automaton for the grammar with axiom S' and productions: 0. $S' \to S\,\$$, 1. $S \to L = R$, 2. $S \to R$, 3. $L \to *R$, 4. $L \to a$, 5. $R \to L$. The label of each state is generated by the Powerset Construction Procedure (see Algorithm 5.2.3 on page 88). State q_3 shows that this grammar is *not* an $SLR(1)$ grammar.

5.4. $LR(1)$ Parsers

In this section we describe a new algorithm for constructing the parsing table of the automaton of Figure 5.2.1 on page 89. This algorithm is similar to Algorithm 5.2.3 on page 88 (which was used for constructing $LR(0)$ parsing tables) and provides the definition of a class of the deterministic context-free languages, the so called $LR(1)$ languages. Actually, one can show (see Theorem 5.4.16 on page 123) that every deterministic context-free language admits an $LR(1)$ grammar which generates it.

ALGORITHM 5.4.1. **Constructing the $LR(1)$ Parsing Table.**
Given a context-free grammar $G = \langle V_T, V_N, P, S \rangle$ we want to construct the $LR(1)$ parsing table for the parsing automaton of Figure 5.2.1 on page 89.
Step (1). First we consider the augmented grammar $G' = \langle V_T \cup \{\$\}, V_N \cup \{S'\}, P', S' \rangle$, where the set P' of productions is $P \cup \{S' \to S\}$. We assume that $\$ \notin V_T$ and $S' \notin V_N$. We have that the start symbol S' of the augmented grammar does not occur on the right hand side of any production of the augmented grammar.

For instance, in the case of the grammar G with axiom S and the three productions

$$1.\ S \to C\,C \qquad 2.\ C \to c\,C \qquad 3.\ C \to d$$

we consider the following augmented grammar G':

$$0.\ S' \to S \qquad 1.\ S \to C\,C \qquad 2.\ C \to c\,C \qquad 3.\ C \to d$$

REMARK 5.4.2. [**Avoiding a New Start Symbol in the Augmented Grammar for $LR(1)$ Parsing**] If the start symbol S of the grammar G does *not* occur on the right hand side of any production of G, then we can take the augmented grammar G' to be G itself. □

Step (2). We construct a set $\mathcal{P}$ of *big productions with lookahead sets* as we now indicate. A big production with a lookahead set is a linear graph like the one described in Step (2) of Algorithm 5.2.3 on page 88 for constructing $LR(0)$ parsing tables, but in the label of each node of the graph there is also a set of symbols in $V_T \cup \{\$\}$, called the *lookahead set*.

The construction of the set $\mathcal{P}$ of big productions with lookahead sets is done incrementally by applying to the following Rules (2.1) and (2.2). The Closure Rule (2.2) should be applied as long as possible.

Initialization Rule 2.1
Initially, the set $\mathcal{P}$ consists of one big production only. It is the following one with lookahead set $\{\$\}$:

$$\boxed{S' \to {}.S,\ \{\$\}} \xrightarrow{\ S\ } \boxed{S' \to S.,\ \{\$\}}$$

If the axiom S does *not* occur on the right hand side of any production, and we take the augmented grammar G' to be G itself, then the set $\mathcal{P}$ initially includes a big production with lookahead set $\{\$\}$ of the form:

$$\boxed{S \to {}.\alpha_1\alpha_2 \ldots \alpha_n,\ \{\$\}} \xrightarrow{\alpha_1} \boxed{S \to \alpha_1.\alpha_2 \ldots \alpha_n,\ \{\$\}} \xrightarrow{\alpha_2} \ldots \xrightarrow{\alpha_n} \boxed{S \to \alpha_1\alpha_2 \ldots \alpha_n.,\ \{\$\}}$$

for each production for the axiom S of the form $S \to \alpha_1 \ldots \alpha_n$, where $n \geq 0$ and for $i = 1, \ldots, n$, $\alpha_i \in V_T \cup V_N$.

Closure Rule 2.2

For every node in the graph constructed so far, of the form:

$\boxed{B \to \alpha \centerdot A\beta,\ L}$ where $A, B \in V_N$ and $\alpha, \beta \in V^*$, and for every production

$A \to \gamma$, with $\gamma = \gamma_1 \ldots \gamma_n$, for $n \geq 0$, where the γ_i's belong to $V_T \cup V_N$, in the augmented grammar G', we add to the set $\mathcal{P}$ the following big production:

$$\boxed{A \to \centerdot\,\gamma_1\gamma_2 \ldots \gamma_n, L'} \xrightarrow{\gamma_1} \boxed{A \to \gamma_1\centerdot\gamma_2 \ldots \gamma_n, L'} \xrightarrow{\gamma_2} \cdots \xrightarrow{\gamma_n} \boxed{A \to \gamma_1\gamma_2 \ldots \gamma_n\centerdot, L'}$$

whose lookahead set L' is defined as follows:

$$L' = \text{if}\ \ \beta - \varepsilon \qquad\qquad\qquad \text{then}\ \ L$$
$$\quad\ \text{if}\ \ \beta \neq \varepsilon\ \text{and}\ \beta \to^* \varepsilon\ \ \text{then}\ \ L \cup (First_1(\beta) - \{\varepsilon\}) \qquad (\dagger 1)$$
$$\quad\ \text{if}\ \ \beta \neq \varepsilon\ \text{and}\ \beta \not\to^* \varepsilon\ \ \text{then}\ \ First_1(\beta) \qquad\qquad\qquad (\dagger 2)$$

Note that:
- in line ($\dagger 1$) we have written $First(\beta) - \{\varepsilon\}$, because ε should not be a member of the lookahead set L' (which is a subset of $V_T \cup \{\$\}$), and yet $\varepsilon \in First(\beta)$ because $\beta \to^* \varepsilon$, and
- line ($\dagger 2$) we have written $First(\beta)$, because $\beta \not\to^* \varepsilon$, and thus $\varepsilon \notin First(\beta)$.

Step (3). We consider the graph constructed at Step (2), made out of all the big productions with lookahead sets. Then, for all nonterminals $A, B \in V_N$, strings $\alpha, \beta, \gamma \in (V_T \cup V_N)^*$, and lookahead sets L, we add an arc labeled by ε from every node of the form:

$\boxed{B \to \alpha \centerdot A\beta,\ L}$ to every node of the form: $\boxed{A \to \centerdot\,\gamma,\ L'}$, where L' is con-

structed from L as indicated at the end of Step (2).
• If the augmented grammar G' is the grammar G itself, then we also add an ε-arc between any two nodes whose label has an item of the form $S \to \centerdot\alpha$, for some production $S \to \alpha$, where S is the start symbol of G.

Step (4). By applying the Powerset Construction Procedure (see, for instance, [21]) to the graph of the big productions with lookahead sets obtained at the end of Step (3), we get a finite automaton. Let that finite automaton be called M.

Note that by the Powerset Construction the label of each state of M is a *set of items* of the grammar G', each item being associated with its lookahead set.

In what follows we use the following notation and terminology.

NOTATION 5.4.3. (1) By abuse of language, we will feel free to say 'an item', instead of 'an item with its lookahead set'.

(2) An item $A \to \beta$ with its lookahead set L will be denoted by $\boxed{A \to \beta,\ L}$, or by

$\boxed{\boxed{A \to \beta,\ L}}$, if that item with its lookahead set L is in a final state.

(3) A state $\boxed{q}$ whose label has the $n\ (\geq 1)$ items $\boxed{A_1 \to \beta_1,\ L_1}, \ldots, \boxed{A_n \to \beta_n,\ L_n}$,

will also be denoted by $\left(q: \begin{array}{c} A_1 \to \beta_1, L_1 \\ \cdots \\ A_n \to \beta_n, L_n \end{array}\right)$, where the order of the items with their

lookahead sets is immaterial (recall that the label of a state is, indeed, a *set* of items with their associated lookahead sets). In this case we also say that any of these n items *is in* the label of the state $\boxed{q}$. □

The initial state of the finite automaton M is the one whose label has the item $\boxed{S' \to \,.\,S,\ \{\$\}}$.

The final state of M is the one whose label has the item $\boxed{\boxed{S' \to S\,.\,,\ \{\$\}}}$.

• If the augmented grammar G' is equal to the given grammar G with axiom S (and thus, as indicated in Remark 5.4.2 on page 108, we have that S does not occur on the right hand side of any production of G), then:

(i) the initial state of M is the one whose label has, possibly among others, the set of items $\{ \boxed{S \to \,.\,\alpha_1\alpha_2 \ldots \alpha_n,\ \{\$\}} \mid S \to \alpha_1\alpha_2 \ldots \alpha_n,\ \text{where for } i=1,\ldots,n,\ \alpha_i \in V_T \cup V_N\}$, and

(ii) a final state of M is every state whose label has an item of the form:

$\boxed{\boxed{S \to \alpha_1\alpha_2 \ldots \alpha_n\,.\,,\ \{\$\}}}$, for some production $S \to \alpha_1\alpha_2 \ldots \alpha_n$, where for $i=1,\ldots,n$, $\alpha_i \in V_T \cup V_N$.

Step (5). The $LR(1)$ parsing table T is then constructed from the automaton M as follows.

(5.1) For each transition $\boxed{q_i} \xrightarrow{\ a\ } \boxed{q_j}$ where a is a terminal symbol,

we insert in the entry $T[q_i, a]$ which is in the *action* part of the table T, the action *sh* q_j (short for *shift* q_j). This means that the parsing automaton of Figure 5.2.1 on page 89 should take the input symbol a at hand, push it on the stack, and push the state q_j on the stack. Then the new input symbol at hand is the one to the right of the previous symbol a at hand. This action of the parsing automaton is called a *shift action*.

(5.2) For the *final* state q_i whose label has the item $\boxed{\boxed{S' \to S\,.\,,\ \{\$\}}}$,

we insert in the entry $T[q_i, \$]$ which is in the *action* part of the table T, the action *acc* (short for *accept*). This means that the parsing automaton of Figure 5.2.1 should accept the given input string. This action of the parsing automaton is called an *accept action*.

Recall that in the final state q_i, instead of the item $\boxed{\boxed{S' \to S\,.\,,\ \{\$\}}}$, we have the item $\boxed{\boxed{S \to \alpha_1 \ldots \alpha_n\,.\,,\ \{\$\}}}$, for some $n \geq 0$ and some $\alpha_1, \ldots, \alpha_n$ in $V_T \cup V_N$, if

according to Remark 5.4.2 on page 108, we take the augmented grammar to be the given grammar itself (and we can do so if the axiom S does *not* occur on the right hand side of any production).

(5.3) For each transition $\boxed{q_i} \xrightarrow{\quad A \quad} \boxed{q_j}$ with the nonterminal A,

we insert in the entry $T[q_i, A]$ which is in the *goto* part of the table T, the state q_j. This means that the parsing automaton of Figure 5.2.1 should push on the stack the state q_j (see Step (5.4) below). This action of the parsing automaton is called a *goto action*.

(5.4) For each complete item $\boxed{A \to \alpha_1 \ldots \alpha_n \bullet, L}$, for some $n \geq 0$ and some $\alpha_1, \ldots, \alpha_n$

in $V_T \cup V_N$, in the label of a (final or not final) state q_i,
for each $a \in L$, if $a \neq \$$, we insert in the entry $T[q_i, a]$ in the *action* part of the table T, the action *red p* (short for *reduce production p*), where p is the number identifying the production $A \to \alpha_1 \ldots \alpha_n$ of the grammar G'. This means that the parsing automaton of Figure 5.2.1 should replace the string $\alpha_1 q_{\alpha_1} \ldots \alpha_n q_{\alpha_n}$ which is on the stack (the top element being state q_{α_n}) by the nonterminal A. This action of the parsing automaton is called a *reduce action* and it is performed during the parsing of the input word when looking at the character a.

We have the condition '$a \neq \$$' because for $a = \$$ during Step (5.2) we have already considered the complete item with $\$$ in its lookahead set and we have inserted the action *acc* in the entry $T[q_i, \$]$ (in this case the state q_i is final).

Note that in this Step (5.4) the nonterminal symbol A on the left hand side of a complete item $\boxed{A \to \alpha_1 \ldots \alpha_n \bullet, L}$ in the label of a state q_i which is *not* final, cannot be the axiom S' of the augmented grammar G' that we have considered at the end of Step (1), because of Hypothesis (i) we have made when performing the $LR(k)$ parsing (see page 87). Similarly, in the case where the augmented grammar G' is equal to the given grammar G, then the nonterminal symbol A cannot be the axiom S.

This conclude the presentation of the algorithm for constructing the $LR(1)$ parsing table.

Having constructed the $LR(1)$ parsing table, we can use the pushdown automaton of Figure 5.2.1 on page 89 with that table, for parsing a given input word w. Initially, the stack has the initial state q_0 only, and the input string is $w\,\$$. Then the pushdown automaton works by using the $LR(1)$ parsing table as it were an $LR(0)$ parsing table.

As in the case of $LR(0)$ parsing (see page 94), the sequence of the stack configurations shows *in the reverse order* the rightmost derivation of the input string $w\,\$$, when that string is generated by the augmented grammar G' (see, for instance, Figure 5.4.4 on page 116). The *accept* action stands for the *reduce* action: *red* 0 $(S' \to S)$.

REMARK 5.4.4. [*Multiple actions*] As for $LR(0)$ grammars, also in the case of the $LR(1)$ grammars, if we have to place more than one action in an entry of the $LR(1)$ parsing table (that is, we have conflicts), then the language generated by the given grammar cannot be parsed by using a pushdown automaton which uses that table and the augmented grammar G' which has been derived from the given grammar G, is *not* an $LR(1)$ grammar.

REMARK 5.4.5. [*Undefined entry*] If during the process of parsing a given input word $w\,\$$, the pushdown automaton requires an entry of the table, but that entry is empty, then the word w does *not* belong to the language generated by the augmented grammar G' and w does *not* belong to the language generated by the given grammar G. □

REMARK 5.4.6. [*Replacing many items by a single item within the same state: union of the lookahead sets*] When applying Algorithm 5.4.1 on page 108, in any state, for any $n \geq 2$, we can replace n items of the form: $\boxed{A \to \gamma, L_1}$, ..., $\boxed{A \to \gamma, L_n}$, where $A \in V_N$ and $\gamma \in (V_T \cup V_N)^* \cup \{\,\boldsymbol{.}\,\} \cup (V_T \cup V_N)^*$ (that is, γ is a string of terminal or nonterminal symbols with a dot $\boldsymbol{.}$ at the beginning, or in between, or at the end), by a single item of the form: $\boxed{A \to \gamma, L_1 \cup \ldots \cup L_n}$. Indeed, this replacement does not modify the outcome of that algorithm (see Step (5.4) on page 111). □

Note that in the $LR(1)$ parsing table there is no column labeled by S', because no arc in the graph representing the finite automaton M constructed at the end of Step (4) of Algorithm 5.4.1 on page 109, has label S'.

We leave it to the reader to check that, if the axiom of the augmented grammar is S' and the axiom of the given grammar is S, when the action *accept* is performed, then the pushdown automaton is in a final state q whose label has the item $\boxed{S' \to S\,\boldsymbol{.}, \ \{\$\}}$, the input symbol at hand is $\$$, and the stack is of the form (the top being the state q):

q_0	S	q

If, according to Remark 5.4.2 on page 108, we take the augmented grammar to be the given grammar itself, then when the action *accept* is performed, (i) the pushdown automaton is in the final state q whose label has the item $\boxed{S \to \alpha_1 \ldots \alpha_n\,\boldsymbol{.}, \ \{\$\}}$,

for some production for the axiom S of the form $S \to \alpha_1 \ldots \alpha_n$, for some $n \geq 0$ and the α_i's in $V_T \cup V_N$, (ii) the input symbol at hand is $\$$, and (iii) the stack is of the form (the top being the state q):

q_0	α_1	q_r	$\ldots$	q_s	α_n	q

The following fact states a property which is enjoyed by the lookahead sets of the items of the $LR(1)$ grammars.

FACT 5.4.7. [**Lookahead Sets and *Follow*$_1$ Sets**] For any item of the form $\boxed{B \to \alpha\,\boldsymbol{.}\,\beta, \ L}$, with $B \in (V_N \cup \{S'\})$ and $\alpha, \beta \in (V_T \cup V_N)^*$, we have that:

$L \subseteq Follow_1(B)$.

PROOF. The proof is by cases and by induction on the number of items to be inserted in the states of the finite automaton constructed for generating the $LR(1)$ parsing table.

Case (1). For the item of the form $\boxed{S' \to .S,\ \{\$\}}$ where S' is the axiom of the augmented grammar and the production $S' \to S$ is the only production for S', we get the thesis because $Follow_1(S') = \{\$\}$.

Case (2). For the item of the form $\boxed{B \to \alpha.A\beta,\ L}$ with $\beta \neq \varepsilon$ and $\beta \to^* \varepsilon$, we have to consider items of the form $\boxed{A \to \ldots,\ L'}$, where $L' = L \cup (First_1(\beta) - \{\varepsilon\})$. The thesis follows from the following Points (2.1) and (2.2).

Point (2.1). By induction hypothesis we have that: $L \subseteq Follow_1(B)$. We also have that $Follow_1(B) \subseteq Follow_1(A)$, by definition of the function $Follow_1$ when $\beta \neq \varepsilon$ and $\beta \to^* \varepsilon$ (see Algorithm 4.2.7 on page 53). Thus, $L \subseteq Follow_1(A)$.

Point (2.2). We have that: $(First_1(\beta) - \{\varepsilon\}) \subseteq Follow_1(A)$, by definition of the function $Follow_1$ when $\beta \neq \varepsilon$ and $\beta \to^* \varepsilon$.

Case (3). For the item of the form $\boxed{B \to \alpha.A\beta,\ L}$ with $\beta \neq \varepsilon$ and $\beta \not\to^* \varepsilon$, we have to consider items of the form $\boxed{A \to \ldots,\ L'}$, where $L' = First_1(\beta)$. The thesis follows because $First_1(\beta) - \{\varepsilon\}) = First_1(\beta)$ (recall that, when $\beta \not\to^* \varepsilon$, we have that $\varepsilon \notin First_1(\beta)$) and $(First_1(\beta) - \{\varepsilon\}) \subseteq Follow_1(A)$ (by definition of the function $Follow_1$ when $\beta \neq \varepsilon$ and $\beta \not\to^* \varepsilon$). $\qquad \square$

One can show that the following is an alternative definition of $LR(1)$ grammars. The proof of this fact is based on Algorithm 5.4.1 on page 108 and can be found in [**10**, page 263].

DEFINITION 5.4.8. [**$LR(1)$ Grammar and $LR(1)$ Language**] A context-free grammar G is an $LR(1)$ grammar iff
(i) the start symbol does *not* occur in the right hand side of any production, and
(ii) if in the label of a state of the automaton M of Step (4) of Algorithm 5.4.1 for constructing the $LR(1)$ parsing tables, there is a complete item of the form $\boxed{A \to \alpha.,\ L}$ (recall that the label of a state is a set of items, each item being associated with its lookahead set), then (ii.1) for any other complete item $\boxed{B \to \beta.,\ M}$ in the same label, $L \cap M = \emptyset$ (that is, there is no reduce-reduce conflict), and (ii.2) for any other incomplete item $\boxed{B \to \beta.a\gamma,\ M}$, with $a \in V_T \cup \{\$\}$ in the same label, we have that $a \notin L$ (that is, there is no shift-reduce conflict).

A language is an $LR(1)$ language if it is generated by an $LR(1)$ grammar.

Now we will present some examples of $LR(1)$ parsing.

EXAMPLE 5.4.9. [**$LR(1)$ Parsing: Example 1**] Let us consider the grammar G with axiom S and the following productions:

$$1.\ S \to CC \qquad 2.\ C \to cC \qquad 3.\ C \to d$$

The augmented grammar G' is:

$$0.\ S' \to S \qquad 1.\ S \to CC \qquad 2.\ C \to cC \qquad 3.\ C \to d$$

Note that for the grammar G we can take the augmented grammar G' to be G itself, because there is only one production for S and S does not occur on the right hand side of any production in G.

The graph of the big productions with the lookahead sets is depicted in Figure 5.4.1.

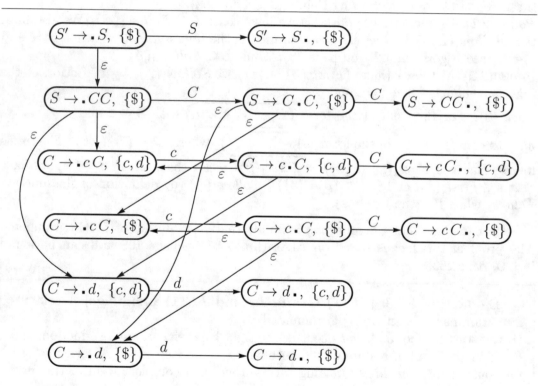

FIGURE 5.4.1. The graph of the big productions with lookahead sets and ε-arcs for the grammar G' with axiom S' and productions: 0. $S' \to S$, 1. $S \to CC$, 2. $C \to cC$, 3. $C \to d$. Each big production with its lookahead set is depicted as a sequence of nodes which are horizontally aligned.

Note the item $\boxed{S \to .CC,\ \{\$\}}$ in the second row from above, has an ε-arc both to the item $\boxed{C \to .cC,\ \{c,d\}}$ in the third row and to the item $\boxed{C \to .d,\ \{c,d\}}$ in the fifth row, both with lookahead set $\{c,d\}$, because $C \not\to^* \varepsilon$ and $First_1(C) = \{c,d\}$. From the graph of Figure 5.4.1 the Powerset Construction Procedure constructs the finite automaton depicted in Figure 5.4.2 on the facing page.

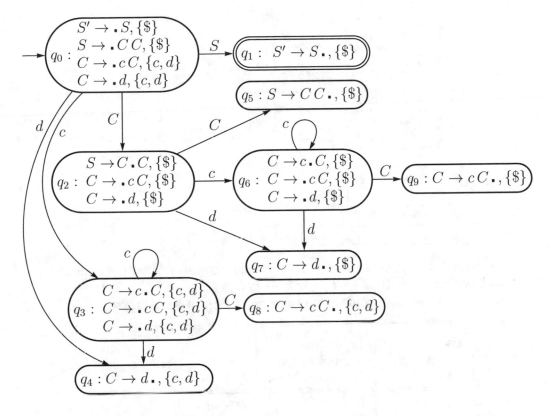

FIGURE 5.4.2. The finite automaton M for the $LR(1)$ parsing of the grammar G' with axiom S' and productions: 0. $S' \to S$, 1. $S \to CC$, 2. $C \to cC$, 3. $C \to d$. The label of each state is a set of items which is computed by the Powerset Construction Procedure from the graph of Figure 5.4.1.

From that automaton we get the $LR(1)$ parsing table of Figure 5.4.3 on the next page. Figure 5.4.4 on the following page shows the behaviour of the automaton of Figure 5.2.1 on page 89, while parsing the input string $d\,c\,d\,\$$ which is read from left to right. In Figure 5.4.4 we use the same conventions of Figure 5.2.5 on page 95 and, in particular, the symbol ▲ points at the input character at hand. The stack grows and shrinks at the right end, and the symbol ▲ points at the top of the stack.   □

| | action | | | goto | |
	c	d	$\$$	S	C
q_0	sh q_3	sh q_4		q_1	q_2
q_1			acc		
q_2	sh q_6	sh q_7			q_5
q_3	sh q_3	sh q_4			q_8
q_4	red 3	red 3			
q_5			red 1		
q_6	sh q_6	sh q_7			q_9
q_7			red 3		
q_8	red 2	red 2			
q_9			red 2		

where:

0. $S' \to S$
1. $S \to C\,C$
2. $C \to c\,C$
3. $C \to d$

FIGURE 5.4.3. $LR(1)$ parsing table for the grammar G' with axiom S' and productions: 0. $S' \to S$, 1. $S \to C\,C$, 2. $C \to c\,C$, 3. $C \to d$. It has been derived from the automaton of Figure 5.4.2 on page 115.

time	stack (the top is marked by ▲)	input (the symbol at hand is marked by ▲)	shift/reduce-goto
0	q_0 ▲	$d\,c\,d\,\$$ ▲	$action(q_0, d) = $ sh q_4
1	$q_0\,d\,q_4$ ▲	$d\,c\,d\,\$$ ▲	$action(q_4, c) = $ red 3 $(C \to d)$ $goto(q_0, C) = q_2$
2	$q_0\,C\,q_2$ ▲	$d\,c\,d\,\$$ ▲	$action(q_2, c) = $ sh q_6
3	$q_0\,C\,q_2\,c\,q_6$ ▲	$d\,c\,d\,\$$ ▲	$action(q_6, d) = $ sh q_7
4	$q_0\,C\,q_2\,c\,q_6\,d\,q_7$ ▲	$d\,c\,d\,\$$ ▲	$action(q_7, \$) = $ red 3 $(C \to d)$ $goto(q_6, C) = q_9$
5	$q_0\,C\,q_2\,c\,q_6\,C\,q_9$ ▲	$d\,c\,d\,\$$ ▲	$action(q_9, \$) = $ red 2 $(C \to c\,C)$ $goto(q_2, C) = q_5$
6	$q_0\,C\,q_2\,C\,q_5$ ▲	$d\,c\,d\,\$$ ▲	$action(q_5, \$) = $ red 1 $(S \to C\,C)$ $goto(q_0, S) = q_1$
7	$q_0\,S\,q_1$ ▲	$d\,c\,d\,\$$ ▲	$action(q_1, \$) = $ accept

FIGURE 5.4.4. Sequence of configurations of the pushdown automaton of Figure 5.2.1 on page 89 while parsing the string $d\,c\,d\,\$$ using the $LR(1)$ parsing table of Figure 5.4.3, for the grammar G' with axiom S' and productions: 0. $S' \to S$, 1. $S \to C\,C$, 2. $C \to c\,C$, 3. $C \to d$.

Before presenting some more examples of $LR(1)$ parsing, let us make the following remark.

REMARK 5.4.10. The label of the final state of the finite automaton M derived at the end of Step (4) of Algorithm 5.4.1 on page 109, may have, together with the complete item $S' \to S\,.\,,\ \{\$\}$ (or $S \to \alpha_1 \ldots \alpha_n\,.\,,\ \{\$\}$, for some production $S \to \alpha_1 \ldots \alpha_n$ for the axiom S, where $n \geq 0$ and, for $i = 1, \ldots, n$, $\alpha_i \in (V_T \cup V_N)^*$, in case we take the augmented grammar to be the given grammar itself), some more complete items. If $\$ $ belongs to one of the lookahead sets of those other complete items, then the given grammar is *not* $LR(1)$ because, together with the *accept action*, we have to insert also a *reduce action* in the same entry of the $LR(1)$ parsing table.

This case occurs, for instance, for the augmented grammar G_1' with axiom S' and productions:

> 0. $S' \to S$ 1. $S \to A$ 2. $S \to c$ 3. $A \to S$ 4. $A \to a$

The grammar G_1' generates the language $\{a, c\}$ and is *not* $LR(1)$. The finite automaton for this grammar G_1' constructed at the end of Step (4) of Algorithm 5.4.1 on page 109, is depicted in Figure 5.4.5 and the associated parsing table is depicted in Figure 5.4.6 on the next page (note the double entry for state q_1 and the symbol $\$ $).

In Theorem 5.4.16 on page 123 we will see that every $LR(1)$ grammar generates a deterministic context-free language, and in Fact 5.8.13 on page 154 we will see that every word of a language generated by an $LR(1)$ grammar has a unique parse tree. This is *not* the case for the word a of the language $\{a, c\}$. Indeed, a has (among infinitely many others) the following two parse trees: $S' \to S \to A \to a$ and $S' \to S \to A \to S \to A \to a$.

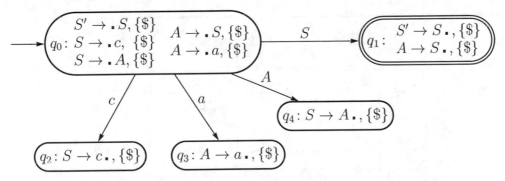

FIGURE 5.4.5. The finite automaton for the grammar G_1' with axiom S' and productions: 0. $S' \to S$,   1. $S \to c$,   2. $S \to A$,   3. $A \to S$ 4. $A \to a$.

On the contrary, the augmented grammar G_2' with axiom S' and productions:

> 0. $S' \to S$ 1. $S \to A\,a$ 2. $S \to c$ 3. $A \to S$ 4. $A \to a$

that generates the language $(a\,a + c)\,a^*$, is $LR(1)$. The finite automaton for this grammar G_2' is depicted in Figure 5.4.7 on the following page and the associated $LR(1)$ parsing table is depicted in Figure 5.4.8 on the next page. □

	action			goto	
	a	c	$\$$	S	A
q_0	sh q_3	sh q_2		q_1	q_4
q_1			red 3/acc		
q_2			red 1		
q_3			red 4		
q_4			red 2		

where:
0. $S' \to S$
1. $S \to c$
2. $S \to A$
3. $A \to S$
4. $A \to a$

FIGURE 5.4.6. Parsing table for the grammar G_1' with axiom S' and productions: 0. $S' \to S$, 1. $S \to c$, 2. $S \to A$, 3. $A \to S$ 4. $A \to a$. It has been derived from the automaton of Figure 5.4.5 on page 117.

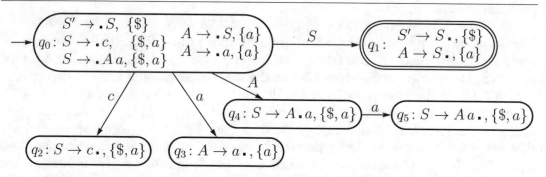

FIGURE 5.4.7. The finite automaton for the augmented grammar G_2' with axiom S' and productions: 0. $S' \to S$, 1. $S \to c$, 2. $S \to Aa$, 3. $A \to S$ 4. $A \to a$.

	action			goto	
	a	c	$\$$	S	A
q_0	sh q_3	sh q_2		q_1	q_4
q_1	red 3		acc		
q_2	red 1		red 1		
q_3	red 4				
q_4	sh q_5				
q_5	red 2		red 2		

where:
0. $S' \to S$
1. $S \to c$
2. $S \to Aa$
3. $A \to S$
4. $A \to a$

FIGURE 5.4.8. $LR(1)$ parsing table for the augmented grammar G_2' with axiom S' and productions: 0. $S' \to S$, 1. $S \to c$, 2. $S \to Aa$, 3. $A \to S$ 4. $A \to a$. It has been derived from the automaton of Figure 5.4.7 on the current page.

EXAMPLE 5.4.11. [**LR(1) Parsing: Example 2**] Let us consider the grammar G with axiom A and the following productions:

$$1.\ A \to B\,A \qquad 2.\ A \to \varepsilon \qquad 3.\ B \to a\,B \qquad 4.\ B \to b$$

The augmented grammar G' with axiom S has the productions:

$$0.\ S \to A \qquad 1.\ A \to B\,A \qquad 2.\ A \to \varepsilon \qquad 3.\ B \to a\,B \qquad 4.\ B \to b$$

(Note that for reasons of simplicity, we have used the symbol S, instead of S'.) The language generated by this grammar is $(a^*b)^*$. The graph of the big productions with the lookahead sets is depicted in Figure 5.4.9. Note that the item $\big(A \to {\scriptstyle\bullet}\,B\,A,\ \{\$\}\big)$ has an ε-arc both to the item $\big(B \to {\scriptstyle\bullet}\,a\,B,\ \{\$,a,b\}\big)$ and to the item $\big(B \to {\scriptstyle\bullet}\,b,\ \{\$,a,b\}\big)$, both with lookahead set $\{\$, a, b\}$, because $A \to \varepsilon$ and $First_1(B) = \{a, b\}$.

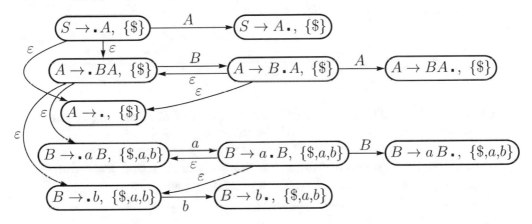

FIGURE 5.4.9. The graph of the big productions with lookahead sets and ε-arcs for the grammar G' with axiom S and productions: 0. $S \to A$, 1. $A \to B\,A$, 2. $A \to \varepsilon$, 3. $B \to a\,B$, 4. $B \to b$. Each big production with its lookahead set is depicted as a sequence of nodes which are horizontally aligned.

The Powerset Construction Procedure constructs from the graph of Figure 5.4.9 the finite automaton depicted in Figure 5.4.10 on the next page.

From that automaton we get the $LR(1)$ parsing table of Figure 5.4.11 on the next page. Figure 5.4.12 on page 121 shows the behaviour of the pushdown automaton of Figure 5.2.1 on page 89 while parsing the input string $a\,a\,b\,b\,\$$ which is read from left to right using the parsing table of Figure 5.4.11 on the next page.

In Figure 5.4.12 we use the same conventions of Figure 5.2.5 on page 95 and, in particular, the symbol ▲ points at the input character at hand. The stack grows and shrinks at the right end, and the symbol ▲ points at the top of the stack.   □

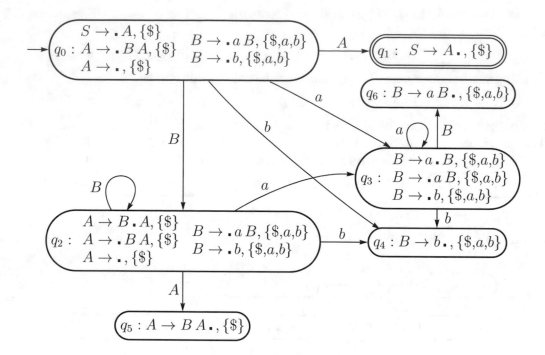

FIGURE 5.4.10. The finite automaton M for the $LR(1)$ parsing of the grammar G' with axiom S and productions: 0. $S \to A$,   1. $A \to BA$, 2. $A \to \varepsilon$,   3. $B \to aB$,   4. $B \to b$. The label of each state is a set of items which is computed by the Powerset Construction Procedure from the graph of Figure 5.4.9 on the preceding page.

	action			*goto*	
	a	b	$\$$	A	B
q_0	sh q_3	sh q_4	red 2	q_1	q_2
q_1			acc		
q_2	sh q_3	sh q_4	red 2	q_5	q_2
q_3	sh q_3	sh q_4			q_6
q_4	red 4	red 4	red 4		
q_5			red 1		
q_6	red 3	red 3	red 3		

where:

0. $S \to A$

1. $A \to BA$

2. $A \to \varepsilon$

3. $B \to aB$

4. $B \to b$

FIGURE 5.4.11. $LR(1)$ parsing table for the grammar G' with axiom S and productions: 0. $S \to A$,   1. $A \to BA$,   2. $A \to \varepsilon$,   3. $B \to aB$, 4. $B \to b$. It has been derived from the finite automaton of Figure 5.4.10.

time	stack (the top is marked by ▲)	input (the symbol at hand is marked by ▲)	*shift/reduce-goto*
0	q_0 ▲	$a\,a\,b\,b\,\$$ ▲	$action(q_0, a) = sh\ q_3$
1	$q_0\,a\,q_3$ ▲	$a\,a\,b\,b\,\$$ ▲	$action(q_3, a) = sh\ q_3$
2	$q_0\,a\,q_3\,a\,q_3$ ▲	$a\,a\,b\,b\,\$$ ▲	$action(q_3, b) = sh\ q_4$
3	$q_0\,a\,q_3\,a\,q_3\,b\,q_4$ ▲	$a\,a\,b\,b\,\$$ ▲	$action(q_4, b) = red\ 4\ (B \to b)$ $goto(q_3, B) = q_6$
4	$q_0\,a\,q_3\,a\,q_3\,B\,q_6$ ▲	$a\,a\,b\,b\,\$$ ▲	$action(q_6, b) = red\ 3\ \ (B \to a\,B)$ $goto(q_3, B) = q_6$
5	$q_0\,a\,q_3\,B\,q_6$ ▲	$a\,a\,b\,b\,\$$ ▲	$action(q_6, b) = red\ 3\ (B \to a\,B)$ $goto(q_0, B) = q_2$
6	$q_0\,B\,q_2$ ▲	$a\,a\,b\,b\,\$$ ▲	$action(q_2, b) = sh\ q_4$
7	$q_0\,B\,q_2\,b\,q_4$ ▲	$a\,a\,b\,b\,\$$ ▲	$action(q_4, \$) = red\ 4\ (B \to b)$ $goto(q_2, B) = q_2$
8	$q_0\,B\,q_2\,B\,q_2$ ▲	$a\,a\,b\,b\,\$$ ▲	$action(q_2, \$) = red\ 2\ (A \to \varepsilon)$ $goto(q_2, A) = q_5$
9	$q_0\,B\,q_2\,B\,q_2\,A\,q_5$ ▲	$a\,a\,b\,b\,\$$ ▲	$action(q_5, \$) = red\ 1\ (A \to B\,A)$ $goto(q_2, A) = q_5$
10	$q_0\,B\,q_2\,A\,q_5$ ▲	$a\,a\,b\,b\,\$$ ▲	$action(q_5, \$) = red\ 1\ (A \to B\,A)$ $goto(q_0, A) = q_1$
11	$q_0\,A\,q_1$ ▲	$a\,a\,b\,b\,\$$ ▲	$action(q_1, \$) = accept$

FIGURE 5.4.12. Sequence of configurations of the pushdown automaton of Figure 5.2.1 while parsing the string $a\,a\,b\,b\,\$$ using the $LR(1)$ parsing table of Figure 5.4.11, for the grammar G' with axiom S and productions: 0. $S \to A$,   1. $A \to B\,A$,   2. $A \to \varepsilon$,   3. $B \to a\,B$, 4. $B \to b$.

EXAMPLE 5.4.12. [**LR(1) Parsing: Example 3**] Let us consider the grammar G with axiom S and the following production only:

$$1.\ S \to \varepsilon$$

The augmented grammar G' with axiom S has the productions:

   0. $S' \to S$ 1. $S \to \varepsilon$

We get the following finite automaton:

and the following $LR(1)$ parsing table for the grammar G':

	action	goto
	$\$$	S
q_0	red 1	q_1
q_1	acc	

where: 0. $S' \to S$
        1. $S \to \varepsilon$

The following Figure 5.4.13 shows the configurations of the pushdown automaton of Figure 5.2.1 on page 89 while parsing the string $\varepsilon\,\$$ (that is, $\$$).

time	stack (the top is marked by ▲)	input (the symbol at hand is marked by ▲)	shift/reduce-goto
0	q_0 ▲	$\$$ ▲	$action(q_0, \$) = red\ 1\ (S \to \varepsilon)$ $goto(q_0, S) = q_1$
1	$q_0\, S\, q_1$ ▲	$\$$ ▲	$action(q_1, \$) = accept$

FIGURE 5.4.13. Sequence of configurations of the pushdown automaton of Figure 5.2.1 on page 89 while parsing the string $\$$ using the $LR(1)$ parsing table for the grammar G' with axiom S' and productions: 0. $S' \to S$,   1. $S \to \varepsilon$.

□

EXAMPLE 5.4.13. [$LR(1)$ **Parsing: Example 4**] Let us consider again the grammar G of Example 5.4.12 on the preceding page with axiom S and the following production only:

$$1.\ S \to \varepsilon$$

If we do not construct the augmented grammar G', as done in the previous Example 5.4.12, we get the following finite automaton:

$$\longrightarrow \boxed{q_0 :\ S \to \boldsymbol{.}\,\varepsilon, \{\$\}}$$

and the following $LR(1)$ parsing table:

	action	goto
	$\$$	S
q_0	acc	

The following Figure 5.4.14 shows the configurations of the pushdown automaton of Figure 5.2.1 on page 89 while parsing the string $\varepsilon\,\$$ (that is, $\$$).

time	stack (the top is marked by ▲)	input (the symbol at hand is marked by ▲)	*shift/reduce-goto*
0	q_0 ▲	$ ▲	$action(q_0, \$) = accept$

FIGURE 5.4.14. Configuration of the pushdown automaton of Figure 5.2.1 on page 89 while parsing the string $ using the $LR(1)$ parsing table for the grammar G with axiom S and production: 1. $S \to \varepsilon$.

□

Now we state the following results concerning the $LR(k)$ grammars and $LR(k)$ languages. For the proofs the interested reader may refer to [**3, 4, 10**].

THEOREM 5.4.14. [**Hierarchy of $LR(k)$ Grammars**] For any $k \geq 0$, the class of the $LR(k)$ grammars is properly contained in the class of the $LR(k+1)$ grammars.

THEOREM 5.4.15. [**Collapse of $LR(k)$ Languages for $k \geq 1$**] (i) The class $LR(0)$ of languages is properly contained in the class of the $LR(1)$ languages. (ii) For any $k \geq 1$, the class of $LR(k)$ languages is equal to the class of $LR(k+1)$ languages (see also Fact 5.8.11 on page 154).

In Section 5.9 on page 158 we will present an algorithm that constructs an $LR(1)$ grammar equivalent to a given $LR(k)$ grammar, for any $k > 1$ (see also [**25**, Section 6.7]), and thus provides a proof of Point (ii) of this Theorem 5.4.15.

The following theorem is important because it relates the class of the $LR(1)$ languages to the class of the deterministic context-free languages (see also Theorem 5.2.17 on page 98).

THEOREM 5.4.16. [**$LR(1)$ Grammars, $LR(1)$ Languages, and Deterministic Context-Free Languages**] (i) A language L is a deterministic context-free language iff there exists $k \geq 1$ such that L is generated by an $LR(k)$ grammar.

(ii) A language L is a deterministic context-free language iff it is generated by an $LR(1)$ grammar.

Point (ii) of this Theorem 5.4.16 follows from Point (i) of the same theorem and from Theorem 5.4.15.

For related results and results concerning ambiguity of $LR(1)$ grammars see Fact 5.8.12 on page 154 and also Fact 5.8.13 on page 154.

THEOREM 5.4.17. [**$LR(1)$ Grammars in Chomsky and Greibach Normal Form**] (i) Every deterministic context-free language has an $LR(1)$ grammar in Chomsky normal form. (ii) Every deterministic context-free language has an $LR(1)$ grammar in Greibach normal form [**4**, page 708] and [**9**, page 567].

The result stated in Theorem 5.4.19 below refers to $LL(k)$ and $LR(k)$ grammars which are *strongly reduced* in the sense specified by the following definition. For a related result about $LL(k)$ and $LR(k)$ languages see Fact 4.3.20 on page 78.

DEFINITION 5.4.18. [**Strongly Reduced Context-Free Grammars Grammars**] A context-free grammar G is said to be *strongly reduced* if

(i) G is reduced, that is, without useless symbols (see Definition 1.2.15 on page 7),

(ii) G is without trivial unit productions, that is, productions of the form $A \to A$, for some nonterminal A, and

(iii) the axiom of G does not occur on the right hand side of any production of G.

THEOREM 5.4.19. [**Strongly Reduced $LL(k)$ Grammars Are Properly Included in Strongly Reduced $LR(k)$ Grammars**] For any $k \geq 0$,

(i) the class of strongly reduced $LL(k)$ grammars is properly contained in the class of strongly reduced $LR(k)$ grammars [**25**, page 248], and

(ii) any strongly reduced $LL(k)$ grammar can be transformed into an equivalent strongly reduced $LR(k)$ in linear time (with respect to the size of the given $LL(k)$ grammar) [**25**, page 352].

5.4.1. Avoiding the Powerset Construction for $LR(1)$ Parsing. Analogously to the case of the $LR(0)$ parsing (see Section 5.2.1 on page 99), we can avoid the application of the Powerset Construction Procedure at Step 4 of Algorithm 5.4.1 (see page 109) by using the five rules in the boxes below.

They construct the finite automaton M which is the outcome of that Step 4. These rules should be applied at the end of Step 1 of Algorithm 5.4.1 (see page 108), that is, after the construction of the augmented grammar G' of the given context-free grammar G.

During the application of these rules, in any given state, for any $n \geq 2$, we can replace n items of the form: $\boxed{A \to \gamma, L_1}$, ..., $\boxed{A \to \gamma, L_n}$, where $A \in V_N$ and $\gamma \in (V_T \cup V_N)^* \cup \{\,\textbf{.}\,\} \cup (V_T \cup V_N)^*$ (these items differ for the lookahead sets only) by a single item of the form: $\boxed{A \to \gamma, L_1 \cup \ldots \cup L_n}$ (see Remark 5.4.6 on page 112).

The correctness of these rules is a consequence of the correctness of the application of the Powerset Construction Procedure.

The Closure Rules (1), (2), and (3) should be applied *as long as possible*, that is, until neither new items nor new states nor new arcs can be added to the finite automaton M under construction.

When constructing the automaton M, priority should be given to the application of the Closure Rule (1) with respect to the Closure rules (2) and (3), in the sense that the Closure Rules (2) and (3) should *not* be applied, if by applying the Closure Rule (1), we add a new item to the label of a state of the automaton.

The Closure Rule (1) should have priority because, before applying the Closure Rules (2) and (3), we should already know the closures of all sets of items considered so far.

Initialization Rule. The initial state q_0 of the finite automaton M has its set of items initialized by the item $\boxed{S' \to \,\text{.}\,S, \; \{\$\}}$.

If the axiom S does *not* occur on the right hand side of any production, and we take the augmented grammar G' to be G itself,

then the label of the initial state q_0 of the finite automaton M has an item of the form $\boxed{S \to \,\text{.}\,\alpha_1 \ldots \alpha_n, \{\$\}}$ for each production of the form $S \to \alpha_1 \ldots \alpha_n$, where $n \geq 0$ and for $i = 1, \ldots, n$, $\alpha_i \in V_T \cup V_N$.

Closure Rule (1). For all $A, B \in V_N$, for all $\alpha, \beta, \gamma \in V^*$, for all states p of the finite automaton M,

if in the label of state p there is an item of the form $\boxed{A \to \alpha \,\text{.}\, B\beta, \; L}$,

then we add to that label *all* items of the form $\boxed{B \to \,\text{.}\,\gamma, \; L'}$, where $B \to \gamma$ is a production of the extended grammar G' and the lookahead set L' is constructed as follows:

$$L' = \begin{array}{llll} \text{if} & \beta = \varepsilon & \text{then} & L \\ \text{if} & \beta \neq \varepsilon \text{ and } \beta \to^* \varepsilon & \text{then} & L \cup (First_1(\beta) - \{\varepsilon\}) \\ \text{if} & \beta \neq \varepsilon \text{ and } \beta \not\to^* \varepsilon & \text{then} & First_1(\beta) \end{array}$$

Similarly to the case of the $LR(0)$ parsing (see page 100), in order to present the Closure Rules (2) and (3), we need the following definitions.

DEFINITION 5.4.20. [**Closure of a Set of Items with their Lookahead Sets**] Given a set I of items with their lookahead sets, the *closure* of I, denoted $\overline{I}$, is the set of items with their lookahead sets that is obtained from I by applying as long as possible Closure Rule (1) below.

Obviously, we have that any set I of items with their lookahead sets is a subset of its closure $\overline{I}$.

DEFINITION 5.4.21. [*use/make* **Operation**] Given a finite automatom M and the closure $\overline{I}$ of a set I of items with their lookahead sets, the *use/make* operation on M and $\overline{I}$, denoted $use/make(M, \overline{I})$, behaves as follows:

if in M there exists a state q with label $\overline{I}$
   then (Case *use*)   it returns this state q
   else (Case *make*)   it returns a new state with label $\overline{I}$.

As in the case of the $LR(0)$ parsing (see page 100), when constructing the finite automaton M, for all closures $\overline{I}$, the state q with label $\overline{I}$ in M, if any, is unique.

Closure Rule (2). For all $A_1, \ldots, A_n, B \in V_N$, for all $\alpha_1, \beta_1, \ldots, \alpha_n, \beta_n \in V^*$, for all lookahead sets $L_1, \ldots, L_n$, for all states p of the finite automaton M,

if in the label of state p all the items with the dot immediately to the left of the nonterminal B are: $\boxed{A_1 \to \alpha_1 \centerdot B\beta_1, L_1}$, ..., $\boxed{A_n \to \alpha_n \centerdot B\beta_n, L_n}$, for some $n > 0$,

then, let q be the state (which may be p itself) returned by $use/make(M, \overline{I})$, where $\overline{I}$ is the closure of the set $\{\boxed{A_1 \to \alpha_1 B \centerdot \beta_1, L_1}, \ldots, \boxed{A_n \to \alpha_n B \centerdot \beta_n, L_n}\}$ of items,

(2.1) we add to M the new state q, if q is returned in the Case *make*, and

(2.2) we add to M a new arc with label B from state p to state q.

Closure Rule (3). For all $a \in V_T$, $A_1, \ldots, A_n \in V_N$, for all $\alpha_1, \beta_1, \ldots, \alpha_n, \beta_n \in V^*$, for all lookahead sets $L_1, \ldots, L_n$, for all states p of the finite automaton M,

if in the label of state p all the items with the dot immediately to the left of the terminal a are: $\boxed{A_1 \to \alpha_1 \centerdot a\beta_1, L_1}$, ..., $\boxed{A_n \to \alpha_n \centerdot a\beta_n, L_n}$, for some $n > 0$,

then, let q be the state (which may be p itself) returned by $use/make(M, \overline{I})$, where $\overline{I}$ is the closure of the set $\{\boxed{A_1 \to \alpha_1 a \centerdot \beta_1, L_1}, \ldots, \boxed{A_n \to \alpha_n a \centerdot \beta_n, L_n}\}$ of items,

(3.1) we add to M the new state q, if q is returned in the Case *make*, and

(3.2) we add to M a new arc with label B from state p to state q.

Final State Rule. The final state of the finite automaton M is the one whose label has the item $\boxed{S' \to S \centerdot, \{\$\}}$.

If the axiom S does *not* occur on the right hand side of any production, and we take the augmented grammar G' to be G itself, then every state of the finite automaton M whose label has an item of the form $\boxed{S \to \alpha_1 \ldots \alpha_n \centerdot, \{\$\}}$, for some production of the form $S \to \alpha_1 \ldots \alpha_n$, where $n \geq 0$ and for $i = 1, \ldots, n$, $\alpha_i \in V_T \cup V_N$, is a final state.

NOTE 5.4.22. Similarly to the case of the $LR(0)$ parsing (see Section 5.2.1 on page 99), we have that the finite automaton M we construct by using the above boxed rules, is minimal, because when applying the Closure Rules (2) and (3), we do not add to M a new state with label $\overline{I}$, if a state with that same label exists in M. $\square$

5.4.2. More Remarks on the Hypotheses for *LR*(*k*) Parsing.

Before closing this section on $LR(1)$, we would like to add some more remarks (besides those made on Section 5.2.2 on page 101) on the hypotheses we made on page 87 for the $LR(k)$ parsing algorithms, for $k \geq 0$.

In particular, we will show that there are grammars for which the $LR(1)$ parsing table is *not correct*, if the start symbol occurs on the right hand side of a production. Here is an example.

Let us consider the grammar G with axiom S and productions:

$$1.\ S \to a\,S \qquad 2.\ S \to b$$

If we construct the finite automaton M for generating the $LR(1)$ parsing table for that grammar and we assume that in the initial state of M there are the items $\boxed{S \to \,.\,a\,S,\ \{\$\}}$ and $\boxed{S \to \,.\,b,\ \{\$\}}$ (see Figure 5.4.15), as indicated at the end of Section 5.2.2 on page 101, then we get an $LR(1)$ parsing table (see Figure 5.4.16 on the next page) which allows the correct parsing of every word in the language $L(G)$ generated by G. However, when accepting a word $w \in L(G)$, the sequence of stack configurations *does not* show the rightmost derivations of w from S in the reverse order (see Figure 5.4.17 on the following page).

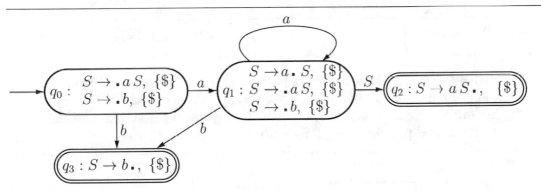

FIGURE 5.4.15. The finite automaton M for the $LR(1)$ parsing of the grammar G with axiom S and productions: 1. $S \to a\,S$, 2. $S \to b$.

Note that, even if the axiom occurs on the right hand side of a production, we may get from a given context-free grammar, an $LR(1)$ parsing table which allows the correct parsing of every word generated by that grammar. Indeed, let us consider the grammar $G1$ with axiom S and the following productions:

$$1.\ S \to A \qquad 2.\ A \to S\,a \qquad 3.\ A \to b$$

The language generated by this grammar is the regular language denoted by the regular expression $b\,a^*$. The finite automaton M to be constructed for generating the $LR(1)$ parsing table, is shown in Figure 5.4.18 on the following page.

The corresponding parsing table is depicted in Figure 5.4.19 on page 129. Note that in row q_4 and column a we have inserted the action *red* 1, even if state q_4 is final (recall Step (5.4) on page 111).

	action			goto
	a	b	$\$$	S
q_0	$sh\ q_1$	$sh\ q_3$		
q_1	$sh\ q_1$	$sh\ q_3$		q_2
q_2			acc	
q_3			acc	

where:
1. $S \to a\,S$
2. $S \to b$

FIGURE 5.4.16. $LR(1)$ parsing table for the grammar G with axiom S and productions: 1. $S \to a\,S$,   2. $S \to Sb$. It has been derived from the finite automaton of Figure 5.4.15 on the previous page.

time	stack (the top is marked by ▲)	input (the symbol at hand is marked by ▲)	shift/reduce-goto
0	q_0 ▲	$a\,b\,\$$ ▲	$action(q_0, a) = sh\ q_1$
1	$q_0\,a\,q_1$ ▲	$a\,b\,\$$ ▲	$action(q_1, b) = sh\ q_3$
2	$q_0\,a\,q_1\,b\,q_3$ ▲	$a\,b\,\$$ ▲	$action(q_3, \$) = acc$

FIGURE 5.4.17. The sequence of configurations of the parsing automaton of Figure 5.4.16 while parsing the string $a\,b\,\$$ using the $LR(1)$ parsing table of Figure 5.4.15 on the previous page for the grammar G with axiom S and productions: 1. $S \to a\,S$,   2. $S \to b$.

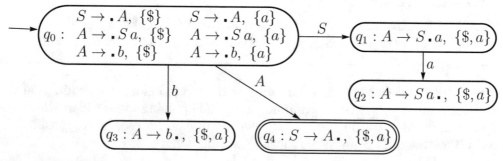

FIGURE 5.4.18. The finite automaton M for the $LR(1)$ parsing of the grammar $G1$ with axiom S and productions: 1. $S \to A$,   2. $A \to S\,a$,   3. $A \to b$.

This parsing table does allow the correct parsing of every word in $L(G1)$. In particular, if we parse the word $b\,a\,\$$ which belongs to $b\,a^*\,\$$, we get the sequence of stack configurations depicted in Figure 5.4.20 on the next page.

	action			goto	
	a	b	$\$$	S	A
q_0		sh q_3		q_1	q_4
q_1	sh q_2				
q_2	red 2		red 2		
q_3	red 3		red 3		
q_4	red 1		acc		

where:
1. $S \to A$
2. $A \to S\,a$
3. $A \to b$

FIGURE 5.4.19. *LR(1)* parsing table for the grammar $G1$ with axiom S and productions: 1. $S \to A$,   2. $A \to S\,a$,   3. $S \to b$. It has been derived from the finite automaton of Figure 5.4.18 on the facing page.

time	stack (the top is marked by ▲)	input (the symbol at hand is marked by ▲)	*shift/reduce-goto*
0	q_0 ▲	$b\,a\,\$$ ▲	$action(q_0, b) = sh\ q_3$
1	$q_0\,b\,q_3$ ▲	$b\,a\,\$$ ▲	$action(q_3, a) = red\ 3\ (A \to b)$ $goto(q_0, A) = q_4$
2	$q_0\,A\,q_4$ ▲	$b\,a\,\$$ ▲	$action(q_4, a) = red\ 1\ (S \to A)$ $goto(q_0, S) = q_1$
3	$q_0\,S\,q_1$ ▲	$b\,a\,\$$ ▲	$action(q_1, a) = sh\ q_2$
4	$q_0\,S\,q_1\,a\,q_2$ ▲	$b\,a\,\$$ ▲	$action(q_2, \$) = red\ 2\ (A \to S\,a)$ $goto(q_0, A) = q_4$
5	$q_0\,A\,q_4$ ▲	$b\,a\,\$$ ▲	$action(q_4, \$) = accept$

FIGURE 5.4.20. The sequence of configurations of the parsing automaton of Figure 5.4.18 on the facing page while parsing the string $b\,a\,\$$ using the *LR(1)* parsing table of Figure 5.4.19 for the grammar $G1$ with axiom S and productions: 1. $S \to A$,   2. $A \to S\,a$,   3. $A \to b$.

We leave it to the reader to check that the grammar $G1'$ obtained from the grammar $G1$ by adding the production $S' \to S$, so that the axiom S' does *not* occur on the right hand side of any production, is an *LR(1)* grammar. Thus, from the grammar $G1'$ we get an *LR(1)* parsing table which allows the correct parsing of every word in $L(G1')$. The grammar $G1'$ has the following productions:

0. $S' \to S$ 1. $S \to A$ 2. $A \to S\,a$ 3. $A \to b$

Let us make a final note concerning the power of unfolding.

By unfolding a grammar which is *not* an $LR(1)$ grammar can be transformed into an equivalent $LR(1)$ grammar. Consider, for instance, the grammar with axiom S' and productions:

0. $S' \to S$ 1. $S \to c$ 2. $S \to A$ 3. $A \to c$

This grammar is not an $LR(1)$ grammar (in particular, the word c has two rightmost derivations). By unfolding S and A, we get a grammar with the single production:

0. $S' \to c$

and, obviously, this grammar is an $LR(1)$ grammar.

Similarly, by unfolding a grammar which is *not* an $LR(0)$ grammar can be transformed into an equivalent $LR(0)$ grammar. Consider, for instance, the grammar with axiom S' and productions:

0. $S' \to S\,\$$ 1. $S' \to A\,\$$ 2. $S \to c$ 3. $A \to c$

This grammar is not an $LR(0)$ grammar (in particular, the word c has two rightmost derivations). By unfolding S and A, we get a grammar with the single production:

0. $S' \to c\,\$$

and obviously this grammar is an $LR(0)$ grammar.

Let us close this section by recalling a property of the $LR(k)$ parsers when they perform either a *shift* action or a *reduce-goto* action.

$LR(k)$ Parsing, for $k \geq 0$.

The action that the $LR(k)$ parser should perform (either a *shift* action or a *reduce-goto* action) is uniquely determined by (see Figure 5.4.21 on the facing page):

  (i) the top of the stack, which is either a *state* or a *symbol* in $V_T \cup V_N \cup \{\$\}$,

  (ii) the prefixes of length $k\ (\geq 0)$ of the words in $V_T^*\,\$$ derivable from $z\,\$$ (these prefixes are needed for constructing the $LR(k)$ parsing table), and

  (iii) the current symbol $\underline{u}_1$ and the leftmost $k\ (\geq 0)$ symbols of u (or u itself if $|u| < k$).

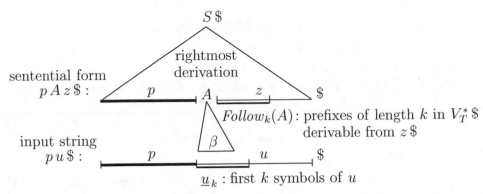

$S\,\$$

rightmost derivation

sentential form
$p\,A\,z\,\$:$

p

A

z

$\$$

$Follow_k(A):$ prefixes of length k in $V_T^*\,\$$
derivable from $z\,\$$

input string
$p\,u\,\$:$

p

β

u

$\$$

$\underline{u}_k:$ first k symbols of u

FIGURE 5.4.21. $LR(k)$ parsing, for $k\geq0$. Note that, if $k=0$, the action of the $LR(0)$ parser is a function of the current symbol which is pointed by the input head, that is, the symbol $\underline{u}_1$. The derivation from S to $p\,A\,z$ is a rightmost derivation. Recall that $Follow_k(A)$ depends on the given grammar only.

5.5. $LALR(1)$ Parsers

In this section we will study the class of $LALR(1)$ grammars and we will present a technique for parsing the languages generated by those grammars.

Basically, $LALR(1)$ parsing is like $LR(1)$ parsing, but it uses parsing tables which are derived by compaction from the $LR(1)$ parsing tables.

There are algorithms for directly constructing the tables for $LALR(1)$ parsing without first constructing the tables for $LR(1)$ parsing [**2**, page 242], but we do not consider them here.

The compaction of an $LR(1)$ parsing table which makes it an $LALR(1)$ parsing table is performed, as we now indicate, on the finite automaton from which the table is derived.

ALGORITHM 5.5.1. **Constructing the $LALR(1)$ Parsing Table.**

Given a context-free grammar $G = \langle V_T, V_N, P, S \rangle$, where $V_T = \{a_1, \ldots, a_r\}$ and $V_N = \{A_1, \ldots, A_s\}$, we consider its augmented grammar G' with the new start symbol S', and the finite automaton M which can be constructed from G' by applying Algorithm 5.4.1 on page 108 for constructing the $LR(1)$ parsing tables.

Then, we replace *as long as possible* (and maybe no times) any subset $\{q_1, \ldots, q_n\}$ of the states of M of the form:

$$q_1: \begin{matrix} item_1, \ L_{11} \\ \cdots \\ item_m, L_{1m} \end{matrix} \quad , \quad \cdots \ , \quad q_n: \begin{matrix} item_1, \ L_{n1} \\ \cdots \\ item_m, L_{nm} \end{matrix}$$

(that is, any subset of states with the same set of items, without considering their lookahead sets) by the following single state $q_{1\ldots n}$

$$q_{1\ldots n}: \begin{matrix} item_1, \ \ L_{11} \cup \ldots \cup L_{n1} \\ \cdots \\ item_m, \ L_{1m} \cup \ldots \cup L_{nm} \end{matrix}$$

Recall that: (i) two items are equal if they refer to the same production and have the dot in the same position, and (ii) the order of occurrence of an item (with its lookahead set) within the label of a state is immaterial, being the label of a state a *set* of items (with their lookahead sets).

After each of these replacements which can be viewed as 'a fusion of states', we readjust the arcs, that is, we replace, for all $k = 1, \ldots, n$, (i) any arc *from* a state q_k by an arc *from* the new state $q_{1\ldots n}$, and (ii) any arc *to* a state q_k by an arc *to* the new state $q_{1\ldots n}$.

Each of the above replacements of states in the finite automaton M, corresponds in the $LR(1)$ parsing table T to the replacement of a set $\{q_1, \ldots, q_n\}$ of rows of the form:

	action				goto		
	a_1	$\ldots$	a_r	$ \$ $	A_1	$\ldots$	A_s
$q_1:$	$T[1,a_1]$	$\ldots$	$T[1,a_r]$	$T[1,\$]$	$T[1,A_1]$	$\ldots$	$T[1,A_s]$
$\vdots$	$\vdots$		$\vdots$	$\vdots$	$\vdots$		$\vdots$
$q_n:$	$T[n,a_1]$	$\ldots$	$T[n,a_r]$	$T[n,\$]$	$T[n,A_1]$	$\ldots$	$T[n,A_s]$

where some of the $T[i,j]$ entries may be absent, by the following single row $q_{1\ldots n}$

	action				goto		
	a_1	$\ldots$	a_r	$ \$ $	A_1	$\ldots$	A_s
$q_{1\ldots n}:$	$T[1,a_1],$ $\vdots,$ $T[n,a_1]$	$\ldots$	$T[1,a_r],$ $\vdots,$ $T[n,a_r]$	$T[1,\$],$ $\vdots,$ $T[n,\$]$	$T[1,A_1],$ $\vdots,$ $T[n,A_1]$	$\ldots$	$T[1,A_s],$ $\vdots,$ $T[n,A_s]$

where in each position of the row $q_{1\ldots n}$ we have kept *one copy only* for each distinct entry, in the sense that for each column $j = a_1, \ldots, a_r, \$, A_1, \ldots, A_s$, and for each $i_1, i_2 = 1, \ldots, n$, we have that $T[i_1, j] \neq T[i_2, j]$.

At the end of all these row replacements, if in the resulting parsing table T for each row i and for each column $j = a_1, \ldots, a_r, \$, A_1, \ldots, A_s$, there exists *at most one* element (that is, there are no conflicts), then the parsing table T is said to be an *LALR(1) parsing table*.

In this case, that is, in the case when there are no conflicts, the augmented grammar G' is an *LALR(1)* grammar and the language generated by G' is an *LALR(1)* language.

REMARK 5.5.2. [*Multiple actions*] As for *LR(1)* grammars, if we have to place more than one action in an entry of the *LALR(1)* parsing table, then there are conflicts and the language generated by the given grammar cannot be parsed by using a pushdown automaton which uses that table, and the augmented grammar G' which has been derived from the given grammar G, is *not* an *LALR(1)* grammar.

REMARK 5.5.3. [*Undefined entry*] If during the process of parsing a given input word $w\,\$$, the pushdown automaton requires an entry of the *LALR(1)* parsing table, but that entry is empty, then the word w does *not* belong to the language generated by the augmented grammar G' and w does *not* belong to the language generated by the given grammar G.

EXAMPLE 5.5.4. [**LALR(1) Parsing: Example 1**] In this example we construct the *LALR(1)* parsing table starting from the *LR(1)* parsing table of Figure 5.4.3 on page 116 relative to Example 5.4.9 on page 113. We have already constructed that *LR(1)* parsing table for the augmented grammar G':

    0. $S' \to S$ 1. $S \to CC$ 2. $C \to cC$ 3. $C \to d$

For $LALR(1)$ parsing we have the finite automaton of Figure 5.5.1, instead of the finite automaton of Figure 5.4.2 on page 115, and we have the $LALR(1)$ parsing table of Figure 5.5.2 on the next page, instead of the $LR(1)$ parsing table of Figure 5.4.3 on page 116.

The states of the finite automaton of Figure 5.4.2 on page 115 which have been fused are:

(i)   states q_3 and q_6, fused into the state q_{36},

(ii) states q_4 and q_7, fused into the state q_{47}, and

(iii) states q_8 and q_9, fused into the state q_{89}.   □

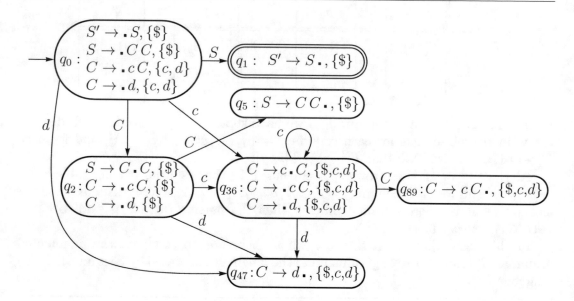

FIGURE 5.5.1. The finite automaton for the $LALR(1)$ parsing of the grammar G' with axiom S' and productions: 0. $S' \to S$,   1. $S \to CC$,   2. $C \to cC$,   3. $C \to d$.

The fusion of the states which is performed by Algorithm 5.5.1 on page 132 does not create conflicts in the *goto* part of the parsing table because in that part the entries depend only on the first components of the $LR(1)$ items which are all equal in the states which are fused.

One can show [**2**, page 237] that when applying Algorithm 5.5.1 for constructing the $LALR(1)$ parsing tables, never *shift-reduce* conflicts may be produced, because *shift* actions depend on the first components of the $LR(1)$ items only. On the contrary, *reduce-reduce* conflicts may be produced.

One can also show [**2**, page 239–240] that for any input word which belongs to the language $L(G')$ generated by the augmented grammar G', the $LALR(1)$ parser mimics the corresponding $LR(1)$ parser, in the sense that, with reference to Example 5.5.4

	action			goto	
	c	d	$\$$	S	C
q_0	sh q_{36}	sh q_{47}		q_1	q_2
q_1			acc		
q_2	sh q_{36}	sh q_{47}			q_5
q_{36}	sh q_{36}	sh q_{47}			q_{89}
q_{47}	red 3	red 3	red 3		
q_5			red 1		
q_{89}	red 2	red 2	red 2		

where:

0. $S' \to S$
1. $S \to C\,C$
2. $C \to c\,C$
3. $C \to d$

FIGURE 5.5.2. *LALR*(1) parsing table for the grammar G' with axiom S' and productions: 0. $S' \to S$,   1. $S \to C\,C$,   2. $C \to c\,C$,   3. $C \to d$. It has been derived from the automaton of Figure 5.5.1 on the facing page.

---

on page 133, it goes through the states q_{36}, q_{47}, and q_{89} iff the *LR*(1) parser goes through the states (q_3 or q_6), (q_4 or q_7), and (q_8 or q_9), respectively.

One can show that for any input word w which does *not* belong to the language $L(G')$, the behaviour of the *LR*(1) parser and the corresponding *LALR*(1) parser, if there exists one, are similar, in the sense that after the *LR*(1) parser has detected an error, the *LALR*(1) parser may do some extra *reduce* actions (but not extra *shift* actions) and then it will also detect an error.

EXAMPLE 5.5.5. [**LALR(1) Parsing: Example 2**] Let us consider the following grammar G:

$$1. \ S \to a\,A \quad 2. \ S \to b\,B \quad 3. \ A \to \varepsilon \quad 4. \ A \to c\,A\,d \quad 5. \ B \to \varepsilon$$

and its augmented version G'':

$$0. \ S' \to S \quad 1. \ S \to a\,A \quad 2. \ S \to b\,B \quad 3. \ A \to \varepsilon \quad 4. \ A \to c\,A\,d \quad 5. \ B \to \varepsilon$$

By applying Algorithm 5.4.1 on page 108 for constructing the *LR*(1) parsing tables, we get the finite automaton of Figure 5.5.3 on the next page and the *LR*(1) parsing table of Figure 5.5.4 on page 137.

By applying Algorithm 5.5.1 on page 132 for constructing the *LALR*(1) parsing tables from the *LR*(1) parsing tables, we get the finite automaton of Figure 5.5.5 on page 137 and the *LALR*(1) parsing table of Figure 5.5.6 on page 138 (see also [**25**, pages 34, 60]).

The states of the finite automaton of Figure 5.5.3 on the following page which have been fused are:

  (i) states q_6 and q_9, fused into the state q_{69},

 (ii) states q_7 and q_{10}, fused into the state q_{710}, and

(iii) states q_8 and q_{11}, fused into the state q_{811}.

Show that if in the given grammar G we replace the production $A \to c\,A\,d$ by the production $A \to c\,A\,c$, then the resulting grammar is not $LR(1)$.   □

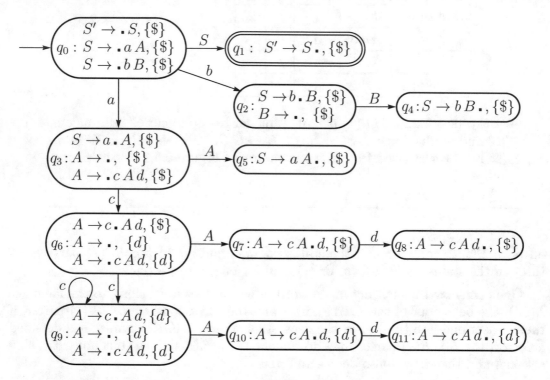

FIGURE 5.5.3. The finite automaton for the $LR(1)$ parsing of the grammar G' with axiom S' and productions: 0. $S' \to S$,   1. $S \to a\,A$, 2. $S \to b\,B$,   3. $A \to \varepsilon$,   4. $A \to c\,A\,d$,   5. $B \to \varepsilon$.

	a	b	c	d	$\$$	S	A	B
	\multicolumn{5}{c}{*action*}	\multicolumn{3}{c}{*goto*}

	a	b	c	d	$\$$	S	A	B
q_0	sh q_3	sh q_2				q_1		
q_1					acc			
q_2					red 5			q_4
q_3			sh q_6		red 3		q_5	
q_4					red 2			
q_5					red 1			
q_6			sh q_9	red 3			q_7	
q_7				sh q_8				
q_8					red 4			
q_9			sh q_9	red 3			q_{10}	
q_{10}				sh q_{11}				
q_{11}				red 4				

where:

0. $S' \to S$
1. $S \to aA$
2. $S \to bB$
3. $A \to \varepsilon$
4. $A \to cAd$
5. $B \to \varepsilon$

FIGURE 5.5.4. *LR(1)* parsing table for the grammar G' with axiom S' and productions: 0. $S' \to S$,   1. $S \to aA$,   2. $S \to bB$,   3. $A \to \varepsilon$,   4. $A \to cAd$,   5. $B \to \varepsilon$. It has been derived from the automaton of Figure 5.5.3 on the preceding page.

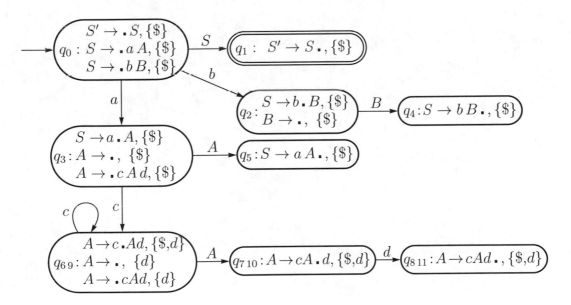

FIGURE 5.5.5. The finite automaton for the *LALR(1)* parsing of the grammar G' with axiom S' and productions: 0. $S' \to S$,   1. $S \to aA$,   2. $S \to bB$,   3. $A \to \varepsilon$,   4. $A \to cAd$,   5. $B \to \varepsilon$.

	\<u>action\</u>					\<u>goto\</u>		
	a	b	c	d	$\$$	S	A	B
q_0	$sh\ q_3$	$sh\ q_2$				q_1		
q_1					acc			
q_2				$red\ 5$				q_4
q_3			$sh\ q_{69}$	$red\ 3$			q_5	
q_4				$red\ 2$				
q_5				$red\ 1$				
q_{69}			$sh\ q_{69}$	$red\ 3$			q_{710}	
q_{710}				$sh\ q_{811}$				
q_{811}				$red\ 4$	$red\ 4$			

where:

0. $S' \rightarrow S$
1. $S \rightarrow a\,A$
2. $S \rightarrow b\,B$
3. $A \rightarrow \varepsilon$
4. $A \rightarrow c\,A\,d$
5. $B \rightarrow \varepsilon$

FIGURE 5.5.6. $LALR(1)$ parsing table for the grammar G' with axiom S' and productions: 0. $S' \rightarrow S$, 1. $S \rightarrow a\,A$, 2. $S \rightarrow b\,B$, 3. $A \rightarrow \varepsilon$, 4. $A \rightarrow c\,A\,d$, 5. $B \rightarrow \varepsilon$. It has been derived from the automaton of Figure 5.5.5 on the preceding page.

EXAMPLE 5.5.6. [***LALR*(1) Parsing: Example 3**] Let us consider the augmented grammar G':

0. $S' \to S$ 1. $S \to L = R$ 2. $S \to R$ 3. $L \to *R$ 4. $L \to a$ 5. $R \to L$

By applying Algorithm 5.4.1 on page 108 we get the finite automaton of Figure 5.5.7 and the $LR(1)$ parsing table of Figure 5.5.8 on the next page.

By applying Algorithm 5.5.1 on page 132 for constructing the $LALR(1)$ parsing table from the $LR(1)$ parsing table, we have to make no changes to that parsing table and thus, the table of Figure 5.5.8 is also the $LALR(1)$ parsing table of the grammar G'. □

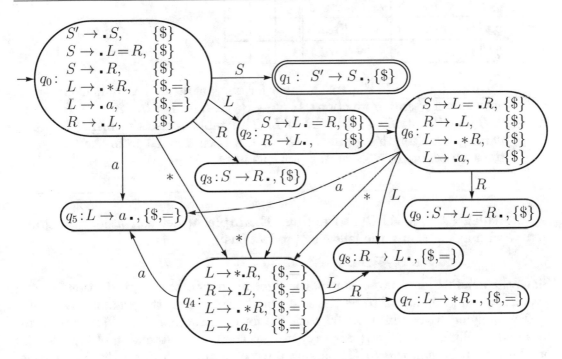

FIGURE 5.5.7. The finite automaton for the $LR(1)$ parsing of the grammar G' with axiom S' and productions: 0. $S' \to S$,   1. $S \to L = R$, 2. $S \to R$,   3. $L \to *R$,   4. $L \to a$,   5. $R \to L$. This automaton is also the $LALR(1)$ parsing automaton for this grammar G'.

	action				goto		
	a	$=$	$*$	$\$$	S	L	R
q_0	sh q_5		sh q_4		q_1	q_2	q_3
q_1				acc			
q_2		sh q_6		red 5			
q_3				red 2			
q_4	sh q_5	sh q_4				q_8	q_7
q_5		red 4		red 4			
q_6	sh q_5		sh q_4			q_8	q_9
q_7		red 3		red 3			
q_8		red 5		red 5			
q_9				red 1			

where:

0. $S' \to S$
1. $S \to L = R$
2. $S \to R$
3. $L \to *R$
4. $L \to a$
5. $R \to L$

FIGURE 5.5.8. $LR(1)$ parsing table for the augmented grammar G' with axiom S' and productions: 0. $S' \to S$, 1. $S \to L=R$, 2. $S \to R$, 3. $S \to *R$, 4. $L \to a$, 5. $R \to L$. This table is also the $LALR(1)$ parsing table for this grammar G'. It has been derived from the automaton of Figure 5.5.7 on the previous page.

EXAMPLE 5.5.7. [**$LALR(1)$ Parsing: Example 4**] Let us consider the grammar G with axiom S and the following productions:

$$1.\ S \to B\,B\,a \qquad 2.\ B \to B\,b \qquad 3.\ B \to c$$

Since the axiom S does not occur on the right hand side of any production, we can take the given grammar G to be the augmented grammar of the grammar G itself.

By applying Algorithm 5.4.1 on page 108 for constructing the $LR(1)$ parsing tables and recalling that $First_1(B) = \{c\}$, we get the finite automaton of Figure 5.5.9 on the next page and the $LR(1)$ parsing table of Figure 5.5.10 on the facing page. By applying Algorithm 5.5.1 on page 132 for constructing the $LALR(1)$ parsing tables from the $LR(1)$ parsing tables, we get the finite automaton of Figure 5.5.11 on page 142 and the $LALR(1)$ parsing table of Figure 5.5.12 on page 142.

The states of the finite automaton of Figure 5.5.9 on the facing page which have been fused are:

(i) states q_4 and q_5, fused into the state q_{45}, and

(ii) states q_6 and q_7, fused into the state q_{67}.   □

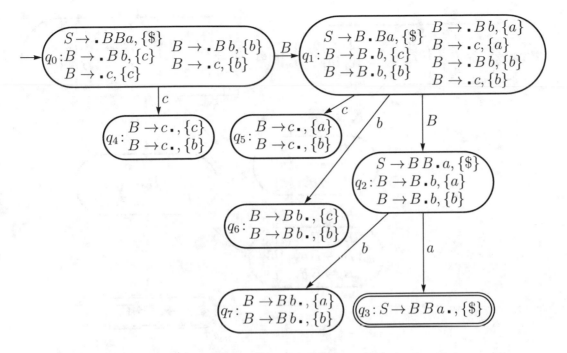

FIGURE 5.5.9. The finite automaton for the $LR(1)$ parsing of the grammar G with axiom S and productions: 1. $S \to BBa$, 2. $B \to Bb$, 3. $B \to c$.

| | \multicolumn{4}{c}{action} | goto |
	a	b	c	\$	B
q_0			sh q_4		q_1
q_1		sh q_6	sh q_5		q_2
q_2	sh q_3	sh q_7			
q_3				acc	
q_4		red 3	red 3		
q_5	red 3	red 3			
q_6		red 2	red 2		
q_7	red 2	red 2			

where: 1. $S \to BBa$
        2. $B \to Bb$
        3. $B \to c$

FIGURE 5.5.10. $LR(1)$ parsing table for the grammar G with axiom S and productions: 1. $S \to BBa$, 2. $B \to Bb$, 3. $B \to c$. It has been derived from the finite automaton of Figure 5.5.9.

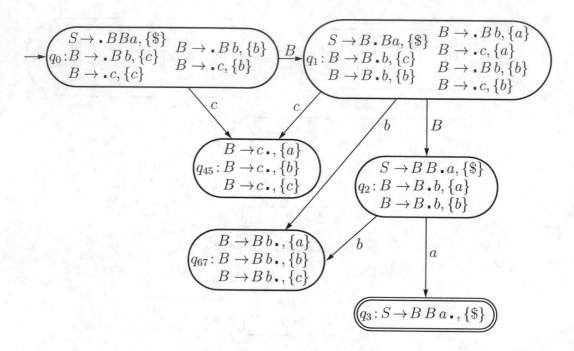

FIGURE 5.5.11. The finite automaton for the $LALR(1)$ parsing of the grammar G with axiom S and productions: 1. $S \rightarrow B\,B\,a$, 2. $B \rightarrow B\,b$, 3. $B \rightarrow c$.

| | \multicolumn{4}{c}{action} | \multicolumn{1}{c}{goto} |
	a	b	c	$\$$	B
q_0			$sh\ q_{45}$		q_1
q_1		$sh\ q_{67}$	$sh\ q_{45}$		q_2
q_2	$sh\ q_3$	$sh\ q_{67}$			
q_3				acc	
q_{45}	$red\ 3$	$red\ 3$	$red\ 3$		
q_{67}	$red\ 2$	$red\ 2$	$red\ 2$		

where:
1. $S \rightarrow B\,B\,a$
2. $B \rightarrow B\,b$
3. $B \rightarrow c$

FIGURE 5.5.12. $LALR(1)$ parsing table for the grammar G with axiom S and productions: 1. $S \rightarrow B\,B\,a$, 2. $B \rightarrow B\,b$, 3. $B \rightarrow c$. It has been derived from the finite automaton of Figure 5.5.11.

EXAMPLE 5.5.8. [***LALR*(1) Parsing: Example 5**] Let us consider the grammar G with axiom S and the following productions:

1. $S \to a\,A\,a$
2. $S \to b\,A\,b$
3. $S \to a\,B\,b$
4. $S \to b\,B\,a$
5. $A \to c$
6. $B \to c$

Since the axiom S does not occur on the right hand side of any production, we can take the given grammar G to be the augmented grammar of the grammar G itself.

By applying Algorithm 5.4.1 on page 108 for constructing the $LR(1)$ parsing tables, we get the finite automaton of Figure 5.5.13 and the $LR(1)$ parsing table of Figure 5.5.14 on the next page.

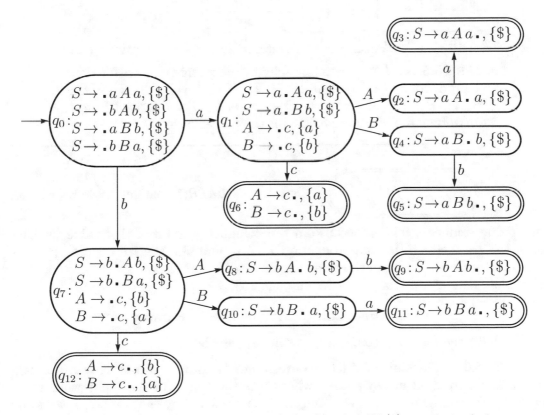

FIGURE 5.5.13. The finite automaton for the $LR(1)$ parsing of the grammar G with axiom S and productions: 1. $S \to a\,A\,a$, 2. $S \to b\,A\,b$, 3. $S \to a\,B\,b$, 4. $S \to b\,B\,a$, 5. $A \to c$, 6. $B \to c$.

By applying Algorithm 5.5.1 on page 132 for constructing the $LALR(1)$ parsing tables from the $LR(1)$ parsing tables, we fuse the states q_6 and q_{12}, thereby getting

	action				goto	
	a	b	c	$\$$	A	B
q_0	$sh\ q_1$	$sh\ q_7$				
q_1			$sh\ q_6$		q_2	q_4
q_2	$sh\ q_3$					
q_3				$red\ 1$		
q_4		$sh\ q_5$				
q_5				$red\ 3$		
q_6	$red\ 5$	$red\ 6$				
q_7			$sh\ q_{12}$		q_8	q_{10}
q_8		$sh\ q_9$				
q_9				$red\ 2$		
q_{10}	$sh\ q_{11}$					
q_{11}				$red\ 4$		
q_{12}	$red\ 6$	$red\ 5$				

where:
1. $S \to a\,A\,a$
2. $S \to b\,A\,b$
3. $S \to a\,B\,b$
4. $S \to b\,B\,a$
5. $A \to c$
6. $B \to c$

FIGURE 5.5.14. $LR(1)$ parsing table for the grammar G with axiom S and productions: 1. $S \to a\,A\,a$, 2. $S \to b\,A\,b$, 3. $S \to a\,B\,b$, 4. $S \to b\,B\,a$, 5. $A \to c$, 6. $B \to c$. It has been derived from the finite automaton of Figure 5.5.13 on the preceding page.

---

the state: $\left(\!\!\left(\begin{array}{l} q_{6\,12}: \begin{array}{l} A \to c\,\textbf{.}\,,\{a,b\} \\ B \to c\,\textbf{.}\,,\{a,b\} \end{array} \end{array}\right)\!\!\right)$. Thus, in the $LALR(1)$ parsing table we will get two reduce-reduce conflicts, because in the columns a and b of that table we have both the $red\ 5$ action (for the production $A \to c$) and also the $red\ 6$ action (for the production $B \to c$). Hence, the given grammar G is *not* an $LALR(1)$ grammar (see also what we state in Example 5.8.7 on page 153). $\qquad\square$

5.6. Time Complexity of $LR(k)$ Parsing

We have the following complexity result [3, page 395].

FACT 5.6.1. [**Parsing of $LR(k)$ Languages in Linear Time**] Any $LR(k)$ language can be parsed in $O(n)$ time, where n is the length of the input word to be parsed. We assume that the time complexity is measured by the number of *shift* and *reduce-goto* actions performed on the stack.

PROOF. We will consider the case of $k=1$ (for $k=0$ and $k>1$ the proof is similar and we leave it to the reader). Let us consider the $LR(1)$ grammar $G = \langle V_T, V_N, P, S \rangle$ and the pda (actually, it is a deterministic pda) that performs the $LR(1)$ parsing of an input word $w \in V_T^*$, using the $LR(1)$ parsing table for the grammar G.

Let us introduce the following definitions which apply to the pda that performs the $LR(1)$ parsing.

A *p-configuration* (short for *parsing configuration*) of the pda is a pair of the form $\langle s, v \rangle$, where:
(i) s is a string in $Q\left((V_T \cup V_N)\,Q\right)^*$, where Q is the set of states of the pda, that denotes the current stack of the pda, and
(ii) v is the suffix of the input word w which remains to be read by the pda.
In a *p*-configuration $\langle s, v \rangle$ the *rightmost* symbol of s is the current state of the pda and the *leftmost* symbol of v is the symbol which is currently read.

The initial *p*-configuration is $\langle q_0, w \rangle$, where q_0 is the initial state of the pda and w is the word to be parsed.

A *sequence of p-configurations* of a pda is the one determined by the sequence of actions (each of which is either a *shift* action or a *reduce-goto* action) performed by the pda while parsing a given input word, starting from the initial *p*-configuration $\langle q_0, w \rangle$.

A *sequence of c-configurations* of a pda is a subsequence of the sequence of the *p* configurations of the pda, made out of the following *p*-configurations only:
- the initial *p*-configuration $\langle q_0, w \rangle$,
- every *p*-configuration immediately after a *shift* action, and
- every *p*-configuration immediately after a *reduce-goto* action that makes the stack shorter than the stack of the previous *c*-configuration of the sequence.

Note that given a sequence π of *p*-configurations, there exists a unique associated sequence of *c*-configurations which, in general, is not a contiguous subsequence of π.

Note also that during the $LR(1)$ parsing of an input word w, there exist at most $1 + 3|w|$ *c*-configurations. Indeed, if we associate with every *c*-configuration $\langle s, v \rangle$ the integer $|s| + 3|v|$, then in any given sequence of *c*-configurations, from every *c*-configuration to the next, the value of $|s| + 3|v|$ decreases by at least one unit (recall that in any *shift* action two symbols are pushed onto the stack), and the integer associated with the initial *c*-configuration $\langle q_0, w \rangle$ is $1 + 3|w|$ (the summand 1 is due to symbol q_0 which, initially, is the only symbol on the stack).

Thus, in order to show that $LR(1)$ parsing can be done in linear time with respect to $|w|$, it remains to show that between any two *c*-configurations, the pda may perform a sequence of actions whose maximal length is independent of the length of the input word w to be parsed.

First we state the following Facts (α) and (β) whose proof is immediate.

Fact (α). If the pda performs a *reduce-goto* action using an ε-production of the form $A \to \varepsilon$, for some nonterminal A, then the stack becomes longer by two cells (say, from stack s to stack $s\,A\,q$, for some state q, the new top of the stack being q).

Only the *reduce-goto* actions which use ε-productions can make the stack longer. □

Fact (β). If the pda performs a *reduce-goto* action by using a unit production of the form $A \to B$, for some nonterminals A and B, then the stack remains of the same length (say, from stack $s\,B\,p$ to stack $s\,A\,q$, for some states p and q, the old top of the stack being p and the new top of the stack being q).

Only the *reduce-goto* actions which use productions of the form either $A \to B$, or $A \to a$, with $a \in V_T$, can keep the stack of the same length. □

Now $LR(1)$ parsing can be done in linear time with respect to $|w|$, because there exists a constant k such that for all *c*-configurations $\langle s, v \rangle$ in the sequence of

c-configurations, there exists a sequence σ of actions, with $|\sigma|=h$ and $0\leq h\leq k$, such that the pda that performs the $LR(1)$ parsing, starting from the c-configuration $\langle s, v\rangle$, after performing the sequence σ, either

(i) stops by accepting w, or

(ii) stops by rejecting w, or

(iii) performs a *shift* action, thereby constructing a new c-configuration, or

(iv) performs a *reduce-goto* action that makes the length of the stack *smaller than* $|s|$, thereby constructing a new c-configuration, or

(v) $h=k$ and every action in the sequence σ is a *reduce-goto* action which returns a stack whose length is *equal to* or *greater than* $|s|$.

As we will see below, we can take the constant k to be $|Q|^2\times|V_N|$.

Suppose that the pda is in the c-configuration $\langle s, v\rangle$ and it performs an action. If that action is: either (i) acceptance, or (ii) rejection, or (iii) a *shift* action, or (iv) a *reduce-goto* action which makes the length of the stack smaller than $|s|$, then the pda produces the next c-configuration in one step. Thus the length h of the sequence σ is 1.

If the action performed by the pda is none of the above, then the pda performs a *reduce-goto* action using a production of the form either $A \to \varepsilon$, or $A \to B$, or $A \to a$, and the length of the derived stack is not decreased (actually, it may increase as shown by Facts (α) and (β) above) and no new c-configuration is generated.

However, as we now show, if no new c-configuration is generated by a sequence σ of at most k actions (because none of the Cases (i)–(iv) occurs during σ), then Case (v) occurs, and the pda enters an infinite run of ε-moves on the input. Hence the parsing process can be stopped by rejecting the input word w is rejected, and thus also in this case the $LR(1)$ parsing is done in linear time.

First we note that, in Case (v), starting from the c-configuration $\langle s, v\rangle$, after the first action of the sequence σ of actions, we have that the stack s has at least three topmost symbols, say $p\,A\,q$, with $p, q\in Q$ and $A\in V_N$, the top symbol being q. Indeed, starting from the initial stack configuration $\left(\begin{smallmatrix} q_0 \\ \blacktriangle \end{smallmatrix}\right)$, where $\blacktriangle$ denotes the top of the stack, the *accept, reject, reduce-goto*, and *shift* actions modify the stack configurations as shown in Figure 5.6.1 on the next page. In that figure: (i) $\left(\cdots p\,a\,q \atop \blacktriangle\right)$ denotes a stack configuration with the three top symbols of the form '*state, terminal symbol, state*', the top being the state q, and (ii) $\left(\cdots p\,A\,q \atop \blacktriangle\right)$ denotes a stack configuration with the three top symbols of the form '*state, nonterminal symbol, state*', the top being the state q.

Now we have that there exists an action in the sequence σ of length k, after which the pda constructs a stack s' such that: (i) $|s'| \geq |s|$, and (ii) s' has the *same* three topmost symbols $p\,A\,q$ that were at the top of the stack after the first action of σ.

This is a consequence of the following facts.

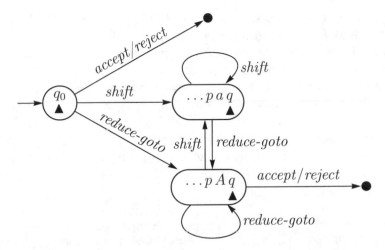

FIGURE 5.6.1. Transitions between stack configurations. ▲ denotes the top of the stack. The *accept* (or *reject*) action can be performed in the initial configuration $\left(\begin{smallmatrix} q_0 \\ \blacktriangle \end{smallmatrix}\right)$, if the input string ε belongs (or does not belong, respectively) to the language of the given grammar. After acceptance or rejection the pda stops.

Fact (1): during σ the pda always performs *reduce-goto* actions (that is, ε-moves on the input) and thus, it always uses the same column of the $LR(1)$ parsing table,

Fact (2): starting from the stack s, a sequence of ε-moves each of which makes the length of the stack *equal to* or *greater than* $|s|$, determines a sequence of stack configurations which depends only on the $LR(1)$ parsing table and the three topmost symbols of the stack s (in particular, the sequence of ε-moves does not depend on the other symbols on the stack), and

Fact (3): there are at most $|Q|^2 \times |V_N|$ different strings of the form $p\,A\,q$ which may occur at the top of the stack s, and

Fact (4): the action of the sequence σ which constructs the stack s' occurs within at most $|Q|^2 \times |V_N|$ actions (note that a sequence of h actions determines a sequence of $h+1$ stack configurations by taking into account also the stack configuration from which the pda performs the first action of the sequence).

The construction of the stack s' from the stack s shows that, if Case (v) occurs, then the pda enters an infinite run of ε-moves (and thus, the input word w can be rejected after k moves). Indeed, since the pda is deterministic, if the pda constructs the stack s' from the stack s, then it will also construct a stack s'' from the stack s', because the stacks s and s' have the same three topmost symbols (recall Fact (2) above). Therefore, an infinite sequence of stack configurations can be constructed by performing always ε-moves on the input word w. □

5.7. Complexity of Parsing Subclasses of Context-Free Languages

In Table 5.1 on the following page we give the measures of the time complexity and the space complexity for testing a grammar and constructing a parser for the following subclasses of context-free grammars: $LL(1)$ grammars, $SLR(1)$ grammars, $LR(1)$ grammars, and $LALR(1)$ grammars [25, page 400].

In that table the size n of the given input grammar is assumed to be the total number of occurrences of symbols in its productions.

Note that, since to fill an entry in the parser table takes at least constant time, for each row of Table 5.1, we have that the complexity class in the second column includes (actually, it properly includes) the complexity class in the third column.

If we know that the given grammar is context-free, the entries of Column 1 of Table 5.1 do not change, because to test whether or not a given grammar is a context-free grammar takes deterministic linear time with respect to the number n of the occurrences of symbols in its productions.

	deterministic time for testing a grammar	deterministic time for constructing the parser	size of the parser
$LL(1)$	$O(n^2)$	$O(2^{n^2+4\log n})$	$O(2^{n^2+2\log n})$
$SLR(1)$	$O(n^2)$	$O(2^{n+3\log n})$	$O(2^{n+2\log n})$
$LR(1)$	$O(n^3)$	$O(2^{n^2+4\log n})$	$O(2^{n^2+2\log n})$
$LALR(1)$	$O(2^{n+3\log n})$	$O(2^{n+3\log n})$	$O(2^{n+2\log n})$

TABLE 5.1. Deterministic time and space complexities (that is, time and space taken by a deterministic Turing Machine) for testing a grammar of size n and for constructing a parser of various classes of grammars: $LL(1)$, $SLR(1)$, $LR(1)$, and $LALR(1)$.

We have that the problem, which we call $P1$, of testing whether or not given an arbitrary context-free grammar G and an integer $k \geq 1$ in unary notation, the grammar G *is not* an $LL(k)$ grammar is NP-complete. The same complexity result holds if we replace $LL(k)$ by:

(i) $SLR(k)$, thereby getting a problem which we call $P2$, or

(ii) $LR(k)$, thereby getting a problem which we call $P3$.

However, if we replace $LL(k)$ by $LALR(k)$, we get a problem which we call $P4$, and we have that problem $P4$ is PSPACE-complete [25, Table 10.1 on page 399].

For the complexity measures of these problems $P1$–$P4$ the size of the input is assumed to be k (in unary notation) plus the size of the grammar G.

Note that since PSPACE is a complexity class which refers to *deterministic* computations, also the complement of Problem $P4$ which is the problem of testing whether or not given an arbitrary context-free grammar G and an integer $k \geq 1$ in unary notation, the grammar G *is* an $LALR(k)$ grammar, is PSPACE-complete [25, page 398].

If $k\,(\geq 1)$ is given in binary notation (not in unary notation), then Problems $P1$–$P4$ all become NEXPTIME-complete (recall that the class of NEXPTIME problems is $\bigcup_{k \geq 0} \text{NTIME}(2^{n^k})$.)

Note also that the entries of Table 5.1 on the facing page are consistent with the complexity results we have now stated about Problems $P1$–$P4$, because the algorithms which justify those entries, take advantage of the fact that k is 1.

Finally, recall that the problem to decide whether or not, given an arbitrary context-free grammar G, there exists $k \geq 0$ such that G is an $LL(k)$ grammar, is undecidable. The same undecidability result holds if we replace $LL(k)$ by $SLR(k)$, or by $LR(k)$, or by $LALR(k)$ [25, page 386].

5.8. Subclasses of Context-free Languages

This section is devoted to the illustration of Figure 5.8.2 on page 156 in which we consider and stratify various subclasses of the context-free languages. We will also discuss some other relationships among subclasses of context-free languages.

First let us recall the notion of an ambiguous context-free grammar which we will need in the sequel.

DEFINITION 5.8.1. [**Ambiguous and Unambiguous Context-Free Grammar**] A context-free grammar such that there exists a word w with at least two distinct parse trees is said to be *ambiguous*. A context-free grammar is not ambiguous is said to be *unambiguous*.

We get an equivalent definition if in the above definition we replace 'two parse trees' by 'two leftmost derivations' or 'two rightmost derivations'.

We have already seen on page 97 that the grammar G with axiom S and the following productions:

$$S \rightarrow A \quad \mid B$$
$$A \rightarrow a\,A\,b \quad \mid 0$$
$$B \rightarrow a\,B\,b\,b \mid 1$$

is $LR(0)$ and it is *not* $LL(k)$, for any $k \geq 0$.

The language generated by that grammar is:

$$L = \{a^n\,0\,b^n \mid n \geq 0\} \cup \{a^n\,1\,(b\,b)^n \mid n \geq 0\}.$$

This language is a deterministic context-free language which enjoys the prefix property. This fact shows the proper containment between the deterministic context-free languages and the union of the $LL(k)$ languages, for all $k \geq 0$, as indicated in Figure 5.8.2 on page 156. This result is due to D. J. Rosenkrantz and R. E. Stearns [22] and it has been stated on Fact 4.3.20 on page 78.

The following notion is necessary for presenting Fact 5.8.3 below. It relates $SLR(k)$ grammars and $LR(k)$ grammars.

DEFINITION 5.8.2. [**Structurally Equivalent Grammars**] Two unambiguous context-free grammars G_1 and G_2 are said to be *structurally equivalent* iff $L(G_1) = L(G_2)$ and for every word $w \in L(G_1)$ (which is equal to $L(G_2)$) the derivation trees of w in G_1 and G_2 are the same except, possibly, for the labeling of the nodes with nonterminal symbols.

For instance, the following two grammars G_1 and G_2 are structurally equivalent:
(i) the grammar G_1 has axiom S and productions:

$$S \to Ac \mid bA \qquad\qquad A \to \varepsilon$$

(ii) the grammar G_2 has axiom S and productions:

$$S \to Ac \mid bB \qquad\qquad A \to \varepsilon \qquad\qquad B \to \varepsilon$$

Indeed, in particular, for the word b we have the following two derivation trees which differ only for the labeling of a node with a nonterminal symbol.

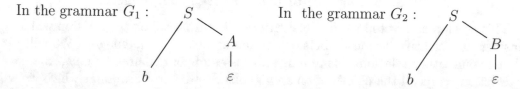

FACT 5.8.3.   [**Transforming $LR(k)$ Grammars into Equivalent $SLR(k)$ Grammars**] For any $k \geq 0$, any context-free grammar G can be transformed into a structurally equivalent grammar which is $SLR(k)$ iff G is $LR(k)$ [**25**, page 84].

Note that, an ambiguous grammar may generate a deterministic context-free language. Consider, for instance, the grammar G with axiom S and productions:

$$S \to A \mid a \qquad A \to a$$

It is an *ambiguous* grammar, but its language $L(G) = \{a\}$ is a deterministic context-free language (because it is a regular language) and it has an $LR(0)$ parser [**25**, page 45].

Recall that if a word w has two distinct parse trees, then it has two distinct parse trees which are generated by leftmost derivations (or, equivalently, rightmost derivations).

Now we will present some hierarchies of grammars (and languages) which are all subclasses of the context-free grammars (and languages).

Unless otherwise specified, until the end of this chapter, we will assume that the grammars we consider are *strongly reduced* (see Definition 5.4.18 on page 124), that is,

(i) they are *reduced grammars*, which means that they are without useless symbols (see Definition 1.2.15 on page 7),

(ii) they are *without trivial unit productions*, and

(iii) the axiom of each of them does not occur on the right hand side of any production.

Let us first recall the different ways in which one can present a class of grammars and, indeed, in this book various classes of grammars has been introduced in these different ways. Figure 5.8.1 on the facing page shows these different ways.

Every class of grammars defines a class of languages in the sense that, given a class $\mathcal{A}$ of grammars, the corresponding class of languages is made out of all languages L such that there exists a grammar in the class $\mathcal{A}$ which generates L. For

A class of grammars (or languages) can be introduced in various ways.

  (i) A first way is to give the conditions which should be satisfied by the productions of the grammars in the class.

  For instance, the class of context-free grammars has been defined in this way by stipulating that their productions are of the form: $A \rightarrow \sigma$, where $A \in V_N$ and $\sigma \in (V_T \cup V_N)^*$.

 (ii) A second way is to give the conditions which should be satisfied by the derivations of the words of the languages generated by the grammars in the class.

  For instance, the class of $LR(k)$ grammars, for any $k \geq 0$, has been introduced in Definition 5.1.2 on page 86 in this way.

(iii) A third way is to present an algorithm for parsing the languages generated by the grammars in the class, and to give the conditions which should be satisfied by the parsing table needed for that algorithm.

  For instance, the class of $LR(0)$ grammars has been introduced in Definition 5.2.8 on page 96 in this way.

  Note that, since the algorithm may modify the given grammar (as in the case of the algorithm which generates the $LR(0)$ parsing table by first constructing the augmented grammar), one should specify whether that algorithm defines the class of the given grammars or the class of the modified grammars.

FIGURE 5.8.1. Different ways of presenting classes of grammars (or languages).

---

instance, the class of the $LR(1)$ languages is made out of all languages L such that there exists an $LR(1)$ grammar which generates L.

We say that a class $\mathcal{A}$ of grammars is contained in a class $\mathcal{B}$ of grammars, and we write $\mathcal{A} \subseteq \mathcal{B}$, if every grammar of the class $\mathcal{A}$ is also a grammar of the class $\mathcal{B}$.

We say that a class $\mathcal{A}$ of languages is contained in the class $\mathcal{B}$ of languages, and we write $\mathcal{A} \subseteq \mathcal{B}$, if for every language L in $\mathcal{A}$ there is a grammar G of the class $\mathcal{B}$ which generates L.

We say that a class $\mathcal{A}$ of grammars (or languages) is incomparable with respect to the class $\mathcal{B}$ of grammars (or languages) iff neither $\mathcal{A} \subseteq \mathcal{B}$ nor $\mathcal{B} \subseteq \mathcal{A}$.

We have the following hierarchies of grammars and languages depicted in the framed diagrams 1.1–2.2 below. As usual,
(i) $\mathcal{A} = \mathcal{B}$ means $\mathcal{A} \subseteq \mathcal{B}$ and $\mathcal{B} \subseteq \mathcal{A}$, and
(ii) $\mathcal{A} \subset \mathcal{B}$ means $\mathcal{A} \subseteq \mathcal{B}$ and $\mathcal{A} \neq \mathcal{B}$.

Since in the hierarchies we also refer to $LL(0)$ grammars and $LL(0)$ languages, let us recall that, by definition:

(i) any $LL(0)$ grammar has a unique production for each nonterminal (and thus the axiom does not occur on the right hand side of any production), and

(ii) if it does not contains useless symbols, then it generates a singleton language. For instance, the grammar with axiom S and productions: $S \rightarrow A\,b\,C$, $A \rightarrow \varepsilon$, and $C \rightarrow c\,A$, is an $LL(0)$ grammar and $L(S) = \{b\,c\}$.

1.1 *Hierarchy of* (*strongly or not strongly*) *reduced grammars.*

For any $k > 1$, $LL(0) \subset LL(1) \subset \ldots \subset LL(k) \subset LL(k+1) \subset \ldots$

$\subset$

$LR(0) \subset LR(1) \subset \ldots \subset LR(k) \subset \ldots$

For any $k \geq 0$, the fact that the class of $LL(k)$ grammars does not include the class of $LR(0)$ grammars is a consequence of Example 5.2.10 on page 96.

The fact that the class of reduced $LR(0)$ grammars does not include the class of reduced $LL(1)$ grammars is shown by the grammar G with axiom S and the productions $S \to a S \mid b$. For all $k \geq 0$, the grammar G is a reduced $LL(1)$ grammar (and thus it is also a reduced $LL(h)$ grammar, for all $h \geq 1$), and it is *not* an $LR(k)$ grammar, because the axiom S occurs on the right hand side of a production.

Thus, for all $k \geq 0$, for all $h \geq 1$, the class of the (strongly or not strongly) reduced $LL(h)$ grammars is incomparable with respect to the class of the (strongly or not strongly) reduced $LR(k)$ grammars.

If we consider *strongly reduced* grammars, by Theorem 5.4.19 on page 124, we have that, for all $k \geq 0$, the class of *strongly reduced* $LL(k)$ grammars is properly contained in the class of *strongly reduced* $LR(k)$ grammars. This result can be depicted as follows.

1.2 *Hierarchy of strongly reduced grammars.*

For any $k \geq 0$, $\ldots \subset LL(k) \subset \ldots$

$\subset$

$\ldots \subset LR(k) \subset \ldots$

We also have the following results. Some of them have been presented in Theorem 4.3.18 on page 77 and some others we will be shown below in this chapter.

1.3 *Hierarchy of strongly reduced grammars.*

$SLR(0) = LALR(0) = LR(0) \subset SLR(1) \subset LALR(1) \subset LR(1)$

In general, for any $k \geq 1$, $SLR(k) \subset LALR(k) \subset LR(k)$

2.1 *Hierarchy of languages.*

For any $k \geq 0$, $SLR(k) = LALR(k) = LR(k)$

For any $k \geq 1$, $SLR(1) = LALR(1) = LR(1) = SLR(k) = LALR(k) = LR(k)$

2.2 *Hierarchy of languages.*

For any $k \geq 1$, $LL(0) \subset LL(1) \subset \ldots \subset LL(k) \subset LL(k+1) \subset \ldots \subset LR(1) = \ldots = LR(k) = \ldots$

$\subset$ $\cup$

$LR(0)$

Every $LL(0)$ language is an $LR(0)$ language, because every singleton language is an $LR(0)$ language (indeed, every singleton language is a prefix-free, deterministic context-free language). We also have that:

(i) $L \in LL(0)$ iff $L = \emptyset$ or L is a singleton (thus, the language generated by a reduced $LL(0)$ grammar is a singleton, because the axiom of that grammar is not useless), and

(ii) $L \in LR(0)$ implies that $L = \{\varepsilon\}$ or $\varepsilon \notin L$ (because L enjoys the prefix-free property) [**9**, page 352].

The fact that, for $k \geq 1$, the class of $LL(k)$ languages is incomparable with the class of $LR(0)$ (this fact has been depicted in the diagram '2.2 *Hierarchy of languages*' above) follows from the following two facts:

(i) for $k \geq 1$, any $LL(1)$ language is an $LL(k)$ language, and the class of $LL(1)$ languages is not a subclass of $LR(0)$ languages because the $LL(1)$ language a^* (which is a regular language, and thus by Fact 4.3.22 on page 79 it is an $LL(1)$ language) is *not* an $LR(0)$ language (because it is *not* prefix-free), and

(ii) for any $k \geq 1$, as an immediate consequence of Fact 4.3.21 on page 78, the language $L = \{a^n b^n \mid n \geq 1\} \cup \{a^n c^n \mid n \geq 1\}$ is an $LR(0)$ language (because it is an $LR(1)$ language and it is prefix-free), and it is *not* an $LL(k)$ language.

We have the following facts.

FACT 5.8.4. [**Relationships Between $SLR(k)$ Grammars and $LALR(k)$ Grammars**] The class of $SLR(0)$ grammars coincides with the class of $LALR(0)$ grammars. For $k \geq 1$ the class of $SLR(k)$ grammars is properly contained in the class of $LALR(k)$ grammars.

EXAMPLE 5.8.5. The grammar with axiom S and productions:

$S \rightarrow Ac \mid bA \mid bc$

$A \rightarrow \varepsilon$

is an $LALR(1)$ grammar which is *not* $SLR(k)$ for any $k \geq 0$ [**25**, page 72].

FACT 5.8.6. [**Relationships Between $LALR(k)$ Grammars and $LR(k)$ Grammars**] The class of $LALR(0)$ grammars coincides with the class of $LR(0)$ grammars. For $k \geq 1$ the class of $LALR(k)$ grammars is properly contained in the class of $LR(k)$ grammars.

EXAMPLE 5.8.7. The grammar with axiom S and productions:

$S \rightarrow aAa \mid bAb \mid aBb \mid bBa$

$A \rightarrow c$

$B \rightarrow c$

is an $LR(1)$ grammar which is *not* $LALR(k)$ for any $k \geq 0$ (see also the Example 5.5.8 on page 143).

FACT 5.8.8. [**Hierarchy of the $LR(k)$ Grammars**] For all $k \geq 0$, the grammar with axiom S and the productions:

$S \rightarrow ab^k c \mid Ab^k d$

$A \rightarrow a$

is an $LR(k+1)$ grammar which is *not* an $LR(k)$ grammar [**25**, page 53].

FACT 5.8.9. [**Relationships Between $LR(k)$ Grammars and $SLR(k)$ Grammars**] For any $k \geq 0$, any language generated by an $LR(k)$ grammar can be generated by an $SLR(k)$ grammar [**25**, page 75].

Actually, we have the following stronger results.

FACT 5.8.10. [**Relationships Between the Classes of $SLR(k)$ Languages, $LR(k)$ Languages, and $LALR(k)$ Languages**] For every $k \geq 0$, we have that the classes of $SLR(k)$ languages, $LR(k)$ languages, and $LALR(k)$ languages are all equal. [**25**, page 84].

FACT 5.8.11. [**Computable Collapse of $LR(k)$ Languages, for $k \geq 1$, to $LR(1)$ Languages and $SLR(1)$ Languages**] (i) For any $k > 1$, given any $LR(k)$ grammar G there exists an equivalent $LR(1)$ grammar G_1 which is Turing computable from G (see also Theorem 5.4.15 on page 123). (ii) Given any $LR(1)$ grammar G_1 it can be transformed in a Turing computable way into an equivalent $SLR(1)$ grammar [**25**, page 84].

As a consequence of the above facts we have also the following facts (see also what we stated in Theorem 5.4.16 on page 123).

FACT 5.8.12. [**Deterministic Context-Free Languages are $LR(1)$ Languages, $SLR(1)$ Languages, and $LALR(1)$ Languages**] (i) Any deterministic context-free language can be generated by an $LR(1)$ grammar. (ii) Any deterministic context-free language can be generated by an $SLR(1)$ grammar. (iii) Any deterministic context-free language can be generated by an $LALR(1)$ grammar.

FACT 5.8.13. [**Deterministic Context-Free Languages are Generated by Unambiguous Grammars**] (i) For every deterministic context-free language L there exists an unambiguous context-free grammar G which generates L and, by the previous Fact 5.8.12, this grammar can be taken to be an $LR(1)$ grammar.
(ii) For all $k \geq 0$, any strongly reduced $LR(k)$ grammar is unambiguous.

Figure 5.8.2 on page 156 shows the relationships among various subclasses of context-free languages.

Note that what we state in that figure about the class of the *Simple Languages*, is consistent with the following two facts about grammars (not languages):

(i) the grammar with axiom S and productions: $S \to a\,S\,A \mid b\,S\,B \mid \varepsilon$, $A \to a$, $B \to b$ (these productions are in Greibach normal form) is *not* an $LR(1)$ grammar, because the axiom S occurs on the right hand side of a production, and

(ii) the grammar with axiom S' and productions: $S' \to S$, $S \to a\,S\,A \mid b\,S\,B \mid \varepsilon$, $A \to a$, $B \to b$ (these productions are *not* in Greibach normal form because:

(ii.1) in the production $S' \to S$ the right hand side does not begin with a terminal symbol, and (ii.2) the left hand side of the production $S \to \varepsilon$ is *not* the axiom S') is *not* an $LR(1)$ grammar.

We state without proof the following results.

FACT 5.8.14. [**Properties of $LR(0)$ Languages**] (i) A language L is an $LR(0)$ language iff (i.1) it is an $LR(1)$ language, and (i.2) for all u, v, x if $u \in L$ and $u x \in L$ and $v \in L$, *then* $v x \in L$ [**9**, page 515] [**25**].
(ii) Given an $LR(0)$ language L *if* $u \in L$ and $u x \in L$ then $u x^* \in L$.

FACT 5.8.15. [**Regular Expressions on Right Hand Sides of Context-Free Grammars**] Every context-free grammar whose productions have their right hand sides written as regular expressions over the alphabet $V_T \cup V_N$, can be transformed into an equivalent context-free grammar whose productions have their right hand sides written, as usual, as strings in $(V_T \cup V_N)^*$.

This transformation can be done in linear time with respect to the size of the given grammar [**25**, page 116].

For instance, the grammar whose axiom is E and whose productions are:

$$E \to T\,(+T)^*$$
$$T \to F\,(\times F)^* \qquad\qquad (G_1)$$
$$F \to a + (E)$$

can be transformed into the equivalent grammar whose axiom is E and whose productions are:

$$E \to T \mid E + T$$
$$T \to F \mid T \times F \qquad\qquad (G_2)$$
$$F \to a \mid (E)$$

Obviously, during this transformation one should be careful about the use of overloaded symbols because, for instance, the symbols which are used for writing regular expressions, such as $+$, $($, and $)$, may also be used as terminal symbols of the given grammar.

For instance, in the case of our grammar G_1 above, the round parentheses (and) are symbols for writing regular expressions in the productions $E \to T\,(+T)^*$ and $T \to F\,(\times F)^*$, while they are terminal symbols in the production $F \to a + (E)$.

Let us conclude this section by stating the following decidability result which follows from [**23**].

FACT 5.8.16. [**Decidability of Equivalence for $LR(k)$ Grammars**] There exists an algorithm which always terminates and for all $h, k \geq 0$, given an $LR(h)$ grammar $G1$ and an $LR(k)$ grammar $G2$, tells us whether or not they are equivalent, that is, $L(G1) = L(G2)$.

More decidability results are listed in Section 10.2 on page 296.

Context-free languages

They are accepted by PDA's by final state or by empty stack.
$\{a^i b^j c^k \mid (i=j \ or \ j=k) \ and \ i,j,k \geq 1\}$ is a nondeterministic context-free, inherently ambiguous language.

⊃ *Non-inherently ambiguous context-free languages*

$\{a^k b^m \mid (m=k \ or \ m=2k) \ and \ k\geq 1 \ and \ m\geq 1\}$ is a nondeterministic context-free, non-inherently ambiguous language. A non-ambiguous grammar with axiom S which generates this language is:
$$S \to L \mid R \qquad L \to aLb \mid ab \qquad R \to aRbb \mid abb$$
In Figure 5.8.3 on the next page we have depicted a pda which accepts this language by final state.

⊃ $\bigcup_{k \geq 0} LR(k)$ *languages (Deterministic context-free languages)*

For all $k\geq 0$, $LR(k)$ languages are accepted by deterministic PDA's by final state. For any deterministic context-free language L, there exists $k \geq 1$ such that L is generated by an $LR(k)$ grammar. In this class of grammars ε-productions are allowed for every nonterminal symbol. For all $k \geq 0$, a language which is generated by an $LR(k)$ grammar, can be generated by an $LR(1)$ grammar. For all $k\geq 0$, every $LR(k)$ grammar is unambiguous.
For any deterministic context-free language L, the language $L\,\$$, with $\$ \notin V_T$, can be generated by an $LR(0)$ grammar. The class of $LR(1)$ languages is strictly larger than the union, for all $k\geq 0$, of the classes of $LL(k)$ languages (see Fact 4.3.20 on page 78) **[22]**.
The language $\{a^n b^n \mid n \geq 1\} \cup \{a^n c^n \mid n \geq 1\}$ is $LR(1)$, and not $LL(k)$, for any $k \geq 0$ (see Fact 4.3.21 on page 78). Recall also Example 5.2.10 on page 97.

⊃ $\bigcup_{k \geq 1} LL(k)$ *languages*

For all $k \geq 0$, the class of $LL(k)$ languages is the class of languages generated by $LL(k)$ grammars. In this class of grammars ε-productions are allowed for every nonterminal symbol. For all $k \geq 0$, the class of $LL(k+1)$ languages properly includes the class of $LL(k)$ languages and the class of $LL(k+1)$ grammars properly includes the class of $LL(k)$ grammars (see Theorem 4.3.18 on page 77). $S \to A$, $A \to aBb \mid b$, $B \to a \mid bAB$ is an $LL(1)$ grammar.

⊃ *Simple languages*

Languages generated by grammars in Greibach normal form such that for each nonterminal A no two productions of the form $A \to a\,\alpha$ and $A \to a\,\beta$ exist, for some $a \in V_T$ and some $\alpha, \beta \in V_N^*$, with $\alpha \neq \beta$. Recall that in grammars in Greibach normal form the only ε-production allowed is $S \to \varepsilon$, where S is the axiom.

⊃ $LL(0)$ *languages* A language is $LL(0)$ iff it is empty or it is a singleton.

FIGURE 5.8.2. Hierarchy of subclasses of context-free languages. All containments ⊃ are proper. We assume, without loss of generality, that the axiom S does *not* occur on the right hand side of any production.

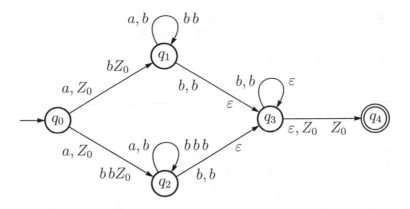

FIGURE 5.8.3. A nondeterministic pda which accepts by final state the language L generated by the grammar with axiom S and productions: $S \to L \mid R$, $L \to a\,L\,b \mid a\,b$, $R \to a\,R\,b\,b \mid a\,b\,b$. The nondeterminism is due to the moves from state q_0. We have that: $L = \{a^k\,b^m \mid (m = k \text{ or } m = 2k) \text{ and } k \geq 1 \text{ and } m \geq 1\}$. An arc from state q_i to state q_j with label '$x, Z\ w$' means that the pda moves from state q_i to state q_j if: (i) the symbol x is read from the input, (ii) the top of the stack is Z, and (iii) the string w is pushed onto the stack so that the leftmost symbol of w will be the new top of the stack. In this move if $x \neq \varepsilon$, then the input head moves one character to the right, otherwise it does not move.

EXERCISE 5.8.17. [**Language of Balanced Parentheses**] (i) Show that the grammar G_1 with axiom S' and productions:

$S' \to S$

$S \to a\,S\,b \mid \varepsilon \mid S\,S$

is *not* an $LR(1)$ grammar. The language generated by G_1 is:

$L(G_1) = \{w \mid w \in \{a, b\}^* \wedge |w|_a = |w|_b \wedge \text{ for all prefixes } u \text{ of } w, |u|_a \geq |u|_b\},$

that is, the grammar G_1 generates the deterministic context-free language of balanced parentheses. For instance, the word $w = a\,a\,a\,b\,a\,a\,b\,b\,b\,b\,a\,b$ belongs to $L(G_1)$ (the symbols a and b play the role of the open parenthesis and the closed parenthesis, respectively). We can depict the word w as follows:

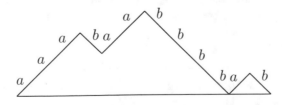

Since the parentheses are balanced, the left and the right end of any word $w \in L(G_1)$ are 'at the same level'.

(ii) Show that the language $L(G_1)$ is a deterministic context-free language by constructing a deterministic pda which accepts it by final state [21].

(iii) Show that the grammar G_2 with axiom S' and productions:

$S' \to S$

$S \to A\,S \mid \varepsilon$

$A \to a\,S\,b$

is an $LR(1)$ grammar and $L(G_2) = L(G_1)$. Recall that for every deterministic context-free language L there exists an $LR(1)$ grammar G which generates L.   □

5.9. Derivation of Equivalent $LR(1)$ Grammars from $LR(k)$ Grammars

As mentioned on page 123, in this section we present an algorithm that, given any given $LR(k+1)$ grammar, for any $k > 0$, constructs an equivalent $LR(1)$ grammar (see [25, Section 6.7]). Such an algorithm provides a constructive proof of Point (ii) of Theorem 5.4.15 on page 123.

Let us consider an $LR(k+1)$ grammar $G = \langle V_T, V_N, P, S \rangle$, for some $k > 0$. We assume that the grammar G is without useless symbols and without trivial unit productions. Let V be $V_T \cup V_N$.

In order to show how to construct an $LR(1)$ grammar which is equivalent to G, we need the following two notions:

(i) $First_k(\alpha)$, for any string $\alpha \in V^*$, and

(ii) $Follow_k(s)$, for any (terminal or nonterminal) symbol $s \in V$.

The former notion is the one we have introduced in Definition 4.3.1 on page 64.

The latter notion is the following variant of the one we have introduced in Definition 4.3.4 on page 71. In this variant:

(i) we define $Follow_1(S)$ to be $\{\varepsilon\}$, (rather than $\{\$\}$, as stated in Definition 4.2.6 on page 52) (by doing so we comply with the notation used in [25, Section 6.7]), and

(ii) we consider s to be a terminal or nonterminal symbol in V (while in Definition 4.3.4 we have assumed that s is a nonterminal symbol).

DEFINITION 5.9.1. [**The Set $Follow_k(s)$ for a Terminal or Nonterminal Symbol s**] Let us consider a context-free grammar $\langle V_T, V_N, P, S \rangle$, possibly with ε-productions, without useless symbols. Let V be $V_T \cup V_N$. For any $k \geq 1$, $Follow_k$ is a function from V to the set of all subsets of V_T^*. For any $s \in V$, $Follow_k(s)$ is the *smallest* set such that for any string $w \in (V_T^0 \cup V_T^1 \cup V_T^2 \cup \ldots \cup V_T^{k-1} \cup V_T^k)$,

if $S \to^* \alpha\, s\, \beta$ for some $\alpha \in V^*$ and $\beta \in V^*$ and $w \in First_k(\beta)$

then $w \in Follow_k(s)$.   □

ALGORITHM 5.9.2. [**Constructing an $LL(1)$ Grammar Equivalent to an $LL(k)$ Grammar, for $k > 1$**]

Given an $LR(k+1)$ grammar $G = \langle V_T, V_N, P, S \rangle$, for some $k > 0$, the equivalent $LR(1)$ grammar $G' = \langle V_T, V'_N, P', S' \rangle$ is constructed as follows:

(i) the set V'_N of nonterminal symbols is made out of the following symbols:

- S', which is the axiom, and
- for each $A \in V_N$, $y \in Follow_k(A)$, $x \in First_k(A\,y)$,

  $[x, A, y]$ (note that a nonterminal symbol is a triple)

(ii) the set P' of productions is made out of the following productions:

- for each $x \in First_k(S)$,

  $S' \to x\,[x, S, \varepsilon]$

- for each production $A \to B_1 B_2 \ldots B_m$ in P, with the B_i's in V,

  $[y_0, A, y_m] \to [y_0, B_1, y_1]\,[y_1, B_2, y_2] \ldots [y_{m-1}, B_m, y_m]$

- for each $a \in V_T$, for each $b \in V_T$, for each $x\,b \in Follow_k(a)$, with $|x\,b| = k$,

  $[a\,x, a, x\,b] \to b$

- for each $a \in V_T$, for each $x \in Follow_k(a)$, with $0 \le |x| < k$,

  $[a\,x, a, x] \to \varepsilon$

(Obviously, the notions of $First_k$ and $Follow_k$ we have used in this algorithm, refer to the given $LR(k{+}1)$ grammar G.) It can be shown that G' is an $LR(1)$ grammar equivalent to the $LR(k)$ grammar G [25, Section 6.7].

Let $L([x, A, y])$ be the language generated by the nonterminal $[x, A, y]$ in G'. We have that:

$$L([x, A, y]) = \{w \mid x\,w \in L(A\,y)\}$$

where $L(A\,y)$ denotes the language generated by A (in the grammar G) followed by the string y.

Now we give an example of derivation of an $LR(1)$ grammar H' which is equivalent to a given $LR(2)$ grammar H.

Let the axiom of the grammar H be S and the productions be the following ones:

$S \to A\,b\,b \mid B\,b$

$A \to a\,A \mid a$

$B \to a\,B \mid a$

In [25, Section 6.7] it is shown that the grammar H is $LR(2)$ and it is not $LR(1)$.

If we take $k = 1$ in Algorithm 5.9.2 on the preceding page, we will derive an equivalent $LR(1)$ grammar H' from the given $LR(k{+}1)$ (that is, $LR(2)$) grammar H.

The grammar H' has axiom S'. We have that:

$First_1(S) = \{a\}$

$Follow_1(S) = \{\varepsilon\}$

$First_1(S\,Follow_1(S)) = \{a\}$

$First_1(A) = First_1(B) = \{a\}$

$Follow_1(A) = Follow_1(B) = \{b\}$

$Follow_1(a) = \{a, b\}$

$Follow_1(b) = \{b, \varepsilon\}$

The productions of the grammar H' are:

1. $S' \rightarrow a\,[a, S, \varepsilon]$

2. $[a, S, \varepsilon] \rightarrow [a, A, b]\,[b, b, b]\,[b, b, \varepsilon]$ (from $S \rightarrow A\,b\,b$)

3. $[a, S, \varepsilon) \rightarrow [a, B, b]\,[b, b, \varepsilon]$ (from $S \rightarrow B\,b$)

4. $[a, A, b] \rightarrow [a, a, a]\,[a, A, b]$ (from $A \rightarrow a\,A$)

5. $[a, A, b] \rightarrow [a, a, b]$ (from $A \rightarrow a$)

6. $[a, B, b] \rightarrow [a, a, a]\,[a, B, b]$ (from $B \rightarrow a\,B$)

7. $[a, B, b] \rightarrow [a, a, b]$ (from $B \rightarrow a$)

8. $[a, a, a] \rightarrow a$

9. $[a, a, b] \rightarrow b$

10. $[b, b, b] \rightarrow b$

11. $[b, b, \varepsilon] \rightarrow \varepsilon$

Let us explain production 1.

(i) The leftmost a on the right hand side is due to $First_1(S) = \{a\}$,

(ii) the third component of the nonterminal is due to $Follow_1(S) = \{\varepsilon\}$, and

(iii) the first component of the nonterminal is due to $First_1(S\,Follow_1(S)) = \{a\}$.

Let us explain production 2. From the production $S \rightarrow A\,b\,b$, we get:

$[a, S, \varepsilon] \rightarrow [a, A, y_1]\,[y_1, b, y_2]\,[y_2, b, \varepsilon]$

for some values of the strings y_1 and y_2. Now, by proceeding from the right to the left, we have that $y_2 \in First_1(b\,\varepsilon)$, and thus $y_2 = b$. We also have that $y_1 \in First_1(b\,b)$, and thus $y_1 = b$.

The productions 8–11 are immediately derived from the rules given in Algorithm 5.9.2 on page 158.

The given grammar H can be transformed into an equivalent $LR(1)$ grammar also by taking $k = 2$, instead of $k = 1$ (any $k \geq 1$ will do). In that case we get a grammar, let us called it H'', with axiom S'' and the following productions:

1. $S'' \rightarrow aa\,[aa, S, \varepsilon]$

1'. $S'' \rightarrow ab\,[ab, S, \varepsilon]$

2. $[aa, S, \varepsilon] \rightarrow [aa, A, bb]\,[bb, b, b]\,[b, b, \varepsilon]$ (from $S \rightarrow A\,b\,b$)

2'. $[ab, S, \varepsilon] \rightarrow [ab, A, bb]\,[bb, b, b]\,[b, b, \varepsilon]$ (from $S \rightarrow A\,b\,b$)

3. $[aa, S, \varepsilon] \rightarrow [aa, B, b]\,[b, b, \varepsilon]$ (from $S \rightarrow B\,b$)

3'. $[ab, S, \varepsilon] \rightarrow [ab, B, b]\,[b, b, \varepsilon]$ (from $S \rightarrow B\,b$)

4. $[aa, A, bb] \rightarrow [aa, a, aa]\,[aa, A, bb]$ (from $A \rightarrow a\,A$)

4'. $[aa, A, bb] \rightarrow [aa, a, ab]\,[ab, A, bb]$ (from $A \rightarrow a\,A$)

5. $[ab, A, bb] \rightarrow [ab, a, bb]$ (from $A \rightarrow a$)

6. $[aa, B, b] \rightarrow [aa, a, aa]\,[aa, B, b]$ (from $B \rightarrow a\,B$)

6'. $[aa, B, b]$ $\rightarrow$ $[aa, a, ab]\,[ab, B, b]$ (from $B \rightarrow a\,B$)

7. $[ab, B, b]$ $\rightarrow$ $[ab, a, b]$ (from $B \rightarrow a$)

8. $[aa, a, aa]$ $\rightarrow$ a

9. $[aa, a, ab]$ $\rightarrow$ b

10. $[ab, a, bb]$ $\rightarrow$ b

11. $[ab, a, b]$ $\rightarrow$ ε

11'. $[bb, b, b]$ $\rightarrow$ ε

11''. $[b, b, \varepsilon]$ $\rightarrow$ ε

Note that the productions 4 and 4' (and also the productions 6 and 6') are due to the fact that $Follow_2(a) = \{aa,\ ab\}$.

The following leftmost derivation shows that $aab \in L(S'')$ (we have underlined the nonterminal which is expanded):

$S'' \rightarrow \{\text{by } 1\}$ $aa\,\underline{[aa, S, \varepsilon]}$

$\rightarrow \{\text{by } 3\}$ $aa\,\underline{[aa, B, b]}\,[b, b, \varepsilon]$

$\rightarrow \{\text{by } 6'\}$ $aa\,\underline{[aa, a, ab]}\,[ab, B, b]\,[b, b, \varepsilon]$

$\rightarrow \{\text{by } 9\}$ $aab\,\underline{[ab, B, b]}\,[b, b, \varepsilon]$

$\rightarrow \{\text{by } 7\}$ $aab\,\underline{[ab, a, b]}\,[b, b, \varepsilon]$

$\rightarrow \{\text{by } 11\}$ $aab\,\underline{[b, b, \varepsilon]}$

$\rightarrow \{\text{by } 11''\}$ $aab.$

5.10. Conventions for $LL(k)$ and $LR(k)$ Parsing

In Table 5.2 on the next page we recall some hypotheses we made concerning the parsing of various kinds of $LL(k)$ languages and $LR(k)$ languages and, in particular:

 (i) the use of a rightmost, new symbol $ in the input string,

 (ii) the use of augmented grammars with the production of the axiom,

 (iii) the initial stack configuration, and

 (iv) the lookahead sets.

Obviously, when we consider augmented grammars, we have that the new axiom S' does not occur on the right hand side of any production.

	input string	augmented grammar	production of the axiom	initial stack	lookahead set
$LL(k)$	ended by \$	no	axiom S	S \$ ▲	none
$LR(0)$ and $SLR(1)$	ended by \$	yes	axiom S' add: $S' \to S$ \$	q_0 ▲	none
$LR(1)$ and $LALR(1)$	ended by \$	yes	axiom S' add: $S' \to S$	q_0 ▲	$\{\$\}$

TABLE 5.2. Our conventions on the input string, the augmented grammar with the production of the axiom, the initial stack configuration (q_0 is the initial state), and the lookahead set for various classes of context-free grammars.

CHAPTER 6

Parsers for Operator Grammars and Parser Generators

In this chapter we will present the parsers for operator grammars and we will show how to make use of the parser generators for generating parsers.

6.1. Operator-Precedence Parsers

Let us introduce the following concept of an operator grammar.

DEFINITION 6.1.1. [**Operator Grammar**] An *operator grammar* is a context-free grammar without ε-productions such that there are no two consecutive nonterminals on the right hand side of the productions.

We have the following fact whose proof is based on the existence of a procedure for generating an equivalent operator grammar from any given unambiguous context-free grammar [**3**].

FACT 6.1.2. Every context-free language L is such that $L - \{\varepsilon\}$ can be generated by an operator grammar.

Instead of presenting the general theory of parsing languages which are generated by operator grammars, we now present an example of parsing a particular expression language, which is generated by an operator grammar where each operator has an associated *precedence*. This notion of precedence is the usual notion of precedence used in Mathematics so that, for instance, the expression $5 + 2 \times 4$ is evaluated to 13 and not to 28, because $\times$ has a higher precedence than $+$. In the literature the operator grammars whose operators have an associated precedence are called *operator-precedence grammars* and the techniques for parsing those grammars are referred to as *operator-precedence parsing techniques*.

Let us consider the operator-precedence grammar with axiom E and the following four productions:

$$E \rightarrow E + E \mid E \times E \mid E \uparrow E \mid a$$

where, as usual, $+$, $\times$, and $\uparrow$ denote sum, product, and exponentiation, respectively.

We first introduce the following augmented grammar G' with axiom E' so to place every generated word between *two* occurrences of the symbol $ which is assumed not to be in $V_T \cup V_N$. Thus, in G' we introduce the extra production $E' \rightarrow \$E\$$. Then we also introduce the following parsing table which encodes the precedence among the operators $+$, $\times$, and $\uparrow$, the symbol $, and the identifier a of the given grammar:

© Springer Nature Switzerland AG 2021
A. Pettorossi, *Techniques for Searching, Parsing, and Matching*, https://doi.org/10.1007/978-3-030-63189-5_6

T:

left \ right	a	$+$	$\times$	$\uparrow$	$\$$
a		$>$	$>$	$>$	$>$
$+$	$<$	$>$	$<$	$<$	$>$
$\times$	$<$	$>$	$>$	$<$	$>$
$\uparrow$	$<$	$>$	$>$	$<$	$>$
$\$$	$<$	$<$	$<$	$<$	

This table T can be generated from the given grammar G' as we will indicate below. We have that: (i) the rows and the columns of that table are labeled by the terminal symbols of the grammar G', (ii) the symbols $<$ and $>$ denote the precedence relation between operators, and (iii) the fact that, for instance, $\times$ as a higher precedence with respect to $+$, is denoted in the table T by the two entries: $+ < \times$ and $\times > +$, as indicated by the subtable:

	$\cdots$	$+$	$\times$	$\cdots$
$\cdots$				
$+$			$<$	
$\times$		$>$		
$\cdots$				

Now we will see how the table T is used for parsing a given word w of the language generated by G'.

Let us consider, for instance, the word $w = a + a \times a$. We add two extra $\$$ symbols as a first and last character of w and we get $\$\, a + a \times a\, \$$. Then we add the symbol $<$ or the symbol $>$ between any two symbols of $\$\, w\, \$$ according to the table T.

We get: $\$ < a > + < a > \times < a > \$$ (for instance, we have: $\$ < a$ because in the table T at row $\$$ and column a we have the symbol $<$, and we have: $+ < a$ because in the table T at row $+$ and column a we have the symbol $<$).

Then the parsing process can be described as a left-to-right move from the leftmost $\$$ until a symbol $>$ is found, followed by a right-to-left move until a symbol $<$ is found. Then the string between the symbols $<$ and $>$ (and including them) is reduced according to the grammar at hand and we erase also the symbols $<$ and $>$.

Then we proceed by a new left-to-right move until a symbol $>$ is found, followed by a new right-to-left move until a symbol $<$ is found. Again the string between the symbols $<$ and $>$ is reduced. We continue with these left-to-right and right-to-left moves and reductions, until all $<$'s and $>$'s have been erased.

At that point the first phase of the parsing process terminates. In the case of our grammar G', we get from $\$\, w\, \$ = \$\, a + a \times a\, \$$ the following sequence of sentential forms:

1. $\$ < a > + < a > \times < a > \$$
2. reducing $< a >$: $\$E + < a > \times < a > \$$
3. reducing $< a >$: $\$E + E \times < a > \$$
4. reducing $< a >$: $\$E + E \times E \$$

Then a second phase of the parsing process begins. We forget about the derived nonterminal symbols, E in our case, and we use again the table T to insert $<$'s and $>$'s in the sentential form at hand. In our case by forgetting E, we get: $\$ + \times \$$, and after the insertion of the $<$'s and $>$'s we get: $\$ < + < \times > \$$.

Now we proceed as in the first phase of the parsing process and we perform a left-to-right move from the leftmost $\$$ until a symbol $>$ is found, followed by a right-to-left move until a symbol $<$ is found. Then we reduce that part of the sentential form which is identified by the substring between the two symbols $<$ and $>$ which have been found.

We repeat this process again by forgetting nonterminals, adding $<$'s and $>$'s, performing moves, and reducing substrings until we are left only with the string $\$\,\$$. In our case we get:

5. $\$ < + < \times > \$$
6. reducing $< \times >$: $\$ < +E\ \$$
7. forgetting E : $\$ < + \$$
8. adding $>$: $\$ < + > \$$
9. reducing $<+>$: $\$\,E\ \$$
10. forgetting E : $\$\,\$$

By recalling the sequence of reductions we can reconstruct the parse tree of the given word w. In our case we get the following parse tree:

Parse tree for

$a + a \times a$

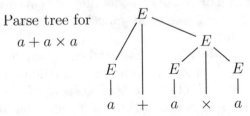

Now we present some heuristics for filling the table T. More can be found in [2, Chapter 4]. Empty entries in the table T denote errors and, during the parsing process, on those entries we have to invoke suitable *error recovery* routines.

(1) If an operator $\times$ has higher priority than an operator $+$, we have the following subtable:

	$+$	$\times$
$+$		$<$
$\times$	$>$	

(2) If an operator $+$ has the same priority as an operator $-$, we have the following subtable:

	+	−
+		>
−		>

This table enforces a *left associative parsing*, that is, for instance, $a - a + a$ is parsed as $(a - a) + a$.

(3) If we want an operator to be right associative (such as, for instance, the exponentiation operator, denoted ↑), we have the following subtable:

	↑
↑	<

The reader may easily verify that, indeed, this subtable enforces a *right associative parsing*, that is, for instance, $a \uparrow a \uparrow a$ is parsed as $a \uparrow (a \uparrow a)$. Analogously, we use > if we want an operator to be *left associative*.

By using the table T we get the following two parse trees for the words $a + a + a$ and $a \uparrow a \uparrow a$, respectively.

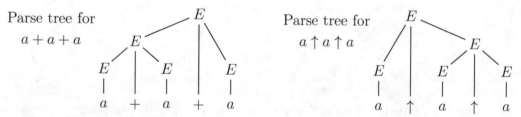

Parse tree for $a + a + a$

Parse tree for $a \uparrow a \uparrow a$

Instead of using the parsing table T which takes quadratic space with respect to the number of operators in the grammar, we may sometimes use two functions which we call the *left function*, denoted ℓ, and the *right function*, denoted r. To store those functions it takes linear space only.

In the rest of this section, by abuse of language when we say 'operator' we mean any element of the set $Op \cup \{\$, a\}$ which labels a row or a column of the table T.

The left function and the right function are used, instead of the parsing table T, as follows. For instance, given two operators α and β, in order to know whether $\alpha < \beta$ or $\alpha > \beta$, we compare the values of $\ell(\alpha)$ and $r(\beta)$, and

(i) if $\ell(\alpha) < r(\beta)$, then we have $\alpha < \beta$,   and

(ii) if $\ell(\alpha) > r(\beta)$, then we have $\alpha > \beta$.

Now we illustrate how to derive the left function and the right function, if they exist, from a parsing table T [**2**, page 209] in the case when between two operators there may be only either the precedence relation < or the precedence relation >. The interested reader may look at [**2**, Chapter 4] to see how to deal with the case in which extra relations, besides < and >, exist between two operators of operator-precedence grammars.

The derivation of the left function and the right function is based on a graph which is constructed as follows.

For each operator α of the grammar we introduce two nodes: ℓ_α and r_α. For each pair of operators α and β, if $\alpha > \beta$, then we draw an edge from ℓ_α to r_β, and if $\alpha < \beta$, then we draw an edge from r_β to ℓ_α.

If the graph we have constructed has a cycle than the *left function* and the *right function* do not exist. If the graph has no cycle, then for each operator α, $\ell(\alpha)$ is the length of the longest path in the graph starting from ℓ_α, and $r(\alpha)$ is the length of the longest path in the graph starting from r_α.

For instance, in the case of the given expression grammar with operators $+, \times, \uparrow, \$$, and a, we get the following graph:

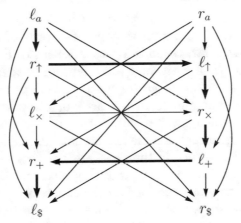

In this drawing of the graph for each operator α, the position of the node ℓ_α and the position of the node r_α has been chosen for minimizing the number of the edge crossings. As the reader may verify, in our case we get the following values for the left function and the right function:

	a	$+$	$\times$	$\uparrow$	$\$$
left function ℓ:	6	2	4	4	0
right function r:	5	1	3	5	0

For instance, the entry 6 for $\ell(a)$ is due to the path (in bold in the graph above):

$$\ell_a \to r_\uparrow \to \ell_\uparrow \to r_\times \to \ell_+ \to r_+ \to \ell_\$$$

which is the longest path in the graph starting from ℓ_a and it has, indeed, 6 edges. In case when we have also the binary operators $-$ (minus) and $/$ (divide), and the round brackets, as usual for arithmetic expressions, we get the following values for the left function and the right function [2, page 209]:

	a	$+$	$-$	$\times$	$/$	$\uparrow$	$($	$)$	$\$$
left function ℓ:	6	2	2	4	4	4	0	6	0
right function r:	5	1	1	3	3	5	5	0	0

As already mentioned, more information on the operator-precedence grammars and their parsing procedures can be found in [2, Chapter 4].

6.2. Use of Parser Generators

In this section we illustrate the use of the parser generator Bison [7] and also the use of the lexical analyzer generator Flex [18]. More information on these tools can be found in http://dinosaur.compilertools.net/. We will end this section by providing some suggestions for constructing parsers in practical cases.

All programs of this section have been executed using: (i) the Bison version 2.3 (GNU), (ii) the Flex version 2.5.35 Apple(flex-32), and (iii) the C++ compiler Apple clang version 11.0.3, under the operating system Mac OS X Catalina 10.15.4.

6.2.1. Generation of Parsers Using Bison.

Bison is a *parser generator*, that is, a program which given a description of a grammar, produces a C or a C++ program that parses words of the language generated by that grammar. In particular, Bison is a parser generator for $LALR(1)$ context-free grammars and it is compatible with Yacc (acronym for 'Yet Another Compiler Compiler') [11], a well-known parser generator for $LALR(1)$ grammars, to which people usually refer when mentioning work in the area of *compiler-compilers*. Compiler-compilers are programs which given a description of the syntax of a programming language, automatically generate compilers for that language.

Bison is compatible with Yacc in the sense that almost all grammar descriptions which can be given in input to Yacc for producing a correct parser, can also be given in input to Bison which will also produce a correct parser.

For reasons of simplicity, we will not discuss here the behaviour of Bison when: (i) the given grammar is *not* an $LALR(1)$ grammar, or (ii) the given grammar is an *ambiguous* grammar, or (iii) the word to be parsed *does not* belong to the language generated by the given grammar. For these issues the interested reader may refer to [7] for the case of Bison, and to [2, page 261–266] for the case of Yacc.

Let us see how to use the parser generator Bison by presenting a few examples.

EXAMPLE 6.2.1.

Generating a parser for a simple $LALR(1)$ language.

Let us consider the following grammar G whose axiom is S and whose productions are:

$$1.\ S \to C\,C \qquad 2.\ C \to c\,C \qquad 3.\ C \to d$$

In order to get a parser for the language $L(G)$ generated for this grammar by Bison, we have first to prepare a file whose extension is '.y'. Let that file be called grammar.y. It should be structured in three parts separated by %% as follows:

```
declarations
%%
productions and semantic actions
%%
lexical analyzer and auxiliary C or C++ functions
```

For instance, in the case of our grammar G, we prepare the following file.

```
/**
 * ==========================================================================
 *                    Use of Bison: an LALR(1) grammar
 * Filename: "grammar.y"
 *
 *                     S ->  C  C '\n'
 *                     C ->  'c' C  |  'd'
 *
 * S is the axiom. 'c' and 'd' are the characters c and d, respectively.
 * '\n' is the carriage-return character. '\t' is the tab character.
 * ==========================================================================
 */
%{
  #include <stdio.h>     /* needed for using printf                       */
%}
%% /* Grammar and Semantic Actions.
    * The semantic value is the number of characters.                     */
S:          C  C  '\n'   { printf ("--> result: %d\n", $1 + $2); }
;
C:          'c'  C       { $$ = 1 + $2; }
      | 'd'              { $$ = 1;       }
;
%%
/* --- Lexical Analyzer ---- */
/* The lexical analyzer returns the numeric code of the character read.
 * It skips all blanks and tabs.                                          */
int yylex (void) {
  int k;
  /* Skip blanks and tabs.  */
  while ((k = getchar ()) == ' ' || k == '\t') ;
  /* Return the numeric code k of a char read.  */
  return k;
}
/* --------------------------------------------------------------------
 * input:      output:
 * --------------------------------------------------------------------
 * $ bison grammar.y
 * $ cc grammar.tab.c -ly -o grammar
 * $ ./grammar
 * ccd cccd
 *              --> result: 7
 * $ ./grammar
 * cdcdd
 *              syntax error
 * -------------------------------------------------------------- */
```

In the first part of the file grammar.y, that is, the declarations part, besides
some comments, we have only the command '#include <stdio.h>'. That command is required for using the printing function printf (see the second part of the
file grammar.y).

In the second part we write the productions of the grammar. The nonterminal of
the left hand side of the first production is assumed to be the axiom of the grammar.
Each production is associated with a C++ command (or, in general, a sequence of
C++ commands) which specifies the so-called *semantic actions*. In our case, we have
chosen that the semantic actions compute the number of c's and d's which occur in
the given string to parse.

Due to the presence of semantic actions, Bison produces, from a given grammar, 'more' than a simple parser. Indeed, it produces a *translator* which, when given in input a word of the language generated by the given grammar, constructs an output value (as it is done by the so-called *attribute grammars* [13]). In the specifications of the semantic actions: (i) the identifier $$ denotes the value associated with the nonterminal in the left hand side of a production, and (ii) $n denotes the value associated with the nonterminal occurring on the n-th position on the right hand side of the production.

For instance, for the production $C \rightarrow cC$ (which is written as C: 'c' C), the associated semantic action '$$ = 1 + $2' computes for the nonterminal C on the left hand side a value which is one unit more than the value computed for the nonterminal C on the right hand side (which occurs in the second position, being the first position that of the character 'c'). Indeed, since we want to count the number of the c's and d's in the string to parse, when we encounter a 'c', we have to add 1 to that number.

In the third part of the file grammar.y we write the *lexical analyzer*, called yylex(), that is, a piece of code for passing to the parser a terminal at a time. In our case a terminal is any character, excluding blank and tab (see the code of yylex()).

The functions printf and getchar are used in the second part and the third part of the file grammar.y.

The function int printf(const char * format, x) prints its second argument x as indicated by the string format specified in its first argument. In particular,
(i.1) if format is "%d\n", then x is printed as a decimal integer,
(i.2) if format is "%g\n", then x is printed as the shorter between a decimal floating point value or as a mantissa-exponent value, and
(i.3) if format is "%s\n", then x is printed as a string of characters.

The newline character \n has the effect that, after printing x the next printing action will take place on the next line.

The function int getchar(void) returns the next character from the standard input as an integer value of type int.

Having prepared the file grammar.y, if we issue the following three commands (where $ denotes the system prompt):

```
$ bison grammar.y
$ cc grammar.tab.c -ly -o grammar
$ ./grammar
```

and we give in input a word $w \in L(G)$, then we will get in output the value specified by the semantic actions. The option '-ly' in the second command invokes suitable library routines for the C++ compiler. In our case, if we input the word w is 'ccd cccd', then we get the number of characters different from blank and tab which are present in 'ccd cccd', that is, 7. In particular, as indicated in the comment lines at the end of the file grammar.y, we get:

```
ccd cccd              (typed in input)
--> result: 7         (printed in output)
```

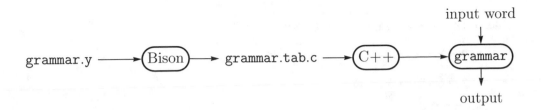

FIGURE 6.2.1. Generation of a parser using Bison for the grammar description in the file grammar.y. The suffixes '.y' and '.tab.c' cannot be modified. If the input word is: ccd cccd, then the output is: --> result: 7.

In Figure 6.2.1 we have depicted the process of generating a parser using Bison as we have indicated above.

REMARK 6.2.2. When invoking Bison, if we add the option '-v', that is, we type the command 'bison -v grammar.y', instead of 'bison grammar.y', we will also get in output a file named grammar.output with a description of the finite automaton which directs the $LALR(1)$ parsing. Indeed, for our grammar G above, we get (modulo some syntactic modifications) the following file which: (i) associates the rule numbers 1, 2, and 3 to the three productions $S \to C\,C$, $C \to c\,C$, and $C \to d$, respectively, and (ii) describes the finite automaton represented in Figure 5.5.1 on page 134:

```
Grammar   rule 1     S -> C C '\n'
          rule 2     C -> 'c' C
          rule 3     C -> 'd'
                          ... omissis ...
state 0
    'c'   shift, and go to state 1
    'd'   shift, and go to state 2
    S     go to state 7
    C     go to state 3
state 1
    C  ->  'c' . C   (rule 2)
    'c'   shift, and go to state 1
    'd'   shift, and go to state 2
    C     go to state 4
state 2
    C  ->  'd' .   (rule 3)
    $default reduce using rule 3 (C)
state 3
    S  ->  C . C '\n'   (rule 1)
    'c'   shift, and go to state 1
    'd'   shift, and go to state 2
    C     go to state 5
state 4
    C  ->  'c' C .   (rule 2)
    $default reduce using rule 2 (C)
state 5
    S  ->  C C . '\n'   (rule 1)
    '\n'shift, and go to state 6
```

```
state 6
    S  ->  C C '\n' .    (rule 1)
    $default reduce using rule 1 (S)
state 7
    $    go to state 8
state 8
    $    go to state 9
state 9
    $default accept
```

As the reader may verify, we have that the initial state 0 corresponds to state q_0 of Figure 5.5.1 on page 134 and, similarly, state 1 corresponds to state q_{36}, state 2 corresponds to state q_{47}, state 3 corresponds to state q_2, state 4 corresponds to state q_{89}, state 5 corresponds to state q_5, and state 7 corresponds to state q_1.

In the above file `grammar.output` we have a description of the finite automaton of Figure 5.5.1 on page 134, but there are also the extra states 6, 8, and 9 which do not occur in that figure. The reason for these extra states is as follows:

(i) state 6 is due to the fact that in the actual representation of the grammar G the production $S \to C\,C$ is terminated by the newline character '\n' and so a transition from state 5 to a new state 6 is required, and

(ii) states 8 and 9 are due to the fact that in $LALR(1)$ parsers we actually use augmented grammars with the extra production $S' \to S$, where S' is the new axiom symbol. In our case this extra production requires a transition from state 7 to state 8 and from state 8 to state 9 (for more details on this point the reader may refer to the Bison manual [7]).

REMARK 6.2.3. When invoking Bison, if we add the option '-y', that is, we type the command 'bison -y grammar.y', instead of 'bison grammar.y', then Bison behaves like Yacc in the sense that we will get in output a file named y.tab.c, instead of grammar.tab.c. Then, in our case, after the command 'cc y.tab.c -ly', we will get in output the file named a.out, instead of the file named grammar.

EXAMPLE 6.2.4.

Generating a parser for an expression calculator.

The following example illustrates the use of Bison in the presence of: (i) tokens, (ii) priorities of operators, and (iii) the yyerror routine which deals with the errors which may occur during parsing.

Let us consider the following grammar whose axiom is *line* and whose productions are:

$$
\begin{array}{ll}
line \to & \varepsilon \quad\quad | \; line \; \backslash n \quad\quad | \; line \; expr \; \backslash n \\
expr \to & \text{NUMBER} \; | \; expr + expr \; | \; expr - expr \; | \; expr * expr \; | \; expr / expr \\
& | -expr \; | \; expr \,\hat{}\, expr \; | \; (expr)
\end{array}
$$

where: (i) ε is the empty word, (ii) \n is the newline character, (iii) $+$, $-$, $\times$, $/$, $*$, and $\hat{}$ denote addition, subtraction, multiplication, division, and exponentiation, respectively, and (iv) NUMBER is a token string and it will be introduced below. We

have to construct the following file, named `calculator.y`, to be given in input to
Bison.

```
/**
 * ======================================================================
 *                    Use of Bison: an expression calculator
 * Filename: "calculator.y"
 *
 * ======================================================================
 */

%{
  #define YYSTYPE double /* YYSTYPE is the type of yylval          */
  #include <stdio.h>      /* needed for using printf               */
  #include <ctype.h>      /* needed for NUMBER                     */
  #include <math.h>       /* needed for using pow (exponential)    */
%}

/* Precedence of operators is determined by the sequence of lines.
 * For instance, * ties more than +, and ^ ties more than UMINUS.   */

%token NUMBER

/*                                                PRECEDENCE        */
%left '+' '-' /* left  associative: 2-1-1 = (2-1)-1     weakest     */
%left '*' '/' /* left  associative                       |          */
%left UMINUS  /* left  associative                       |          */
%right '^'    /* right associative: 2^3^2 = 2^(3^2)     strongest   */

%%
/* Grammar for input to calculator and Semantic Actions.           */

line:             // empty production //
        | line '\n'
        | line expr '\n'     { printf ("--> result: %.10g\n", $2);}
//      | error '\n'         { yyerror(": bad input line!\n"); } // <-- ERR
/*  uncomment this line ERR if parsing should continue upon error     */
        ;
expr:   NUMBER                  { $$ = $1;            } // default action //
        | expr '+' expr         { $$ = $1 + $3;    }
        | expr '-' expr         { $$ = $1 - $3;    }
        | expr '*' expr         { $$ = $1 * $3;    }
        | expr '/' expr         { $$ = $1 / $3;    }
        | '-' expr %prec UMINUS { $$ = - $2;       } // unary minus    //
        | expr '^' expr         { $$ = pow($1,$3); } // exponentiation //
        | '(' expr ')'          { $$ = $2;         }
        ;
%%

/* ----- Lexical Analyzer ------ */
/* The lexical analyzer returns a double floating point number
 * on the stack and the token NUMBER, or the numeric code of
 * the character read, if not a number. It skips all blanks and tabs.   */

int yylex (void) {
  int k;
  /* Skip blanks and tabs.  */
  while ((k = getchar ()) == ' ' || k == '\t') ;
```

```
   /* Process numbers.        */
   if (k == '.' || isdigit (k))
     { ungetc (k, stdin);
       scanf ("%lf", &yylval);   /* value of token */
       return NUMBER;            /* type  of token */
     }
   /* Return the numeric code k of a char read.   */
   return k;
}

/* Function needed if line ERR above is uncommented */
/* Called by yyparse on error.                      */
int yyerror (char const *s) {
  printf ("%s", s);
}

/* -------------------------------------------------------------------
 * input:       output:
 * -------------------------------------------------------------------
 * $ bison calculator.y
 * $ cc calculator.tab.c -ly -o calculator
 * $ ./calculator
 * 3.2^2.3
 *             --> result: 14.51593284
 * b
 *             syntax error: bad input line! // if line ERR is uncommented
 * 3+2
 *             --> result: 5
 * ------------------------------------------------------------------- */
```

In the first part of the file `calculator.y` we have, together with the command '#include <stdio>.h' which is needed for using the function `printf`, also the commands:

(i) '#include <ctype>.h' which is needed for using token strings which are of the form NUMBER, and

(ii) '#include <math>.h' which is needed for using the function `pow` which performs the exponentiation.

All these commands are included between the delimiters %{ and %}. Between these delimiters we also have the command '#define YYSTYPE double' which specifies the type of the variable `yylval` which is used by Bison for returning the value of a token (see below). Outside the delimiters %{ and %} in the first part of the file `calculator.y` there are also:

(i) the token declarations, and

(ii) the declarations of precedence between operators.

In our case we have the declaration of the token NUMBER. As specified by the third part of the file `calculator.y`, a token NUMBER is generated by the lexical analyzer `yylex()` from a sequence of non-blank and non-tab characters read from the standard input, by using the functions `ungetc` and `scanf` which we will present below.

A token NUMBER is a string generated by the following grammar (which is equivalent to a regular grammar):

$$\text{NUMBER} \rightarrow digit^+ \mid digit^* \,.\, digit^+ \mid digit^+ \,.\, digit^*$$
$$digit \quad \rightarrow 0 \mid \dots \mid 9$$

(Note that in view of Fact 5.8.15 on page 155 we have allowed ourselves to use regular expressions in the right hand sides of the productions.)

In general, the lexical analyzer returns: (i) a *value* which is stored in the variable `yylval`, and (ii) a *type* of that value which is the name of the token. In our case the type is `NUMBER` and it corresponds to a `double` number in C++, that is, a double-precision floating point number as specified by the command '#define YYSTYPE double' in the first part of the file `calculator.y`.

Tokens are generated by the lexical analyzer `yylex()` by calling the function `scanf`. However, before calling `scanf` the lexical analyzer calls the function `ungetc` for taking into account the last character read by the function `getchar` which was required for skipping blanks and tabs.

The function `int ungetc(int character, FILE * stream)` puts back the first argument `character` into the second argument `stream`, and it puts it back into the same position where the last character was read from the `stream`. When the next reading operation from the `stream` is performed, one gets that `character` again. Note, however, that the physical content of the `stream` is *not* modified by the execution of the function `ungetc`: only the next reading operation is affected.

The function `int scanf(const char * format, &x)` reads a sequence of characters from the standard input. That sequence has to be understood as a value according to the first argument `format`. Then that value is stored in the location x. For instance, given in input `28.7` and having defined `yylval` as a double-precision floating point number by the command '#define YYSTYPE double', the function call `scanf("%lf", &yylval)` assigns to the variable `yylval` a number which will be printed as `28.700000` when using the command `printf("%lf",yylval)` (`lf` stands for *long float*).

Analogously, given in input the string `abca`, `scanf("%s", str)` generates a string `str` whose value is `abca`.

Ambiguity of the grammar is resolved by adding priorities to the operators. These priorities are specified in the first part of the file `calculator.y` after the part between the delimiters `%{` and `%}`. In particular, we write the command `%left op1` for specifying that the operator `op1` is left associative, and we write the command `%right op2` for specifying that the operator `op2` is right associative.

The precedence between operators is established by their relative order in the list of commands which specifies the associativity of the operators: the operator with the weakest precedence is listed first, and the operator with strongest precedence is listed last. The unary minus '-' is denoted by the identifier `UMINUS` and its precedence is indicated by the position of `UMINUS` in the list of precedences. In our case unary minus ties more than the binary minus, also denoted as '-'. For instance, the value of `-6-4` is `-10` (not `-2`), because it is equal to `(-6)-4`.

In the third part of the file `calculator.y` we write the function `yyerror`. This function is invoked when a parsing error occurs. In our case, when a parsing error occurs, the parser skips symbols until the next '\n' (the newline character) is encountered and then, after printing an error message as specified by the semantic action, if any, the parser continues as no error had occurred. In our case, we can type a new input line with a new expression to be evaluated.

At the end of the file `calculator.y` we have listed, as lines of comments, some examples of execution of the executable file named `calculator`. For the input `3.2^2.3` we get in output: `--> result: 14.51593284`, and for the input `b` we get in output: `syntax error: bad input line!`

EXAMPLE 6.2.5.

Generating a parser for a simple assignment language.

This example illustrates: (i) the use of Flex [18] as a generator of lexical analyzers which can be used in conjunction with Bison, and (ii) the use of a symbol table during parsing.

The lexical analyzer, also called a *scanner*, or a *tokenizer*, produced by Flex passes to Bison a token at a time, so that Bison can perform the successive parsing phase according to a given $LALR(1)$ grammar. Flex is a lexical analyzer generator similar to Lex [15].

In order to produce a lexical analyzer we have first to prepare for Flex a file whose extension is '.lex'. As in the case of Bison, that file is structured in three parts separated by %%. In the first part there are declarations, in the second part there are productions and semantic actions, and in the third part there are auxiliary functions. Each production takes the form of a regular expression.

Flex generates as output a C++ program named `lex.yy.c`, which defines a function `yylex()`. Once the program `lex.yy.c` is compiled, if from the standard input (or a given input file) `yylex()` recognizes a word which belongs to the language denoted by a regular expression of the list of productions, then `yylex()` executes the corresponding semantic actions.

If we use Flex in conjunction with Bison, the corresponding semantic action returns a *value* for the variable `yylval` and a *type* identifying the token which has been recognized (in our example either the token `VARIABLE` or the token `NUMBER`).

The grammar we will consider in this example is a grammar which defines a simple programming language of assignments.

$$line \to \varepsilon \mid line\ expr\ \backslash n \mid line\ \mathtt{VARIABLE} := expr\ \backslash n$$
$$expr \to \mathtt{NUMBER} \mid \mathtt{VARIABLE} \mid expr + expr \mid expr - expr \mid expr * expr \mid expr / expr$$
$$\mid - expr \mid expr\ \hat{}\ expr \mid (expr)$$

where: (i) ε is the empty word, (ii) \n is the newline character, (iii) $+$, $-$, $\times$, $/$, $*$, and $\hat{}$ denote addition, subtraction, multiplication, division, and exponentiation, respectively, (iv) `NUMBER` is a double-precision floating point number, and (v) `VARIABLE` is a single character variable identifier in the set $\{\mathtt{a}, \ldots, \mathtt{z}\}$.

There are three files to be prepared:
(1) one for Bison, which we name `fSAL.y` (the extension `.y` is mandatory),

(2) one for Flex, which we name `fSAL.lex` (the extension `.lex` is mandatory), and
(3) one for operating on the symbol table storing the values of the variables. We
name this file `fSAL.h` (the extension `.h` is mandatory).

In Figure 6.2.2 on page 179 we have depicted the process of generating a parser
using Bison in conjunction with the lexical analyzer generator Flex.

Let us first consider the file `fSAL.y` which we now list.

```
/**
 * =======================================================================
 *            Use of Bison: a simple assignment language SAL  (1)
 * Filename: "fSAL.y"
 *
 * Parser with Lexical Analyzer. Running Flex and then Bison.
 * This file uses the file: "fSAL.lex"
 *
 * Note: variables have names made out of one character only.
 * =======================================================================
 */
%{
#include <stdio.h>
#include <math.h> /* needed for using pow (exponential)            */
#include "fSAL.h" /* needed for using putVar, getVar, and printTable  */

/* see file "fSAL.lex":
 * structure for information on VARIABLE's and NUMBER's             */

struct tokenInfo
{ char *name;   /* the name of a NUMBER is assumed to be NULL         */
  double value; /* the initial value of a VARIABLE is assumed to be 0 */
};
%}

%union { struct tokenInfo ti; }    // type of yylval
%token <ti> VARIABLE               // VARIABLE is a token of type ti
%token <ti> NUMBER                 // NUMBER is a token of type ti
%type  <ti> expr                   // expr has type ti

%token ASSIGN_SYMB PLUS MINUS MULTIPLY DIVIDE POWER OPEN CLOSED NEWLINE

%left  PLUS MINUS       /* left  associative */
%left  MULTIPLY DIVIDE  /* left  associative */
%left  UMINUS           /* left  associative */
%right POWER            /* right associative */

%%
line:   // empty production //
      | line expr NEWLINE
                { printf("--> result: %.10g\n", $2.value); }
      | line VARIABLE ASSIGN_SYMB expr NEWLINE
                { putVar($2.name, $4.value); }
//    | error NEWLINE {yyerror(": bad input line!\n");}        // <-- ERR
/* uncomment this line ERR if parsing should continue upon error.     */
      ;
expr:   NUMBER   { $$ = $1; }
      | VARIABLE { if (getVar($1.name) != NULL) {
                  $$.value = (getVar($1.name))->value; }
                }
```

```
         | expr PLUS expr           { $$.value = $1.value + $3.value;    }
         | expr MINUS expr          { $$.value = $1.value - $3.value;    }
         | expr MULTIPLY expr       { $$.value = $1.value * $3.value;    }
         | expr DIVIDE expr         { $$.value = $1.value / $3.value;    }
         | MINUS expr %prec UMINUS  { $$.value = - $2.value;             }
         | expr POWER expr          { $$.value = pow($1.value,$3.value); }
         | OPEN expr CLOSED         { $$.value = $2.value;               }
         ;
%%
#include "lex.yy.c"
/* Function needed if the above line ERR is uncommented  */
int yyerror (char const *s) {
  printf ("%s", s);
}
/* --------------------------------------------------------------------
 * Execution tests with the line "ERR" (in this file "fSAL.y") and the two
 * lines "SYMB_TABLE" (in the file "fSAL.h") uncommented: we notify errors
 * and we print the Symbol Table after inserting new values for the
 * variables.
 * input:      output:
 * --------------------------------------------------------------------
 * $ flex   fSAL.lex
 * $ bison fSAL.y   (or: bison -v fSAL.y)
 * $ cc fSAL.tab.c -ly -o fSAL
 * $ ./fSAL
 * b := 3
 *             Symbol Table after putVar: (b,3) nil
 * a := 2
 *             Symbol Table after putVar: (b,3) (a,2) nil
 * c:=2+a
 *             Symbol Table after putVar: (b,3) (a,2) (c,4) nil
 * a:=1
 *             Symbol Table after putVar: (b,3) (a,1) (c,4) nil
 * a+b^(-2+c)
 *             --> result: 10                           // 1+3^2 = 10
 * b3
 *             syntax error: bad input line!
 * 2+b
 *             --> result: 5
 * ------------------------------------------------------------------- */
```

The value of the variable yylval is *not* a double-precision floating point number as in the previous Example 6.2.1 on page 168, but it is a pointer to a structure named tokenInfo. That structure has two fields: (i) a *name* and (ii) a *value*.
(i) For a token VARIABLE the structure tokenInfo stores the name of the variable and its value (which is initialized to 0), and
(ii) for a token NUMBER the structure tokenInfo stores the fictitious name NULL and the numeric value of the token NUMBER.

The %union declaration specifies the list of the possible types of the variable yylval. In our case we have one type only: ti which is the type of the structure tokenInfo.

In the first part of the file fSAL.y we also have the list of the tokens which are returned by Flex (see the file fSAL.lex). For instance, OPEN denotes the open parenthesis '('.

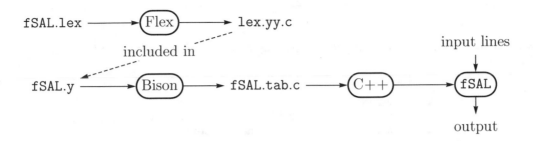

FIGURE 6.2.2. Generation of a parser using Bison, in conjunction with the lexical analyzer generator Flex, for the grammar description in the file `fSAL.y`. The name `lex.yy.c` and the suffixes '.lex', '.y', and '.tab.c' cannot be modified. If the input lines are: `a:=1` and `2+a`, then the output is: `--> result: 3`.

In the second part of the file `fSAL.y` we have the productions and the associated semantic actions. Note that, since the values of the variable `yylval` are instances of the structure `tokenInfo`, we need to refer to the fields `.name` and `.value`. If a line is an expression `expr`, the semantic action prints the value of that expression. If the line is an assignment of the form `a:=expr`, the semantic action initializes a record (or updates the record) for the variable `a` with the value of the expression `expr` using the command '`putVar($2.name, $4.value)`'. If a record for the variable `a` is already present in the symbol table, then the value of the record for `a` is updated with the value of the expression `expr`.

If the expression is a `VARIABLE` token, say `a`, the semantic action looks in the symbol table for a structure `tokenInfo` whose name field is `a`, if any, and returns the value field of that structure.

In the third part of the file `fSAL.y` we have specified the lexical analyzer. The specification is *not* done via the definition of the function `yylex()`. It is done, instead, via the command '`#include "lex.yy.c"`' which has the effect of including the lexical analyzer `lex.yy.c` generated by Flex.

Here is the file `fSAL.lex`. When it is given in input to Flex, we get in output the file `lex.yy.c` to be included in the file `fSAL.y`.

```
/**
 * ========================================================================
 *              Use of Bison: a simple assignment language SAL      (2)
 * file: "fSAL.lex" (flex_SimpleAssignmentLanguage)
 *
 * This file has to be given in input to Flex which will produce in output
 * the file "lex.yy.c" which contains the code of the lexical analyzer
 * (also called the scanner).
 *
 * The file "lex.yy.c" has to be included in the file "fSAL.y"
 * which is processed by Bison.
 * ------
```

```
 * This version of the lexical analyzer is NOT for STAND ALONE use.
 * ======================================================================
 */
%{
#include <string.h> /* needed for using char *strdup( const char *str ) */
%}

%%
[a-z]    { yylval.ti.value = 0;
                  /* yytext contains the matched character in [a-z]     */
             yylval.ti.name =  (char *) strdup(yytext);
             return VARIABLE;
           }
[0-9]+|[0-9]*\.[0-9]+|[0-9]+\.[0-9]*  {
                  /* yytext contains the matched number              */
             yylval.ti.value = atof(yytext);      /* from string to double */
             yylval.ti.name = NULL;
             return NUMBER;
            }
:=       return ASSIGN_SYMB;
\+       return PLUS;
\-       return MINUS;
\*       return MULTIPLY;
\/       return DIVIDE;
\^       return POWER;
\(       return OPEN;
\)       return CLOSED;
\n       return NEWLINE;
[ \t]    ;         /* nothing to return in case of blank or tab         */
                   /* . (dot) matches any input character except \n     */
  .      printf("Invalid character.\n");

%%
int yywrap() {          // Flex terminates after processing the input file
 return 1;
}
/* ------------------------------------------------------------------------
 * input:       output:
 * ------------------------------------------------------------------------
 * $ flex fSAL.lex
 * $ bison fSAL.y   (or: bison -v fSAL.y)
 * $ cc fSAL.tab.c -ly -o fSAL
 * $ ./fSAL
 * 3+2
 *             --> result: 5
 * ------------------------------------------------------------------------ */
```

As in the case of the file with extension '.y' to be given in input to Bison, the file
fSAL.lex is structured in three parts separated by %%. As already mentioned,
(i) in the first part there are declarations,
(ii) in second part there is a list of regular expressions and semantic actions which
are self-explanatory, and
(iii) in the third part of the file fSAL.lex there is the function yywrap which is
required for making Flex to terminate when the input file has been processed.

Let us note only the following few points concerning the file fSAL.lex.

(i) When a character of the set $\{a,\ldots,z\}$ is found, it is recognized as the name of a variable. A `tokenInfo` structure is constructed with name field which is the character found (stored in the variable `yytext`) and a value field initialized to 0. Then a token `VARIABLE` is returned.

(ii) When a string in the language denoted by the regular expression

$$digit^+ + digit^* . \, digit^+ + digit^+ . \, digit^*$$

is recognized as double-precision floating point number, a `tokenInfo` structure is constructed with the fictitious name field `NULL` and and a value field initialized to the value produced by `atof(yytext)`.

The function `double atof(const char * str)`, given a string of characters, produces the corresponding floating point value. For instance, `double w = atof("43.3")` produces a double-precision floating point number `w` whose value will be printed, by using `printf("%f",w)`, as `43.3`.

Then a token `NUMBER` is returned.

(iii) `\+` denotes the symbol '+'.

(iv) `[ \t]` denotes a regular expression which matches either the blank symbol ' ' (note the blank symbol between '[' and '\t') or the tab symbol '\t'.

(v) The dot '.' denotes a regular expression which matches any symbol except the newline symbol '\n'.

Now we present the file `fSAL.h` which is required for manipulating the symbol table which contains a record for each variable.

```
/**
 * ============================================================================
 *                Use of Bison: a simple assignment language SAL    (3)
 * Filename: "fSAL.h"
 * This file is required by "fSAL.y" (which is input to Bison)
 * It contains the code for the Symbol Table for variables
 * with the auxiliary functions: printTable, getVar, and putVar.
 * ============================================================================
 */
#include <stdlib.h>
#include <string.h>   /* for using strlen, strcpy, and strcmp           */

/* ----------------------------------------------------------------------
 *    varRec: a record for a variable in the Symbol Table              */

struct varRec   /* this structure is a record for a variable           */
{ char   *name; /* the name  of the variable                           */
  double value; /* the value of the variable is a double               */
  struct varRec *next;
             /* a pointer to the next record of the Symbol Table        */
};
typedef struct varRec varRecType;

/* ----------------------------------------------------------------------
 *    varTable and lastRec are global variables initialized to NULL.
 *    varTable points to the first varRec of the Symbol Table.
 *    lastRec  points to the last varRec of the Symbol Table.           */
varRecType *varTable = NULL;
varRecType *lastRec  = NULL;
```

```
/*
 *  varTable                                        lastRec
 *     |                                               |
 *     |      +------+-------+-------+          +--->+------+-------+------+
 *     +--->| name | value | next--|---->...----->| name | value | NULL |
 *            +------+-------+-------+                +------+-------+------+
 *
 * -------------------------------------------------------------------- */
/* printTable prints the Symbol Table.                                   */
void printTable(varRecType *T) {
    if (T==NULL) {printf(" nil");}
    else {printf(" (%s",T->name); printf(",%g",T->value); printf(")");
          printTable(T->next);}; 
};
/* -------------------------------------------------------------------- */
/* getVar returns a pointer to the record of the argument variable name. */

varRecType *getVar(char *varName) {
  varRecType *ptr=NULL;

  for (ptr = varTable; ptr != NULL; ptr = (varRecType *) ptr->next) {
     // strcmp(s1,s2) returns 0 iff the string s1 is equal to the string s2
     if (strcmp(ptr->name, varName) == 0)
   return ptr;
   }
   return NULL;
};
/* -------------------------------------------------------------------- */
/* Given a variable name and a value, putVar updates the value in the
 * record of that variable in the Symbol Table. If there is no record
 * for that variable in the Symbol Table, putVar initializes a new
 * record for that variable using the given value.
 * -------------------------------------------------------------------- */
varRecType *putVar( char *varName, double varValue ) {
  varRecType *ptr = getVar(varName);

  if ( ptr == NULL ) {
    ptr = (varRecType *) malloc (sizeof(varRecType));

    if (varTable == NULL) { //If varTable == NULL the Symbol Table is empty
      varTable = ptr;
      lastRec = ptr;
    } else lastRec->next = ptr; // new record at the end of the list.

    ptr->name = (char *) malloc(strlen(varName) + 1);
    strcpy(ptr->name, varName);
    ptr->value = varValue;
    ptr->next = (varRecType *) NULL;
    lastRec = ptr;
  } else { ptr->value = varValue;
  }
// printf("Symbol Table after putVar:");     // <-- SYMB_TABLE
// printTable(varTable); printf("\n");        // <-- SYMB_TABLE
  return ptr;
};
/* -------------------------------------------------------------------- */
```

The symbol table is a list of structures each of which, called `varRec`, contains the information relative to a variable.

A structure `varRec` has three fields:

(i)   a field `name` for the name of the variable,
(ii) a field `value` for the numeric value of the variable, and
(iii) a field `next` which has a pointer to the next structure in the list.

The pointer to the first structure of the list is `varTable` and the pointer to the last structure in the list is `lastRec`. Both are initialized to `NULL`. The field `next` of the record pointed by `lastRec` is always `NULL`.

6.2.2. Generation of Lexical Analyzers Using Flex.

In this section we see how Flex can be used for generating a lexical analyzer in a stand-alone mode, that is, without necessarily providing an input to Bison for generating a parser. We will see this use of Flex through an example. Let us assume that we want to construct a lexical analyzer for a simple assignment language similar to that of Example 6.2.5 on page 176.

The tokens to be recognized are:

(i)   single character variable names in the set $\{a, \ldots, z\}$
(ii)   integer numbers as a sequence of 1 or more digits in the set $\{0, \ldots, 9\}$
(iii) `:=`
(iv)   `+`
(v)   `*`
(vi)   `\n` (newline)
(vii) ` ` (blank)
(viii) `\t` (tab).

When tokens are recognized they will not be returned to Bison as in Example 6.2.5 on page 176, but they will be printed out by a `printf(...)` command.

Below we present a file, called `faSAL.lex`, which can be given in input to Flex for producing of the desired lexical analyzer. This file is structured in three parts separated by `%%` as follows:

```
declarations
%%
productions and semantic actions
%%
auxiliary C or C++ functions and main program
/**
 * =======================================================================
 *                    SIMPLE ASSIGNMENT LANGUAGE
 * Filename: "faSAL.lex"  (faSAL = flex_alone_SimpleAssignmentLanguage)
 *
 * Lexical Analyzer for the input to "fSAL.y" in STAND ALONE mode.
 *
 * ------
 * This version of the lexical analyzer is for STAND ALONE use.
 * =======================================================================
 */
```

```
%{
#include <stdlib.h>
#include <stdio.h>
#include <string.h>       // needed for using char *strdup( const char *str )

struct tokenInfo
{ char *name;
  int value;
};

struct tokenInfo  yylval;
%}

%%
[a-z]    { yylval.value = 0;
                    /* yytext contains the matched character in [a-z]     */
           yylval.name =  (char *) strdup(yytext);
           printf("VARIABLE: %s\n", yylval.name);
         }
[0-9]+   {          /* yytext contains the matched number in [0-9]+       */
           yylval.value = atoi(yytext);                /* from string to int */
           yylval.name = NULL;
           printf("INTEGER: %d\n", yylval.value);
         }
:=       printf("ASSIGN_SYMB\n");
\+       printf("PLUS\n");
\*       printf("MULTIPLY\n");
\n       printf("NEWLINE\n");
[ \t]    ;          /* nothing to return in case of blank and tab         */
                    /* . (dot) matches any input character except \n      */
.        printf("Invalid character.\n");
%%
int yywrap() {           // Flex terminates after processing the input file
 return 1;
}
int main() {
  yylex();
}
/* -----------------------------------------------------------------------
 * Compiling and executing in STAND ALONE mode.
 * input:        output:
 * -----------------------------------------------------------------------
 * $ flex faSAL.lex
 * $ cc lex.yy.c -o faSAL
 * $ ./faSAL
 * 3:=8a
 *          // This is not a valid expression, but the scanner works
 *          // correctly and the tokens are recognized in a correct way.
 *               INTEGER: 3
 *               ASSIGN_SYMB
 *               INTEGER: 8
 *               VARIABLE: a
 *               NEWLINE
 * ----------------------------------------------------------------------- */
```

In Figure 6.2.3 on the facing page we have represented the process of generating a lexical analyzer using Flex as we have illustrated above.

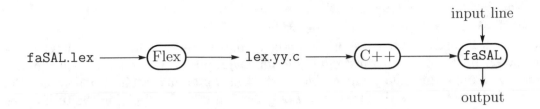

FIGURE 6.2.3. Generation of a *lexical analyzer* using Flex for the grammar description in the file `faSAL.y`. The suffix '.lex' and the name `lex.yy.c` cannot be modified. If the input line is: `3:=`, then the output are the three lines: `INTEGER: 3`, `ASSIGN_SYMB`, and `NEWLINE`.

With respect to the file `fSAL.lex` that we have presented in Example 6.2.5 on page 179, the reader will note in the above file `faSAL.lex`:

(i) the introduction of the definition of the structure `tokenInfo` and

(ii) the declaration of the type '`struct tokenInfo`' of the variable `yytext`. This variable stores the string which matches the pattern of a production during the lexical analysis.

Variables are treated as in Example 6.2.5 on page 176, while numbers are now integer numbers, rather than double-precision floating point numbers. Given a string of characters, the function `int atoi(const char * str)` produces the corresponding integer value. For instance, `int n = atoi("52")` produces the integer number `n` whose value is 52. Note that the lexical analyzer works correctly also for inputs which are not legal expressions of Example 6.2.5. For instance, if we issue the following three commands (where $ denotes the system prompt):

```
$ flex faSAL.lex
$ cc lex.yy.c -o faSAL
$ ./faSAL
```

and then we type in input the string `8c:=\n`, (that is, `8c:=` followed by the newline character), we will get the following output:

```
INTEGER: 8
VARIABLE: c
ASSIGN_SYMB
NEWLINE
```

Finally, in the file `fSAL.lex` we have the main function `main()` which consists only of the function call `yylex()` which performs the lexical analysis.

6.2.3. Suggestions for Constructing Parsers.

We close this section by providing suggestions for constructing parsers in some practical cases.

The first suggestion for constructing parsers is to use a *parser generator*, such as Yacc or Bison [7, 11]. If we decide not to use a parser generator, we have the choice between constructing either (1) a *top-down parser*, or (2) a *bottom-up parser*. This choice depends on the manipulations we have to make after the parse tree has been generated by the parser (see [4, Chapter 9]).

Case (1). If we choose to construct a *top-down* parser, then an $LL(1)$ parser is recommended. In this case we transform the grammar, if possible, into an $LL(1)$ grammar and then we produce the parsing table for the $LL(1)$ grammar we have generated. We may also try to reduce the size of the $LL(1)$ parsing table by applying the techniques indicated in [4, page 662].

Case (2). If we choose to construct a *bottom-up* parser, then an $LALR(1)$ parser is recommended (or an $SLR(1)$ parser, if possible). We can also construct a recursive descent parser (see, for instance, the examples of Sections 7.1 on page 193, 7.2 on page 203, 7.3 on page 214, and 7.4 on page 227).

6.3. Summary on Parsers of Context-Free Languages

In this section we recall a few basic results and ideas on context-free parsing (see also the companion book [21]).

(A) **General Parsers**. We have the following general algorithms for context-free parsing.

- The *Cocke-Younger-Kasami parser*. This algorithm requires the context-free grammar to be given in Chomsky normal form [21]. It has $O(n^3)$ time complexity, where n is the size of the input string to be parsed. It is basically a dynamic programming algorithm that solves a problem of size k by solving p problems of size $k-1$. Actually, one can show that this algorithm has the same complexity of the $n \times n$ matrix multiplication [28].

- The *Earley parser*. It has $O(n^3)$ time complexity, where n is the size of the input string to be parsed [21]. The Earley parser has $O(n^2)$ time complexity if the given context-free grammar is strongly unambiguous (recall that a context-free grammar is said to be *strongly unambiguous* if for every nonterminal symbol A, for every string w of terminal symbols, there exists *at most one* leftmost derivation from A to w). If a language L is a deterministic context-free language (that is, L can be generated by an $LR(1)$ grammar), then there exists a grammar G that generates L for which the Earley parser has $O(n)$ time complexity.

(B) **Chop-and-Expand Parsers**. We have the following algorithms for parsing non-left recursive, context-free grammars.

- The algorithm that uses the *higher order* function *existsev* with the three arguments: p, f, and L (see Section 2.3 on page 24 and Chapter 3 on page 31). This function explores a tree whose root is the node n, looking for a leaf satisfying the predicate p such that every node generates a list of son-nodes using the function f. The initial value of the list L is $[n]$.

    The higher order function *existsev* can be avoided if p and f do not depend on the node being visited. The tail recursive program keeps the list of the *frontier nodes* to be visited. Thus, we get the Chop-and-Expand parsers (thanks to Burstall-Dijkstra) on page 31 and page 35.

- The *backtracking* algorithm for right linear regular grammars corresponding to *nondeterministic* finite automata [21, Section 2.10]. This algorithm searches the space of all possible derivations by backtracking using a do-while command and recursion (see Section 2.2 on page 15). But, in fact, (i) the do-while command is avoided in favour of tail recursion, and (ii) recursion is implemented by keeping the list of the *ancestor nodes*.

- The algorithms with lookahead. These algorithms all have $O(n)$ time complexity, where n is the size of the input string to be parsed.

  - $LL(1)$ parsers: Chop-and-Expand parsers of non-left recursive context-free grammars.

  - *Recursive descent parsers*: bottom-up deterministic parsers for non-left recursive context-free grammars (see, for instance, the parser we have used for Propositional Theorem Prover on page 214).

  - Parsers of right linear regular grammars corresponding to *deterministic* finite automata [**21**, Section 2.10].

(C) **Shift-and-Reduce Parsers.** We have the following algorithms for parsing deterministic context-free languages with lookahead. These algorithms all have $O(n)$ time complexity, where n is the size of the input string to be parsed.

  - $LR(0)$ parsers: for prefix-free, deterministic context-free languages.

  - $LR(1)$ parsers: for deterministic context-free languages (and $LALR(1)$ parsing).

(D) **Operator-Precedence Grammar Parsers**. These algorithms have been presented in Section 6.1 on page 163. They are based on the fact that for every context-free language L, the language $L - \{\varepsilon\}$ can be generated by an operator-precedence grammar.

Now let us recall a few basic results related to the problem of parsing context-free languages.

- Rosenkrantz-Stearns' result about $LL(k)$ and $LR(k)$ languages [**22**]:

  $LL(1) \subset LL(2) \subset \ldots \subset LL(k) \subset \ldots \subset LR(1) =$ deterministic context-free languages.

  Note that the class $LR(0)$ is not inserted in this inclusions of classes of languages.

- For all $k \geq 1$,

  $$S \to a\,T$$
  $$T \to S\,A \quad | \ A$$
  $$A \to b\,B \quad | \ c$$
  $$B \to b^{k-1}\,d \mid \varepsilon$$

  is an $LL(k)$ grammar and *not* an $LL(k-1)$ grammar.

- For all $k \geq 1$,

  $$\{a^n\,w \mid n \geq 1 \text{ and } w \in \{b, c, b^k, d\}^n\}$$

  is an $LL(k)$ language and it is *not* an $LL(k-1)$ language.

- A language is $LL(0)$ iff it is empty or it is a singleton. If we assume that in the grammars there are no useless symbols, then a language is $LL(0)$ iff it is a singleton.

  Note that we do not define the parsing tables for $LL(0)$ parsing. The following two examples show how to construct the parsers for $LL(0)$ languages.

EXAMPLE 6.3.1. Given the alphabet $\Sigma = \{a, b\}$, the algorithm for accepting the $LL(0)$ language which is empty, is any finite automaton without final states (see Figure 6.3.1).

FIGURE 6.3.1. A finite automaton accepting the empty language. S is not a final state.

Given the alphabet $\Sigma = \{a, b\}$, the algorithm for accepting the $LL(0)$ language which is the singleton $\{a\,b\,a\,a\}$, is a finite automaton with a sequence of states, no cycles and exactly one final state (see Figure 6.3.2). There are $n+1$ states in the sequence if n is the length of the word in the singleton.

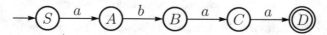

FIGURE 6.3.2. The finite automaton accepting the word $a\,b\,a\,a$ only.

- For all $k \geq 1$, every $LR(k)$ language is an $LR(1)$ language. That is, for every $k \geq 1$, for every $LR(k)$ language L (that is, for every language L generated by an $LR(k)$ grammar), there exists an $LR(1)$ grammar which generates L.

- For all $k \geq 0$, there are $LR(k+1)$ grammars which are *not* $LR(k)$ grammars.

- For all $k \geq 0$,

$$S \to a\,b^k\,c \mid A\,b^k\,d$$
$$A \to a$$

is an $LR(k+1)$ grammar and not an $LR(k)$ grammar.

6.3.1. Summary on $LR(0)$ and $LR(1)$ Parsing.

A language L is deterministic context-free, that is, it is parsable by a deterministic pda (dpda, for short) with acceptance by final state

iff L is $LR(1)$

iff $L\$$, with $\$ \notin V_T$, is $LR(0)$ (recall Theorem 5.2.17 on page 98).

For a deterministic pda, acceptance *by final state* is more powerful than acceptance *by empty stack*.

A language L enjoys the *prefix property* (or it is *prefix-free*) iff no word in L is a proper prefix of another word in L.

Every deterministic context-free language L which enjoys the prefix property is recognized by a dpda by final state

    iff L is recognized by a dpda by empty stack

    iff L is $LR(0)$.

- $D = \{0^i\,1^k\,a\,2^i \,|\, i,k \geq 1\} \cup \{0^i\,1^k\,b\,2^k \,|\, i,k \geq 1\}$ is a deterministic context-free language

    and every grammar for D in Greibach normal form must have at least two productions of the form $A \to a\,\alpha$ and $A \to a\,\beta$, with $\alpha \neq \beta$,

    and the dpda which accepts by final state should make at least an ε-move.

We can always take this dpda such that if it has to make an ε-move, then it makes it while the input is not completely read. (This follows from a theorem holding for any dpda which: (i) accepts a language by final state, and (ii) should perform at least one ε-move [21].)

Note that the language D enjoys the prefix property.

A context-free grammar which generates the language D has axiom S and the following productions:

$$
\begin{array}{lll}
S \to 0\,L\,T \mid\ \ 0\,R & L \to 0\,L\,T \mid 1\,A & R \to 0\,R \ \ \mid 1\,B\,T \\
T \to 2 & A \to 1\,A \ \ \mid a & B \to 1\,B\,T \mid b
\end{array}
$$

- The language $\{a^n b^n \mid n > 0\}$ generated by the grammar with axiom S and the following productions:

    $S \ \to \ a\,S\,b \ \mid \ a\,b$

  is a prefix-free deterministic context-free language (it is in zone (B) of Figure 6.3.3).

- The language $D \cup \{c,\ c\,c\}$ is a deterministic context-free language, but it is not prefix-free (it is in zone (A) of Figure 6.3.3).

- Let w^R denote the reverse of the word w. For instance, $(a\,b\,c\,b)^R = b\,c\,b\,a$ and $\varepsilon^R = \varepsilon$. The language $\{0\,w\,w^R\,\$\,0 \mid w \in \{0,1\}^*\} \cup \{1\,w\,w^R\,\$\,1 \mid w \in \{0,1\}^*\}$ generated by the grammar with axiom S and the following productions:

    $S \ \to \ \ 0\,A\,\$\,0 \ \mid \ 1\,A\,\$\,1$

    $A \ \to \ \ 0\,A\,0 \ \ \mid \ 1\,A\,1 \ \ \mid \ \varepsilon$

  is prefix-free, but it is not deterministic context-free (it is in zone (C) of Figure 6.3.3).

It is decidable whether or not a deterministic context-free language, given by a dpda accepting by final state or an $LR(k)$ grammar, for some $k \geq 0$ (recall that, without loss of generality, we may assume $k=1$), is prefix-free [9, page 355].

It is undecidable whether or not a context-free language (given by a context-free grammar) is prefix-free [9, page 262].

The class of the deterministic context-free languages (see zone (A)+(B) of Figure 6.3.3) is a proper superset of the class of the deterministic context-free languages which are prefix-free (see zone (B) of Figure 6.3.3). Deterministic context-free languages which are prefix-free are also called *strict deterministic context-free languages* in [9, pages 355–358].

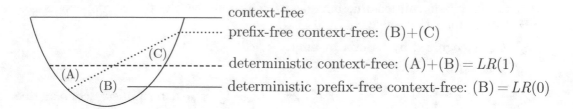

FIGURE 6.3.3. Various subclasses of context-free languages.
Prefix-free context-free languages: (B)+(C). Deterministic context-free languages: (A)+(B). Deterministic, prefix-free context-free languages: (B).

We have the following two characterization of the languages which are in zone (B):
(i) the languages in zone (B) are all the languages generated by $LR(0)$ grammars, and
(ii) the languages in zone (B) are all the languages generated by *strict deterministic context-free grammars* [**9**, page 347]. Let us now define this subclass of the context-free grammars. First we need the following definitions.

DEFINITION 6.3.2. [**Partition on a Set**] A *partition* on a set D based on an equivalence relation ρ, is the set of disjoint non-empty subsets D_i's of D such that: (i) the union of the D_i's is D, and (ii) every D_i is a ρ-equivalence class, that is, for all $x, y \in D$, we have that $x \rho y$ iff $(x \in D_i$ and $y \in D_i)$.

DEFINITION 6.3.3. [**Strict Partition on the Nonterminals of a Context-free Grammar**] Given a context-free grammar $G = \langle V_T, V_N, P, S \rangle$, a partition π on V_N based on the equivalence $\equiv$, is said to be *strict* if
for all (not necessarily distinct) nonterminals $A, A' \in V_N$,
$A \equiv A'$ iff
  for all $\alpha, \beta, \beta' \in (V_T \cup V_N)^*$,
  for all two distinct productions $A \to \alpha \beta$ and $A' \to \alpha \beta'$, we have that:
$\beta \neq \varepsilon$ and $\beta' \neq \varepsilon$ and $\left((\underline{\beta}_1 \equiv \underline{\beta}'_1) \text{ or } (\underline{\beta}_1 \text{ and } \underline{\beta}'_1 \text{ are possibly distinct terminals}) \right)$.
(Recall that given an alphabet V and a word $w \in V^+$, by $\underline{w}_1$ we denote the leftmost symbol of V occurring in w.)

DEFINITION 6.3.4. [**Strict Deterministic Context-free Grammar**] A context-free grammar $G = \langle V_T, V_N, P, S \rangle$ is said to be *strict deterministic* if there exists a strict partition of the set V_N [**9**, page 347].

For instance, the grammar G_0 with axiom S and the following productions:

$$S \to a\,A \quad | \; a\,B$$
$$A \to a\,A\,a \; | \; b\,C \qquad\qquad C \to b\,C \quad | \; a$$
$$B \to a\,B \quad | \; b\,D \qquad\qquad D \to b\,D\,c \; | \; c$$

has the strict partition $\{\{S\}, \{A, B\}, \{C, D\}\}$ on V_N.

The grammar G_1 for arithmetic expressions with axiom S and the following productions:

$$S \rightarrow (E)$$
$$E \rightarrow T \qquad | \ E+T$$
$$T \rightarrow F \qquad | \ T*F$$
$$F \rightarrow S \qquad | \ a$$

does not have a strict partition on V_N (this is due to the two productions for F).

The grammar G_2, which is equivalent to G_1, with axiom S and the following productions:

$$S \ \rightarrow \ (E$$
$$E \ \rightarrow \ T_1 E \ | \ T_2 \qquad\qquad F_1 \rightarrow (E* \ | \ a*$$
$$T_1 \rightarrow F_1 T_1 \ | \ F_2 \qquad\qquad F_2 \rightarrow (E+ \ | \ a+$$
$$T_2 \rightarrow F_1 T_2 \ | \ F_3 \qquad\qquad F_3 \rightarrow (E) \ | \ a)$$

has the strict partition $\{\{S\}, \{E\}, \{T_1, T_2\}, \{F_1, F_2, F_3\}\}$ on V_N.

CHAPTER 7

Visits of Trees and Graphs and Evaluation of Expressions

In this chapter we will consider a few programs for parsing expressions and visiting trees and graphs. In particular, we will consider programs for: (i) parsing strings written according to a given context-free grammar, and then visiting the trees they denote, (ii) parsing and evaluating boolean expressions, and (iii) testing whether or not propositional formulas are tautologies.

We will also describe an algorithm for encoding n-ary trees using binary trees, and two algorithms proposed by E. W. Dijkstra: (i) an algorithm which given an *undirected*, connected, weighted graph, constructs one of its minimal spanning trees, and (ii) an algorithm which given a *directed*, connected, weighted graph, and one of its nodes p, constructs all paths from the node p to every other node of the graph.

7.1. Depth First Visit of Trees

The program presented in this section: (i) first, parses using the recursive descent technique a given input string denoting a tree, (ii) then, generates an internal form of that tree, and (iii) finally, visits that tree in a depth first manner according to the so called *postorder traversal* (not the preorder traversal we have described on page 17). In particular, for a binary tree we first visit the left son node, then the right son node, and finally, the root node. The productions of the context-free grammar which generates the input string are the following ones:

```
tree  ::=  char | - char tree | (tree char tree)
char  ::=  '0' | '1' |...| '9'
```

The axiom is `tree`. No blank characters are allowed before, in between, and after the input string.

A string which is a single character c, denotes a leaf with the character c. A string of the form '- c s' denotes a node with the character c and a single son node denoted by the string s (short for *son* node). A string of the form '(l c r)' denotes a node with the character c, a left son node denoted by the string l (short for *left* son node), and a right son node denoted by the string r (short for *right* son node). For instance, (57-62) denotes the tree:

```
        7
      /   \
     5     6
           |
           2
```

The internal tree which corresponds to a given input string, is printed as a string which is generated by the following productions with axiom `tree`:

© Springer Nature Switzerland AG 2021
A. Pettorossi, *Techniques for Searching, Parsing, and Matching*, https://doi.org/10.1007/978-3-030-63189-5_7

```
tree  ::=  n | (n.tree) | (tree.n.tree)
n     ::=  0 | 1 |...| 9
```

(i) The first production `tree ::= n` is for the case of a leaf, (ii) the second production `tree ::= (n.tree)` is for the case of a unary tree, and (iii) the third production `tree ::= (tree.n.tree)` is for the case of a binary tree. For instance, the tree denoted by the string (57-62), is printed as: (5.7.(6.2))

If we issue the following two commands:

```
javac DepthFirstVisit.java
java  DepthFirstVisit
```

we get the following sentence in output:

Input a tree according to the grammar given in the program, please.

Then, if we type the following input string (note the absence of blank characters):

```
(-231(-564-78))
```

we get:

```
Tree in input:
((2.3).1.((5.6).4.(7.8)))

Depth first visit of the tree:
3 2 6 5 8 7 4 1
```

Indeed, the string (-231(-564-78)) denotes the tree:

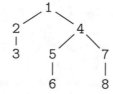

whose depth first visit is given by the sequence: 3 2 6 5 8 7 4 1.

REMARK 7.1.1. [**Terminology for Nodes and Trees**] In our context here, we will consider the words 'node' and 'tree' as interchangeable, because every node in a tree can be viewed as the root of the subtree rooted in that node (see also Remark 7.4.1 on page 227).

In the class `DepthFirstVisit` of the program below, we have that the expression
`Character.getNumericValue(c)`
is the same as `c-48`, and returns the integer value corresponding to the character `c` representing that value. For instance, the integer value corresponding to the character '8' is 8 (= 56−48).

Here is the program for parsing a string denoting a tree and computing the first depth visit of that tree.

```
/**
 * =============================================================================
 *                      DEPTH FIRST VISIT OF A TREE
 * Filename: "DepthFirstVisit.java"
 *
 * Grammar G for the input tree:
 *
 *                   tree ::= char | - char tree | (tree char tree)
 *                   char ::= '0' | '1' | ... | '9'
```

```
 * Grammar for printing the input tree:
 *                     tree ::= n | (n.tree) | (tree.n.tree)
 *                     n    ::= 0 | 1 | ... | 9
 * No blanks are allowed before, in between, and after the input string.
 * A tree is input as a string generated by the grammar G and then
 * it is visited in the depth first manner.
 * =======================================================================
 */
import java.io.*;
/**
 * =======================================================================
 *                  Class which constructs a Node
 *
 * This class is used for constructing a Node of a binary tree.
 * By default, a Node is a binary node.
 *
 * A Node can be extended for constructing a Node which is
 * either a binary node, or a unary node, or a leaf node.
 * =======================================================================
 */

class Node {
    public Object  value;       // value field
    public Node    left;        // reference to the left  child node
    public Node    right;       // reference to the right child node

  /**
   * @param v : value at the node
   * @param l : reference to the left  child node
   * @param r : reference to the right child node
   */                           // constructor of a node
    public Node( Object v, Node l, Node r) {
        if ( v == null )  throw new IllegalArgumentException( );
        value = v;
        left  = l;
        right = r;
    }
}
/**
 * =======================================================================
 *          Class which constructs a binary node with two child nodes
 * =======================================================================
 */

class BinaryNode extends Node {
                                // constructor of a binary node
  /**
   * @param v : value at the node
   * @param l : reference to the left  child node
   * @param r : reference to the right child node
   */
    public BinaryNode(Object v, Node l, Node r) {
        super(v, l, r);
    }
  /**
   * @return a string representing the tree whose root is the given node
   */
    public String toString(){
        return "("+ left.toString() +"."+ value +"."+ right.toString() +")";
    }
}
```

```java
/**
 * ================================================================
 *              Class which constructs a unary node with one child node
 * ================================================================
 */

class UnaryNode extends Node {
                                        // constructor of a unary node
  /**
   * @param v       : value at the node
   * @param child : reference to the child node
   */

  public UnaryNode(Object v, Node child) {
        super(v, child, null);
  }
  /**
   * @return a string representing the tree whose root is the given node
   */
    public String toString() {
        return "(" + value + "." + left.toString() + ")";
    }
}
/**
 * ================================================================
 *              Class which constructs a leaf node
 * ================================================================
 */

class LeafNode extends Node {
                                        // constructor of a leaf
  /**
   * @param v : value at the node
   */
  public LeafNode(Object v) {
        super(v, null, null);
  }

  /**
   * @return a string representing the leaf node
   */
  public String toString() {
        return "" + value;
  }
}

/**
 * ================================================================
 *              Class ParseException
 * ================================================================
 */

class ParseException extends Exception {

                        // constructor of a new instance of ParseException
  public ParseException() {
        super("Parse  exception!");
  }
}
// ----------------------------------------------------------------
```

```java
public class DepthFirstVisit {
// ==========================================================================
    /**
     * This class DepthFirstVisit transforms the input string into a tree
     * of type Node. Parsing is done using the recursive descent technique.
     * The string encodes the tree as indicated by the grammar G.
     * @param  string: the string which encodes the given tree
     * @return the root of the tree generated by the parsing
     * @throws IOException or ParseException
     */      // stringReader is a sequence of characters, which are read one
             // at a time, by the method read() of the class StringReader.
             //           RECURSIVE DESCENT PARSING
    public static Node parse(BufferedReader stringReader)
                                    throws IOException, ParseException {
        char c = (char)stringReader.read();
        if ( ('0' <= c ) && ( c <= '9') ) {
            return new LeafNode(new Integer(Character.getNumericValue(c)));
        } else
        if ( c == '-') {
            char c2        = (char)stringReader.read();
            Integer value  = new Integer(Character.getNumericValue(c2));
            Node childTree = parse(stringReader);
            UnaryNode node = new UnaryNode(value, childTree);
            return node;
        } else
        if ( c == '(' ) {
            Node leftTree   = parse(stringReader);
            char c2         = (char)stringReader.read();
            Integer value   = new Integer(Character.getNumericValue(c2));
            Node rightTree  = parse(stringReader);
            BinaryNode node = new BinaryNode(value, leftTree, rightTree);
            c2              = (char)stringReader.read();
            return node;
        } else {
        throw new ParseException();
        }
    }
    /** Depth first visit of the given tree
     *  @param tree : tree to be visited in a depth first manner
     *  @return the sequence of nodes which is the depth first visit of
     *          the given tree
     */
    public static String depthFirstVisit(Node tree) {
        StringBuffer buffer = new StringBuffer();
// ---------------------- RECURSIVE VERSION ---------------------------
    if ( tree instanceof LeafNode ) {                                    //
            buffer.append(((LeafNode)tree).value + " ");                 //
        } else                                                           //
        if ( tree instanceof UnaryNode ) {                               //
            buffer.append(depthFirstVisit(((UnaryNode)tree).left)        //
                    + tree.value + " ");                                 //
        } else                                                           //
        if ( tree instanceof BinaryNode ) {                              //
            buffer.append(depthFirstVisit(((BinaryNode)tree).left)       //
                    + depthFirstVisit(((BinaryNode)tree).right)          //
                    + tree.value + " ");                                 //
        };                                                               //
// ---------------------- END OF RECURSIVE VERSION ---------------------
        return buffer.toString();
    }
```

```
// ---------------------------------------------------------------------
    public static void main(String[] args) throws IOException {

        System.out.println("Input a tree according to the grammar given "
                                + "in the program, please.");
        Node tree = null;
        try {
        tree = parse(new BufferedReader(new InputStreamReader(System.in)));
        } catch ( IOException e ) {
            e.printStackTrace();
        } catch ( ParseException pex ) {
            System.out.println(pex.getMessage());
        }
        if (tree != null) {
            System.out.println("\nTree in input:\n" + tree);
            System.out.println("\nDepth first visit of the tree:");
            System.out.println(depthFirstVisit(tree));
        }
    }
}

/**
 * input:  output:
 * ---------------------------------------------------------------------
 * javac DepthFirstVisit.java
 * java  DepthFirstVisit
 *
 *     Input a tree according to the grammar given in the program, please.
 * (-231(-564-78))
 *
 *     Tree in input:
 *     ((2.3).1.((5.6).4.(7.8)))
 *
 *     Depth first visit of the tree:
 *     3 2 6 5 8 7 4 1
 * ---------------------------------------------------------------------
 */
```

The following program is like the above one: it parses a string denoting a tree and computes the first depth visit of that tree, but it uses a graphical interface. It can be run by typing the following three commands:

```
javac DepthFirstVisit.java
javac DepthFirstVisitGUI.java
java  DepthFirstVisitGUI
```

```
/**
 * =====================================================================
 *                    DEPTH FIRST VISIT OF A TREE
 *                    with a Graphical User Interface
 * Filename: "DepthFirstVisitGUI.java"
 *
 * This program should be compiled after the compilation of the program
 * DepthFirstVisit.java.
 * See also the initial comments in the file DepthFirstVisit.java
 *
 * This program uses the class DepthFirstVisit in the file named
 * DepthFirstVisit.java. The file DepthFirstVisit.java should be stored
 * in the same folder where this file DepthFirstVisitGUI.java is stored.
 *
```

```
 * To get a dialog window with font size 14 (instead of 28): set the
 * boolean variable bw (short for big_window) to false (see line ***)
 * ======================================================================
 */
import java.io.*;
import javax.swing.JFrame;
import java.awt.Font;                               // needed for changing fonts

// ----------------------------------------------------
public class DepthFirstVisitGUI extends JFrame {
    /** Creates new form DepthFirstVisitGUI */
    public DepthFirstVisitGUI() {
        initComponents();
    }
    /** This method initComponents() is called from within the constructor
     *  to initialize the form.
     */
    private void initComponents() {//GEN-BEGIN:initComponents
        jLabel1    = new javax.swing.JLabel();
        jLabel2    = new javax.swing.JLabel();
        jLabel3    = new javax.swing.JLabel();
        jLabel4    = new javax.swing.JLabel();
        txInput    = new javax.swing.JTextField();
        txOutTree  = new javax.swing.JTextField();
        txOutDPF   = new javax.swing.JTextField();
        btParse    = new javax.swing.JButton();
        menuBar    = new javax.swing.JMenuBar();
        fileMenu   = new javax.swing.JMenu();
        exitMenuItem = new javax.swing.JMenuItem();
// ------------------------------------------------------------

        boolean bw = true;  // true (false) for big (small) window.   ***
        Font sansSerifFont =
            bw ? (new Font("SansSerif",Font.PLAIN,28)):
                 (new Font("SansSerif",Font.PLAIN,14));
// ------------------------------------------------------------
        txInput.setFont(sansSerifFont);
        txOutTree.setFont(sansSerifFont);
        txOutDPF.setFont(sansSerifFont);

        getContentPane().setLayout(null);
        setTitle("DEPTH FIRST VISIT OF A TREE");
        setLocationRelativeTo(null);
        addWindowListener(new java.awt.event.WindowAdapter() {
            public void windowClosing(java.awt.event.WindowEvent evt) {
                exitForm(evt);
            }
        });
// ------------------------------------------------------------
        jLabel1.setBackground(new java.awt.Color(255, 255, 150));
        jLabel1.setFont(sansSerifFont);
        jLabel1.setText("<HTML>\n<PRE>\n"
        +" Grammar for the input tree:\n"
        +"                  tree ::= char | - char tree |"
        +" (tree char tree)\n"
        +"                  char ::= '0' | '1' | ... | '9'\n"
        +" Grammar for the internal tree:\n"
        +"                  tree ::= n | (n.tree) | (tree.n.tree)\n"
        +"                  n    ::= 0 | 1 | ... | 9\n"
        +"<PRE>\n</HTML>");
```

```
        jLabel1.setVerticalAlignment(javax.swing.SwingConstants.TOP);
        jLabel1.setOpaque(true);
        getContentPane().add(jLabel1);
        if (bw) {jLabel1.setBounds(10, 10, 1080, 190);}
            else {jLabel1.setBounds(5, 5, 525, 95);}
// -------------------------------------------------------------
        jLabel2.setFont(sansSerifFont);
        jLabel2.setText("Input Tree:");
        getContentPane().add(jLabel2);
        if (bw) {jLabel2.setBounds(20, 208, 180, 32);}
            else {jLabel2.setBounds(10, 104, 90, 16);}
        getContentPane().add(txInput);
        if (bw) {txInput.setBounds(270, 208, 810, 40);}
            else {txInput.setBounds(140, 104, 380, 20);}
// -------------------------------------------------------------
        jLabel3.setFont(sansSerifFont);
        jLabel3.setText("Internal Tree:");
        getContentPane().add(jLabel3);
        if (bw) {jLabel3.setBounds(20, 288, 200, 32);}
            else {jLabel3.setBounds(10, 144, 110, 16);}
        txOutTree.setBackground(new java.awt.Color(25, 255, 25));
        getContentPane().add(txOutTree);
        if (bw) {txOutTree.setBounds(270, 288, 810, 40);}
            else {txOutTree.setBounds(140, 144, 380, 20);}
// -------------------------------------------------------------
        jLabel4.setFont(sansSerifFont);
        jLabel4.setText("Depth First Visit:");
        getContentPane().add(jLabel4);
        if (bw) {jLabel4.setBounds(20, 368, 280, 32);}
            else {jLabel4.setBounds(10, 184, 140, 16);}
        txOutDPF.setBackground(new java.awt.Color(25, 255, 25));
        getContentPane().add(txOutDPF);
        if (bw) {txOutDPF.setBounds(270, 368, 810, 50);}
            else {txOutDPF.setBounds(140, 184, 380, 20);}
// -------------------------------------------------------------
        btParse.setFont(sansSerifFont);
        btParse.setText("Parse and Visit");
        btParse.addActionListener(new java.awt.event.ActionListener() {
            public void actionPerformed(java.awt.event.ActionEvent evt) {
                btParseActionPerformed(evt);
            }
        });
        getContentPane().add(btParse);
        if (bw) {btParse.setBounds(340, 440, 576, 52);}
            else {btParse.setBounds(240, 210, 138, 25);}
// -------------------------------------------------------------
        fileMenu.setText("FILE_MENU");
        exitMenuItem.setText("Exit");
        exitMenuItem.addActionListener(
                                new java.awt.event.ActionListener() {
            public void actionPerformed(java.awt.event.ActionEvent evt) {
                exitMenuItemActionPerformed(evt);
            }
        });

        fileMenu.add(exitMenuItem);// adding a File Menu with an Exit button
        menuBar.add(fileMenu);     //
        setJMenuBar(menuBar);      //
```

```
        java.awt.Dimension screenSize =
            java.awt.Toolkit.getDefaultToolkit().getScreenSize();
        if (bw) {setBounds((screenSize.width-944)/2,
                (screenSize.height-700)/2, 1095, 600);}
            else {setBounds((screenSize.width-944)/2,
                (screenSize.height-700)/2, 544, 300);}
} //GEN-END:initComponents

private void btParseActionPerformed(java.awt.event.ActionEvent evt) {
  //GEN-FIRST:event_btParseActionPerformed
  // Add your handling code here:
        Node tree = null;
        try {    // from String to StringReader and to BufferedReader
            BufferedReader inputline
                = new BufferedReader(
                            new StringReader(txInput.getText()));
            tree = DepthFirstVisit.parse(inputline);
        } catch ( IOException e ) {
            e.printStackTrace();
            txOutTree.setText("IOException!");
        } catch ( ParseException pex ){
            txOutTree.setText(pex.getMessage());
        }
        if (tree != null) {
            txOutTree.setText(tree.toString());
            txOutDPF.setText(DepthFirstVisit.depthFirstVisit(tree));
        }
} //GEN-LAST:event_btParseActionPerformed

private void exitMenuItemActionPerformed(
                                java.awt.event.ActionEvent evt) {
  //GEN-FIRST:event_exitMenuItemActionPerformed
    System.exit(0);
} //GEN-LAST:event_exitMenuItemActionPerformed

/** Exit the Application */
private void exitForm(java.awt.event.WindowEvent evt) {
  //GEN-FIRST:event_exitForm
    System.exit(0);
} //GEN-LAST:event_exitForm
/**
 * @param args the command line arguments
 */
public static void main(String args[]) {
    new DepthFirstVisitGUI().show();
}
// Variables declaration - do not modify    //GEN-BEGIN:variables
private javax.swing.JMenuItem exitMenuItem;
private javax.swing.JMenu fileMenu;
private javax.swing.JLabel jLabel1;
private javax.swing.JLabel jLabel2;
private javax.swing.JLabel jLabel3;
private javax.swing.JLabel jLabel4;
private javax.swing.JMenuBar menuBar;
private javax.swing.JTextField txInput;
private javax.swing.JTextField txOutTree;
private javax.swing.JTextField txOutDPF;
private javax.swing.JButton btParse;
// End of variables declaration              //GEN-END:variables
}
```

```
/**
 * input:          output:
 * ------------------------------------------------------------------------
 * javac DepthFirstVisit.java                      // This compilation is needed
 * javac DepthFirstVisitGUI.java
 * java  DepthFirstVisitGUI
 *
 *               (see figures below)
 * ------------------------------------------------------------------------
 */
```

After typing the string (-231(-564-78)) we have:

Then by clicking the button 'Parse and Visit' we get:

7.2. Evaluator of Boolean Expressions

The program presented in this section: (i) first, parses using the recursive descent technique a given input string denoting a boolean expression, (ii) then, generates the internal tree which represents that expression, and (iii) finally, returns the value of that boolean expression by evaluating every node of that internal tree.

In this section, as concrete instances of boolean expressions, we take the formulas of the propositional calculus built out of the atoms **true** and **false** and the operators ¬, ∨, ∧, and →, which, respectively, denote negation, disjunction, conjunction, and implication. The productions of the context-free grammar which generates the input string are the following ones:

```
b  ::=  c  |  c>b          (b is a boolean expression)
c  ::=  l  |  l+c  |lxc    (c is a condition)
l  ::=  a  |  -l           (l is a literal)
a  ::=  't'  |  'f'  |  (b) (a is an atom)
```

The axiom is b. 't' stands for **true**, 'f' stands for **false**, - denotes negation, + denotes disjunction, x denotes conjunction, and > denotes implication. We assume that: (i) + and x bind more than >, and (ii) - binds more than + and x. We also assume right associativity for subexpressions involving + and x. Parentheses override priorities. No blanks are allowed before, in between, and after the input string.

For instance, the string -t>f+t denotes the boolean expression:

¬ true → (false ∨ true)

The internal tree which corresponds to the input string is then printed as a string which is generated by the following productions from the axiom b:

```
b  ::=  true | false | (-b) | (b + b) | (b x b) | (b > b)
```

For instance, the boolean expression: ¬true → (false ∨ true) is printed as:

((-true) > (false + true))

If we execute the following two commands:

```
javac BooleanExpression.java
java  BooleanExpression
```

we get the following sentence in output:

Input a boolean expression according to the given grammar, please.

Then, if we type the following input string (note the absence of blank characters):

t>(f+f)+-tx-f

we get:

```
Parse tree of the boolean expression:
(true > ((false + false) + ((-true) x (-false))))

Value of the boolean expression:
false
```

Indeed, we have that the string t>(f+f)+-tx-f represents according to our conventions, the boolean expression true → ((false ∨ false) ∨ (¬ true ∧ ¬ false)).

That boolean expression can be depicted as a tree as follows:

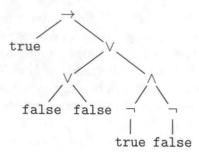

Its value is: false.

The following program parses and evaluates boolean expressions.

```
/**
 * =========================================================================
 *                    EVALUATOR OF BOOLEAN EXPRESSIONS
 * Filename: "BooleanExpressionEvaluator.java"
 *
 * Grammar G for the input boolean expression b:
 *
 *    boolean expressions  b ::=  c  | c>b          <-- bexprParse
 *    conditions           c ::=  l  | l+c  | lxc    <-- condParse
 *    literals             l ::=  a  | -l            <-- litParse
 *    atoms                a ::= 't' | 'f' | (b)      <-- atomParse
 *
 * 't' stands for true, 'f' stands for false, - denotes negation,
 * + denotes disjunction, x denotes conjunction, and > denotes implication.
 * The grammar should not be left recursive.
 * Internal tree:
 * -------------
 *    b ::= true  |  false  |  (-b)  |  (b x b)  |  (b + b)  |  (b > b)
 *          (Leaf)    (Leaf)   (Unary)  (Binary)   (Binary)    (Binary)
 * Output value:
 * ------------
 *    value ::= true | false
 * ------------
 * Priorities: + and x bind more than >
 *             - binds more than + or x
 *             Right associativity for + and x
 *             Parentheses override priorities.
 * No blanks are allowed before, in between, and after the input string.
 *
 * A boolean expression is given in input as a string generated by
 * the grammar G and then it is parsed and evaluated.
 * The word 'node' is assumed to be equivalent to the word 'tree'.
 *
 * ----------
 * If "C2 extends C1" then the class C2 has the methods of the class C1.
 * This may not be desirable, but it allows the use of objects of the class
 * C1 and then the use of "instanceof" to test whether or not an object of
 * the class C1 is indeed of the class C2.
 *
 * ----------
 * Line (1) below checks whether or not the input boolean expression is
 * terminated by a carriage-return '\n'.
 * =========================================================================
 */

import java.io.*;
```

```
/**
 * ==========================================================================
 *                      Class which constructs a Node
 * This class is used for constructing a Node of a binary tree.
 * By default, a Node is a binary node.
 * A Node can be extended for constructing a Node which is
 * either a binary node, or a unary node, or a leaf node.
 * ==========================================================================
 */
class Node {
   public Object  value;       // value field
   public Node    left;        // reference to the left  child node
   public Node    right;       // reference to the right child node
                                        // constructor
  /**
   * @param v : value at the node
   * @param l : reference to the left  child node
   * @param r : reference to the right child node
   */                                    // constructor of a binary node
   public Node( Object v, Node l, Node r) {
       if ( v == null )  throw new IllegalArgumentException( );
       value = v;
       left  = l;
       right = r;
   }
}
/**
 * ==========================================================================
 *              Class which constructs a binary node with two child nodes
 * ==========================================================================
 */
class BinaryNode extends Node {
  /**                              // constructor of binary node
   * @param v : value at the node
   * @param l : reference to the left  child node
   * @param r : reference to the right child node
   */
   public BinaryNode(Object v, Node l, Node r) {
       super(v, l, r);
   }
  /**
   * @return a string representing the tree whose root is the given node
   */
   public String toString(){
       return "("+ left.toString() +" "+ value +" "+ right.toString() +")";
   }
}
/**
 * ==========================================================================
 *              Class which constructs a unary node with one child node
 * ==========================================================================
 */
class UnaryNode extends Node {
  /**                              // constructor of unary node
   * @param v       : value at the node
   * @param child : reference to the child node
   */

   public UnaryNode(Object v, Node child) {
           super(v, child, null);
   }
```

```
  /**
   * @return a string representing the tree whose root is the given node
   */
    public String toString() {
        return "(" + value + left.toString() + ")";
    }
}

/**
 * =============================================================================
 *                    Class which constructs a leaf node
 * =============================================================================
 */
class LeafNode extends Node {
  /**                                     // constructor of a leaf
   * @param v : value at the node
   */
    public LeafNode(Object v) {
        super(v, null, null);
    }
  /**
   * @return a string representing the leaf node
   */
    public String toString() {
        return "" + value;
    }
}
/**
 * =============================================================================
 *                    Class ParseException
 * =============================================================================
 */
class ParseException extends Exception {
                           // constructor of a new instance of ParseException
    public ParseException() {
        super("parse exception!");
    }
}
/**
 * =============================================================================
 *                    Class EvalException
 * =============================================================================
 */
class EvalException extends Exception {
                           // constructor of a new instance of EvalException
    public EvalException() {
        super("eval exception!");
    }
}
// -----------------------------------------------------------------------------
public class BooleanExpressionEvaluator {
// =============================================================================
  /**
   * This class BooleanExpressionEvaluator transforms the input string
   * into a tree of type Node. Parsing is done using the recursive descent
   * technique.
   * The string encodes the tree as indicated by the grammar G.
   * @param  string: the string which encodes the given tree
   * @return the root of the tree generated by the parsing
   * @throws IOException or ParseException or EvalException.
   */
```

```
    public static char c; // static field.
                          // inputLine is a sequence of characters,
                          // which are read one at a time, by
                          // the method read() of the class StringReader
//                    RECURSIVE DESCENT PARSING
    public static Node bexprParse(BufferedReader inputLine)
                                   throws IOException, ParseException {
       Node node1 = condParse(inputLine);
       if ( c == '>' ) {
          c = (char)inputLine.read();
          Node node2 = bexprParse(inputLine);
          return new BinaryNode(new Character('>'), node1, node2);
       } else { return node1; }
    }

    public static Node condParse(BufferedReader inputLine)
                                   throws IOException, ParseException {
       Node node1 = litParse(inputLine);
       if ( c == 'x' ) {
          c = (char)inputLine.read();
          Node node2 = condParse(inputLine);
          return new BinaryNode(new Character('x'), node1, node2);
       } else
       if ( c == '+' )    {
          c = (char)inputLine.read();
          Node node2 = condParse(inputLine);
          return new BinaryNode(new Character('+'), node1, node2);
       } else { return node1; }
    }

    public static Node litParse(BufferedReader inputLine)
                                   throws IOException, ParseException {
       Node node = null;
       if ( c == '-' ) {
          c = (char)inputLine.read();
          Node node1 = litParse(inputLine);
          node = new UnaryNode(new Character('-'), node1);
       } else { node = atomParse(inputLine); };
       return node;
    }

    public static Node atomParse(BufferedReader inputLine)
                                   throws IOException, ParseException {
       Node node1 = null;
       if ((c == 't') || (c == 'f')) {
          node1 = new LeafNode(new Boolean((c=='t')?true:false));
          c = (char)inputLine.read();
          return node1;
       } else {
       if ( c=='(' ) {
          c = (char)inputLine.read();
          node1 = bexprParse(inputLine);
          if ( c==')' ) { c = (char)inputLine.read(); }// reads past ')'
          else { throw new ParseException(); };
          return node1;
          };
       };
       throw new ParseException();
    }
```

```
// ----------------------------------------------------------------------

  /** Evaluation of the tree which represents the input boolean expression
   *  @param tree : tree to be evaluated
   *  @return the boolean value of the tree
   */
  public static boolean evalTree(Node tree)
                               throws EvalException {

// --------------------- RECURSIVE VERSION ----------------------------

  if ( tree instanceof LeafNode ) {                                    //
        return ((Boolean)((LeafNode)tree).value).booleanValue();       //
  } else                                                               //
  if ( tree instanceof UnaryNode ) {                                   //
        return !(evalTree(((UnaryNode)tree).left));                    //
  } else                                                               //
  if ( tree instanceof BinaryNode ) {                                  //
        boolean left  = evalTree(((BinaryNode)tree).left);             //
        boolean right = evalTree(((BinaryNode)tree).right);            //
        if (((Character)(((BinaryNode)tree).value)).charValue() == '+')//
           { return left || right; } else                             //
        if (((Character)(((BinaryNode)tree).value)).charValue() == 'x')//
           { return left && right; } else                             //
        if (((Character)(((BinaryNode)tree).value)).charValue() == '>')//
           { return (!left) || right; } else {                        //
        throw new EvalException();                                     //
        }                                                              //
  } else {                                                             //
  throw new EvalException();                                           //
  }                                                                    //
// --------------------- END OF RECURSIVE VERSION ---------------------
  }

// ----------------------------------------------------------------------
    public static void main(String[] args)
                              throws IOException, ParseException {

      System.out.println("Input a boolean expression according to the "
                    + "given grammar, please.");
      Node tree = null;
      try {     // from String to StringReader and to BufferedReader
          BufferedReader inputLine =
                  new BufferedReader(new InputStreamReader(System.in));
          c = (char)inputLine.read();
          tree = bexprParse(inputLine);
          if (c != '\n') { throw new ParseException(); };        // <--- (1)
      } catch ( IOException e ) {
          e.printStackTrace();
          System.out.println("IOException!");
      } catch ( ParseException pex ) {
          System.out.println(pex.getMessage());
          return;
      };
      // ------

      if (tree != null) {
          System.out.println("\nParse tree of the boolean expression:\n"
                        + tree);
          System.out.println("\nValue of the boolean expression:");
```

```
        try {
            System.out.println(evalTree(tree));
        } catch ( EvalException evalex ) {
            System.out.println(evalex.getMessage());
        }
        }
    }
}

/**
 * input: output:
 * ----------------------------------------------------------------
 * javac BooleanExpressionEvaluator.java
 * java  BooleanExpressionEvaluator
 *
 *       Input a boolean expression according to the given grammar, please.
 * t>(f+f)+-tx-f
 *
 *       Parse tree of the boolean expression:
 *       (true > ((false + false) + ((-true) x (-false))))
 *
 *       Value of the boolean expression:
 *       false
 * ----------------------------------------------------------------
 */
```

The following program is like the above one: it parses and evaluates boolean expressions, but it uses a graphical interface. It can be run by typing the following three commands:

```
    javac BooleanExpressionEvaluator.java
    javac BooleanExpressionEvaluatorGUI.java
    java  BooleanExpressionEvaluatorGUI
```

```
/**
 * =======================================================================
 *                   EVALUATOR OF BOOLEAN EXPRESSIONS
 *                     with a Graphical User Interface
 * Filename: "BooleanExpressionEvaluatorGUI.java"
 *
 * This program should be compiled after the compilation of the program
 * BooleanExpressionEvaluator.java.
 * See also the initial comments of the file BooleanExpressionEvaluator.java
 *
 * This program uses the class BooleanExpressionEvaluator in the file named
 * BooleanExpressionEvaluator.java. The file BooleanExpressionEvaluator.java
 * should be stored in the same folder where this file
 * BooleanExpressionEvaluatorGUI.java is stored.
 *
 * To get a dialog window with font size 14 (instead of 28): set the
 * boolean variable bw (short for big_window) to false (see line ***)
 * =======================================================================
 */

import java.io.*;
import javax.swing.JFrame;
import java.awt.Font;                              // needed for changing fonts

// ---------------------------------------------------------------
```

```
public class BooleanExpressionEvaluatorGUI extends JFrame {
    /** Creates new form BooleanExpressionEvaluatorGUI */
    public BooleanExpressionEvaluatorGUI() {
        initComponents();
    }
    /** This method initComponents() is called from within the constructor
     * to initialize the form.                                              */
    private void initComponents() {//GEN-BEGIN:initComponents
        jLabel1   = new javax.swing.JLabel();
        jLabel2   = new javax.swing.JLabel();
        jLabel3   = new javax.swing.JLabel();
        jLabel4   = new javax.swing.JLabel();
        txInExpr  = new javax.swing.JTextField();
        txOutExpr = new javax.swing.JTextField();
        txOutVal  = new javax.swing.JTextField();
        btParse   = new javax.swing.JButton();
        menuBar   = new javax.swing.JMenuBar();
        fileMenu  = new javax.swing.JMenu();
        exitMenuItem = new javax.swing.JMenuItem();
// --------------------------------------------------------------
        boolean bw = true;  // true (false) for big (small) window.  ***
        Font sansSerifFont =
            bw ? (new Font("SansSerif",Font.PLAIN,28)):
                 (new Font("SansSerif",Font.PLAIN,14));
// --------------------------------------------------------------
        txInExpr.setFont(sansSerifFont);
        txOutExpr.setFont(sansSerifFont);
        txOutVal.setFont(sansSerifFont);

        getContentPane().setLayout(null);
        setTitle("EVALUATION OF A BOOLEAN EXPRESSION");
        setLocationRelativeTo(null);
        addWindowListener(new java.awt.event.WindowAdapter() {
            public void windowClosing(java.awt.event.WindowEvent evt) {
                exitForm(evt);
            }
        });
// --------------------------------------------------------------
        jLabel1.setBackground(new java.awt.Color(255, 255, 150));
        jLabel1.setFont(sansSerifFont);
        jLabel1.setText("<HTML>\n<PRE>\n"
        +" Grammar for the input boolean expression b:\n"
        +"   b ::= c | c>b       c ::= l | l+c | lxc       l ::= a | -l\n"
        +"   a ::= 't' | 'f' | (b)\n"
        +"   't' stands for true. 'f' stands for false.\n"
        +" Internal tree: \n"
        +"   b ::= true  |  false  |  (-b)  |  (b + b)\n"
        +"         | (b x b)  |   (b > b)\n"
        +" Evaluation of the boolean expression:\n"
        +"    true | false\n"
        +"<PRE>\n</HTML>");
        jLabel1.setVerticalAlignment(javax.swing.SwingConstants.TOP);
        jLabel1.setOpaque(true);
        getContentPane().add(jLabel1);
        if (bw) {jLabel1.setBounds(10, 10, 1164, 288);}
            else {jLabel1.setBounds(5, 5, 582, 144);}
// --------------------------------------------------------------
        jLabel2.setFont(sansSerifFont);
        jLabel2.setText("Input Expression:");
        getContentPane().add(jLabel2);
```

```
        if (bw) {jLabel2.setBounds(20, 336, 312, 40);}
           else {jLabel2.setBounds(10, 168, 156, 20);}
        getContentPane().add(txInExpr);
        if (bw) {txInExpr.setBounds(280, 336, 800, 50);}
           else {txInExpr.setBounds(10, 168, 156, 20);}
// ----------------------------------------------------------
        jLabel3.setFont(sansSerifFont);
        jLabel3.setText("Internal Tree:");
        getContentPane().add(jLabel3);
        if (bw) {jLabel3.setBounds(20, 416, 312, 40);}
           else {jLabel3.setBounds(10, 208, 156, 20);}
        txOutExpr.setBackground(new java.awt.Color(25, 255, 25));
        getContentPane().add(txOutExpr);
        if (bw) {txOutExpr.setBounds(280, 416, 800, 50);}
           else {txOutExpr.setBounds(140, 208, 400, 25);}
// ----------------------------------------------------------
        jLabel4.setFont(sansSerifFont);
        jLabel4.setText("Evaluation:");
        getContentPane().add(jLabel4);
        if (bw) {jLabel4.setBounds(20, 496, 280, 32);}
           else {jLabel4.setBounds(10, 253, 140, 16);}
        txOutVal.setBackground(new java.awt.Color(25, 255, 25));
        getContentPane().add(txOutVal);
        if (bw) {txOutVal.setBounds(280, 496, 800, 50);}
           else {txOutVal.setBounds(140, 253, 400, 25);}
// ----------------------------------------------------------
        btParse.setFont(sansSerifFont);
        btParse.setText("Parse and Evaluate");
        btParse.addActionListener(new java.awt.event.ActionListener() {
            public void actionPerformed(java.awt.event.ActionEvent evt) {
                btParseActionPerformed(evt);
                }
            });
        getContentPane().add(btParse);
        if (bw) {btParse.setBounds(460, 596, 388, 50);}
           else {btParse.setBounds(230, 288, 194, 26);}
// ----------------------------------------------------------
        fileMenu.setText("FILE_MENU");
        exitMenuItem.setText("Exit");
        exitMenuItem.addActionListener(new java.awt.event.ActionListener() {
            public void actionPerformed(java.awt.event.ActionEvent evt) {
                exitMenuItemActionPerformed(evt);
                }
            });
        fileMenu.add(exitMenuItem);// adding a File Menu with an Exit button
        menuBar.add(fileMenu);      //
        setJMenuBar(menuBar);      //
        java.awt.Dimension screenSize =
            java.awt.Toolkit.getDefaultToolkit().getScreenSize();
        if (bw) {setBounds((screenSize.width-944)/2,
                (screenSize.height-700)/2, 1112, 748);}
           else {setBounds((screenSize.width-944)/2,
                (screenSize.height-700)/2, 556, 374);}
    } //GEN-END:initComponents
private void btParseActionPerformed(java.awt.event.ActionEvent evt) {
    //GEN-FIRST:event_btParseActionPerformed
    // Add your handling code here:
    // This part is like the main of the class BooleanExpressionEvaluator
    // in the file BooleanExpressionEvaluator.java.
        Node tree = null;
```

```
            try {// from String to StringReader and to BufferedReader. Added
                 // an extra '\n' at the end of the input for terminating the
                 // input as in the BooleanExpressionEvaluator class.
                 BufferedReader inputLine
                  = new BufferedReader(
                    new StringReader((txInExpr.getText()) + '\n'));
                 BooleanExpressionEvaluator.c = (char)inputLine.read();
                 tree = BooleanExpressionEvaluator.bexprParse(inputLine);
                 if (BooleanExpressionEvaluator.c != '\n')
                     { throw new ParseException(); };
            } catch ( IOException e ) {
                 e.printStackTrace();
                 txOutExpr.setText("IOException!");
            } catch ( ParseException pex ){
                 txOutExpr.setText(pex.getMessage());
                 return;
            } // ------
            if (tree != null) {
                 txOutExpr.setText(tree.toString());
            try { txOutVal.setText(
                 (BooleanExpressionEvaluator.evalTree(tree))?"true":"false");
            } catch ( EvalException evalex ) {
                 System.out.println(evalex.getMessage());
            }
            }
    } //GEN-LAST:event_btParseActionPerformed
    private void
            exitMenuItemActionPerformed(java.awt.event.ActionEvent evt) {
      //GEN-FIRST:event_exitMenuItemActionPerformed
        System.exit(0);
    } //GEN-LAST:event_exitMenuItemActionPerformed
    /** Exit the Application */
    private void exitForm(java.awt.event.WindowEvent evt) {
      //GEN-FIRST:event_exitForm
        System.exit(0);
    } //GEN-LAST:event_exitForm
    /**
     * @param args the command line arguments  */
    public static void main(String args[]) {
        new BooleanExpressionEvaluatorGUI().show();
    }
    // Variables declaration - do not modify   //GEN-BEGIN:variables
    private javax.swing.JMenuItem exitMenuItem;
    private javax.swing.JMenu fileMenu;
    private javax.swing.JLabel jLabel1;
    private javax.swing.JLabel jLabel2;
    private javax.swing.JLabel jLabel3;
    private javax.swing.JLabel jLabel4;
    private javax.swing.JMenuBar menuBar;
    private javax.swing.JTextField txInExpr;
    private javax.swing.JTextField txOutExpr;
    private javax.swing.JTextField txOutVal;
    private javax.swing.JButton btParse;
    // End of variables declaration            //GEN-END:variables
}
/**
 * input:                 output:
 * -----------------------------------------------------------------------
 * javac BooleanExpressionEvaluator.java       // This compilation is needed
 * javac BooleanExpressionEvaluatorGUI.java
```

```
 *  java  BooleanExpressionEvaluatorGUI
 *
 *              (see figures below)
 *  -------------------------------------------------------------------
 */
```

After typing the string t>(f+f)+-tx-f we have:

```
○ ○ ○                    EVALUATION OF A BOOLEAN EXPRESSION
FILE_MENU
─────────────────────────────────────────────────────────────────
  Grammar for the input boolean expression b:
    b ::= c | c>b        c ::= 1 | 1+c | 1xc        1 ::= a | -1
    a ::= 't' | 'f' | (b)
    't' stands for true. 'f' stands for false.
  Internal tree:
    b ::= true  | false  |  (-b)  |  (b + b)
        | (b x b)  |  (b > b)
  Evaluation of the boolean expression:
    true | false
```

Input Expression: | t>(f+f)+-tx-f |

Internal Tree: | |

Evaluation:

Parse and Evaluate

Then by clicking the button 'Parse and Evaluate' we get:

```
○ ○ ○                    EVALUATION OF A BOOLEAN EXPRESSION
FILE_MENU
─────────────────────────────────────────────────────────────────
  Grammar for the input boolean expression b:
    b ::= c | c>b        c ::= 1 | 1+c | 1xc        1 ::= a | -1
    a ::= 't' | 'f' | (b)
    't' stands for true. 'f' stands for false.
  Internal tree:
    b ::= true  | false  |  (-b)  |  (b + b)
        | (b x b)  |  (b > b)
  Evaluation of the boolean expression:
    true | false
```

Input Expression: | t>(f+f)+-tx-f |

Internal Tree: | (true > ((false + false) + ((-true) x (-false)))) |

Evaluation: | false |

Parse and Evaluate

7.3. A Theorem Prover for the Propositional Calculus

The program presented in this section: (i) first, parses using the recursive descent technique a given input string denoting a propositional formula, (ii) then, generates the internal tree which represents that formula, and (iii) finally, tells us whether or not that formula is a tautology. In case it is not a tautology the program returns the values of the propositional variables for which the given formula evaluates to `false`. The productions of the context-free grammar which generates the input string are the following ones:

```
p  ::=  c | c>p              (p is a propositional formula)
c  ::=  l | l+c |lxc         (c is a condition)
l  ::=  a | -l               (l is a literal)
a  ::=  '0' | ... | '9' | (p)   (a is an atom)
```

The axiom is p. The propositional variables are denoted by the characters '0', ..., '9', and thus, we assume that there are at most ten of them.

As in Section 7.2 on page 203, - denotes negation, + denotes disjunction, x denotes conjunction, and > denotes implication. For reasons of brevity, we will also write `true` as t and `false` as f. We assume that: (i) + and x bind more than >, and (ii) - binds more than + and x. We also assume right associativity for subexpressions involving + and x. Parentheses override priorities. No blank characters are allowed before, in between, and after the input string.

For instance, the string 1x3+1 denotes the propositional formula $P_1 \wedge (P_3 \vee P_1)$ where we have used the propositional variables P_1 and P_3, instead of '1' and '3', respectively.

The internal tree which corresponds to the input string is then printed as a string which is generated by the following productions from the axiom p:

```
p  ::=  d | (-p) | (p + p) | (p x p) | (p > p)
d  ::=  0 | 1 |...| 9
```

Note that the propositional variables '0', ..., '9' are printed as the digits 0, ..., 9, respectively . For instance, the propositional formula $P_1 \wedge (P_3 \vee P_1)$ is printed as (1 x (3 + 1)). If we execute the following two commands:

```
javac PropositionalTheoremProver.java
java  PropositionalTheoremProver
```

we get the following sentence in output:

```
Input a propositional formula according to the given grammar, please.
The variables should be between 0 and 3.
```

The value 3 is due to the fact that in our implementation we have set the value of the variable DIM (which tells us the maximum number of the propositional variables which may occur in the input formula) to 4. Thus, our propositional variables are: '0', '1', '2', and '3'. The value of DIM can be modified by the programmer and in our implementation it is a positive integer which it can be at most 10.

Then, if we type the following input string (note the absence of blank characters):

```
0>(1+1)+-0x-2
```

we get:

Parse tree of the propositional formula:
(0 > ((1 + 1) + ((-0) x (-2)))))

Is it a tautology? NO.
The falsity assignment is:

0=true; 1=false; 2=false; 3=false;

Indeed, the string (0 > ((1 + 1) + ((-0) x (-2)))) represents, according to our conventions, the propositional formula $P_0 \to ((P_1 \vee P_1) \vee (\neg P_0 \wedge \neg P_2))$, where we have used the propositional variables P_0, P_1, and P_2, instead of '0', '1', and '2', respectively. That propositional formula can be depicted as a tree as follows:

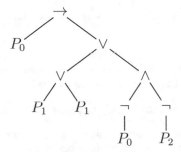

The value of that formula is **false** if $P_0 =$**true**, and $P_1 = P_2 =$ **false**.

Here is the program for parsing a given propositional formula and checking whether or not it is a tautology.

```
/**
 * ==============================================================================
 *                   PROPOSITIONAL THEOREM PROVER
 * Filename: "PropositionalTheoremProver.java"
 *
 * Grammar G for the input propositional formula p:
 *
 *     propositional formulas  p  ::=  c  | c>p                <-- propParse
 *     conditions              c  ::=  l  | l+c | lxc          <-- condParse
 *     literals                l  ::=  a  | -l                 <-- litParse
 *     atoms                   a  ::=  '0' | ... | '9' | (p)   <-- atomParse
 * Propositional variables are named: '0', ..., '9'.
 * The value of DIM is set to the maximum number of propositional variables
 * which are actually present in any given formula.
 * If DIM = 4, then the variables are: '0', '1', '2', and '3'.
 * (see line (1) below). DIM should be at most 10.
 * - denotes negation, + denotes disjunction, x denotes conjunction, and
 * > denotes implication.
 * Internal tree:
 * -------------
 *    p ::=  0   | ... |  9  |  (-p)  |  (p x p)  |  (p + p)  |  (p > p)
 *          (Leaf)        (Leaf)  (Unary)   (Binary)    (Binary)    (Binary)
 *
 * Output value of a propositional formula:
 * ---------------------------------------
 *    value ::= true | false
 * -------------
 * Priorities: + and x bind more than >
 *             - binds more than + or x
```

```
 *               Right associativity for + and x
 *               Parentheses override priorities.
 * No blanks are allowed before, in between, and after the input string.
 * The propositional formula in input should be a string generated by
 * the grammar G and then it is parsed and evaluated for all assignments
 * of the propositional variables.
 *
 * The word 'node' is assumed to be equivalent to the word 'tree'.
 * ---------
 * If "C2 extends C1" then the class C2 has the methods of the class C1.
 * This may not be desirable, but it allows the use of objects of the class
 * C1 and then the use of "instanceof" to test whether or not an object of
 * the class C1 is indeed of the class C2.
 * ---------
 * Line (1) below depends on the number of propositional variables.
 * Line (2) below checks whether or not the input propositional formula is
 * terminated by a carriage-return '\n'.
 * =======================================================================
 */
import java.io.*;
/**
 * =======================================================================
 *                  Class which constructs a Node
 *
 * This class is used for constructing a Node of a binary tree.
 * By default, a Node is a binary node.
 * A Node can be extended for constructing a Node which is
 * either a binary node, or a unary node, or a leaf node.
 * =======================================================================
 */
class Node {
   public Object  value;      // value field
   public Node    left;       // reference to the left  child node
   public Node    right;      // reference to the right child node
                                       // constructor
  /**
   * @param v : value at the node
   * @param l : reference to the left  child node
   * @param r : reference to the right child node
   */                               // constructor of a binary node
   public Node( Object v, Node l, Node r) {
      if ( v == null )  throw new IllegalArgumentException( );
      value   = v;
      left    = l;
      right   = r;
   }
}
/**
 * =======================================================================
 *             Class which constructs a binary node with two child nodes
 * =======================================================================
 */
class BinaryNode extends Node {
  /**                              // constructor of binary node
   * @param v : value at the node
   * @param l : reference to the left  child node
   * @param r : reference to the right child node
   */
   public BinaryNode(Object v, Node l, Node r) {
      super(v, l, r);
   }
```

```java
    /**
     * @return a string representing the tree whose root is the given node
     */
    public String toString(){
        return "("+ left.toString() +" "+ value +" "+ right.toString() +")";
    }
}

/**
 * =============================================================================
 *                  Class which constructs a unary node with one child node
 * =============================================================================
 */
class UnaryNode extends Node {
    /**                              // constructor of unary node
     * @param v        : value at the node
     * @param child : reference to the child node
     */

    public UnaryNode(Object v, Node child) {
        super(v, child, null);
    }
    /**
     * @return a string representing the tree whose root is the given node
     */
    public String toString() {
        return "(" + value + left.toString() + ")";
    }
}

/**
 * =============================================================================
 *                  Class which constructs a leaf node
 * =============================================================================
 */
class LeafNode extends Node {
    /**                              // constructor of a leaf
     * @param v : value at the node
     */
    public LeafNode(Object v) {
        super(v, null, null);
    }
    /**
     * @return a string representing the leaf node
     */
    public String toString() {
        return "" + value;
    }
}
/**
 * =============================================================================
 *                  Class ParseException
 * =============================================================================
 */
class ParseException extends Exception {
                        // constructor of a new instance of ParseException
    public ParseException() {
        super("parse exception!");
    }
}
```

```java
/**
 * ===============================================================
 *                   Class EvalException
 * ===============================================================
 */
class EvalException extends Exception {
                          // constructor of a new instance of EvalException
    public EvalException() {
          super("eval exception!");
    }
}
// -------------------------------------------------------------------
public class PropositionalTheoremProver {
// ===============================================================
    /**
     * This class PropositionalTheoremProver transforms the input string
     * into a tree of type Node using the recursive descent technique.
     * The string encodes the tree as indicated by the grammar G.
     * @param  string: the string which encodes the given tree
     * @return the root of the tree generated by the parsing
     * @throws IOException or ParseException or EvalException.
     */
// Three static fields of the class PropositionalTheoremProver
                      // DIM: maximum number of the distinct variables
                      // in the propositional formula
    public static final int DIM = 4;                         // <--- (1)
                      // At most DIM propositional variables in the
                      // propositional formula. By default, every
                      // element of tValues is initialized to "false"
    public static boolean [] tValues = new boolean [DIM];

    public static char c;// static field (global variable).
                      // inputLine is a sequence of characters,
                      // which are read one at a time, by
                      // the method read() of the class StringReader
// ----------------------- RECURSIVE DESCENT PARSING ---------------------
    public static Node propParse(BufferedReader inputLine)
                              throws IOException, ParseException {
      Node node1 = condParse(inputLine);
      if ( c == '>' ) {
        c = (char)inputLine.read();
        Node node2 = propParse(inputLine);
        return new BinaryNode(new Character('>'), node1, node2);
      } else { return node1; }
    }

    public static Node condParse(BufferedReader inputLine)
                              throws IOException, ParseException {
      Node node1 = litParse(inputLine);
      if ( c == 'x' ) {
        c = (char)inputLine.read();
        Node node2 = condParse(inputLine);
        return new BinaryNode(new Character('x'), node1, node2);
      } else
      if ( c == '+' )   {
        c = (char)inputLine.read();
        Node node2 = condParse(inputLine);
        return new BinaryNode(new Character('+'), node1, node2);
      } else { return node1; }
    }
```

```java
    public static Node litParse(BufferedReader inputLine)
                              throws IOException, ParseException {
        Node node = null;
        if ( c == '-' ) {
            c = (char)inputLine.read();
            Node node1 = litParse(inputLine);
            node = new UnaryNode(new Character('-'), node1);
        } else { node = atomParse(inputLine); };
        return node;
    }

    public static Node atomParse(BufferedReader inputLine)
                              throws IOException, ParseException {
        Node node1 = null;
        if (('0' <= c) && (c <= '9')) {
                              // from the character to the integer: -48 //
            node1 = new LeafNode(new Integer(Character.getNumericValue(c)));
            c = (char)inputLine.read();
            return node1;
        } else {
        if ( c=='(' ) {
            c = (char)inputLine.read();
            node1 = propParse(inputLine);
            if ( c==')' ) { c = (char)inputLine.read(); } // reads past ')'
            else { throw new ParseException(); };
            return node1;
            };
        };
        throw new ParseException();
    }

// --------------------------------------------------------------------
    /** Evaluation of the tree which represents the input boolean expression
    *   @param tree : tree to be evaluated
    *   @return the boolean value of the tree
    */
    public static boolean evalTree(Node tree)
                              throws EvalException {
// -------------------- RECURSIVE VERSION ------------------------------
    if ( tree instanceof LeafNode ) {                               //
        return tValues[(Integer)(((LeafNode)tree).value)];          //
        } else                                                      //
        if ( tree instanceof UnaryNode ) {                          //
            return !(evalTree(((UnaryNode)tree).left));             //
        } else                                                      //
        if ( tree instanceof BinaryNode ) {                         //
            boolean left  = evalTree(((BinaryNode)tree).left);      //
            boolean right = evalTree(((BinaryNode)tree).right);     //
            if (((Character)(((BinaryNode)tree).value)).charValue() == '+')//
                { return left || right; } else                      //
            if (((Character)(((BinaryNode)tree).value)).charValue() == 'x')//
                { return left && right; } else                      //
            if (((Character)(((BinaryNode)tree).value)).charValue() == '>')//
                { return (!left) || right; }                        //
        };                                                          //
        throw new EvalException();                                  //
// -------------------- END OF RECURSIVE VERSION ----------------------
    }
// --------------------------------------------------------------------
```

```java
    public static void main(String[] args)
                            throws IOException, ParseException {
        boolean answer = true;
        boolean bval   = true;
        System.out.println("Input a propositional formula according to the "
                        + "given grammar, please.");
        System.out.println("The variables should be between 0 and "
                        + (DIM-1) +".");
        Node tree = null;
        try {      // from String to StringReader and to BufferedReader
            BufferedReader inputLine =
                    new BufferedReader(new InputStreamReader(System.in));
            c = (char)inputLine.read();
            tree = propParse(inputLine);
            if (c != '\n') { throw new ParseException(); };      // <--- (2)
        } catch ( IOException e ) {
            e.printStackTrace();
            System.out.println("IOException!");
        } catch ( ParseException pex ) {
            System.out.println(pex.getMessage());
            return;
        };
    // ====== (begin 0) ===================================
        if (tree != null) {
            System.out.println("\nParse tree of the propositional formula:\n"
                            +tree);
            System.out.print("\nIs it a tautology? ");
/** -------------------------------------------------------------------
 * The following fragment computes the dispositions for tValues[0],...,
 * tValues[DIM-1] from false,...,false to true,...,true until we finds
 * a disposition which makes bval == false, if any. In that case the given
 * formula is NOT a tautology. If, otherwise, all dispositions make
 * bval == true, then the given formula is a tautology.
 * ------------------------------------------------------------------ */
            for (int i = 0; i < (int)Math.pow(2,DIM); i++) {
                try {
                  bval = evalTree(tree);
                } catch ( EvalException evalex ) {
                    System.out.println(evalex.getMessage());
                };
                if (!bval) { answer = false; break; }
                else {
                    for (int k = 0; k < DIM; k++) {
                        if (tValues[k]) { tValues[k] = false; }
                        else { tValues[k] = true; break; }
                    }
                }
            };
    // ----------------------------------------------------------
            if (answer) { System.out.println("YES."); } else {
                System.out.println("NO.\nThe falsity assignment is:\n");
                for (int k = 0; k < DIM; k++) {
                    System.out.print(k + "=" + tValues[k] + "; ");};
                System.out.println();
            }
    // ----------------------------------------------------------
        }
    // ====== (end 0)  ===================================
    }
}
```

```
/**
 * input:  output:
 * ------------------------------------------------------------------
 * javac PropositionalTheoremProver.java
 * java  PropositionalTheoremProver
 *
 *      Input a propositional formula according to the given grammar, please.
 *      The variables should be between 0 and 3.
 * 0>1>0
 *
 *      Parse of the propositional formula:
 *      (0 > (1 > 0))
 *
 *      Is it a tautology? YES.
 * ------------------------------------------------------------------
 *      Input a propositional formula according to the given grammar, please.
 *      The variables should be between 0 and 3.
 * 0>-1
 *
 *      Parse of the propositional formula:
 *      (0 > (-1))
 *
 *      Is it a tautology? NO.
 *      The falsity assignment is:
 *
 *      0=true; 1=true; 2=false; 3=false;
 * ------------------------------------------------------------------
 *      Input a propositional formula according to the given grammar, please.
 *      The variables should be between 0 and 3.
 * 0>(1+1)+-0x-2
 *
 *      Parse tree of the propositional formula:
 *      (0 > ((1 + 1) + ((-0) x (-2))))
 *
 *      Is it a tautology? NO.
 *      The falsity assignment is:
 *
 *      0=true; 1=false; 2=false; 3=false;
 * ------------------------------------------------------------------
 */
```

The following program is like the above one: it parses a given propositional formula
and checks whether or not it is a tautology, but it uses a graphical interface. It can
be run by typing the following three commands:

```
javac PropositionalTheoremProver.java
javac PropositionalTheoremProverGUI.java
java  PropositionalTheoremProverGUI
```

```
/**
 * ==================================================================
 *                   PROPOSITIONAL THEOREM PROVER
 *                   with a Graphical User Iterface
 * Filename: "PropositionalTheoremProverGUI.java"
 *
 * This program should be compiled after the compilation of the program
 * PropositionalTheoremProver.java.
 *
 * See also the initial comments of the file PropositionalTheoremProver.java
```

```
 *
 * This program uses the class PropositionalTheoremProver in the file named
 * PropositionalTheoremProver.java. The file PropositionalTheoremProver.java
 * should be stored in the same folder where this file
 * PropositionalTheoremProverGUI.java is stored.
 * ------------
 * Lines (1) below depend on the number of propositional variables.
 * Line (2) below checks whether or not the input propositional formula
 * is terminated by a carriage-return '\n'.
 * ------------
 * To get a dialog window with font size 14 (instead of 28): set the
 * boolean variable bw (short for big_window) to false (see line ***).
 * This program has been generated by a graphical tool with which one can
 * draw windows and add buttons.
 * =====================================================================
 */
import java.io.*;
import javax.swing.JFrame;
import java.awt.Font;                                  // needed for changing fonts
// -----------------------------------------------------------
public class PropositionalTheoremProverGUI extends JFrame {
    /** Creates new form PropositionalTheoremProverGUI */
    public PropositionalTheoremProverGUI() {                    // constructor
        initComponents();
    }
    /** This method initComponents() is called from within the constructor
     * to initialize the form.
     */
    private void initComponents() {//GEN-BEGIN:initComponents
        jLabel1     = new javax.swing.JLabel();
        jLabel2     = new javax.swing.JLabel();
        jLabel3     = new javax.swing.JLabel();
        jLabel4     = new javax.swing.JLabel();
        txInForm    = new javax.swing.JTextField();
        txParsedForm = new javax.swing.JTextField();
        txAnswTaut  = new javax.swing.JTextField();
        btParse     = new javax.swing.JButton();
        menuBar     = new javax.swing.JMenuBar();
        fileMenu    = new javax.swing.JMenu();
        exitMenuItem = new javax.swing.JMenuItem();

        getContentPane().setLayout(null);
        setTitle("PROPOSITIONAL THEOREM PROVER");
        setLocationRelativeTo(null);
        addWindowListener(new java.awt.event.WindowAdapter() {
            public void windowClosing(java.awt.event.WindowEvent evt) {
                exitForm(evt);
            }
        });
// -----------------------------------------------------------
        boolean bw = true;  // true (false) for big (small) window.  ***
        Font sansSerifFont =
            bw ? (new Font("SansSerif",Font.PLAIN,28)):
                (new Font("SansSerif",Font.PLAIN,14));
// -----------------------------------------------------------
        txInForm.setFont(sansSerifFont);
        txParsedForm.setFont(sansSerifFont);
        txAnswTaut.setFont(sansSerifFont);

// -----------------------------------------------------------
```

```
      jLabel1.setBackground(new java.awt.Color(255, 255, 150));
      jLabel1.setFont(sansSerifFont);
      jLabel1.setText("<HTML>\n\n<PRE>\n"
     +" Grammar for the input propositional formula p:\n"
     +"    prop:   p ::= c | c>p        cond:   c ::= l | l+c | lxc\n"
     +"    lit:    l ::= a | -l"
     +"      atom:    a ::= '0' | ... | '3' | (p)\n"          // <--- (1)
     +" Internal tree: p ::= 0 | ... | 3 | (-p) | (p x p)\n"// <--- (1)
     +"                   | (p + p) | (p > p)\n"
     +" Abbreviations: f/false  t/true  -/not  x/and  +/or  >/implies"
     +"<PRE>\n</HTML>");
      jLabel1.setVerticalAlignment(javax.swing.SwingConstants.TOP);
      jLabel1.setOpaque(true);
      getContentPane().add(jLabel1);

      if (bw) {jLabel1.setBounds(10, 10, 1200, 190);}
         else {jLabel1.setBounds(5, 5, 565, 97);}
// -----------------------------------------------------------
      jLabel2.setFont(sansSerifFont);
      jLabel2.setText("Input Formula:");
      getContentPane().add(jLabel2);
      if (bw) {jLabel2.setBounds(20, 208, 200, 32);}
         else {jLabel2.setBounds(10, 104, 130, 16);}
      getContentPane().add(txInForm);
      if (bw) {txInForm.setBounds(280, 208, 860, 40);}
         else {txInForm.setBounds(130, 104, 430, 20);}
// -----------------------------------------------------------
      jLabel3.setFont(sansSerifFont);
      jLabel3.setText("Parsed Formula:");
      getContentPane().add(jLabel3);
      if (bw) {jLabel3.setBounds(20, 288, 220, 32);}
         else {jLabel3.setBounds(10, 144, 130, 16);}
      txParsedForm.setBackground(new java.awt.Color(25, 255, 25));
      getContentPane().add(txParsedForm);
      if (bw) {txParsedForm.setBounds(280, 288, 860, 40);}
         else {txParsedForm.setBounds(130, 144, 430, 20);}
// -----------------------------------------------------------
      jLabel4.setFont(sansSerifFont);
      jLabel4.setText("Is it a tautology?");
      getContentPane().add(jLabel4);
      if (bw) {jLabel4.setBounds(20, 368, 280, 32);}
         else {jLabel4.setBounds(10, 184, 140, 16);}
      txAnswTaut.setBackground(new java.awt.Color(25, 255, 25));
      getContentPane().add(txAnswTaut);
      if (bw) {txAnswTaut.setBounds(280, 368, 860, 50);}
         else {txAnswTaut.setBounds(130, 184, 430, 20);}
// -----------------------------------------------------------
      btParse.setFont(sansSerifFont);
      btParse.setText("Parse and Evaluate");
      btParse.addActionListener(new java.awt.event.ActionListener() {
          public void actionPerformed(java.awt.event.ActionEvent evt) {
            btParseActionPerformed(evt);
            }
          });
      getContentPane().add(btParse);
      if (bw) {btParse.setBounds(430, 440, 576, 52);}
         else {btParse.setBounds(240, 215, 158, 26);}

// -----------------------------------------------------------
```

```
    fileMenu.setText("FILE_MENU");
    exitMenuItem.setText("Exit");
    exitMenuItem.addActionListener(new java.awt.event.ActionListener() {
        public void actionPerformed(java.awt.event.ActionEvent evt) {
            exitMenuItemActionPerformed(evt);
            }
        });
    fileMenu.add(exitMenuItem);// adding a File Menu with an Exit button
    menuBar.add(fileMenu);        //
    setJMenuBar(menuBar);         //
    java.awt.Dimension screenSize =
        java.awt.Toolkit.getDefaultToolkit().getScreenSize();
    if (bw) {setBounds((screenSize.width-1300)/2,
            (screenSize.height-700)/2, 1160, 590);}
        else {setBounds((screenSize.width-444)/2,
            (screenSize.height-300)/2, 580, 300);}
} //GEN-END:initComponents

private void btParseActionPerformed(java.awt.event.ActionEvent evt) {

    // GEN-FIRST:event_btParseActionPerformed
    // Add your handling code here:
    // This part is like the main of the class PropositionalTheoremProver
    // in the file PropositionalTheoremProver.java.

        boolean answer = true;
        boolean bval   = true;
        int DIM        = PropositionalTheoremProver.DIM;        // <--- (1)
        Node tree = null;
        try {   // from String to StringReader and to BufferedReader.
                // Added an extra '\n' at the end of the input for
                // terminating the input as in the
                // PropositionalTheoremProver class.
          BufferedReader inputLine
          = new BufferedReader(
            new StringReader((txInForm.getText()) + '\n'));
          PropositionalTheoremProver.c = (char)inputLine.read();
          tree=PropositionalTheoremProver.propParse(inputLine);// <--- (2)
          if (PropositionalTheoremProver.c != '\n')
                { throw new ParseException(); };
        } catch ( IOException e ) {
            e.printStackTrace();
            txParsedForm.setText("IOException!");
        } catch ( ParseException pex ){
            txParsedForm.setText(pex.getMessage());
            return;
        };

        // ------ (begin Parse and Evaluate)
        if (tree != null) {
            txParsedForm.setText(tree.toString());
// ----------------------------------------------------------
        for (int i = 0; i < (int)Math.pow(2,DIM);
                     i++) {
            try {
              bval = PropositionalTheoremProver.evalTree(tree);
            } catch ( EvalException evalex ) {
              txAnswTaut.setText(evalex.getMessage());
            };
            if (!bval) { answer = false; break; }
```

```
                else {
                    for (int k = 0; k < DIM; k++) {
                        if (PropositionalTheoremProver.tValues[k])
                            { PropositionalTheoremProver.tValues[k] = false; }
                        else { PropositionalTheoremProver.tValues[k] = true;
                            break; }
                    }
                }
            };
// -----------------------------------------------------------

        if (answer) { txAnswTaut.setText("YES."); } else {
            String outstring = "NO. False if: ";
            for (int k = 0; k < DIM; k++) {
            outstring = outstring + k + "="
                + ((PropositionalTheoremProver.tValues[k])?"t; ":"f; ");}
            txAnswTaut.setText(outstring);
        }

// -----------------------------------------------------------
        }
            // ------ (end Parse and Evaluate)
    } //GEN-LAST:event_btParseActionPerformed

    private void
            exitMenuItemActionPerformed(java.awt.event.ActionEvent evt) {
      //GEN-FIRST:event_exitMenuItemActionPerformed
        System.exit(0);
    } //GEN-LAST:event_exitMenuItemActionPerformed

    /** Exit the Application */

    private void exitForm(java.awt.event.WindowEvent evt) {
      //GEN-FIRST:event_exitForm
        System.exit(0);
    } //GEN-LAST:event_exitForm

    /**
     * @param args the command line arguments
     */

    public static void main(String args[]) {
        new PropositionalTheoremProverGUI().show();
    }

    // Variables declaration - do not modify    //GEN-BEGIN:variables
    private javax.swing.JMenuItem exitMenuItem;
    private javax.swing.JMenu fileMenu;
    private javax.swing.JLabel jLabel1;
    private javax.swing.JLabel jLabel2;
    private javax.swing.JLabel jLabel3;
    private javax.swing.JLabel jLabel4;
    private javax.swing.JMenuBar menuBar;
    private javax.swing.JTextField txInForm;
    private javax.swing.JTextField txParsedForm;
    private javax.swing.JTextField txAnswTaut;
    private javax.swing.JButton btParse;
    // End of variables declaration             //GEN-END:variables
}
```

```
/**
 * input:               output:
 * ----------------------------------------------------------------------
 * javac PropositionalTheoremProver.java      // This compilation is needed
 * javac PropositionalTheoremProverGUI.java
 * java  PropositionalTheoremProverGUI
 *
 *            (see figures below)
 * ----------------------------------------------------------------------
 */
```

After typing the string `0>(1+1)+-0x-2` we have:

```
 ○ ○ ○                    PROPOSITIONAL THEOREM PROVER
FILE_MENU
  Grammar for the input propositional formula p:
     prop:     p ::= c │ c>p        cond:    c ::= l │ l+c │ lxc
     lit:      l ::= a │ -l         atom:    a ::= '0' │ ... │ '3' │ (p)
  Internal tree: p ::= 0 │ ... │ 3 │ (-p) │ (p x p)
                    │ (p + p) │ (p > p)
  Abbreviations: f/false  t/true  -/not  x/and  +/or  >/implies

  Input Formula:    0>(1+1)+-0x-2

  Parsed Formula:

  Is it a tautology?

                         Parse and Evaluate
```

Then by clicking the button 'Parse and Evaluate' we get:

```
 ○ ○ ○                    PROPOSITIONAL THEOREM PROVER
FILE_MENU
  Grammar for the input propositional formula p:
     prop:     p ::= c │ c>p        cond:    c ::= l │ l+c │ lxc
     lit:      l ::= a │ -l         atom:    a ::= '0' │ ... │ '3' │ (p)
  Internal tree: p ::= 0 │ ... │ 3 │ (-p) │ (p x p)
                    │ (p + p) │ (p > p)
  Abbreviations: f/false  t/true  -/not  x/and  +/or  >/implies

  Input Formula:    0>(1+1)+-0x-2

  Parsed Formula:   (0 > ((1 + 1) + ((-0) x (-2))))

  Is it a tautology?  NO. False if: 0=t; 1=f; 2=t; 3=f;

                         Parse and Evaluate
```

7.4. Encoding of n-ary Trees Using Binary Trees

Before formalizing the problem of encoding n-ary trees using binary trees, let us first present the following three data structures which are used in that formalization:
  (i) binary trees with objects of type T in the nodes,
  (ii) n-ary trees with objects of type T in the nodes, and
  (iii) lists of n-ary trees with objects of type T in the nodes.
  For reasons of brevity, instead of saying 'binary trees with objects of type T in the nodes', we will also say: 'binary trees with nodes of type T'. Analogous terminology will also be used for n-ary trees and lists of n-ary trees.

REMARK 7.4.1. [**Terminology for Nodes and Trees**] When referring to trees, we will equivalently use the term 'node' and 'tree', because every node in a tree denotes the subtree rooted in that node (see also Remark 7.1.1 on page 194).

BINARY TREES WITH NODES OF TYPE T

Let V denote the set of objects of type T. We define the set B of the binary trees with objects of type T in the nodes, to be the solution of the following domain equation (see [**20**, pages 107–124]):

$$B = 1 + B \times V \times B \tag{1}$$

The empty binary tree in the domain 1 is the element $e \in B$, and a non-empty binary tree in the domain $B \times V \times B$ is a triple $(\mathtt{lb}, \mathtt{v}, \mathtt{rb})$, where: $\mathtt{v} \in V$ is an object of type T, and $\mathtt{lb}$ and $\mathtt{rb}$ are two binary trees in B with objects of type T. These two trees are said to be the *left* and *right* subtrees, respectively, of the given binary tree $(\mathtt{lb}, \mathtt{v}, \mathtt{rb})$.
  In the Java 1.5 implementation which we will present below, we have that:
($\bullet$) the empty binary tree e with nodes of type T is constructed by the nullary constructor BinNode<T>() by using the command

    new BinNode<T>(), and

($\bullet$) the non-empty binary tree $(\mathtt{lb}, \mathtt{v}, \mathtt{rb})$ with nodes of type T is constructed by the ternary constructor BinNode<T>(lb,v,rb) by using the command

    new BinNode<T>(lb,v,rb)

where v is an object of type T, and lb and rb denote two already constructed binary trees with nodes of type T. The selector which tests whether or not a binary tree with nodes of type T is empty, is:

    isEmpty()

Thus, for instance, in the case of binary trees with nodes of type Integer we have that

    new BinNode<Integer>().isEmpty() returns true.

Here is a program which constructs binary trees with nodes of type T.

```
/**
 * ==========================================================================
 *           Class which constructs a binary node with two child nodes
 * Filename: "BinNode.java"
 *
 * Binary trees with nodes of type T are internally represented as follows:
 *
 *      bt<T>    ::= e | (bt<T>, val, bt<T>)    where val is of type T
 *
```

```
 * e is the empty binary node
 * constructors: new BinNode<T>() | new BinNode<T>(-,-,-)
 * selector:     new BinNode<T>().isEmpty() is true  (the BinNode<T> is e)
 *
 * ------------
 * constructing e: new BinNode()
 *
 * constructing an non-empty binary node of type Integer, which is
 *    7 with empty child nodes:
 *
 *    new BinNode<Integer>(new BinNode<Integer>(),7, new BinNode<Integer>())
 *
 * Notice that Java 1.5 accepts: 7, instead of: new Integer(7).
 * =======================================================================
 */
public class BinNode<T> {

    private T value;          // value field of type T
    private BinNode left;     // reference to the left  child node
    private BinNode right;    // reference to the right child node

    public BinNode ( ) {      // constructor 1:  empty BinNode e
      this.value = null;      // for constructor 1: this.left  == null is true
     }                        // for constructor 1: this.right == null is true

    /*
     * Constructor of a Node with:
     * - value v,
     * - parameters l and r, which are references to the left and right
     *   child nodes, respectively.
     */
    public BinNode ( BinNode l, T v, BinNode r ) {     // constructor 2
       this.left  = l;
       this.value = v;
       this.right = r;
     }

    /**
     * @return the value.
     */
    public T getValue() {
       return value;
     }

    /**
     * @return the left child node.
     */
    public BinNode getLeftChild(){
        return left;
     }

    /**
     * @return the right child node.
     */
    public BinNode getRightChild(){
        return right;
     }
    /**
     * @return true iff the value of the BinNode is the null reference.
     *
     * Each of the following prints: true
```

```
 *      System.out.print(new BinNode().isEmpty());
 *      System.out.print(new BinNode<Integer>().isEmpty());
 *      System.out.print(new BinNode(null,null,null).isEmpty());
 *      System.out.print(new BinNode<Integer>(null,null,null).isEmpty());
 *
 *  The following two instructions:
 *      BinNode<Integer> b = null;
 *      System.out.println(b.isEmpty());
 *  give a NullPointerException
 */
public boolean isEmpty() {
   return value == null;
}
/**
 * This method prints the tree whose root is the given node.
 * We assume that 'value' can be printed as a string.
 */
public void binNodePrint(){
   if (value == null) {System.out.print("e");}
   else {
   System.out.print("("); left.binNodePrint();
   System.out.print(" "+value+" ");
   right.binNodePrint(); System.out.print(")");
   }
}
}
// ----------------------------------------------------------------------
```

N-ARY TREES WITH NODES OF TYPE T

Let V denote the set of objects of type T. We define the set T of the *n*-ary trees with objects of type T in the nodes, to be the solution of the following domain equations:

$$
\begin{aligned}
T &= 1 + V \times \textit{Tlist} \\
\textit{Tlist} &= 1 + T \times \textit{Tlist}
\end{aligned}
\tag{2}
$$

The empty *n*-ary tree with nodes of type T in the domain 1 is the element $E \in T$, and a non-empty *n*-ary tree with nodes of type T in the domain $V \times \textit{Tlist}$ is a pair (v, L), where: $v \in V$ is an object of type T, and $L \in \textit{Tlist}$ is a list of *n*-ary trees with nodes of type T, which is constructed as indicated on page 232.

In the Java 1.5 implementation which we will present below, we have that:
($\bullet$) the empty *n*-ary tree E with nodes of type T is constructed by the nullary constructor NaryNode<T>() by using the command

   new NaryNode<T>(), and

($\bullet$) the non-empty *n*-ary tree (v, L) with nodes of type T is constructed by the binary constructor NaryNode<T>(v,L) by using the command

   new NaryNode<T>(v,L)

where v is an object of type T and L is a list of *n*-ary trees with nodes of type T. The selector which tests whether or not an *n*-ary tree with nodes of type T is empty, is:

   isEmpty()

Thus, for instance, in the case of *n*-ary trees with nodes of type Integer we have that

   new NaryNode<Integer>().isEmpty() returns true.

Here is a program which constructs n-ary trees with nodes of type T.

```
/**
 * ==============================================================================
 *       Class which constructs an n-ary node with a list of child nodes
 * Filename: "NaryNode.java"
 *
 * N-ary trees with nodes of type T are internally represented as follows:
 *
 *     nt<T>     ::= E  | (val, list_nt<T>)       where val is of type T
 *
 * E is the empty n-ary tree.
 * list_nt<T> is a list of n-ary trees with nodes of type T.
 * constructors: new NaryNode<T>() | new NaryNode<T>(-,-)
 * selector:     new NaryNode<Integer>().isEmpty() is true
 *                                     (indeed, the NaryNode<Integer> is E)
 * ---------
 * Lists of n-ary trees are internally represented as follows:
 *
 *   list_nt<T> ::= [] | nt<T> : list_nt<T>
 *
 * cons is denoted by the infix ':'. In the implementation using ArrayList
 * the last element which is cons-ed is to the right (not to the left).
 *
 * constructors: new List<T>() | l.cons(nt) where l is a list of n-ary trees
 *                        of type <T> and nt is an n-ary tree of type <T>
 * selector:     new List<Integer>().isEmpty() is true
 *                                     (indeed, the List<Integer> is [])
 * ----------------------------------------------------------------------
 * constructing E: new NaryNode<Integer>()
 *
 * constructing a non-empty n-ary node of type Integer, which is
 *    8 with an empty list of child nodes:
 *
 *    new NaryNode<Integer>(8, new List<NaryNode<Integer>>())
 *
 * Notice that Java 1.5 accepts: 8, instead of: new Integer(8).
 * ==============================================================================
 */
import java.util.*;        // needed for using ArrayList<T> and Iterator

public class NaryNode<T> {

    private T value;                     // value of the n-ary node of type T
    private List <NaryNode<T>> list;     // list of child nodes

    /*
     * Constructor of a Node with:
     * - value v,
     * - parameter l, which is a reference to the list of child nodes.
     */

    public NaryNode ( ) {     // constructor 1: empty NaryNode E
      this.value = null;      // for constructor 1: this.list == null is true
    }

    public NaryNode ( T value, List<NaryNode<T>> list ) {  // constructor 2
      this.value = value;     // for: NaryNode <Integer> n1
      this.list  = list;      //         = new NaryNode(1,new List())
    }                         // n1.list.isEmpty() is true
```

```
/**
 * @return the list of child nodes.
 */
public List <NaryNode<T>> getListOfChildren(){
    return list;
}

/**
 * @return the value at the node.
 */
public T getValue(){
    return value;
}

/**
 * @return true iff the value is the null reference.
 *
 * The following two instructions:
 *     System.out.println(new NaryNode().isEmpty());
 *     System.out.println(new NaryNode(null,null).isEmpty());
 * both return true.
 */
public boolean isEmpty() {
    return value == null;
}

/**
 * This method prints the tree whose root is the given node.
 * We assume that 'value' can be printed as a string.
 */
public void naryNodePrint(){
    if (value == null) { System.out.print("E"); } // empty n-ary tree
    else { System.out.print(value+" [");
            for (int i=list.size()-1; i>=0; i--) {
                ((NaryNode)(list.get(i))).naryNodePrint();
                if (i > 0) {System.out.print(", ");}
                };
            System.out.print("]");
    }
}
}
/**
 * ----------------------------------------------------------------------
 * We have that:
 *
 * NaryNode <Integer> n0 = new NaryNode();
 * System.out.println(n0.list == null);     // prints: true
 * System.out.println((n0.list).isEmpty());// raises a NullPointerException!
 *
 * System.out.println(new NaryNode().isEmpty());            // prints: true
 * System.out.println(new NaryNode<Integer>().isEmpty()); // prints: true
 *
 * NaryNode <Integer> n1 = new NaryNode(1,new List());
 * System.out.println(n1.list == null);     // prints: false
 * System.out.println(n1.list.isEmpty())    // prints: true
 * ----------------------------------------------------------------------
 */
```

LISTS OF N-ARY TREES WITH NODES OF TYPE T

The lists of n-ary trees with objects of type T are elements of the domain *Tlist* which has been defined by the domain equations (2) on page 229. For any type T, the empty list of n-ary trees with nodes of type T in the domain 1 is the element [], and a non-empty list of n-ary trees with nodes of type T is a pair h : H, where:

  (i) h $\in T$ is an n-ary tree with nodes of type T,

 (ii) ':' denotes the infix *cons* operation on lists, and

(iii) H $\in$ *Tlist* is a list of n-ary trees with nodes of type T.

In the Java 1.5 implementation of the lists with nodes of trees of type T which we will present below, we have that:

(•) the empty list [] of n-ary trees with nodes of type T is constructed by the nullary constructor List<NaryNode<T>>() by using the command

   new List<NaryNode<T>>(), and

(•) the non-empty list of n-ary trees with nodes of type T is constructed from an already constructed, shorter list H of n-ary trees with nodes of type T, by *cons*-ing onto it an n-ary tree nt with nodes of type T by using the following command:

   H.cons(nt)

The selector which tests whether or not a list of n-ary trees with nodes of type T is empty, is:

   isEmpty()

Thus, for instance, in the case of lists of n-ary trees with nodes of type Integer we have that

   new List<NaryNode<Integer>>().isEmpty() returns true,

because new List<NaryNode<Integer>>() is the empty list [] of n-ary trees with nodes of type Integer.

Here is the program List.java which is the Java 1.5 implementation of the *generic class* of the lists of elements of type T. It is similar to the program, also called List.java, presented in Section 3.2 on page 35 where the reader may found some examples of use of the methods of the generic class List.

```
/** ========================================================================
 *                 Generic Class List <T> (class used for encoding trees)
 * Filename: "List.java"
 *
 * Every object of the class List<T> is a list of elements of type T.
 * The following methods are available:
 *    cons(T d), head(), tail(), size(), get(int i), isSingleton(),
 *    isEmpty(), makeEmpty(), copy(), and listPrint().
 * Also cloneCopy() is available if we uncomment line (***) below and
 * comment the previous line.
 *
 * Notice that the tail() method is destructive.
 * After a tail operation, if we need the original value of the list, we
 * should reconstruct it by 'consing' the head of the list.
 * ---------------------
 * Lists of elements nt of type T are internally represented as follows:
 *
 *    list_nt<T> ::= [] | nt<T> : list_nt<T>
 *
 * cons is denoted by the infix ':'. In the implementation using ArrayList
```

```
* the last element which is cons-ed is to the right (not to the left).
*
* constructors: new List<T>() | l.cons(t)  where l is a list of objects
*                                  type <T> and t is an object of type <T>
* selector:     new List<Integer>().isEmpty() is true
*                                  (indeed, the new List<Integer> is [])
*               new List().isEmpty() is true
* ---------------------
* List la = new List();   la.cons(3);   la.listPrint(); // prints: [ 3 ]
* List lb = new List<Integer>();
* lb.cons(6);   lb.listPrint();                         // prints: [ 6 ]
* ======================================================================
*/

import java.util.*;           // needed for using ArrayList<T> and Iterator

 public class List<T> {       // it is ok if we do not use cloneCopy()

// public class List<T> implements Cloneable { // (***) In order to use
//          // cloneCopy(), uncomment this line and comment the previous one.

    private ArrayList<T> list;

    public List() {
       list = new ArrayList<T>();// constructor
    }

    public void cons(T datum) {  // the head of the list is to the right,
       list.add(datum);          // not to the left.
    }                            // add(_) is a method of ArrayList<T>

    public T head() {         // the head of the list is to the right.
       if (list.isEmpty())    // It is the last element:  >---------------+
          {System.out.println("Error: head of empty list!");};//         |
          T obj = list.get(list.size() - 1);  //    <--------------------+
       return obj;            // isEmpty(), size(), and get(int i)
    }                         // are methods of ArrayList<T>

    public void tail() {      // destructive tail() method
       if (list.isEmpty())
          {System.out.println("Error: tail of empty list!");};
       list.remove(list.size() - 1); // isEmpty(), size(), and remove(int i)
    }                              // are methods of ArrayList<T>

    public int size() {
       return list.size();       // size() is a method of ArrayList<T>
    }

    public T get(int i) {        // 0 <= i <= size() - 1
       return list.get(i);       // get(int i) is a method of ArrayList<T>
    }

    public boolean isSingleton() {
       return list.size() == 1;  // size() is a method of ArrayList<T>
    }

    public boolean isEmpty() {
       return list.isEmpty();    // isEmpty() is a method of ArrayList<T>
    }
```

```
    public void makeEmpty() {
        list.clear();              // clear() is a method of ArrayList<T>
    }

    // ----------------------- Printing a list ---------------------------
    // We assume that an element of the list has a toString() method.

    public void listPrint() {
        if ( !isEmpty() ){
        System.out.print("[ ");
        for (Iterator iter = list.iterator(); iter.hasNext(); ) {
            System.out.print((iter.next()).toString() + " ");
            };
        System.out.print("]");
        }
        else {System.out.print("[]");}
    }
    // ----------------------- Making a copy of a list without clone() ----
    // ----------------------- The given list is NOT destroyed. -----------
    public List<T> copy() {
        List<T> copyList = new List<T>();
        for (Iterator<T> iter = list.iterator(); iter.hasNext(); ) {
            copyList.list.add(iter.next());
        };
        return copyList;
    }
    // ----------------------- Making a copy of a list with clone() -------
    // ----------------------- The given list is NOT destroyed. -----------
    public List<T> cloneCopy() {                    // see (***) above
        try { List<T> copyList = (List<T>)super.clone();
              copyList.list = (ArrayList<T>)list.clone();
              return copyList;
        } catch (CloneNotSupportedException e) {
          throw new InternalError();
        }
    }
}
/* --------------------------------------------------------------------- */
```

SOLVING THE ENCODING PROBLEM

Let us consider the set N of the natural numbers. In what follows by B and T we denote, respectively, the set of the binary trees and n-ary trees with natural numbers in the nodes which we have defined on pages 227 and 229.

Every n-ary tree in T can be encoded into a binary tree in B via the encoding function Kin : $T \to B$, and can be decoded from a binary tree via the decoding function Hin : $B \to T$. These two functions, which are defined in the Java program EncodingTrees.java listed on page 235, are such that for every n-ary tree nt, we have that: Hin(Kin(nt)) = nt. In order to execute the program EncodingTrees.java we need the following Java programs:

    (i)   BinNode.java,

    (ii) NaryNode.java, and

    (iii) List.java,

which implement, respectively, (i) the binary trees in B with nodes of type T (see page 227), (ii) the n-ary trees in T with nodes of type T (see page 229), and (iii) the lists in *Tlist* of elements of type T, for some type parameter T (see page 232). The actual type of those trees and lists is given by instantiating the type parameter T, as allowed in Java 1.5. For instance, in the case of lists, if we instantiate the type T to <NaryNode <Integer>>, we get the lists of n-ary trees with nodes of type Integer.

In the program EncodingTrees.java an n-ary tree with nodes of type Integer to be encoded into a binary tree with nodes of type Integer, is given as a string nt generated by the following productions:

```
nt        ::=  E     |  ne_nt
ne_nt     ::=  m     |  m ( ne_list )
ne_list   ::=  ne_nt  |  ne-nt , ne_list
```

where: (i) E is the empty n-ary tree, (ii) comma and parentheses are terminal symbols, and (iii) m is any integer number in the set {...,-2,-1,0,1,2,...}. In this representation we have used the notions of an ne_nt (that is, a non-empty n-ary tree) and ne_list (that is, a non-empty list of non-empty n-ary trees). This choice of using non-empty n-ary trees has the advantage that a node with value m and no son nodes, can be given in input as the string m, rather than the longer string m([]).

The internal representation of an n-ary tree nt is done according to domain equations (2) (see page 229), that is, it is generated by the following productions:

```
nt    ::=  E   |  m ( list )
list  ::=  []  |  nt : list
```

where we have used the empty list [] and the infix *cons* operation denoted ':'.

Here is a program for encoding n-ary trees into binary trees and decoding binary trees back to n-ary trees by using the functions Kin and Hin.

```
/**
 * ==============================================================================
 *                 ENCODING n-ARY TREES INTO BINARY TREES
 * Filename: "EncodingTrees.java"
 *
 * This program defines the encoding method Kin from n-ary trees to binary
 * trees. It also defines an inverse method Hin such that
 * for every n-ary tree nt, we have that Hin(Kin(nt)) = nt.
 * Grammar of the input n-ary tree nt:
 * n-ary tree:            nt       ::= E | ne_nt
 *
 * non-empty n-ary tree:  ne_nt    ::= m | m(ne_list)
 *
 * non-empty list of non-empty n-ary trees:
 *                        ne_list ::= ne_nt | ne_nt , list_list
 *
 * where: E is the empty n-ary tree,
 *        m can be any integer in {...,-2,-1,0,1,2,...}
 * Comma and parentheses are terminal symbols.
 * ------------------------------------------------------------------------------
 * The internal representations of binary trees, n-trees, and lists of n-ary
 * trees are provided by objects of the classes: BinNode, NaryNode, and List
 * ==============================================================================
 */

import java.io.*;
import java.util.*;         // needed for using ArrayList<T> and Iterator
```

```
/**
 * ============================================================
 *                    Class ParseException
 * ============================================================
 */
class ParseException extends Exception {
                        // constructor of a new instance of ParseException
    public ParseException() {
          super("parse exception!");
    }
};
public class EncodingTrees {
/**
 * ------------------------------------------------------------
 * In order to define the encoding and decoding functions Kin, K, Hin, and H
 * which are given below, we use the following representation of binary
 * trees and n-ary trees. These representations make use of the ternary
 * constructor b(-,-,-) and the binary constructor T(-,-). These
 * constructors are used only for this purpose and in the comments below.
 *
 * binary tree:    bt = e  | b(bt1,n,bt2)
 * n-ary  tree:    nt = E  | T(n,list_nt) (list_nt is the list of sons of n)
 *           list_nt = [] | nt : list_nt
 *
 *      e is the empty binary tree
 *      E is the empty n-ary tree
 *      n is a natural number
 * ------------------------------------------------------------
 * +++ Kin : nt -> bt                         // Kin encodes an nt into a bt
 * --- Kin(E)            = e
 * --- Kin(T(n,l))       = K(T(n,l),[])
 *
 * +++ K : nt x list_nt -> bt                 // nt is not equal to E
 * --- K(T(n,[]),[])     = b(e,n,e)           // ex: node 9
 * --- K(T(n,[]),h:l)    = b(e,n,K(h,l))      // ex: node 2
 * --- K(T(n,h:l),[])    = b(K(h,l),n,e)      // ex: node 4
 * --- K(T(n,h:l),h1:11) = b(K(h,l),n,K(h1,11))// ex: node 3
 * ------------------------------------------------------------
 */

    public static BinNode<Integer> Kin (NaryNode<Integer> nt) {
        if (nt.isEmpty()) { return new BinNode(); }
        else { return K(nt, new List <NaryNode<Integer>> ());}
    }

    public static BinNode<Integer> K (NaryNode <Integer> nt,
                               List <NaryNode <Integer>> lnt ) {

        if ( nt.getListOfChildren().isEmpty() && lnt.isEmpty())
           { return new BinNode(new BinNode(), nt.getValue(), new BinNode());}
        else if ( nt.getListOfChildren().isEmpty() && !lnt.isEmpty() )
           { NaryNode<Integer> hd1 = lnt.head();
             lnt.tail();
             BinNode<Integer>
                 res = new BinNode(new BinNode(), nt.getValue(), K(hd1, lnt));
             lnt.cons(hd1);                     // restoring the list
             return res; }
        else if ( !nt.getListOfChildren().isEmpty() && lnt.isEmpty() )
            { NaryNode<Integer> hd2 = (nt.getListOfChildren()).head();
              (nt.getListOfChildren()).tail();
```

```
          BinNode<Integer>
             res = new BinNode(K(hd2, nt.getListOfChildren()),
                               nt.getValue(),
                               new BinNode());
          (nt.getListOfChildren()).cons(hd2);  // restoring the list
          return res; }
    else { NaryNode<Integer> hd3 = (nt.getListOfChildren()).head();
          (nt.getListOfChildren()).tail();
          NaryNode<Integer> hd4 = lnt.head();
          lnt.tail();
          BinNode<Integer>
             res = new BinNode(K(hd3, nt.getListOfChildren()),
                               nt.getValue(),
                               K(hd4, lnt));
          (nt.getListOfChildren()).cons(hd3);  // restoring the list
          lnt.cons(hd4);                       // restoring the list
          return res;
       }
 }
/**
 * -----------------------------------------------------------------------
 * +++ Hin : bt -> nt
 * --- Hin(e)          = E
 * --- Hin(b(bt1,n,e)) = T(n,H(bt1))         //bt1 may be equal to e
 *
 * +++ H   : bt -> list_nt
 * --- H(e)            = []
 * --- H(b(bt1,n,bt2)) = T(n,H(bt1)) : H(bt2)//bt1 and bt2 may be equal to e
 * -----------------------------------------------------------------------
 */
  public static NaryNode <Integer> Hin (BinNode <Integer> bt) {
     if (bt.isEmpty()) { return new NaryNode(); }
     else { return new NaryNode(bt.getValue(), H(bt.getLeftChild()) );}
  }
  public static List <NaryNode <Integer>> H (BinNode <Integer> bt) {

     if ( bt.isEmpty())
        { return new List(); }
     else { NaryNode<Integer>
               hd = new NaryNode(bt.getValue(), H(bt.getLeftChild()) );
          List <NaryNode<Integer>> lnt = new List();
          lnt = H(bt.getRightChild());
          lnt.cons(hd);
          return lnt; }
  }
// ------------------- parsing the input n-ary node --------------------
//                     RECURSIVE DESCENT PARSING
  public static char c;
                       // inputLine is a sequence of characters,
                       // which are read one at a time, by
                       // the method read() of the class StringReader

  public static NaryNode <Integer> nodeParse(BufferedReader inputLine)
                          throws IOException, ParseException {
     NaryNode <Integer> node1 = new NaryNode();
     if ( c == 'E' ) { c = (char)inputLine.read(); return node1; } else
     if (('0' <= c) && (c <= '9')) {
        int v = c-48;
        node1 = new NaryNode(v, new List());
        c = (char)inputLine.read();
```

```
        if ( c == '(' ) {
        c = (char)inputLine.read();
        List <NaryNode <Integer>> listNodes = listNodeParse(inputLine);
        node1 = new NaryNode(v, listNodes);
        if ( c==')' ) { c = (char)inputLine.read(); } // reads past ')'
        else { throw new ParseException(); };
        return node1;
        }
        else { return node1; }
    }; throw new ParseException();
    }

  public static List <NaryNode <Integer>> listNodeParse(
                            BufferedReader inputLine)
                            throws IOException, ParseException {
      List <NaryNode <Integer>> listNodes = new List();
      NaryNode <Integer> node1 = nodeParse(inputLine);
      if ( c == ',' ) {
        c = (char)inputLine.read();
        listNodes = listNodeParse(inputLine);
      };
      listNodes.cons(node1);
      return listNodes;
    }
// ---------------- end of parsing -------------------------------------------
// ---------------- main ------------------------------------------------------
  public static void main(String [] args ) {

    System.out.println("Input an n-ary tree nt according to the given "
                        + "grammar, please.");
    NaryNode <Integer> nNode = new NaryNode();
    BinNode  <Integer> bNode = new BinNode();
    try {     // from String to StringReader and to BufferedReader
        BufferedReader inputLine =
                new BufferedReader(new InputStreamReader(System.in));
        c = (char)inputLine.read();
        nNode = nodeParse(inputLine);
        if (c != '\n') { throw new ParseException(); };
    } catch ( IOException e ) {
        e.printStackTrace();
        System.out.println("IOException!");
    } catch ( ParseException pex ) {
        System.out.println(pex.getMessage());
        return;
    };
    // ------
    System.out.print("\nParsing of the n-ary tree:\n   nt = ");
    nNode.naryNodePrint();
    System.out.print("\nBy applying Kin "
                    + "we get the encoding binary tree:\n   bt = ");
    bNode = Kin(nNode);
    bNode.binNodePrint();
    NaryNode <Integer> nNode1 = new NaryNode();
    nNode1 = Hin(bNode);
    System.out.print("\nBack to the n-ary tree nt using Hin:\n"
                    +"   nt = ");
    nNode1.naryNodePrint();
    System.out.println();
  }
}
```

```
/**
 *  input:      output
 *  ------------------------------------------------------------------
 *  javac EncodingTrees.java
 *  java  EncodingTrees
 *              Input an n-ary tree nt according to the given grammar, please.
 *  E
 *
 *              Parsing of the n-ary tree:
 *                  nt = E
 *              By applying Kin we get the encoding binary tree:
 *                  bt = e
 *              Back to the n-ary tree nt using Hin:
 *                  nt = E
 *
 *  ------------------------------------------------------------------
 *  1(2)
 *
 *              Parsing of the n-ary tree:
 *                  nt = 1 [2 []]
 *              By applying Kin we get the encoding binary tree:
 *                  bt = ((e 2 e) 1 e)
 *              Back to the n-ary tree nt using Hin:
 *                  nt = 1 [2 []]
 *
 *  ------------------------------------------------------------------
 *  1(2,3(5,6),4(7(9),8))
 *
 *              Parsing of the n-ary tree:
 *                  nt = 1 [2 [], 3 [5 [], 6 []], 4 [7 [9 []], 8 []]]
 *              By applying Kin we get the encoding binary tree:
 *                  bt - ((e 2 ((e 5 (e 6 e)) 3 (((e 9 e) 7 (e 8 e)) 4 e))) 1 e)
 *              Back to the n-ary tree nt using Hin:
 *                  nt = 1 [2 [], 3 [5 [], 6 []], 4 [7 [9 []], 8 []]]
 *
 *  --------
 *  that is:  nt                                    bt
 *
 *                1                                  1
 *              / | \          Kin                 / \
 *              2 3 4         ----->              2   e
 *              /|  | \       <-----             / \
 *              5 6 7  8        Hin             e   3
 *                  |                              / \
 *                  9                             5   4
 *                                               /|   |\
 *                                              e 6   7 e
 *                                               /|   |\
 *                                              e e   9 8
 *                                                   /| |\
 *                                                  e e e e
 *
 *  ------------------------------------------------------------------
 */
```

We have the following properties.

(1) In T(n,list-nt), that is, in NaryNode(n,list-nt) we have that list-nt is the list of the son nodes, if any, of the node n in the left-to-right order.

(2) In K(t,lt) the list lt is the list of the brother nodes, if any, of the node t in the left-to-right order.

(3) The first argument of K is never equal to the empty n-ary tree E. The proof of this property is based on the fact that for each call of K(T(n,l1),l2), the tree E is a member of neither the list l1 nor the list l2. The easy proof by computational induction is left to the reader.

EXERCISE 7.4.2. Define the domain B' of the binary trees and the domain T' of the n-ary trees to be the solutions of the following domain equations, where N denotes the set of natural numbers and $Tlist'$ denotes the domain of the list of the n-ary trees in T':

$$B' = 1 + N + B' \times N \times B'$$
$$T' = 1 + N + N \times Tlist'$$
$$Tlist' = 1 + T' \times Tlist'$$

Define the functions Rin : $T' \rightarrow B'$ and Sin : $B' \rightarrow T'$ such that for every n-ary tree nt we have that: Sin(Rin(nt)) = nt.

Hint: A possible implementation of these domains is as follows:

```
/**
 *  --------------------------------------------------------------
 *     binary tree:       bt = e  | l(n) | b(bt1,n,bt2)
 *     n-ary  tree:       nt = E  | L(n) | T(n,list_nt)
 *                   list_nt = [] | nt : list_nt
 *  --------------------------------------------------------------
 */
```

Here are some examples of how the functions Rin and Sin should behave:

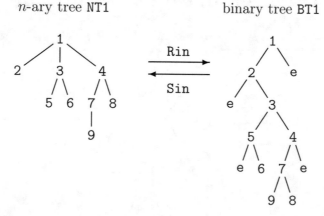

n-ary tree NT1   binary tree BT1

The following picture shows that: Rin(T(L(1),[L(3)])) = b(l(3),1,e).

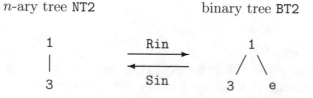

n-ary tree NT2   binary tree BT2

The following picture shows that: `Rin(L(1)) = 1(1)`.

n-ary tree NT3		binary tree BT3
	Rin	
1	$\xrightarrow{\qquad}$ $\xleftarrow{\qquad}$	1
	Sin	

Here are the definitions of the functions `Rin` and `Sin`. They use the auxiliary functions `R` and `S`, respectively.

The example nodes 2, ..., 9 which we will consider in the comments of these auxiliary definitions, refer to the *n*-ary tree NT1 and the binary tree BT1 we have depicted above.

```
----------------------------------------------------------------

+++ Rin : nt -> bt            // Rin encodes an nt into a bt
--- Rin(E)      = e
--- Rin(L(n))   = 1(n)
--- Rin(T(n,l)) = R(T(n,l),[])   // empty list of brothers of t

+++ R : nt x list_nt -> bt        // list_nt is the list of brothers of nt
--- R(L(n),[])       = 1(n)               // example: node 9
--- R(L(n),a:l)      = b(e,n,R(a,l))      // example: node 5
--- R(T(n,a:l),[])   = b(R(a,l),n,e)      // example: node 4
--- R(T(n,a:l),a1:l1) = b(R(a,l),n,R(a1,l1)) // example: node 3

----------------------------------------------------------------

+++ Sin : bt -> nt
--- Sin(e)         = E
--- Sin(1(n))      = L(n)
--- Sin(b(bt1,n,e)) = T(n,S(bt1))          // bt1 is not equal to e

+++ S : bt -> list_nt
--- S(1(n))        = [L(n)]              // nodes 6, 9, and 8:
                                         // leaves with no younger brothers.
--- S(b(e,n,bt1))  = L(n) : S(bt1)       // nodes 2 and  5:
                                         // leaves with younger brothers.
--- S(b(bt1,n,e))  = [T(n,S(bt1)]        // node 4.
--- S(b(bt1,n,bt2) = T(n,S(bt1)) : S(bt2)// nodes 3 and 7.

----------------------------------------------------------------
```

We have the following properties.

(1) The first argument of `R` is never equal to the empty *n*-ary tree `E`. The proof of this property is based on the fact that for each call of `R(T(n,l1),l2)` and `R(L(n),l2)`, the tree `E` is a member of neither the list `l1` nor the list `l2`. The easy proof by computational induction is left to the reader.

(2) Let us assume that `Sin` takes as input a binary tree which can be obtained as the result of applying `Rin` to an *n*-ary tree. Then, in the above equations defining the function `S` (the ones preceded by `---`'s), the trees `bt1` and `bt2` are not equal to the empty binary tree `e`.   □

We will end this section by providing the definitions of the binary trees and the *n*-ary trees in Pascal and C++. In Pascal using variant records, binary trees are realized by the following type definition:

```
type B = ^cell;
cell = record case tag : (no_son, two_sons) of
                  no_son: ();
                two_sons: (value: integer; lson, rson: B)
       end;
```

In C++ binary trees are realized by the following class definition:

```
class cell {
public :
   int value; cell* lson; cell* rson;
   cell(int v, cell* l, cell* r) : value(v), lson(l), rson(r) { };
};
typedef cell* B;
```

EXERCISE 7.4.3. Define in Pascal and in C++ the domain B of the binary trees which are solutions of the following domain equation, where N denotes the set of natural numbers:

$$B = 1 + N + B \times N \times B \qquad \square$$

In Pascal using variant records n-ary trees are realized by the following type definition:

```
type    T = ^Tcell;
    Tlist = ^Tlistcell;
    Tcell = record case tag :  (empty, non_empty) of
                         empty:  ();
                       non_empty:  (atom: integer; next: Tlist)
              end;
Tlistcell = record case tag :  (emptyl, non_emptyl) of
                        emptyl:  ();
                      non_emptyl: (value: T; sons: Tlist)
              end;
```

We could have also defined the record `Tlistcell` as follows:

`Tlistcell = record value:  T; sons:  Tlist end;`

In this case: (i) a pointer to `Tlistcell` implements an element of the domain $T \times Tlist$ (see page 229), and (ii) the NULL pointer implements the element of the domain 1 in the equation $Tlist = 1 + T \times Tlist$ (see again page 229).

In C++ n-ary trees are realized by the following class definition:

```
class Tlistcell;
typedef Tlistcell* Tlist;
class Tcell {
public : int atom; Tlist next;
        Tcell(int at, Tlist nx) : atom(at), next(nx) { };
};
typedef Tcell* T;
class Tlistcell {
public : T value; Tlist sons;
        Tlistcell(T val, Tlist ss) : value(val), sons(ss) { };
};
```

EXERCISE 7.4.4. Define in Pascal and in C++ the domain T of the n-ary trees which are solutions of the following domain equations, where N denotes the set of natural numbers and *Tlist* denotes the domain of the list of the n-ary trees in T:

$$T = 1 + N + N \times Tlist$$
$$Tlist = 1 + T \times Tlist \qquad \qquad \square$$

7.5. Minimal Spanning Tree of an Undirected Graph

In this section we describe an algorithm for constructing a minimal spanning tree of an undirected, connected, weighted graph with N nodes. The *weight* (also called *length*) of any arc is an integer which can be either positive or null or negative. The lengths can be *non-Euclidean*, in the sense that if the arc $i-j$ has length d_{ij} and the arc $j-k$ has length d_{jk}, then the length d_{ik} of the arc $i-k$, if it exists, need not be related to the values of d_{ij} and d_{jk}. The length of an arc $i-j$ is also called the *distance* from node i to node j (which is equal to the distance from node j to node i because the graph is undirected). There could be cycles with total negative length. In the adjacency matrix $N \times N$ which represents the lengths of the arcs of the graph, the entry '∞' at row i and column j, for $i, j = 0, \ldots, N-1$, denotes the absence of the arc from node i to node j. We assume that there is no arc from node i to node i itself, for $i = 0, \ldots, N-1$, but in the adjacency matrix at row i and column i, we have put the value 0 (because 0 is the neutral element for addition).

In the program below, for simplicity reasons, we have assumed that the lengths are all non-negative integers, and we have encoded the absence of an arc by the value '-1'.

A brute force algorithm for constructing a minimal spanning tree of an undirected, connected, weighted graph consists in: (i) constructing all possible spanning trees, and then (ii) taking a minimal one. This obvious algorithm is very inefficient because, by Caley's formula, there are N^{N-2} distinct spanning trees of a given undirected, connected graph with N nodes. In Figure 7.5.1 on the following page we have depicted the 16 spanning trees of a graph with four nodes placed at the vertexes of a square and the six arcs connecting every pair of nodes. Such graphs with all possible arcs are called *clicks*.

Now we will present an algorithm which is much more efficient than the brute force one. This efficient algorithm was first proposed by R. C. Prim and independently by E. W. Dijkstra. We will call this algorithm the *Minimal Spanning Tree algorithm*, or *MST algorithm*, for short.

The basic idea of the algorithm is as follows. We start from a node, say p, of the given graph whose nodes can be colored either red or blue. We assume that initially all nodes are blue, except for the chosen node p which is red. Then we choose a blue node, say q, which is connected to node p by an arc which has a minimal length among all the arcs which have node p as one of their two vertexes. We color red this second node q. By doing so we have a first red arc between p and q which will be part of the minimal spanning tree to be constructed. We proceed by acquiring in the red part of the graph a new blue node which will then be colored red together with the arc which connects this new red node to the red part, until all nodes are colored red.

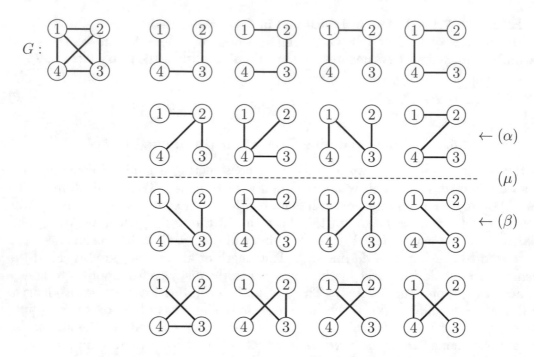

FIGURE 7.5.1. The 16 ($= 4^{4-2}$) spanning trees of a undirected, connected graph G with four nodes. The spanning trees of rows (α) and (β) are mirror images (modulo the names of the nodes) w.r.t. the line (μ).

Thus, during the execution of the algorithm the given graph of which we must compute a minimal spanning tree, is divided into two parts: (i) a red part, called *Red*, for which we have already computed a minimal spanning tree, and (ii) a blue part, called *Blue*, from which we have to choose a node which will become red and by doing so, a new arc is added to the minimal spanning tree to be computed.

Ties of the length of the arcs can be resolved in any way we like, and this is why through this algorithm we actually compute *a* minimal spanning tree, rather than *the* minimal spanning tree. (Obviously, for all minimal spanning trees the total length of the arcs is the same.) In what follows, for reasons of simplicity, we will free to say 'the minimal spanning tree', instead of 'a minimal spanning tree'. Similarly, we will feel free to say 'the shortest arc', instead of 'a shortest arc'. The correctness of the MST algorithm can be derived, as shown in [**6**], from the following three points.

Point (i).   The *local optimum* is a *global optimum*.

Point (ii).   The use of the *function inversion technique*.

Point (iii).   The use of an $(N-1) \times 2$ array.

Point (i). The *local optimum* is a *global optimum*.

This fact allows us to derive a *greedy algorithm* for computing the spanning tree which we compute 'by addition of nodes', as described above.

Suppose that V is the shortest arc connecting a red node to a blue node (see Figure 7.5.2 on the next page).

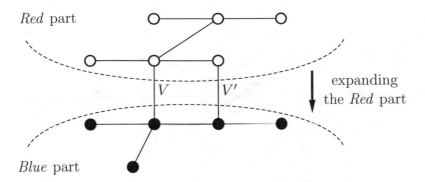

FIGURE 7.5.2. Construction of a minimal spanning tree. The *Red* part shows the portion of the final minimal spanning tree for the points which now are red. The *Blue* part shows the portion of the final minimal spanning tree for the points which now are blue.

This arc V must be an arc of the spanning tree. We prove this fact by contradiction. Let us assume that: (i) a different arc, call it V', instead of V, is in the minimal spanning tree connecting a red node to a blue node, and (ii) the weight of V' is greater than the weight of V. Call T' this pretending minimal spanning tree which includes the arc V', instead of the arc V. Now from the tree T' we construct a different spanning tree T which is shorter than T' by replacing the arc V' by the arc V. Indeed, (i) T connects all nodes of the graph because the blue node of V is connected to the blue node of V', and (ii) T is a tree because no loops are generated by the substitution of V' by V, because if a loop is generated, it should go through another arc from the red nodes to the blue nodes and there is no such arc, simply because we took the arc V' away.

At this point the structure of the algorithm is as follows, where we called *violet* an arc which has a red node and a blue node. Recall that N is the number of nodes in the given undirected graph.

color red one node and color blue all the remaining nodes;
while the number of red nodes is less than N **do**
    begin *Step* (1). Select the shortest violet arc.
            Step (2). Color it red and color red its blue node.
    end

Point (*ii*). The use of the *function inversion technique.*

The choice of the shortest violet arc can be done in two ways: either (ii.1) for each red node we compute the shortest arc from it to a blue node, and then we take the shortest arc among these minimal arcs, one for each red node, or (ii.2) for each blue node we compute the shortest arc from it to a red node, and then we take the shortest arc among these minimal arcs, one for each blue node.

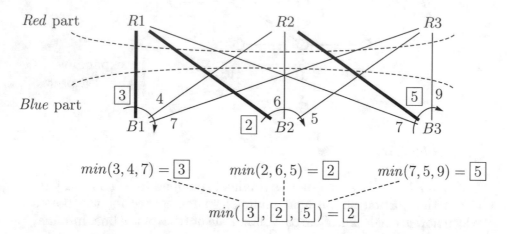

FIGURE 7.5.3. Computation of the minimal arc connecting the *Red* part to the *Blue* part. The arcs with thicker lines are the so called *ultraviolet arcs*. There is exactly one ultraviolet arc for each blue node. Given a blue node its ultraviolet arc is the shortest arc from that blue node to a red node. We did not draw every arc: more arcs may be present within the *Red* part or the *Blue* part.

Since the given graph is undirected, these two choices are both correct. However, from a complexity point of view they are *not* equivalent, because we are computing the spanning tree by making the *Red* part larger, while the *Blue* part is shrinking. Indeed, in the case of Choice (ii.2), when a blue node becomes red, the computation of the shortest arc for each blue node requires one comparison only, while in the case of Choice (ii.1), when a blue node becomes red, the computation of the shortest arc for each blue node requires a number of comparisons which is the product 'current number of red nodes' × 'current number of blue nodes'.

This technique which looks at the distances *for each blue node* towards to red nodes, instead of looking at the distances *from each red node* towards the blue nodes, is called *function inversion*. The word 'inversion' comes from the fact that we are extending the *Red* part, while looking at the distances from each *blue* node.

Note that for the application of the function inversion technique it is crucial that the given graph is undirected.

In Figure 7.5.3 we show how the computation of the shortest violet arc is done in the case of three red nodes: $R1$, $R2$, and $R3$, and three blue nodes: $B1$, $B2$, and $B3$. First, we compute the shortest violet arc for the node $B1$, the node $B2$, and the node $B3$. These three shortest arcs, which are called *ultraviolet arcs*, are drawn with thicker lines in that figure. The ultraviolet arc of a blue node is the shortest arc which connects that blue node to a red node. Then we compute the shortest arc among these three shortest ultraviolet arcs. In our case it is the arc from node $B2$ to node $R1$ whose length is 2. When the node $B2$ becomes red, we have to recompute: (•) the ultraviolet arc for the node $B1$, that is, the shortest violet arc from the blue node $B1$ to the *Red* part (this is done by comparing the length of the ultraviolet arc $B1 - R1$ with the length of the arc $B1 - B2$, if any), and

($\bullet$) the ultraviolet arc for the node $B3$, that is, the shortest violet arc from the blue node $B3$ to the *Red* part (this is done by comparing the length of the arc $B3-R2$ with the length of the arc $B3-B2$, if any).

Note that, instead of saying '*the* shortest violet (or ultraviolet) arc' we should say '*a* shortest violet (or ultraviolet) arc' because there may be ties. Indeed, as already mentioned, Algorithm 7.5.1 for computing minimal spanning trees is a nondeterministic algorithm and computes *a* minimal spanning tree.

Thus, while the computation of the minimal spanning tree progresses, in order to make Choice (ii.2), for each node which is presently blue, we have to store its ultraviolet arc and the length of this ultraviolet arc. This is done by keeping an array of ultraviolet arcs as described in Point (iii) below.

We have the following version of the algorithm.

Algorithm 7.5.1.

Computation of a Minimal Spanning Tree of an Undirected Graph. (Dijkstra's MST algorithm)

color red one node and color blue all the remaining nodes;
while the number of red nodes is less than N **do**
  begin *Step* (1). Select the shortest ultraviolet arc.
        Step (2). Color it red and color red its blue node, say P.
        Step (3). Adjust the set of ultraviolet arcs: for each blue node B,
             compare the length ℓ of its ultraviolet arc with the length m
             of the arc $B-P$ which, if $m < \ell$, becomes the new ultraviolet
             arc for the node B.
  end

Point (iii). *The use of an* $(N-1) \times 2$ *array.*

This array, called `uvArcs` in the program `MST.java` on page 251, keeps the ultraviolet arcs, each arc being a pair of nodes which are stored in a row of the array. The array `uvArcs` is initialized by the arcs from the chosen initial red node, say A, to the other $N-1$ blue nodes. Thus, initially the array `uvArcs` looks like this:

$$
\begin{array}{cc}
(1) & (2)
\end{array}
$$

$$
Red \quad
\begin{array}{cc}
A & B \\
A & C \\
A & \ldots \\
A & \ldots
\end{array}
\quad Blue
$$

where the left part is of red nodes and the right part is of blue nodes. Initially, the only red node is A and all other nodes are blue nodes. The number of rows of the array `uvArcs` is the number of the nodes which are initially blue, that is, $N-1$.

Now let us see how the array `uvArcs` is modified during the computation of the minimal spanning tree (see also Example 7.5.2 on page 249).

Suppose that we have constructed the minimal spanning tree of the subgraph whose nodes are colored red, and supposed that the arcs of that minimal spanning trees are stored in the upper part, named *Red*, of the array `uvArcs`. The lower part, named *Blue*, of that array stores the ultraviolet arcs, one for each blue node. In the following array `uvArcs` the blue nodes are C, D, and B.

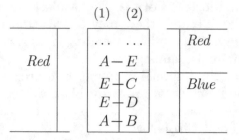

Every node which occurs in the left-upper part (that is, the nodes either in the column (1), or in the column (2) of the *Red* rows) of the array `uvArcs` is colored red, while every node which occur in the lower-right part (that is, the nodes in the column (2) of the *Blue* rows) of the array `uvArcs` is colored blue. In our case the only blue nodes are C, D, and B. Let us now consider the three steps of the body of the while-do loop of our Algorithm 7.5.1 on the previous page.

Step (1). *Select the shortest ultraviolet arc.* Among the arcs in the lower part of the array `uvArcs` (in our case, $E-C$, $E-D$, and $A-B$) we select the arc with the shortest length. Let us assume that it is the arc $E-D$.

Step (2). *Color it red and color red its blue node.* In our case we color red the arc $E-D$ and its blue node D. We do so by swapping the rows $E-D$ and $E-C$. We get the following array `uvArcs` where: (i) the blue part now has two arcs only, namely, $E-C$ and $A-B$, and (ii) the arc $E-D$ and the node D now are red and they belong to the *Red* part:

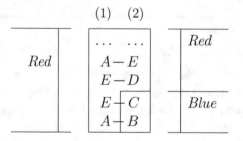

Step (3). *Adjust the set of ultraviolet arcs.* For each arc $X-Y$ in the set *Blue* of ultraviolet arcs (that is, in the *Blue* rows), we compare its length ℓ with the length m of the arc, if any, from the blue node Y to the node D which has been colored red at the preceding Step (2). If $m<\ell$, then we write D, instead of X. If we assume that length($D-B$) < length($A-B$) and length($D-C$) $\not<$ length($E-C$), we get:

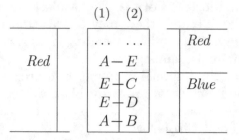

At the end of Step (3) we have extended the red part of the given graph by one more node (in our case the node D), having preserved the invariant that:

($\bullet$) the *Red* part stores the arcs of the minimal spanning tree of the subgraph whose nodes are currently red, and

($\bullet$) the *Blue* part stores the ultraviolet arcs of the nodes which are currently blue, that is, the shortest arc which connects the blue node in column (2) to a red node of the graph.

Note also that during the computation of the minimal spanning tree, we have the following invariant:

   $number\text{-}of\text{-}red\text{-}arcs + number\text{-}of\text{-}blue\text{-}nodes = N-1$

where: (i) *number-of-red-arcs* is the current number of the arcs of the minimal spanning tree of the subgraph whose nodes are colored red, and (ii) *number-of-blue-nodes* is the current number of the blue nodes (which is equal to the current number of the ultraviolet arcs).

The time complexity of our algorithm $O(N^2)$ and the space complexity is $O(N)$ where N is the number of nodes in the given graph.

Another possible algorithm for computing a minimal spanning tree of an undirected graph is Kruskal's algorithm (see, for instance, [20, page 101]) whose worst case time complexity is $O(N^2 \log N)$, where N is the number of nodes in the given graph and thus, the number of arcs is of order $O(N^2)$. In Kruskal's algorithm the extra $\log N$ factor is due to the need of sorting the arcs of the graph according to their length.

EXAMPLE 7.5.2. [**Minimal Spanning Tree of an Undirected Graph**] Let us consider the undirected, connected, weighted graph of Figure 7.5.4.

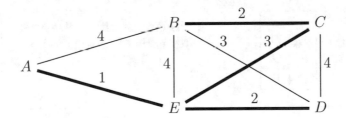

FIGURE 7.5.4. A five node graph of which we compute a minimal spanning tree starting from node A. The successive configurations of the array storing the ultraviolet arcs are shown on page 250. The arcs with thicker lines are those belonging to the resulting minimal spanning tree.

We have the following symmetric matrix of distances:

	A	B	C	D	E
A	0	4	∞	∞	1
B	4	0	2	3	4
C	∞	2	0	4	3
D	∞	3	4	0	2
E	1	4	3	2	0

Let us consider node A as first red node. All other nodes are blue. Thus, we have the following array `uvArcs` of ultraviolet arcs (actually, some of them are not existing, that is, they have length ∞):

Then, we have the following sequence of pairs of actions: (i) take a shortest ultraviolet arc, and (ii) adjust the ultraviolet arcs.

(1.i) Take $A-E$ which is a shortest ultraviolet arc and swap rows:

$$\begin{array}{c} A-E \\ A-C \\ A-D \\ A-B \end{array}$$

(1.ii) Adjust ultraviolet arcs after node E became red:

$$\begin{array}{c} A-E \\ E-C \\ E-D \\ A-B \end{array}$$

(2.i) Take $E-D$ which is a shortest ultraviolet arc and swap rows:

$$\begin{array}{c} A-E \\ E-D \\ E-C \\ A-B \end{array}$$

(2.ii) Adjust ultraviolet arcs after node D became red:

$$\begin{array}{c} A-E \\ E-D \\ E-C \\ D-B \end{array}$$

(3.i) Take $E-C$ which is a shortest ultraviolet arc and swap rows:

$$\begin{array}{c} A-E \\ E-D \\ E-C \\ D-B \end{array}$$

(3.ii) Adjust ultraviolet arcs after node C became red:

$$\begin{array}{c} A-E \\ E-D \\ E-C \\ C-B \end{array}$$

Finally, we take the only available ultraviolet arc $C-B$ and we get the following arrays `uvArcs` (no swap of rows is required and hence, the array is not changed):

$$\begin{array}{c} A-E \\ E-D \\ E-C \\ C-B \end{array}$$

Therefore, at the end of the MST algorithm (see Algorithm 7.5.1 on page 247) we get the minimal spanning tree which is indicated in Figure 7.5.4 on page 249 by ticker lines. That minimal spanning tree consists of the following four arcs:

$A-E$, $E-D$, $E-C$, and $C-B$.   □

```
/**
 * ============================================================================
 *              MINIMAL SPANNING TREE OF A UNDIRECTED GRAPH
 *
 * Filename: "MST.java"
 *
 * N is the number of nodes of the graph. We assume that N > 1. N1 is N-1.
 * The element graph[i][j] holds the distance, which is an integer number,
 * from node i to node j of the graph.
 * The algorithm is correct also for distances which are negative, null, or
 * positive, and even for non-Euclidean distances, but some changes should
 * be made to the code.
 * We assume that for any node i, distance[i][i]=0.
 * For distances which are real numbers, instead of integer numbers, we
 * should write 'double', instead of 'int'.
 * The algorithm is taken from E. W. Dijkstra:
 * 'A Short Introduction to the Art of Programming', EWD 316 August 1971.
 * Note. We stipulate that distance[i][i] == -1 when there is no arc from
 * node i to node j. Thus, when the algorithm is used for distances which
 * are negative, null, or positive, and even for non-Euclidean distances,
 * suitable changes are to be made (see lines -1- and -2-) because -1 can no
 * longer be used for encoding the absence af an arc.
 * If all distances are >= 0 then
 * line  -1- becomes: if (1 < uvMinLength) and
 * lines -2- should be suitably changed.
 * ============================================================================
 */
public class MST {                    // MST : Minimal Spanning Tree

    public static void main(String[] args) {
        int N = 0;                    // - to be read from the input: args[0]
        int initNode = 0;             // - to be read from the input: args[1]

// -------------------------------- N: number of Nodes of the graph.
//                                  N > 1.
    try {N = Integer.parseInt(args[0]);
        if ( N < 2) { throw new RuntimeException (); };
    } catch (Exception e) {System.out.print("*** Wrong number of nodes!\n");}
// -------------------------------- initNode: initial node.
//                                  0 <= initNode <= N-1.
    try {initNode = Integer.parseInt(args[1]);
        if ( ( 0 > initNode ) || ( initNode > N-1 ) ) {
            throw new RuntimeException ();
        };
    } catch (Exception e) {System.out.print("*** Wrong initial node!\n");}

// ----------------------------------------------------------------
// MAXLENGTH: maximum length of the arcs. 1 <= length <= MAXLENGTH.
        final int MAXLENGTH = 9;
// ----------------------------------------------------------------
// PerCentPROB: probability of connectivity. 0 < PerCentPROB <= 100.
// If PerCentPROB = k, every node is connected with probability k/100 to the
// other N-1 nodes.
        final int PerCentPROB = 60;
// ----------------------------------------------------------------
// Generation of a random graph with N nodes.
// The length of each arc belongs to the set {1,..., MAXLENGTH}.
// Every node has (N-1) x PerCentPROB / 100 successor nodes (in average).

        UGraph g =
            new UGraph(N, initNode, MAXLENGTH, PerCentPROB);
```

```
    g.graphPrint();
    System.out.println("Every node is connected to the other nodes with " +
                       "probability " + PerCentPROB + " percent.");
    System.out.println("The length of each arc belongs to the set {1,..., "
                       + MAXLENGTH + "}.");
    System.out.println("The initial node is: " + initNode);
//
    int i, uvMin, p, N1 = N-1;
    int l, uvMinLength;          // 'double', not 'int', for real distances
//---------------------------------------------------------------------------
//    The g.uvArcs are the ultraviolet arcs of the graph g (see Dijkstra)
//---------------------------------------------------------------------------
    int k = 0;
    while (k < N1) {g.uvArcs[k][0] = 0; g.uvArcs[k][1] = k+1; k++;};
    k = 0;
    while (k < N1) {           //                  <<=========================
      uvMin = k;
      uvMinLength = g.graph[g.uvArcs[k][0]] [g.uvArcs[k][1]];//it may be -1
//---------------------------------------------------------------------------

      i = k+1;
      while (i < N1) {           //                  <<-------------------+
         l = g.graph[g.uvArcs[i][0]] [g.uvArcs[i][1]];            // |
         if ( (l < uvMinLength && l >= 0) || uvMinLength == -1 ) // |    -1-
            { uvMin = i; uvMinLength = l; };                     // |
         i++;                                                    // |
      };                         // end of while <<-------------------+
      if (uvMinLength >= 0) { //                                  //     -2-
      p = g.uvArcs[uvMin][1];  // nearest blue node to red zone

//---------------------------------------------------------------------------

      if (uvMin != k) {g.swap(k,uvMin);};
      i = k+1;
      while (i < N1) {           //                  <<-------------------+
         if (   (g.graph[g.uvArcs[i][0]] [g.uvArcs[i][1]]        // |
               > g.graph[p] [g.uvArcs[i][1]]                    // |
               && g.graph[p] [g.uvArcs[i][1]] >= 0              // |    -2-
               )                                                // |
            || (g.graph[g.uvArcs[i][0]] [g.uvArcs[i][1]] == -1  // |    -2-
               && g.graph[p] [g.uvArcs[i][1]] >= 0)             // |    -2-
            ) { g.uvArcs[i][0] = p; };                          // |
         i++;                                                    // |
      };                         // end of while <<-------------------+
      k++;
      } else { break;}           //                             //     -2-
    };                           // end of while <<=========================
    g.uvPrint(k);  }
}

/**
 * input:
 * --------------------------------------------------------------------------
 * javac MST.java
 * java  MST 9 0
 *
 * output:
 * ------
 * The random undirected graph has 9 node(s) (from node 0 to node 8).
 * The symmetric matrix of the arc lengths is:
```

```
* 0 :   0 4 7 - - - 2 4 9
* 1 :   4 0 - 1 7 - - 4 -
* 2 :   7 - 0 5 - 7 3 6 3
* 3 :   - 1 5 0 - 5 8 3 4
* 4 :   - 7 - - 0 8 5 4 6
* 5 :   - - 7 5 8 0 - - 6
* 6 :   2 - 3 8 5 - 0 6 5
* 7 :   4 4 6 3 4 - 6 0 -
* 8 :   9 - 3 4 6 6 5 - 0
*
* Every node is connected to the other nodes with probability 60 percent.
* The length of each arc belongs to the set {1, ..., 9}.
* The initial node is: 0
*
* The arcs of the minimal spanning tree,
* starting from node 0 and reaching all reachable nodes, are:
* 0 -- 6
* 6 -- 2
* 2 -- 8
* 0 -- 1
* 1 -- 3
* 3 -- 7
* 7 -- 4
* 3 -- 5
* -------------------------------------------------------------------
*/

/**
* ============================================================================
*                         The UGraph class
* Filename: "UGraph.java"
*
* This class UGraph defines a undirected, weighted graph.
* The class UGraph is not a monitor, because not all fields are "private".
* However, the non-private fields are read, but never assigned to.
* All methods are "synchronized".
* Thus, this class  UGraph is "almost" a monitor.
* For real distances, instead of integer distances, write 'double', instead
* of 'int'.
* ============================================================================
*/
import java.util.Random;

public class UGraph {
    final  int N;            // N = number of nodes of the graph
    final  int initNode;     // initial node of the minimal spanning tree
    static int [][] graph;   // an N x N array
    static int [][] uvArcs;  // an N-1 x 2 array: arcs of the minimal
                             // spanning tree

// -------------------- beginning of constructor -------------------------

    public UGraph(int N, int initNode, int MAXLENGTH, int PerCentPROB) {

    /** Generation of a random, undirected graph with N nodes.
     *
     * The random variable randomConnect controls the connectivity:
     *      node i is connected with node j, for i != j, with percent
     *      probability PerCentPROB:  0 <= PerCentPROB <= 100
     * The random variable randomLength controls the length of the arcs:
     *      1 <= length of an arc <= MAXLENGTH
     */
```

```
      this.N             = N;
      this.initNode      = initNode;
      this.graph         = new int [N][N];
      this.uvArcs        = new int [N-1][2];

      Random randomConnect = new Random();   // random graph connectivity
      Random randomLength  = new Random();   // random arc length

   // initializing the graph: -1 (printed as "-") means "unconnected node"
   // graph[i][j] = m with m >= 0
   //     iff m is the length of the arc from node i to node j
    for(int i=0;i<N;i++) {
      for(int j=i;j<N;j++) {
         if ((i != j) && (randomConnect.nextInt(100) < PerCentPROB))
                 { graph[i][j] = 1 + randomLength.nextInt(MAXLENGTH);
                   graph[j][i] = graph[i][j];                 // symmetric graph
                 }
         else if (i == j ) { graph[i][j] = 0; }
         else   { graph[i][j] = -1; graph[j][i] = -1; };// symmetric graph
      }
    }
  }
// ------------------- end of constructor -----------------------------

// ------------------- swapping two rows of the array uvArcs -----------
  public static void swap (int i, int j) {
     int temp;
     temp = uvArcs[i][0]; uvArcs[i][0] = uvArcs[j][0]; uvArcs[j][0] = temp;
     temp = uvArcs[i][1]; uvArcs[i][1] = uvArcs[j][1]; uvArcs[j][1] = temp;
  }

// ------------------- printing the graph ----------------------------------
  public synchronized void graphPrint () {
    System.out.println("The random undirected graph has "+ N +" node(s) " +
                      "(from node 0 to node " + (N-1) + ").\n" +
                      "The symmetric matrix of the arc lengths is:");
    for(int i=0;i<N;i++) {
      System.out.print(i + " : ");
      for(int j=0;j<N;j++) {
         if (graph[i][j] < 0) { System.out.print("- "); }
         else System.out.print( graph[i][j] + " ");
      }; System.out.println();
    }; System.out.println();
  }

// -------------- printing the arcs of the minimal spanning tree ----------

  public synchronized void uvPrint (int N) {
     if (N==0) {System.out.println("\nThe minimal spanning tree is the "+
                             "initial node "+ initNode +" only.");}
     else { System.out.print("\nThe arcs of the minimal spanning tree,\n" +
                   "starting from node " + initNode + " and reaching " +
                   "all reachable nodes, are: \n");
          for (int k=0; k<N; k++)
            {System.out.print(uvArcs[k][0] + " -- " +
             uvArcs[k][1] + "\n");};}
  }
}
// -----------------------------------------------------------------------
```

CHAPTER 8

Path Problems in Directed Graphs

In this chapter we present some techniques for solving path problems in directed graphs. We will first recall some algorithms for matrix multiplication because, as we will see, matrix multiplication can be used for solving path problems, when directed graphs are represented by adjacency matrices (see, for instance, [20, pages 8–10]).

By definition, we have that given a graph G with n nodes, its adjacency matrix M is an $n \times n$ matrix made out of 0's and 1's such that for all i, j, with $1 \le i, j \le n$, $M[i, j] = 1$, that is, an element of M in position $\langle i, j \rangle$ is 1, iff in the graph G there is an arc from node i to node j. In particular, $M[i, i] = 1$ iff there exists an arc from node i to node i itself. We assume that the length of a path is given by the number of its arcs. Thus, in particular, in any graph G there is a path of length 0 from any node of G to that same node.

We have that there exists in G a path of length $k \, (\ge 0)$ from node i to node j iff the in k-th power of M, denoted M^k, the element in position $\langle i, j \rangle$, denoted $M^k[i, j]$, is 1.

8.1. Matrix Multiplication Algorithms

The matrix multiplication problem can be formalized as follows.

PROBLEM 8.1.1. *Matrix Multiplication.*
Input: two $n \times n$ matrices of integers

$$A = \begin{vmatrix} a_{11} & \dots & a_{1n} \\ \dots & \dots & \dots \\ a_{n1} & \dots & a_{nn} \end{vmatrix} \text{ and } B = \begin{vmatrix} b_{11} & \dots & b_{1n} \\ \dots & \dots & \dots \\ b_{n1} & \dots & b_{nn} \end{vmatrix}$$

Output: the $n \times n$ matrix $C = A \times B$, that is,
for every $i, j = 1, \dots, n$, $c_{ij} = \sum_{1 \le k \le n} a_{ik} b_{kj}$.

In the sequel we will feel free to write the multiplication of the matrices A and B as $A \, B$, instead of $A \times B$.

The elementary matrix multiplication algorithm is as follows.

ALGORITHM 8.1.2. *Elementary Algorithm for Matrix Multiplication.*

Given any two $n \times n$ matrices A and B, the matrix $C = A \times B$ is obtained by performing the n multiplications and $n-1$ additions for each $c_{ij} = \sum_{1 \le k \le n} a_{ik} b_{kj}$, as indicated in the specification of the Matrix Multiplication Problem (see Problem 8.1.1 above).

© Springer Nature Switzerland AG 2021
A. Pettorossi, *Techniques for Searching, Parsing, and Matching*, https://doi.org/10.1007/978-3-030-63189-5_8

This elementary algorithm takes $n^2(2n-1) = 2n^3 - n^2$ arithmetic operations for $n \geq 2$. Let us now consider the following algorithm for matrix multiplication.

ALGORITHM 8.1.3. *Matrix Multiplication by Partition.*

Consider the following $n \times n$ matrices A, B, and C, and the partitions of each of these matrices into four $(n/2) \times (n/2)$ blocks:

$$A = \begin{vmatrix} A_{11} & A_{12} \\ A_{21} & A_{22} \end{vmatrix}, \ B = \begin{vmatrix} B_{11} & B_{12} \\ B_{21} & B_{22} \end{vmatrix}, \text{ and } C = \begin{vmatrix} C_{11} & C_{12} \\ C_{21} & C_{22} \end{vmatrix}.$$

Perform the 8 multiplications of $(n/2) \times (n/2)$ matrices and the 4 additions of $(n/2) \times (n/2)$ matrices as indicated by the equalities:

$$C_{11} = A_{11}B_{11} + A_{12}B_{21}, \quad C_{12} = A_{11}B_{12} + A_{12}B_{22},$$
$$C_{21} = A_{21}B_{11} + A_{22}B_{21}, \quad C_{22} = A_{21}B_{12} + A_{22}B_{22}.$$

This algorithm takes $O(n^3)$ arithmetic operations, because their number $T(n)$ satisfies the following recurrence relation for $n \geq 2$:

$$T(n) = 8T(n/2) + 4(n^2/4), \text{ with } T(1) = 1,$$

whose solution is: $T(n) = 2n^3 - n^2$.

We have also the following algorithm.

ALGORITHM 8.1.4. *Strassen Matrix Multiplication.*

Consider the following $n \times n$ matrices A, B, and C, and the partitions of each of these matrices into four $(n/2) \times (n/2)$ blocks:

$$A = \begin{vmatrix} A_{11} & A_{12} \\ A_{21} & A_{22} \end{vmatrix}, \ B = \begin{vmatrix} B_{11} & B_{12} \\ B_{21} & B_{22} \end{vmatrix}, \text{ and } C = \begin{vmatrix} C_{11} & C_{12} \\ C_{21} & C_{22} \end{vmatrix}.$$

Perform the 7 multiplications of $(n/2) \times (n/2)$ matrices and the 10 additions of $(n/2) \times (n/2)$ matrices (we count the subtractions as additions of negated values) indicated by the following equalities:

$$m_1 = (A_{12} - A_{22})(B_{21} + B_{22}), \quad m_2 = (A_{11} + A_{22})(B_{11} + B_{22}),$$
$$m_3 = (A_{11} - A_{21})(B_{11} + B_{12}), \quad m_4 = (A_{11} + A_{12})B_{22},$$
$$m_5 = A_{11}(B_{12} - B_{22}), \quad m_6 = A_{22}(B_{21} - B_{11}),$$
$$m_7 = (A_{21} + A_{22})B_{11},$$

Then, by performing the following 8 additions of $(n/2) \times (n/2)$ matrices, we get:

$$C_{11} = m_1 + m_2 - m_4 + m_6, \quad C_{12} = m_4 + m_5,$$
$$C_{21} = m_6 + m_7, \quad C_{22} = m_2 - m_3 + m_5 - m_7.$$

This algorithm due to V. Strassen in 1969 takes $O(n^{\log_2 7})$, which is about $O(n^{2.81})$, because their number satisfies the following recurrence relation for $n \geq 2$:

$$T(n) = 7T(n/2) + 18(n^2/4), \text{ with } T(1) = 1.$$

Indeed, we have that:

$$T(n) = (18/4)[n + (7/4)n^2 + (7/4)^2n^2 + \ldots + (7/4)^{(\log_2 n)-1}n^2] + 7^{\log_2 n}T(1) =$$
$$= (18n^2/4)[((7/4)^{\log_2 n} - 1)/((7/4) - 1)] + 7^{\log_2 n} =$$
$$= 6n^{\log_2 7} - 6n^2 + n^{\log_2 7} < 7n^{\log_2 7}.$$

(Recall that $x^{\log_y z} = z^{\log_y x}$ for all $x, y, z > 0$ and $y \neq 1$.)

If n is not an exact power of 2 we can pad the given matrix with extra rows (on the bottom) and columns (on the right) made out of all 0's, so that it becomes an $m \times m$ matrix, where $m = 2^{\lceil \log_2 n \rceil}$, where $\lceil x \rceil$ denotes the least integer k such that $k \geq x$.

A better method is as follows: if n is even, then make a recursive call to $n/2$, and if n is odd, then pad with one row and one column of 0's (thereby getting an $(n+1) \times (n+1)$ matrix) and make a recursive call to $(n+1)/2$.

Following Strassen's idea, new algorithms have being discovered which multiply matrices even faster than $O(n^{\log_2 7})$. The current asymptotic upper bound is about $O(n^{2.55})$. However, we cannot hope to multiply two $n \times n$ matrices faster than $O(n^2)$, because there are n^2 elements to compute.

8.2. Comparing Matrix Multiplication Algorithms

Let us recall some definitions from Abstract Algebra for comparing the above algorithms for matrix multiplication.

DEFINITION 8.2.1. [**Semiring**] A *semiring* is an algebra $(S, +, \cdot)$ with carrier set S and the two operations $+$ and $\cdot$, such that:

(i) $+$ is associative and commutative,
(ii) $\cdot$ is associative, and
(iii) $\cdot$ distributes over $+$ on both sides, that is, for all $a, b, c \in S$,
    $a \cdot (b + c) = (a \cdot b) + (a \cdot c)$ and $(b + c) \cdot a = (b \cdot a) + (c \cdot a)$.

An element u of S is an *identity* for the operation op iff
    for all $x \in S$, $x \; op \; u = u \; op \; x = x$.
An element z of S is an *absorbent element* for the operation op iff
    for all $x \in S$, $x \; op \; z = z \; op \; x = z$.
It can be shown that in any semiring:
- if an identity for $+$ exists, then it is unique,
- if an identity for $\cdot$ exists, then it is unique, and
- if an absorbent element for $\cdot$ exists, then it is unique.

DEFINITION 8.2.2. [**Semiring with 0 and 1**] A *semiring with* 0 *and* 1 is a semiring $(S, +, \cdot)$ with the identity for $\cdot$, denoted 1, and the absorbent element for $\cdot$, denoted 0, which is also the identity for $+$. We will write $(S, +, \cdot, 0, 1)$-semiring to denote such a semiring.

DEFINITION 8.2.3. [**Ring**] A *ring* is a semiring $(S, +, \cdot)$ where the algebra $(S, +)$ is a commutative group, that is, $+$ is associative and commutative, $+$ has an identity, denoted 0, and every element x has an additive inverse, denoted $-x$, that is, for all $x \in S$, $x + (-x) = (-x) + x = 0$.

As for any group, we have that in a ring the additive inverse of any element is unique.

One can prove that in any ring the identity for $+$ is the absorbent element for $\cdot$, that is, for all $x \in S$, $x \cdot 0 = 0 \cdot x = 0$. As proved in [8], one can also show that:

for all $x \in S$, $x \cdot (-y) = (-x) \cdot y = -(x \cdot y)$ and $(-x) \cdot (-y) = x \cdot y$.

DEFINITION 8.2.4. [**Ring with 1**] A ring $(S, +, \cdot)$ with the identity for $\cdot$, denoted 1, is said to be *a ring with* 1. Such a ring will be denoted by $(S, +, \cdot, 0, 1)$-ring.

DEFINITION 8.2.5. [**Field**] An $(S, +, \cdot, 0, 1)$-ring is said to be a *field* iff $\cdot$ is commutative, and every element x different from 0, has a multiplicative inverse, denoted x^{-1}, that is, for all $x \in S$, $x \cdot x^{-1} = x^{-1} \cdot x = 1$.

Given any $(S, +, \cdot, 0, 1)$-semiring, we may consider the set, denoted M_n, of the $n \times n$ matrices whose elements are taken from the set S. M_n is said to be the set of the $n \times n$ *matrices over the* $(S, +, \cdot, 0, 1)$-*semiring* (or *over* S, for short).

Let 0_n denote the $n \times n$ matrix with all 0's, and I_n denote the $n \times n$ matrix which is like 0_n, except that for all i, with $1 \le i \le n$, $(I_n)_{ii} = 1$, that is, each element of the main diagonal of I_n is 1.

One can show that $(M_n, +_n, \cdot_n, 0_n, I_n)$ is a semiring with 0 and 1, denoted $(M_n, +_n, \cdot_n, 0_n, I_n)$-semiring, where:

(i) $+_n$ is defined elementwise, that is, for all $n \times n$ matrices A and B, we have that $A +_n B$ is the $n \times n$ matrix C such that for all i, j, with $1 \le i, j \le n$, $C_{ij} = A_{ij} + B_{ij}$, and

(ii) $\cdot_n$ is defined as follows: for all $n \times n$ matrices A and B, we have that $A \cdot_n B$ is the $n \times n$ matrix C such that

for all i, j, with $1 \le i, j \le n$, $C_{ij} = (A_{i1} \cdot B_{1j}) + (A_{i2} \cdot B_{2j}) + \ldots + (A_{in} \cdot B_{nj})$.

Analogously, we have that, given any $(S, +, \cdot, 0, 1)$-ring, instead of any $(S, +, \cdot, 0, 1)$-semiring, we get the ring with 1 of the $n \times n$ matrices over S, instead of the semiring with 0 and 1 of the $n \times n$ matrices over S. The ring of the $n \times n$ matrices over a given $(S, +, \cdot, 0, 1)$-ring will be denoted by $(M_n, +_n, \cdot_n, 0_n, I_n)$-ring.

Notice that any $(M_n, +_n, \cdot_n, 0_n, I_n)$-ring of matrices is *not* commutative even if the corresponding $(S, +, \cdot, 0, 1)$-ring of their elements is commutative.

FACT 8.2.6. [**Comparing the Matrix Multiplication Algorithms**] The Elementary Algorithm and the Partition Algorithm for matrix multiplication work for all $n \times n$ matrices whose elements are taken from any $(S, +, \cdot, 0, 1)$-semiring. Strassen algorithm for matrix multiplication works for all $n \times n$ matrices whose elements are taken from any $(S, +, \cdot, 0, 1)$-ring.

8.3. Fast Boolean Matrix Multiplication

If we look for an asymptotically fast method for multiplying boolean matrices, we cannot use Strassen algorithm because the boolean values 1 and 0 with the additive operation $\vee$ (that is, the least upper bound) and the multiplicative operation $\wedge$ (that is, the greatest lower bound), do *not* form a ring with 1. Indeed, there is no inverse w.r.t. the operation $\vee$.

However, given two $n{\times}n$ boolean matrices A and B, we can multiply them together as they were matrices of elements in $\mathbb{Z}_{n+1}$, that is, the integers modulo $n{+}1$, for $n\geq 2$, where we consider $\vee$ as $+$ (i.e., addition), and $\wedge$ as $\cdot$ (i.e., multiplication).

It can be shown that if we multiply the two $n \times n$ boolean matrices A and B as they were matrices of elements in $\mathbb{Z}_{n+1}$, thereby getting the matrix $\widetilde{C}$, then the boolean matrix $C = A \wedge_n B$ can be computed as follows:

for all i,j, with $1\leq i,j\leq n$, if $\widetilde{C}_{ij}=0$ then $C_{ij}=0$ $\;and\;$ if $1\leq\widetilde{C}_{ij}\leq n$ then $C_{ij}=1$.

Thus, also boolean matrices can be multiplied within the same time complexity (counting the number of arithmetic operations) which is required for multiplying two integer matrices, that is, they can by multiplied with time complexity $O(n^{\log_2 7})$.

If, instead, we count the number of bit operations, as it is reasonable for boolean matrices, then the time complexity is $O(n^{\log_2 7}\, I_M(\log_2 n))$, where $I_M(n)$ is the time complexity for multiplying two integers, each of which being made out of n digits in base 2. (Recall that for all i,j, with $1\leq i,j\leq n$, $\widetilde{C}_{ij}$ has at most $\lceil\log_2(n+1)\rceil$ bits, because $\widetilde{C}_{ij}$ is at most n.)

Recalling that by the Schönhage-Strassen method we have that

$$I_M(n) = O(n\,(\log_2 n)\,\log_2(\log_2 n)),$$

we get that the time complexity for multiplying two $n{\times}n$ boolean matrices is:

$$O(n^{\,\log_2 7}\,(\log_2 n)\,(\log_2\log_2 n)\,(\log_2\log_2\log_2 n)).$$

We will see below that fast algorithms for boolean matrix multiplication allow us to construct fast algorithms for computing both the transitive closure of binary relations and the paths between nodes in graphs.

8.4. IC-Semirings and Path Problems in Directed Graphs

In order to study path problems in labeled directed graphs it is convenient to consider the $n \times n$ matrices whose elements are taken from suitable semirings, called *ic-semirings*, which we will introduce in this section. We will have that the algebra of the $n{\times}n$ matrices whose elements are taken from an ic-semiring, is an ic-semiring as well.

We assume that paths of labeled directed graphs are represented as elements of matrices associated with the graphs and, in particular, we assume that a path with label p from node h to node k of a graph G with n nodes, is represented by the element p taken from the semiring $(S,+,\,\cdot\,,0,1)$ and placed in row h and column k of an $n{\times}n$ matrix M associated with the graph G. Thus, for the matrix M we have that $M_{hk}=p$.

In order to motivate our definitions below, we now list a few properties that we want to hold for the paths of labeled directed graphs whose labels are taken from the semiring $(S,+,\,\cdot\,,0,1)$.

(i) Two paths from node m to node n, the first one with label p and the second one with label q, are equal to a single path from m to n with label $p+q$.

(ii) For any node n_1, n_2, and n_3, a path from n_1 to n_2 with label p followed by a path from n_2 to n_3 with label q, is equal to a path from n_1 to n_3 with label $p\cdot q$.

(iii) The absence of a path from node m to node n is equal to a path from node m to node n with label 0.

(iv) The path of length 0 (that is, a path of no arcs) from a node to itself is equal to a path from that node to itself with label 1.

(v) For any node n_1, n_2, and n_3, a path from n_1 to n_2 with label p, followed by a path from n_2 to n_3 with label $q_1 + q_2$, is equal to a path from n_1 to n_3 with label $(p \cdot q_1) + (p \cdot q_2)$ (this property is the distributivity of $\cdot$ over $+$).

(vi) Two paths both with label p, between the same two nodes, are equal to a single path with label p (this property is the idempotency of $+$).

(vii) A path from a node to itself with label p, that is, a *loop* with label p, is equal to a path from that node to itself with label p^*, that is, $1 + p + p \cdot p + p \cdot p \cdot p + \ldots$ (this property motivates the need for countably infinite sums).

DEFINITION 8.4.1. [**ic-semiring**] An $(S, +, \cdot, 0, 1)$-semiring, that is, a semiring with 0 and 1, is said to be *idempotent complete semiring* (or *ic-semiring*, for short) iff

(i) $+$ is idempotent, that is, for all $x \in S$, $x + x = x$, and

(ii) there are countably infinite sums, that is, there exists the value of $\sum_{i \geq 0} a_i$, that is, $a_0 + a_1 + \ldots$ for any infinite sequence $\langle a_0, a_1, \ldots \rangle$ of elements of S, and

(iii) $\cdot$ distributes on both sides over countably infinite sums, that is,

$$
\begin{aligned}
(a_0 + a_1 + a_2 + \ldots) \cdot (b_0 + b_1 + b_2 + \ldots) = \quad & (a_0 \cdot b_0) + (a_0 \cdot b_1) + (a_0 \cdot b_2) + \ldots \\
+ \quad & (a_1 \cdot b_0) + (a_1 \cdot b_1) + (a_1 \cdot b_2) + \ldots \\
+ \quad & (a_2 \cdot b_0) + (a_2 \cdot b_1) + (a_2 \cdot b_2) + \ldots \\
+ \quad & \ldots
\end{aligned}
$$

These semirings are called *closed semirings* in [**1**]. We prefer to call them *idempotent complete semirings* to recall that the operation $+$ is idempotent and there exist countably infinite sums.

For ic-semirings we will use the unary postfixed operation * to denote the infinite sum of all powers, that is, for all $s \in S$, $s^* =_{def} \sum_{i \geq 0} s^i$, that is, $s^* =_{def} 1 + s + s \cdot s + s \cdot s \cdot s + \ldots$ (recall that there is no need for parentheses among the summands and the factors, because $+$ and $\cdot$ are associative). Thus, $0^* = 1$. (One can informally state this property by saying that a loop of no path from a node m to itself is the same as the path of length 0 from m to itself.)

Here are three examples of ic-semirings with 0 and 1.

(i) $(\{0, 1\}, \vee, \wedge, 0, 1)$-semiring, called the *boolean ic-semiring*, where:
$x \vee y =_{def}$ *if* $x = 1$ or $y = 1$ *then* 1 *else* 0, and
$x \wedge y =_{def}$ *if* $x = 1$ and $y = 1$ *then* 1 *else* 0.
This ic-semiring is used for testing whether or not in a given directed graph there is a path from node i to node j.

(ii) $(R^{\geq 0} \cup \{+\infty\}, min, +, +\infty, 0)$-semiring, called the *non-negative ic-semiring*, where $R^{\geq 0}$ is the set of the non-negative reals, and for all x in $R^{\geq 0} \cup \{+\infty\}$ we have that $min(x, +\infty) = min(+\infty, x) = x$.

This ic-semiring is used for computing, given any directed graph whose arcs are labeled by non-negative reals, the minimum distance from any node to any node of the given graph.

(iii) $(REG(\Sigma^*), \cup, \cdot, \emptyset, \{\varepsilon\})$-semiring, called the *Regular Expressions ic-semiring*, where Σ is any given finite alphabet, Σ^* is the set of all words over Σ, that is, the set of all sequences of symbols in Σ, and $REG(\Sigma^*)$ is the set of all regular languages over Σ.

In what follows we will denote a regular language also by its corresponding regular expression (hence the name *Regular Expressions ic-semiring* for this ic-semiring).

Recall that, given two languages L_1 and L_2, their concatenation $L_1 \cdot L_2$ is defined in terms of concatenation of words, also denoted $\cdot$, as follows:

$$L_1 \cdot L_2 = \{w_1 \cdot w_2 \mid w_1 \in L_1 \text{ and } w_2 \in L_2\}.$$

This ic-semiring can be used for computing, given any directed graph whose arcs are labeled by regular expressions, the regular expression which denotes the set of all paths from any node to any node of the given graph.

From any given ic-semiring $(S, +, \cdot, 0, 1)$ we may get, as specified in Section 8.2 on page 258, the $(M_n, +_n, \cdot_n, 0_n, I_n)$-semiring of the $n \times n$ matrices whose elements are taken from the given semiring. It can be shown that $(M_n, +_n, \cdot_n, 0_n, I_n)$-semiring is an ic-semiring.

Let us now look at some problems for which the matrices over ic-semirings we have introduced, are particularly useful.

8.5. Transitive Closure in Directed Graphs: the Reachability Problem

Given a directed graph G with n nodes, the reachability problem in G consists in testing for each pair of nodes i and j whether or not there exists a path from i to j. We can solve this problem by considering the ic-semiring of the $n \times n$ matrices over the boolean ic-semiring $\langle \{0, 1\}, \vee, \wedge, 0, 1 \rangle$ as follows.

We associate with G the $n \times n$ boolean matrix $A(G)$, called *adjacency matrix*, (see, for instance, [20, Chapter 1]) such that for all i and j with $1 \leq i, j \leq n$,

$A(G)_{ij} =_{def}$ *if* there is an arc from node i to node j *then* 1 *else* 0.

In particular, $A(G)_{ii} = 0$ if there is no arc from node i to itself. From now on the matrix $A(G)$ will also be simply called A when the graph to which it refers, is understood from the context.

We assume that $A^0 = I_n$ (where I_n is the identity matrix, that is, the $n \times n$ matrix with all elements 0's except those in the main diagonal which are 1's). The definition of the identity boolean matrix I_n is based on the facts that:

(•) for all i and j with $1 \leq i, j \leq n$, there is no path of one or more arcs from a node i to a node j, and

(•) *if* $i = j$ *then* node j is reachable from node i (and this fact is encoded by the values 1's in the main diagonal of I_n) *else* node j is not reachable from node i (and this is encoded by the values 0's outside the main diagonal of I_n).

Then, given any two $n \times n$ boolean matrices A and B, we stipulate that, for all i, j with $1 \leq i, j \leq n$,

$$(A \wedge_n B)_{ij} = (A_{i1} \wedge B_{1j}) \vee (A_{i2} \wedge B_{2j}) \vee \ldots \vee (A_{in} \wedge B_{nj}).$$

We have that: $A^1 = A$ and $A^{n+1} = A^n \wedge_n A = A \wedge_n A^n$.

Below we will feel free to omit writing the operators $\wedge_n$ and $\wedge$, and we will use juxtaposition, instead. Often, for reasons of simplicity, we will also write $\wedge$, instead of $\wedge_n$. Analogously, we will also write $\vee$, instead of $\vee_n$.

One can show by induction on $r\,(\geq 0)$ that $A^r_{ij} = 1$ iff in the graph G there exists a path of length r from node i to node j. Thus, let us consider the matrix

$$A^* =_{def} I_n \vee A \vee A^2 \vee A^3 \vee \ldots \vee A^n \vee \ldots$$

We have that given any two nodes i and j, the node j is reachable from node i (that is, there is a path from node i to node j) iff $A^*_{ij} = 1$. One can also show that:

$$A^* = I_n \vee A \vee A^2 \vee A^3 \vee \ldots \vee A^{n-1}$$

This result follows from the fact that any path which, so to speak, touches more than n nodes of the graph G, should touch at least twice a node of G.

Moreover, we have that:

$$A^* = (I_n \vee A)^{n-1}. \tag{\#1}$$

This result follows from the fact that $A^* = I_n \vee A \vee A^2 \vee A^3 \vee \ldots \vee A^{n-1}$ and $I_n \vee A \vee A^2 \vee A^3 \vee \ldots \vee A^{n-1} = (I_n \vee A)^{n-1}$ because any path p of length k, with $0 \leq k \leq n-1$, can be viewed as a path of length $n-1$ which is the concatenation of the given path p of length k and a path of length $(n-1)-k$ from the final node of p to that same final node.

As a consequence of Equation (#1), the matrix A^* can be computed by successive squaring of $(I_n \vee A)$ for $\lceil \log_2(n-1) \rceil$ times, because $(I_n \vee A)^{n-1} = (I_n \vee A)^b$, where b is the smallest power of 2 such that $b \geq n-1$. (For any real number x, by $\lceil x \rceil$ we denote the least integer m such that $m \geq x$.) For instance, if $n=7$, then $(I_n \vee A)^6 = (I_n \vee A)^8$, and by performing 3 $(= \lceil \log_2(7-1) \rceil)$ successive squarings, starting from $(I_n \vee A)$, we get: (i) $(I_n \vee A)^2$, (ii) $(I_n \vee A)^4$, and (iii) $(I_n \vee A)^8$. Thus, the time needed for computing $(I_n \vee A)^*$ is $T(n) \leq M(n)\lceil \log_2 n \rceil$, where $M(n)$ denotes the time complexity for $n \times n$ boolean matrix multiplication. In the following section we will see that the $\lceil \log_2 n \rceil$ factor is actually redundant, that is, $T(n) \leq M(n)$.

8.6. Reducing Transitive Closure to Boolean Matrix Multiplication

We have the following fact.

FACT 8.6.1. [**Reducing Boolean Transitive Closure to Boolean Matrix Multiplication**] Given a directed graph G with n nodes, let us consider the corresponding $n \times n$ adjacency, boolean matrix A, and its partition into four $(n/2) \times (n/2)$ blocks (assume that n is even): $A = \begin{vmatrix} A_{11} & A_{12} \\ A_{21} & A_{22} \end{vmatrix}$. We have that:

$$A^* = \begin{vmatrix} A^*_{11} \vee (A^*_{11} \wedge A_{12} \wedge E^* \wedge A_{21} \wedge A^*_{11}) & A^*_{11} \wedge A_{12} \wedge E^* \\ E^* \wedge A_{21} \wedge A^*_{11} & E^* \end{vmatrix} \tag{\#2}$$

where $E = (A_{21} \wedge A^*_{11} \wedge A_{12}) \vee A_{22}$.

PROOF. It is based on the interpretation of the matrix E and the four submatrices in the block partition of A^* via the diagrams of Figure 8.6.1 on the next page and Figure 8.6.2 on the facing page.

Let A_{11} denote a subgraph G_1 of G with $n/2$ nodes, and A_{22} denote the subgraph G_2 of G with the remaining $n/2$ nodes. In Figure 8.6.1 on the next page and Figure 8.6.2 on the facing page we use the following conventions:

Paths from G_2 to G_2 : E^*, where $E = (A_{21} \wedge A_{11}^* \wedge A_{21}) \vee A_{22}$
can be depicted as follows:

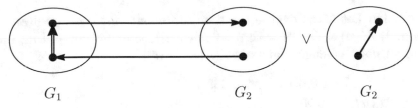

FIGURE 8.6.1. The set E of paths that go from the subgraph G_2 to the same subgraph G_2. They provide an interpretation of the matrix $E = (A_{21} \wedge A_{11}^* \wedge A_{12}) \vee A_{22}$.

Paths from G_1 to G_2:
$A_{11}^* \wedge A_{12} \wedge E^*$

Paths from G_2 to G_1:
$E^* \wedge A_{21} \wedge A_{11}^*$

Paths from G_1 to G_1:
$A_{11}^* \vee$
$(A_{11}^* \wedge A_{12} \wedge E^* \wedge A_{21} \wedge A_{11}^*)$

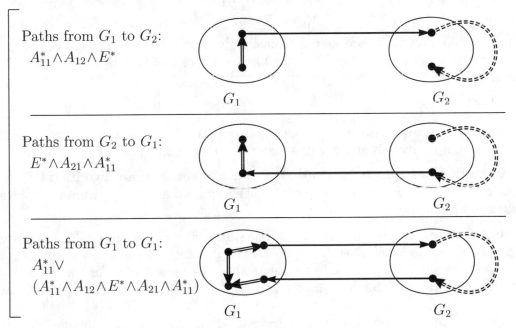

FIGURE 8.6.2. Three sets of paths that provide an interpretation of the three matrices $A_{11}^* \wedge A_{12} \wedge E^*$, $E^* \wedge A_{21} \wedge A_{11}^*$, and $A_{11}^* \vee (A_{11}^* \wedge A_{12} \wedge E^* \wedge A_{21} \wedge A_{11}^*)$, respectively.

(i) a *solid* arrow ⟶ denotes an arc of the graph G,

(ii) a *solid double* arrow ⟹ in the graph G_1 or G_2 denotes a path of any length (≥ 0) within the subgraph G_1 or G_2, respectively, and

(iii) a *dashed double* arrow ⇒ denotes a path of any length (≥ 0) going anywhere through the graph G.

Thus, for instance, the left upper corner of A^*, that is, $A_{11}^* \vee (A_{11}^* \wedge A_{12} \wedge E^* \wedge A_{21} \wedge A_{11}^*)$, can be interpreted as a path going from a node in G_1 to a node in G_1 (see also Figure 8.6.2). It is *either* entirely inside G_1 (see A_{11}^*) *or* it is inside G_1 (see A_{11}^*) and then it goes to G_2 (see A_{12}), it returns zero or more times to G_2 (see E^*), it returns to G_1 (see A_{21}), and finally, it continues entirely inside G_1 (see A_{11}^*). Analogous interpretation can be done for the other blocks of the matrix A^* (see again Figure 8.6.2 on the preceding page). $\qquad\square$

FACT 8.6.2. Let $M(n)$ denote the time complexity for $n \times n$ boolean matrix multiplication. If $M(n) = O(n^\alpha)$ with $\alpha > 2$, then the time for computing the transitive closure of an $n \times n$ boolean matrix is $T(n) = O(n^\alpha)$.

PROOF. From Fact 8.6.1 on page 262 we get that:
$$T(n) \le 2T(n/2) + 6M(n) + O(n^2).$$
Thus, $T(n) = O(n^\alpha)$ if $M(n) = O(n^\alpha)$ with $\alpha > 2$. The factor 6 comes from the following six matrix multiplications which are necessary for obtaining the elements of the matrix A^*:

$$M_1 = A_{11}^* \wedge A_{12} \qquad M_2 = A_{21} \wedge A_{11}^* \qquad M_3 = M_1 \wedge E^*$$
$$M_4 = M_3 \wedge M_2 \qquad M_5 = E^* \wedge M_2 \qquad M_6 = A_{21} \wedge M_1.$$

If n is not a power of 2, then we can embed a given $n \times n$ boolean matrix, say A, into an $m \times m$ boolean matrix, say D, with m being a power of 2, with $m > n$, which has the form:
$$D = \begin{vmatrix} A & 0 \\ 0 & I \end{vmatrix}$$
where I is the $(m-n) \times (m-n)$ boolean identity matrix. Since m is not larger than $2n$ the time complexity will increase of at most 2^3 times, which is a constant factor. $\qquad\square$

From this Fact 8.6.2 it follows that, in order to obtain a fast algorithm for computing the transitive closure of a graph, we simply need a fast algorithm for boolean matrix multiplication.

REMARK 8.6.3. The matrix A^* in Equation (#2) of the above Fact 8.6.1 on page 262 is *not* symmetric with respect to the partition of the given graph G into the two subgraphs G_1 and G_2 in the sense that the second row *cannot* be derived from the first row by interchanging the subscripts 1 and 2 and interchanging the two columns.

On the contrary, the following expression of the matrix A^* is symmetric with respect to that partition (and thus, in this expression of the matrix A^* the second row *can* be derived from the first row by interchanging the subscripts 1 and 2 and interchanging the two columns):

$$A^* = \begin{vmatrix} D^* & D^* \wedge A_{12} \wedge A_{22}^* \\ E^* \wedge A_{21} \wedge A_{11}^* & E^* \end{vmatrix} \qquad\qquad (\#3)$$

where $D = (A_{12} \wedge A_{22}^* \wedge A_{21}) \vee A_{11}$ and $E = (A_{21} \wedge A_{11}^* \wedge A_{12}) \vee A_{22}$.

In the expression $D^* \wedge A_{12} \wedge A_{22}^*$ the matrix A_{12} denotes the last time the path from the subgraph G_1 enters the subgraph G_2. Other moves from G_1 to G_2, if any, are denoted within D^*.

Note also that the value of E can be derived from the value of D by interchanging the subscripts 1 and 2. Using the symmetric expression (#3), the evaluation of A^* requires $T(n)$ time units where $T(n)$ satisfies the following inequation:
$$T(n) \le 4T(n/2) + 6M(n) + O(n^2).$$

Thus, again, we have that $T(n) = O(n^\alpha)$ if $M(n) = O(n^\alpha)$ with $\alpha > 2$. The factor 4 comes from the four transitive closures we have to compute: E^*, D^*, A_{11}^*, and A_{22}^*. The factor 6 comes from the following six matrix multiplications we have to perform:

$$M_1 = A_{12} \wedge A_{22}^* \qquad\qquad M_2 = M_1 \wedge A_{21} \qquad\qquad M_3 = D^* \wedge M_1$$

$$M_4 = A_{21} \wedge A_{11}^* \qquad\qquad M_5 = M_4 \wedge A_{12} \qquad\qquad M_6 = E^* \wedge M_4. \qquad\qquad \square$$

The proof of Fact 8.6.1 on page 262 is based only on the property that the boolean ic-semiring is indeed an ic-semiring. Thus, if we consider directed graphs with labels which are elements of a non-negative ic-semiring (see page 260) or a Regular Expressions ic-semiring (see page 261), we have that the statements analogous to Fact 8.6.1 on page 262 and Fact 8.6.2 on the preceding page hold also for the matrices whose elements are non-negative reals or regular expressions.

The following fact shows that we can reduce the multiplication of two boolean matrices to the computation of the transitive closure of a boolean matrix.

FACT 8.6.4. [**Reducing Boolean Matrix Multiplication to Boolean Transitive Closure**] Let $T(n)$ denote the time complexity for computing the transitive closure of an $n \times n$ boolean matrix. If $T(n) = O(n^\alpha)$ with $\alpha > 2$, then the time complexity for the $n \times n$ boolean matrix multiplication is $M(n) = O(n^\alpha)$.

PROOF. It is easy to verify that

$$\begin{vmatrix} 0 & A & 0 \\ 0 & 0 & B \\ 0 & 0 & 0 \end{vmatrix}^* = \begin{vmatrix} I & 0 & A \wedge B \\ 0 & I & 0 \\ 0 & 0 & I \end{vmatrix}$$

Thus, in order to multiply two given $n \times n$ boolean matrices A and B, it is enough to compute the transitive closure of the $(3n) \times (3n)$ boolean matrix $T = \begin{vmatrix} 0 & A & 0 \\ 0 & 0 & B \\ 0 & 0 & 0 \end{vmatrix}$. It

takes $O((3n)^\alpha)$ time. Now $O((3n)^\alpha)$ is equal to $O(n^\alpha)$, and this time complexity is the time complexity required for computing the transitive closure of an $n \times n$ boolean matrix. Having computed that transitive closure T^* of the matrix T, we then consider the top right corner of T^* (which is equal to $A \wedge B$). $\qquad\qquad \square$

8.7. Transitive Closure in IC-Semirings: the Shortest Path Problem

Given a labeled (or weighted) directed graph G with n nodes, the problem of finding the shortest paths in G consists in finding for each pair of nodes i and j, a path with minimum sum of the labels of its arcs. If the labels of G form a non-negative ic-semiring (see Definition 8.4.1 on page 260), we can solve this problem by considering the $n \times n$ matrices over that semiring as follows.

Given a labeled directed graph G with n nodes, we associate with G the $n \times n$ matrix $M(G)$ such that for all i and j, with $1 \le i, j \le n$, $M(G)_{ij} = \lambda(i, j)$, where $\lambda(i, j)$ is the label of the arc from node i to node j. We assume that for all i and j, with $1 \le i, j \le n$, $\lambda(i, j) = +\infty$ if there is no arc from node i to node j (even if $i = j$).

In what follows the matrix $M(G)$ will also be called M when the graph to which it refers, is understood from the context.

Then, for any two nodes i and j of G, we can find a path from i to j with the minimum sum of the labels of its arcs by applying the analogous of Fact 8.6.1 on page 262 for matrices over a non-negative ic-semiring.

Notice that in the identity matrix over the non-negative ic-semiring, each element of the main diagonal is 0 (which is the identity for $+$), while every other element is $+\infty$ (which is the identity for min). This definition of the identity matrix for the non-negative ic-semiring $(R^{\geq 0} \cup \{+\infty\}, min, +, +\infty, 0)$ is based on the fact that for all i and j, with $1 \leq i, j \leq n$,

($\bullet$) if $i = j$, then a shortest path from node i to node j is a path of length 0 whose sum of the labels is 0 and, otherwise,

($\bullet$) if $i \neq j$ and there is no path from node i to node j, then a shortest path from i to j is assumed to have the sum of the labels equal to $+\infty$ (because from node i it is not possible to reach node j).

It can be shown that one can compute the shortest paths between every pair of nodes of a labeled directed graph G by computing the transitive closure of the matrix M over the non-negative ic-semiring of the labels of G.

We have the following fact which is analogous to Fact 8.6.2 on page 264.

FACT 8.7.1. Let $M(n)$ denote the time complexity for multiplying $n \times n$ matrices. If $M(n) = O(n^\alpha)$ with $\alpha > 2$, then the time for computing a shortest path between any two nodes in labeled direct graph whose labels are non-negative reals is $T(n) = O(n^\alpha)$.

EXAMPLE 8.7.2. Let us consider the labeled directed graph with three nodes depicted in Figure 8.7.1. We have that:

$$min(I, M) = \begin{vmatrix} 0 & 8 & 5 \\ 3 & 0 & \infty \\ \infty & 2 & 0 \end{vmatrix} \quad \text{and} \quad (min(I, M))^* = (min(I, M))^{3-1} = \begin{vmatrix} 0 & 7 & 5 \\ 3 & 0 & 8 \\ 5 & 2 & 0 \end{vmatrix}. \quad \square$$

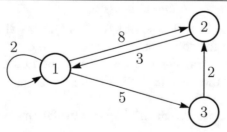

FIGURE 8.7.1. A directed graph with non-negative labels on the arcs.

We leave it to the reader to show that if the labels of the arcs of the given directed graph G are not taken from a non-negative ic-semiring, as for instance in the case of labels which may have negative values, the technique based on the computation of $(min(I, M))^*$ for finding the shortest paths between every pair of nodes of G, is still correct, provided that there are no *negative cycles*, that is, cycles whose sum of the labels of the arcs is a negative value.

If there are negative cycles in the given graph, the technique based on the computation of $(min(I, M))^*$ is *not* correct, and we have to apply other algorithms, like the Floyd-Warshall's algorithm or a variant of Algorithm 8.8.1 (Dijkstra's SSSP algorithm) which we will present on this page. If there are negative cycles, the time complexity of those algorithms goes up to $O(n^3)$ [**16**, Chapter 6, page 133].

8.8. Single Source Shortest Paths in Directed Graphs

In this section we consider the problem of finding, given a labeled directed graph, the shortest paths starting from an initial node, also called the *source*, to all other nodes of the graph. This problem is called the *Single Source Shortest Path problem*. For solving this problem there exists an algorithm which is faster than the one based on the computation of the transitive closure of the adjacency matrix associated with the graph, which we have considered in the previous Section 8.7. We will call this faster algorithm the *Single Source Shortest Path algorithm*, or the *SSSP algorithm*, for short.

This algorithm is based on the Dynamic Programming idea. It is due to E. W. Dijkstra, as the algorithm we have presented in Section 7.5 for computing a minimal spanning tree of an undirected graph (see Algorithm 7.5.1 on page 247), and it takes $O(n^2)$ time for graphs of n nodes, if the labels on the arcs are taken from a nonnegative ic-semiring. Dijkstra's SSSP algorithm is correct also for any labeled directed graph provided that there are no negative cycles, that is, there are no cycles with negative sum of the labels of their arcs.

Dijkstra's SSSP algorithm can be viewed as a particular instance of the *Primal-Dual algorithm* (see [**16**, Capter 5]) and thus, its correctness can be derived from that of the Primal-Dual algorithm.

Note that between any two given nodes of the graph there could be more than one path with the minimal sum of the labels of its arcs. In this case Dijkstra's SSSP algorithm computes one of these minimal paths. However, by abuse of language, in what follows we will feel free to say 'the shortest path', instead of 'a shortest path'.

Now, for reasons of simplicity, we will present Dijkstra's SSSP algorithm in the case when the labels of the arcs are non-negative reals.

ALGORITHM 8.8.1.
Computation of the Single Source Shortest Paths in Directed Graphs. (Dijkstra's SSSP *algorithm*)

Input: We are given a labeled, directed, connected graph G with n nodes. We are also given a node n_0 of G, called the *source*. No assumptions are made on the arcs which depart from n_0 or arrive at n_0.
For each arc $\langle p, q \rangle$, we assume that there exists a label $\lambda(p, q)$ which is a non-negative real number. That label is also called the *length* of the arc.
For each node p, we assume that there exists the arc $\langle p, p \rangle$ whose label $\lambda(p, p)$ is 0.

Output: for each node q in G, we compute a *shortest path* from node n_0 to node q, that is, a path from n_0 to q with minimal *length*. That path has minimal sum of the labels of its arcs, being the minimum taken over all paths from n_0 to q.

Step A. With each node $q \in G$ we associate a label $\Lambda(q)$ which is the length of a shortest path from n_0 to q.

1. $\Lambda(n_0) := 0;$ $Reach := \{n_0\};$
2. for each arc $\langle n_0, q \rangle$, $\Lambda(q) := \lambda(n_0, q);$
3. *Repeat* | among all nodes not in *Reach* with a label, take a node, say p,
         | with *minimal* label $\Lambda(p);$
         | 3.1 $Reach := Reach \cup \{p\};$
         | 3.2 for each arc $\langle p, m \rangle$ with m not in *Reach*,
         | *if* m has already a label
         | *then*   (3.2.1) $\Lambda(m) := min\{\Lambda(p) + \lambda(p, m), \Lambda(m)\}$
         | *else*   (3.2.2) $\Lambda(m) := \Lambda(p) + \lambda(p, m);$

Step B. We find by backtracking a shortest path from node n_0 to a node $q \in G$.

4. Choose *any* node p, different from q, such that $\Lambda(p) = -\lambda(p, q) + \Lambda(q);$
5. Recursively, find a shortest path from n_0 to p by performing Step B.

The following points illustrate a few important facts about of the above SSSP algorithm.

(i) The source node n_0 can be any node of the given graph G. In particular, there may be arcs going into the source node.

(ii) At Point 4 if there exists more than one node p, different from q, such that $\Lambda(p) = -\lambda(p, q) + \Lambda(q)$, then we may choose *any* one of them. If this is the case, then there exists more than one path from n_0 to q with minimal length.

(iii) If $\langle n_0, n_1, \ldots, n_{k-1}, n_k \rangle$ is a shortest path from n_0 to n_k,

then $\Lambda(n_k) = \sum_{i \geq 0}^{k-1} \lambda(n_i, n_{i+1})$.

(iv) This SSSP algorithm is similar to Dijkstra's MST algorithm [6] for computing a minimal spanning tree of undirected graphs with labels on the arcs (see also Algorithm 7.5.1 on page 247). Analogously to Dijkstra's MST algorithm:

($\bullet$) the SSSP algorithm is a *greedy* algorithm, that is, the local optimum is a global optimum (recall what has been said for the MST algorithm on page 244),

($\bullet$) according to what we have said about the MST algorithm, the nodes in *Reach* may be viewed as *red* nodes and the nodes not in *Reach* may be viewed as *blue* nodes, and

($\bullet$) the SSSP algorithm, after transforming a blue node p into a red node (see Point 3.1), readjusts (see Point 3.2.1) or generates (see Point 3.2.2) the label of each blue node m such that there exists an arc $\langle p, m \rangle$.

Now we present the invariants of the loops of the above Dijkstra's SSSP Algorithm 8.8.1. Those invariants clarify the way in which that algorithm works and are the basis of the proof of its correctness which we leave to the reader.

The invariant of the *Repeat* statement at Point 3 is:

«the label of any node q in the set *Reach* is the length of a shortest path from the source node n_0 to q».

The invariant of the for loop at Point 3.2 is:

«each node m *not* in *Reach* such that there is an arc $\langle p, m \rangle$ with $p \in Reach$, has a label which is the length of a shortest path $\langle n_0, \ldots, p, m \rangle$ from the source node n_0 to m such that the nodes $n_0, \ldots, p$ are all in *Reach*».

The assertion after Point 4 is:

«in a shortest path from the source node n_0 to the node q, the last arc is $\langle p, q \rangle$».

The correctness of Dijkstra's SSSP algorithm is based on the following property.

Let us assume that we have computed a shortest path from the source node n_0 to every node in a subset W of the nodes such that $n_0 \in W$. Let us consider a shortest path, say π, from the node n_0 to any node y not in W such that for every node x if there is the arc $\langle x, y \rangle$ in G, then $x \in W$. Then the path π has the property that it goes through nodes of W (except for y itself).

Note that if at Point 3 we take a node p whose label $\Lambda(p)$ is not *minimal*, the algorithm is *not* correct.

EXAMPLE 8.8.2. Given the graph of Figure 8.8.1 on the next page and the node n_0, after Point 3 of Dijkstra's SSSP algorithm we get the 'boxed labels' at each node. Then, having labeled all nodes with the boxed labels, we may find *by backtracking* every arc whose label is exactly the difference of the boxed labels of its nodes. By doing so (see Points 4 and 5 of the SSSP algorithm), we get the following two sequences of values:

(i) $\boxed{12} \xleftarrow{\ 6\ } \boxed{6} \xleftarrow{\ 1\ } \boxed{5} \xleftarrow{\ 2\ } \boxed{3} \xleftarrow{\ 3\ } \boxed{0}$ and

(ii) $\boxed{12} \xleftarrow{\ 3\ } \boxed{9} \xleftarrow{\ 4\ } \boxed{5} \xleftarrow{\ 2\ } \boxed{3} \xleftarrow{\ 3\ } \boxed{0}$

which correspond to the following two shortest paths from node n_0 to node n_6 (see the thicker arcs of the graph of Figure 8.8.1):

(i) $n_0 \longrightarrow n_2 \longrightarrow n_3 \longrightarrow n_5 \longrightarrow n_6$ and

(ii) $n_0 \longrightarrow n_2 \longrightarrow n_3 \longrightarrow n_4 \longrightarrow n_6$, respectively.

The total length of each of those shortest paths is 12 which is, indeed, the boxed label of the final node n_6. Note that by backtracking, from node n_6 we do *not* go back to node n_3 (because $12-9 \neq 5$) and, instead, we go back either to node n_4 (because $12-6=6$) or to node n_5 (because $12-3=9$). $\qquad\square$

For a graph of n nodes the time complexity of Dijkstra's SSSP algorithm is $O(n^2)$ and this is due to the fact that: (i) the body of the *Repeat* statement (see Point 3) is performed at most n times because there are at most n nodes not in *Reach*, and (ii) for each node p not in *Reach* there exist at most n arcs of the form $\langle p, m \rangle$ with m not in *Reach* (see Point 3.2).

Dijkstra's SSSP algorithm shows that if we fix the initial node and the labels of the given graph are taken from a non-negative ic-semiring, we may solve the Single Source Shortest Path problem in $O(n^2)$ time. This is an improvement over the time complexity for solving the shortest path problem between any two nodes. Indeed,

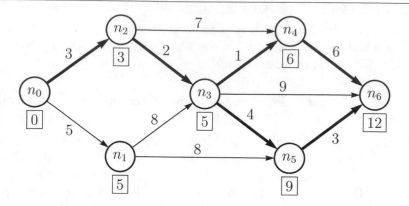

FIGURE 8.8.1. A directed graph with non-negative labels (also called lengths) on the arcs. The thicker arcs are those belonging to the two shortest paths of length 12 from node n_0 to node n_6.

Worst Case Time Complexity

Shortest paths from *any* node to *any* node: (the complexity is that of matrix multiplication)	$O(n^{2.81})$
Shortest paths from a *fixed* node to *any* node:	$O(n^2)$
Shortest path from a *fixed* node to a *fixed* node: (it is an open problem whether or not one can do better)	$O(n^2)$

FIGURE 8.8.2. Time complexity of the computation of the shortest paths in directed graphs with n nodes.

as we have shown in Section 8.6 on page 262, this last problem requires the same amount of time which is needed for matrix multiplication, say $O(n^{2.81})$ time (see also Figure 8.8.2).

One may wonder whether or not it is possible to derive an even faster algorithm for the shortest path problem when we fix both the initial node and the target node. This is the so called *Single Source Single Target Shortest Path* problem. The answer, to our knowledge, is still open, in the sense that no algorithm has been found for this last problem which has a better time performance, in the worst case, than the best algorithm known for the Single Source Shortest Path problem which has an $O(n^2)$ time complexity for graphs of n nodes.

A final point is worth noticing. Let us consider an *undirected graph* with weights on its arcs as a particular case of directed graph, where for each arc from node x to node y with label w, there exists a symmetric arc from node y to node x with the same label w. In an undirected graph any pair of directed arcs from node x to node y and vice versa will be denoted by $x - y$.

Now, given an undirected graph G with non-negative weights on its arcs, we have that a shortest path between two nodes may be made out of arcs none of which belongs to the minimal spanning tree of G. This fact is illustrated in the graph of Figure 8.8.3. In that figure we use the usual convention of drawing every pair of directed arcs of an undirected graph by a single arc without arrowheads. In Figure 8.8.3 a shortest path from node b to node c is the arc $b-c$ with weight 3, while a minimal spanning tree of the graph G has total weight 4 and it is made out of the arcs $a-b$ and $a-c$.

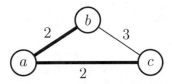

FIGURE 8.8.3. An undirected graph with non-negative labels on the arcs. The thicker arcs are those of the minimal spanning tree.

In what follows we present a Java program which implements Dijkstra's Single Source Shortest Path algorithm. It is made out of two files: SSSP.java and Graph.java, which are located in the same folder.

```
/**
 * =============================================================================
 *                    Single Source Shortest Path: Main Program
 * Filename: "SSSP.java"
 *
 * This program computes a shortest path from a node to any other node
 * of a weighted, directed graph. The weight of an arc is the length of the
 * arc.
 *
 * In what follows we will feel free to say 'the shortest path' (or 'the
 * shortest distance'), instead of 'a shortest path' (or 'a shortest
 * distance'), even if the shortest path may not be unique.
 *
 * In the command:
 *    java SSSP nn in fn
 * the integers nn, in, and fn denote the number of nodes, the initial
 * node, and the final node, respectively.
 * For instance, we should issue the command: java SSSP 5 0 3
 * for a graph of 5 nodes in which we look for a shortest path from node 0
 * to node 3.
 * =============================================================================
 */

import java.util.ArrayList;
import java.util.Iterator;

public class SSSP {                    // SSSP : Single Source Shortest Path

    public static int min (int a, int b) {
       if (a>b) {return b;} else {return a;}
    }

    public static void main(String[] args) {

       int N = 0;                       // - to be read from the input: args[0]
       int initNode = 0;                // - to be read from the input: args[1]
       int finalNode = 0;               // - to be read from the input: args[2]


// -------------------------------- N: number of Nodes of the graph.
//                                  N >= 1.

       try {N = Integer.parseInt(args[0]);
           if ( N < 1) { throw new RuntimeException (); };
       } catch (Exception e)
                  {System.out.print("*** Wrong number of nodes!\n");}

// -------------------------------- initNode: initial node.
//                                  0 <= initNode <= N-1.

       try {initNode = Integer.parseInt(args[1]);
           if ( ( 0 > initNode ) || ( initNode > N-1 ) ) {
              throw new RuntimeException ();
              };
       } catch (Exception e)
                  {System.out.print("*** Wrong initial node!\n");}

// -------------------------------- finalNode: final node.
//                                  0 <= finalNode <= N-1.
```

```
      try {finalNode = Integer.parseInt(args[2]);
          if ( ( 0 > finalNode ) || ( finalNode > N-1 ) ) {
              throw new RuntimeException ();
              };
      } catch (Exception e) {System.out.print("*** Wrong final node!\n");}

// -----------------------------------------------------------------
// MAXLENGTH: maximum length of the arcs. 1 <= length <= MAXLENGTH.
      final int MAXLENGTH = 9;

// -----------------------------------------------------------------
// PerCentPROB: probability of connectivity. 0 < PerCentPROB <= 100.
// If PerCentPROB = k, every node is connected with probability k/100 to
// the other N-1 nodes.
      final int PerCentPROB = 40;

// -----------------------------------------------------------------
// Generation of a random graph with N nodes.
// The length of each arc belongs to the set {1,..., MAXLENGTH}.
// Every node has (N-1) x PerCentPROB / 100 successor nodes (in average).
      Graph g =
          new Graph(N, initNode, finalNode, MAXLENGTH, PerCentPROB);
      g.graphPrint();
      System.out.println("Every node is connected to the other nodes with " +
                         "probability " + PerCentPROB + " percent.");
      System.out.println("The length of each arc belongs to the set {1,..., "
                         + MAXLENGTH + "}.");
      System.out.println("The initial node is: " + initNode);
      System.out.println("The final node is: " + finalNode);

      // ---------------------------------------------
      int p = g.nearestOutsideNode();

      while (p >= 0) {            // <<-------------------------------------+
          g.reach[p] = true;      // Reach = Reach U {p}              // |
          for (int m=0; m<N; m++) {                                   // |
              if (!g.reach[m] && g.graph[p][m] >= 0) {                // |
                  if (g.shortestDistances[m] >= 0)                    // |
                      {g.shortestDistances[m] =                       // |
                       min (g.shortestDistances[p] + g.graph[p][m],   // |
                            g.shortestDistances[m]);}                 // |
                  else {g.shortestDistances[m] =                      // |
                        g.shortestDistances[p] + g.graph[p][m];};     // |
              };                                                      // |
          };                                                          // |
          p = g.nearestOutsideNode();                                 // |
      }                           // end of while <<----------------------+
      // ---------------------------------------------

      // add(0,e) inserts the element e at position 0, and shifts
      // the element at position 0 and all subsequent elements to the right
      // (adds 1 to their indices).

      g.itinerary.add(0, new Integer(finalNode));
      int m = finalNode;
      while (m != initNode) {     // <<-------------------------------------+
          int j=0;                                                    // |
          while ( j == m || g.shortestDistances[j] !=                 // |
                      -g.graph[j][m]+g.shortestDistances[m] ) { j++;};  // |
          g.itinerary.add(0, new Integer(j));                         // |
```

```
            m=j;                                                    // |
         };                        // end of while <<---------------------+
      g.shortestDistancesPrint();
      g.itineraryPrint();
   }
}

// -----------------------------------------------------------------------

/**
 * input:
 * -----------------------------------------------------------------------
 * javac SSSP.java
 * java   SSSP 5 0 3
 *
 * output:
 * -------
 *
 * The random graph has 5 node(s) (from node 0 to node 4).
 * The matrix of the arc lengths is:
 * 0 :   0 - 9 - -
 * 1 :   - 0 - - 7
 * 2 :   - - 0 4 -
 * 3 :   - - 6 0 -
 * 4 :   - - 6 - 0
 *
 * Every node is connected to the other nodes with probability 40 percent.
 * The length of each arc belongs to the set {1, ..., 9}.
 * The initial node is: 0
 * The final node is: 3
 *
 * The shortest distances from the initial node 0 to every node of
 * the graph are ('-' means 'unreachable node'):
 * 0 - 9 13 -
 *
 * The nodes of the shortest path from node 0 to node 3 are:
 * 0 2 3
 *
 * The cumulative distances of the shortest path from node 0 to node 3 are:
 * 0 9 13
 *
 * -----------------------------------------------------------------------
 */
```

```
/**
 * =========================================================================
 *                        The Graph class
 * Filename: "Graph.java"
 *
 * This class Graph is not a monitor, because not all fields are "private".
 * However, the non-private fields are read, but never assigned to.
 * All methods are "synchronized".
 * We can say that this class Graph is "almost" a monitor.
 *
 * In what follows we will feel free to say 'the shortest path' (or 'the
 * shortest distance'), instead of 'a shortest path' (or 'a shortest
 * distance'), even if the shortest path may not be unique.
 * =========================================================================
 */

import java.util.Random;
import java.util.ArrayList;
import java.util.Iterator;

public class Graph {

    final   int N;              // N = number of nodes of the graph
    final   int initNode;       // 0 <= initNode  <= N-1
    final   int finalNode;      // 0 <= finalNode <= N-1
    static int [][] graph;      // an N x N array

    // shortestDistances is an array of N integers belonging to the object
    // of the class Graph

    static int     [] shortestDistances;
    static boolean [] reach;
    static ArrayList itinerary = new ArrayList();

// --------------- beginning of constructor ---------------------------

    public Graph(int N, int initNode, int finalNode, int MAXLENGTH,
                 int PerCentPROB) {

    /** Generation of a random, directed graph with N nodes.
     *  The random variable randomConnect controls the connectivity:
     *      node i is connected with node j, for i != j, with percent
     *      probability PerCentPROB:  0 <= PerCentPROB <= 100
     *  The random variable randomLength controls the length of the arcs:
     *      1 <= length of an arc <= MAXLENGTH
     */

        this.N                = N;
        this.initNode         = initNode;
        this.finalNode        = finalNode;
        this.graph            = new int [N][N];
        this.shortestDistances = new int [N];     // \Lambda(n) for each node n
        this.reach            = new boolean [N];// the Reach set
        Random randomConnect  = new Random();   // random graph connectivity
        Random randomLength   = new Random();   // random arc length
```

```
        // initializing the graph: -1 (printed as "-") means "unconnected node"
        // graph[i][j] = m with m >= 0
        //     iff m is the length of the arc from node i to node j
        for(int i=0;i<N;i++) {
          for(int j=0;j<N;j++) {
              if ((i != j) && (randomConnect.nextInt(100) < PerCentPROB))
                  { graph[i][j] = 1 + randomLength.nextInt(MAXLENGTH); }
              else if (i == j ) { graph[i][j] = 0; }
              else  { graph[i][j] = -1; };
          }
        }

        // initializing the array shortestDistances:
        //    -1 (printed as "-") means "unreached node".
        // shortestDistances[i] = d with d >= 0
        //     iff d is the shortest distance from the initial node to node i
        //        computed so far.

        for(int j=0;j<N;j++) shortestDistances[j] = graph[initNode][j];

        // initializing the array reach
        //    -1 (printed as "-") means "node not in the array reach"
        // initially

        for(int j=0;j<N;j++) reach[j] = false; reach[initNode] = true;

        // initializing the shortest path, called 'itinerary',
        // from initNode to finalNode

        ArrayList itinerary = new ArrayList();
    }
// --------------- end of constructor -------------------------------------

// --------------- updating the array shortestDistances --------------------
    public synchronized void shortestDistancesUpdate (int i, int distance) {
        shortestDistances[i] = distance;
    }

// --------------- accessing the array shortestDistances -------------------
    public synchronized int shortestDistancesAt (int i) {
        return shortestDistances[i];
    }

// --------------- finding a p node ----------------------------------------
// if node == -1 there is no such nearest node outside the array reach.
    public synchronized int nearestOutsideNode () {
        int min = -1; int node = -1;
        for(int j=0; j<N; j++)
           { if (reach[j] == false && shortestDistances[j] >= 0
                && min == -1)
             { node = j; min = shortestDistances[j]; }
             else
             if (reach[j] == false && shortestDistances[j] >= 0
                && shortestDistances[j] < min)
             { node = j; min = shortestDistances[j]; };
           };
        return node;
    }
```

```
// -------------------- printing the graph -------------------------------

   public synchronized void graphPrint () {
     System.out.println("The random graph has "+ N +" node(s) " +
                        "(from node 0 to node " + (N-1) + ").\n" +
                        "The matrix of the arc lengths is:");

     for(int i=0;i<N;i++) {
        System.out.print(i + " :  ");
        for(int j=0;j<N;j++) {
           if (graph[i][j] < 0) { System.out.print("- "); }
           else System.out.print( graph[i][j] + " ");
        }; System.out.println();
      }; System.out.println();
   }


// -------------- printing the array shortestDistances  ------------------

   public synchronized void shortestDistancesPrint () {
      System.out.println("\nThe shortest distances from the initial node "
                         + initNode + " to every node of\nthe graph " +
                         "are ('-' means 'unreachable node'):");

      for(int i=0;i<N;i++) {
           if (shortestDistances[i] < 0) { System.out.print("- "); }
           else System.out.print( shortestDistances[i] + " "); }
      System.out.println();
   }


// -------------- printing the array reach  -----------------------------

// This method is NOT needed. This method is useful for debugging.

   public synchronized void reachPrint () {
      System.out.print("\nThe reach array is: \n");
      for(int i=0;i<N;i++) {
           if (!reach[i]) { System.out.print("- "); }
           else System.out.print("1 "); };
      System.out.println();
   }


// -------------- printing the shortest path from initNode to finalNode ---

// the shortest path from initNode to finalNode is called 'itinerary'
//
   public synchronized void itineraryPrint () {
      if ( shortestDistances[finalNode] >= 0 ) {
         System.out.println("\nThe nodes of the shortest path from node "
                            + initNode + " to node "+finalNode + " are:");

         for (Iterator iter = itinerary.iterator(); iter.hasNext(); ) {
             System.out.print((iter.next()).toString() + " ");
         };
         System.out.println();
```

```
    // --------------------

      System.out.println("\nThe cumulative distances of the shortest "
                     + "path from node "
                     + initNode + " to node "+finalNode + " are:");

      int d = 0; int i = initNode; int j = 0;

      for (Iterator iter1 = itinerary.iterator(); iter1.hasNext(); ) {
          j = ((Integer)iter1.next()).intValue();
          d = d + graph[i][j]; i = j;
          System.out.print(d + " ");
      };
      System.out.println();
      // --------------------
   }
  else { System.out.println("There is no path from node " + initNode +
                     " to node " + finalNode + ".");
      };
  }
}
// -----------------------------------------------------------------------
```

8.9. From Nondeterministic Finite Automata to Regular Expressions

Given a directed graph G of n nodes with every arc labeled by a regular expression over an alphabet Σ (in particular, a single symbol of Σ), let us consider the problem of finding for each pair of nodes i and j in G, the regular expression which denotes the language made out of all words which take from node i to node j as we now specify. A word w takes from node i to node j iff (i) w is $a_0 \ldots a_{m+1}$, where for all $i = 0, \ldots, m$, $a_i \in \Sigma$, and (ii) there is a path $\langle n_0, n_1, \ldots, n_{m+1} \rangle$ such that: (ii.1) $n_0 = i$, (ii.2) $n_{m+1} = j$, and (ii.3) for all $i = 0, \ldots, m$, a_i belongs to the language denoted by the regular expression which is the label of the arc $\langle n_i, n_{i+1} \rangle$.

This problem of finding regular expressions can be solved by applying the analogous of Fact 8.6.1 on page 262 for matrices over the Regular Expressions ic-semiring (see page 261).

Given a directed graph G with n nodes with regular expressions as labels of the arcs, let us associate with G the $n \times n$ matrix $R(G)$ such that for all i, j, with $1 \leq i, j \leq n$, $R(G)_{ij} = expr(i, j)$, where $expr(i, j)$ is the regular expression which labels the arc from node i to node j.

For all i, j (not necessarily distinct), with $1 \leq i, j \leq n$, we have that $expr(i, j) = \emptyset$ if there is no arc from node i to node j.

It can be shown that, given any pair $\langle i, j \rangle$ of nodes of the graph G, one may compute the language made out of the words which take from i to j by computing the transitive closure of the matrix $R(G)$ over the Regular Expressions ic-semiring of the labels of G.

Notice that in the identity matrix over the Regular Expressions ic-semiring each element of the main diagonal is $\{\varepsilon\}$ (which is the identity for $\cdot$), while every other element is $\emptyset$ (which is the identity for $\cup$). This definition of the identity matrix is based on the facts that:

(1) for all i and j with $1 \leq i, j \leq n$, there is no path of one or more arcs from a node i to a node j, and

(2) *if $i = j$, then* node i is reachable from node i itself via a path of length 0 (and this explains why $\{\varepsilon\}$ is in the main diagonal of the identity matrix) *else* node j is not reachable from node i (and this is why $\emptyset$ is outside the main diagonal of the identity matrix).

For the case of matrices over the Regular Expressions ic-semiring it is not natural to establish a fact analogous to Fact 8.6.2 on page 264, because the operations $\cup$ and $\cdot$ cannot reasonably be considered as atomic computation steps. However, by using a fact analogous to Fact 8.6.1 on page 262, we can prove Kleene Theorem which states that for every finite automaton there exists an equivalent regular expression, that is, a regular expression which denotes the language accepted by the finite automaton. Indeed, if we assume that each element of the matrices A_{11}, A_{12}, A_{21}, and A_{22} is a symbol in Σ, the graph is a (deterministic or nondeterministic) finite automaton. Let that automaton be called A. The transitive closure of $\begin{vmatrix} A_{11} & A_{12} \\ A_{21} & A_{22} \end{vmatrix}$ computes the language from a node to any other node by using the operations $\cdot$, $+$, and *, instead of the operations $\wedge$, $\vee$, and * occurring in the statement of Fact 8.6.1. Thus, in particular, we get a regular expression from the initial state to any final state of the finite automaton A. The regular expression denoting the language accepted by A is the sum of all regular expressions from the initial state to a final state of A.

CHAPTER 9

String Matching

In this chapter we present two matching algorithms for testing whether or not a pattern occurs in string. The first algorithm is a naive algorithm (see page 281) whose Prolog implementation will be given in Section 9.2 on page 291. The second algorithm is the Knuth-Morris-Pratt algorithm [14].

9.1. Knuth-Morris-Pratt Pattern Matching

In this section we present a pattern matching algorithm taken from [14]. This algorithm detects all occurrences, possibly overlapped, of a substring p, called the *pattern*, in a string s, called the *subject*.

The main idea of this algorithm is the construction of a finite automaton. We will clarify this point in what follows. The time complexity of this algorithm is $O(m+n)$, where m is the length of the string s and n is the length of the substring p.

First we present the naive pattern matching algorithm which has time complexity $O(n\,m)$. It can be expressed as follows.

ALGORITHM 9.1.1. *Naive Pattern Matcher.*

Input: the *subject* string $s[0], \ldots, s[n-1]$ and the *pattern* string $p[0], \ldots, p[m-1]$. We assume that $n \geq 1$ and $m \geq 1$.
Output: a list $\lambda = [i_1, \ldots, i_k]$ of non-negative integers such that for all i in λ, we have that p occurs in position i in the subject s, that is, for all $j = 0, \ldots, m-1$ we have that $s[i+j] = p[j]$.

$\lambda := [\,]$;
for $i = 0, \ldots, n-m$ **do**

$\quad$ $occurs := true$;
$\quad$ **for** $j = 0, \ldots, m-1$ **do if** $s[i+j] \neq p[j]$ **then** $occurs := false$;
$\quad$ **if** $occurs$ **then** $\lambda := append(\lambda, [i])$ $\hfill (\dagger)$

In the instruction ($\dagger$) of the external for-loop we have used the *append* function, instead of the less expensive *cons* function, because we want that a pattern occurrence i_1 which is located in the subject string on the left of another pattern occurrence i_2, that is, $i_1 < i_2$, should be listed in λ on the left of i_2.

This naive pattern matcher works by repeating, for each position in the subject string, a test which checks whether or not the substring of the subject string starting at that position coincides with the given pattern.

We can improve over this naive pattern matcher algorithm by using the Knuth-Morris-Pratt pattern matcher which we now present. This algorithm improves the

© Springer Nature Switzerland AG 2021
A. Pettorossi, *Techniques for Searching, Parsing, and Matching*, https://doi.org/10.1007/978-3-030-63189-5_9

naive pattern matcher because, if during the process of checking an occurrence of
the pattern in the subject we find a mismatch between the character of the pattern
and the character of the subject string, then we resume the matching process *not*
by a right-shift of the pattern by one position only, but by performing a right-shift
of $r\,(\geq 1)$ positions, as indicated by the so called *failure function* which we will
introduce below.

The failure function determines the value of r by taking into account the structure
of the pattern and, by doing so, it allows us to reduce the total number of character
comparisons required during the matching process.

Here is the Knuth-Morris-Pratt pattern matcher. It is made out of two parts that
have a very similar structure:

(i) the computation of the failure function, and
(ii) the computation of the occurrences of the pattern.

ALGORITHM 9.1.2. *Knuth-Morris-Pratt Pattern Matcher.*

Input: the subject string $s[0], \ldots, s[n-1]$ and the pattern string $p[0], \ldots, p[m-1]$. We
assume that $n \geq 1$ and $m \geq 1$.
Output: a list $\lambda = [i_1, \ldots, i_k]$ of $k\,(\geq 0)$ non-negative integers such that for all i in
λ, we have that the pattern p occurs at position i in the subject s, that is, for all
$j = 0, \ldots, m-1$ we have that $s[i+j] = p[j]$.

Computation of the failure function: $\pi[0], \ldots, \pi[m-1]$.

$\pi[0] := 0;$
$j := 0;$ $(1.\alpha)$
for $i = 1, \ldots, m-1$ **do**
  while $j > 0$ and $p[j] \neq p[i]$ **do** $j := \pi[j-1];$ $(1.\beta)$
  if $p[j] = p[i]$ **then** $j := j+1;$ $(1.\gamma)$
  $\pi[i] := j;$ $(1.\delta)$

Computation of the occurrences of the pattern: $p[0], \ldots, p[m-1]$.

$\lambda := [\,];$
$j := 0;$ $(2.\alpha)$
for $i = 0, \ldots, n-1$ **do**
  while $j > 0$ and $p[j] \neq s[i]$ **do** $j := \pi[j-1];$ $(2.\beta)$
  if $p[j] = s[i]$ **then** $j := j+1;$ $(2.\gamma)$
  if $j = m$ **then begin** $\lambda := append(\lambda, [i-m+1]); \ j := \pi[j-1]$ **end** $(2.\delta)$

Now we introduce the failure function π. It is represented as the array $\pi[0, \ldots, m-1]$
which has the same length m of the pattern p. We first need the following notions.

DEFINITION 9.1.3. [**Prefix and Suffix**] Let us consider a pattern $p[0, 1, \ldots, m-1]$ of length m. The non-empty *prefixes* of that pattern are: $p[0]$, $p[0, 1]$, $\ldots$, and $p[0, 1, \ldots, m-1]$. For $j = 0, \ldots, m-1$, the prefix $p[0, \ldots, j]$ is also denoted by p_{0j}. A *proper prefix* of that pattern is a prefix which is different from the pattern itself.

The *suffixes* of the pattern $p[0, 1, \ldots, m-1]$ are: $p[0, 1, \ldots, m-1]$, $p[1, \ldots, m-1]$, $\ldots$, $p[m-2, m-1]$, $p[m-1]$. A *proper suffix* of that pattern is a suffix which is different from the pattern itself.

Given the pattern $p[0, 1, \ldots, m-1]$, for $j = 0, \ldots, m-1$, we have that the prefix p_{0j} is the sequence of the $j+1$ leftmost characters of the pattern. The following tables shows the prefixes of the pattern $p[0, 1, \ldots, m-1]$. For $j = 0$, the prefix p_{00} is the leftmost character $p[0]$ of the pattern.

	prefixes p_{0j} of the pattern $p[0, 1, \ldots, m-1]$		length of the prefix
$j = 0$	p_{00}	$= p[0]$	1
$j = 1$	p_{01}	$= p[0, 1]$	2
$\ldots$	$\ldots$	$\ldots$	$\ldots$
$j = m-1$	$p_{0\,m-1}$	$= p[0, 1, \ldots, m-1]$	m

DEFINITION 9.1.4. [**Failure Function**] Given a pattern p of length m, its *failure function* π is defined for each $j = 0, \ldots, m-1$, and $\pi[j]$ is the length of the longest *proper prefix* of p_{0j} which is also a *proper suffix* of p_{0j}.

We have that:
$\pi[0] = 0$
$\pi[1] = $ *if* $p[0] = p[1]$ *then* 1 *else* 0

If we consider the pattern $a\,a\,b\,a\,a$, whose length m is 5, we get the failure function which is represented in the following table where, for $j = 0, \ldots, m-1$, the value of $p[j]$ is written in column j of the row named '*pattern p*', and the value of $\pi[j]$ is written in column j of the row named '*failure function* π':

	$p[0]$	$p[1]$	$p[2]$	$p[3]$	$p[4]$
pattern p:	a	a	b	a	a
failure function π:	0	1	0	1	2
	$\pi[0]$	$\pi[1]$	$\pi[2]$	$\pi[3]$	$\pi[4]$

Let us explain the entries of the above table. We have that:

(i) p_{00} is a and the longest proper prefix of a which is also a proper suffix of a, is ε and the length of ε is 0. Thus, $\pi[0] = 0$.

(ii) p_{01} is $a\,a$ and the longest proper prefix of $a\,a$ which is also a proper suffix of $a\,a$, is a and the length of a is 1. Thus, $\pi[1] = 1$.

(iii) p_{02} is $a\,a\,b$ and the longest proper prefix of $a\,a\,b$ which is also a proper suffix of $a\,a\,b$, is ε and the length of ε is 0. Thus, $\pi[2] = 0$.

(iv) p_{03} is $a\,a\,b\,a$ and the longest proper prefix of $a\,a\,b\,a$ which is also a proper suffix of $a\,a\,b\,a$, is a and the length of a is 1. Thus, $\pi[3] = 1$.

(v) p_{04} is $a\,a\,b\,a\,a$ and the longest proper prefix of $a\,a\,b\,a\,a$ which is also a proper suffix of $a\,a\,b\,a\,a$, is $a\,a$ and the length of $a\,a$ is 2. Thus, $\pi[4] = 2$.

If all characters in the pattern p are equal, that is, $p[0] = p[1] = \ldots = p[m-1]$, then the failure function π is such that: $\pi[0] = 0$, $\pi[1] = 1$, $\pi[2] = 2, \ldots, \pi[m-1] = m-1$. Thus, if we assume that the pattern p is a sequence of a's, we get the following table, where for $j = 0, \ldots, m-1$, the j-th column indicates that $p[j] = a$ and $\pi[j] = j$:

	$p[0]$	$p[1]$	$p[2]$	$\ldots$	$p[m-1]$
pattern p:	a	a	a	$\ldots$	a
failure function π:	0	1	2	$\ldots$	$m-1$
	$\pi[0]$	$\pi[1]$	$\pi[2]$	$\ldots$	$\pi[m-1]$

The failure function derived at the end of the first part of the Knuth-Morris-Pratt algorithm, called *Computation of the failure function*, is used during the second phase, called *Computation of the occurrences of the pattern*, as we now indicate.

Let us consider the above pattern $a\,a\,b\,a\,a$ and suppose that we have found the matching substring $a\,a\,b\,a$ and we get a mismatch on the last character which should be a. That is, $s[i] \neq a$. The value of j is 4. This mismatch tells us that we have to consider a new value for j which is $\pi[j-1]$ (see instruction $(2.\beta)$). In our case we get $j = 1$. Then, we check whether or not the current character in the subject string is a (because $p[1]$ is a). We fail again and we get the new value of j which is 0. Indeed, according to the instruction $(2.\beta)$, we have to take as new value of j the value of $\pi[j-1]$, that is, $\pi[0]$ which is 0. At this point it is not the case that $j > 0$, we exit the loop of instruction $(2.\beta)$, and we perform instruction $(2.\gamma)$.

Since $p[0] = a$ and $s[i] \neq a$ and $j \neq m$, we increase i by 1 (which corresponds to a shift of the pattern on the subject string by one character) and we execute again the instructions $(2.\beta)$, $(2.\gamma)$, and $(2.\delta)$ with this new value of i (actually, in our case, since $j = 0$, the instruction $(2.\beta)$ will not be executed).

The failure function for a pattern $p[0]\,p[1]\,\ldots\,p[m-1]$ can be represented as a finite automaton whose states are $0, 1, \ldots, m-1, m$ (see in Figure 9.1.1 on the next page the failure function for the pattern $a\,a\,b\,a\,a$).

For each $k = 0, \ldots, m-1$, there is a *forward arc* from state k to state $k+1$ labeled by the predicate '$= p[k]$'.

For each $k = 1, \ldots, m$, there is a *backward arc* from state k to state $\pi[k-1]$ labeled by the predicate '$\neq p[k]$'. The label of the backward arc from state m to state $\pi[m-1]$ is labeled by the predicate *true*. From state 0 there is an arc to state 0 itself labeled by '$\neq p[0]$'.

This automaton is used as an acceptor of the subject string in the second part of the Knuth-Morris-Pratt algorithm called *Computation of the occurrences of the pattern*, according to the following rule:

if for the input subject string s the automaton gets from the initial state 0 to the final state m, *then* there is an occurrence of the pattern p in the subject string s.

The predicate in each arc of the automaton allows the transition iff it is satisfied by the current character of the subject string.

For the pattern $a\,a\,b\,a\,a$ of length $m = 5$ the automaton which represents the failure function is depicted in Figure 9.1.1 on the facing page. For the pattern $a\,b\,a\,b\,a\,a\,a$

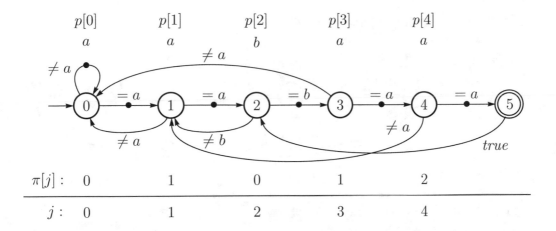

FIGURE 9.1.1. The finite automaton corresponding to the failure function for the pattern $a\,a\,b\,a\,a$. We have that $m = 5$. When the characters of the subject string are fed into this automaton for finding the occurrences of the pattern, we consider the next character in input only when we make a transition with the dot $\bullet$.

of length $m = 7$ the automaton which represents the failure function is depicted in Figure 9.1.2 on the next page.

At each state the automaton which represents the failure function, reads the character at hand and that character is used for making the transition to the next state. As already stated, in the figures representing the failure functions as finite automata, the failure function is used for drawing the backward arcs according to the following rules:

(i) for all i, j, with $i \geq j$, if $\pi[i-1] = j$, then there is a backward arc from state i to state j, and

(ii) there is a backward arc from state 0 to itself labeled by the negation of the label of the arc from state 0 to state 1.

For instance, in Figure 9.1.1 we have drawn a backward arc from state 4 to state 1 because $\pi[4-1] = 1$.

Now we would like to make the following two remarks.

REMARK 9.1.5. When an occurrence of the pattern has been found (see, for instance, the arc labeled by *true* from state 5 to state 2 in the automaton of Figure 9.1.1), the automaton representing the failure function makes a state transition as if a failure occurred. Indeed, the pattern occurrence we have found and the next pattern occurrence may overlap.

REMARK 9.1.6. Some of the tests which the failure function forces us to make, can be avoided because we know in advance the results of these tests. Let us consider, for instance, the case of the failure function represented by the automaton of Figure 9.1.1. If in state 4 we have a character of the subject which is different from a we go to state 1 where the test '$= a$' is bound fail and we have to go to state 0. By avoiding all

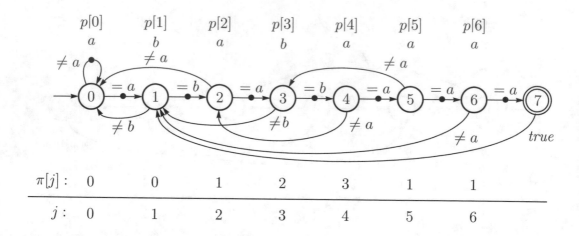

FIGURE 9.1.2. The finite automaton corresponding to the failure function for the pattern $a\,b\,a\,b\,a\,a\,a$. We have that the length m of the pattern is 7. When the characters of the subject string are fed into this automaton for finding the occurrences of the pattern, we consider the next character in input only when we make a transition with the dot •.

redundant tests such as the test '$= a$', we get the automaton of Figure 9.1.3, instead of the automaton of Figure 9.1.1 on the preceding page.

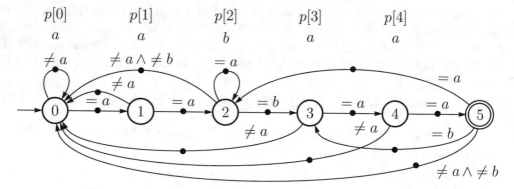

FIGURE 9.1.3. The finite automaton corresponding to the failure function for the pattern $a\,a\,b\,a\,a$. When the characters of the subject string are fed into this automaton for finding the occurrences of the pattern, we always consider the next character in input (indeed, all transitions have the dot •).

Note, however, that if we use the automaton of Figure 9.1.3, instead of the one of Figure 9.1.1, we do not improve the asymptotic time complexity of the Knuth-Morris-Pratt algorithm (see Section 9.1.1 on the next page).

It is interesting to notice that the first part of the Knuth-Morris-Pratt algorithm which computes the failure function, that is, the length of the longest proper prefix of the pattern which is also a proper suffix of pattern, is very similar to the second part of the algorithm which computes the occurrences of the pattern in the subject string. The only differences between the two parts are the following ones.

(i) The for-do loop in instruction $(1.\alpha)$ starts with $i=1$ and not $i=0$, because for every pattern the value of $\pi[0]$ is 0 and thus, we can skip the loop for $i=0$.

(ii) We record the fact that an occurrence of the pattern has been found, by inserting in the list λ the initial position of the occurrence of the pattern in the subject string (see instruction $(2.\delta)$). Then we continue our matching process by looking for a new, possibly overlapping, occurrence of the pattern, and we do so by acting as if a matching failure did occur. Indeed, as in the case of a failure, we update the value of j and the new value of j is set to $\pi[j-1]$.

We have that the Knuth-Morris-Pratt algorithm for the input subject

$s = a\,a\,b\,a\,c\,a\,a\,b\,a\,a\,b\,a\,a$

with length $n=13$ and the input pattern

$p = a\,a\,b\,a\,a$

computes the list $[5, 8]$ of occurrence positions (see Figure 9.1.4).

$$
\begin{array}{ccccccccccccc}
a & a & b & a & c & a & a & b & a & a & b & a & a \\
0 & 1 & 2 & 3 & 4 & 5 & 6 & 7 & 8 & 9 & 10 & 11 & 12
\end{array}
$$

FIGURE 9.1.4. The two occurrences at positions 5 and 8 of the pattern $a\,a\,b\,a\,a$ in the subject string $a\,a\,b\,a\,c\,a\,a\,b\,a\,a\,b\,a\,a$.

9.1.1. Time Complexity Analysis of the Knuth-Morris-Pratt Algorithm.

We start off by evaluating the time complexity for computing the failure function. We will measure this time complexity in terms of the number of assignments to the variable j.

The for-loop of the computation of the failure function is performed from $i=1$ to $i=m-1$. The while-loop at instruction $(1.\beta)$ in the body of the for-loop is controlled by the value of j which may be at most $m-1$ (and this case occurs when the characters in the pattern are all equal) and at each execution of the body of the loop, as we will prove in Lemma 9.1.7 below, the value of j can only be decreased. Thus, we conclude that the time complexity of the computation of the failure function is $O(m^2)$.

The following analysis, based on an the so called amortized analysis, shows that the cost of the computation of the failure function is, in fact, $O(m)$. First we prove the following lemma.

LEMMA 9.1.7. For all $i=1,\ldots,m-1$, for all $h=0,\ldots,i$, $0\le\pi[h]\le h$ and $0\le j\le i$.

PROOF. By induction.

(*Basis*: $i=1$). We want to show that after the execution of instruction $(1.\delta)$ in the first iteration of the for-loop, that is, for $i=1$, we have that: for $h = 0, 1$, $0\le\pi[h]\le h$ and $0\le j\le 1$. Indeed, since initially $j=0$, instruction $(1.\beta)$ is not performed. Thus, (i) by $(1.\gamma)$ we have that if $p[0]=p[1]$ then $j=1$ else $j=0$, and (ii) by $(1.\delta)$ we have that $\pi[1]=j$. By recalling that: (i) $\pi[0]=0$, and (ii) if $p[0]=p[1]$, then $\pi[1]=1$, we get, as desired, that $0\le\pi[0]\le0$, $0\le\pi[1]\le1$, and $0\le j\le1$.

(*Step*: $i \geq 1$) We assume that for $i = k$, we have that, for all $h = 0, \ldots, i$, $0 \leq \pi[h] \leq h$ and $0 \leq j \leq i$ hold, and we show that for $i = k+1$ we have that, for all $h = 0, \ldots, i$, $0 \leq \pi[h] \leq h$ and $0 \leq j \leq i$ hold.

In order to do so, it suffices to show the validity of the following Hoare's triple, where k is the value of the index i of the external for-loop, and the assertion I_k is an invariant of the while-loop (we have also assumed that $\pi[0] = 0$, as shown above, and we wrote the assertions holding after the instructions $(1.\beta)$ and $(1.\gamma)$):

$\{I_k \ \equiv \ \pi[0] = 0 \ $ and $ \ $ for $h = 0, \ldots, k, \ 0 \leq \pi[h] \leq h \ $ and $ \ 0 \leq j \leq k\}$

$\qquad$ **while** $j > 0$ and $p[j] \neq p[k+1]$ **do** $j := \pi[j-1]$; $\qquad\qquad (1.\beta)$

$\{I_k \ \equiv \ \pi[0] = 0 \ $ and $ \ $ for $h = 0, \ldots, k, \ 0 \leq \pi[h] \leq h \ $ and $ \ 0 \leq j \leq k\}$

$\qquad$ **if** $p[j] = p[k+1]$ **then** $j := j+1$; $\qquad\qquad\qquad (1.\gamma)$

$\qquad \{\pi[0] = 0 \ $ and $ \ $ for $h = 0, \ldots, k, \ 0 \leq \pi[h] \leq h \ $ and $ \ 0 \leq j \leq k+1\}$

$\qquad \pi[k+1] = j$ $\qquad\qquad\qquad\qquad\qquad\qquad\qquad\qquad (1.\delta)$

$\{I_{k+1} \equiv \pi[0] = 0 \ $ and $ \ $ for $h = 0, \ldots, k+1, \ 0 \leq \pi[h] \leq h \ $ and $ \ 0 \leq j \leq k+1\}$

The validity of the triple $\{I_k\}$ $(1.\beta)$ $\{I_k\}$ can be shown by retropropagation because $\pi[0] = 0$ and for $h = 0, \ldots, k, \ 0 \leq \pi[h] \leq h$ and $0 \leq j \leq k$ and $j > 0$ implies $\pi[0] = 0$ and for $h = 0, \ldots, k, \ 0 \leq \pi[h] \leq h$ and $0 \leq \pi[j-1] \leq k$.

With reference to the instruction $(1.\beta)$ we have the following two properties.

Property (1). By executing the instruction $(1.\beta)$, the value of j may only decrease or remain unchanged. Indeed, the assignment $j := \pi[j-1]$ does not increase j, because it is performed only for *some* j's in $\{1, \ldots, k\}$ (see the precondition $0 \leq j \leq k$ and the test $j > 0$ of the while-loop) and for *all* j's in $\{1, \ldots, k\}$, we have that $0 \leq \pi[j] \leq j$ holds (see again the precondition). During the while-loop, *before* any assignment of the form $j := \pi[j-1]$, since $\pi[0] = 0$, we have that, for all j's in $\{1, \ldots, k\}$, $\pi[j-1] \leq j-1 < j$.

Property (2). By executing the instruction $(1.\beta)$, the value of j never becomes negative. Indeed, for h in $\{0, \ldots, k\}$, $0 \leq \pi[h]$ and we assign to j the value of $\pi[j-1]$, for some j in $\{1, \ldots, k\}$.

The validity of the triple $\{I_k\}$ $(1.\gamma)$; $(1.\delta)$ $\{I_{k+1}\}$ is immediate by retropropagation, because in I_{k+1} we have that: for $h = 0, \ldots, k+1, \ 0 \leq \pi[h] \leq h$ is equivalent to: for $h = 0, \ldots, k, \ 0 \leq \pi[h] \leq h$ and $0 \leq \pi[k+1] \leq k+1$. $\qquad\qquad \square$

During the computation of the failure function, j is initially 0 and it may be increased by at most $m-1$ units during the $m-1$ iterations of the body of the for-loop. During the execution of the while-loop at instruction $(1.\beta)$, we have that j is strictly decreased (by Lemma 9.1.7 on the previous page). Thus, during the whole computation of the failure function the variable j is assigned at most $2(m-1)$ times, that is, the time complexity of the failure function is $O(m)$.

Since the first part of the Knuth-Morris-Pratt algorithm which computes the failure function, has the same structure of the second part which computes the occurrences of the pattern, in order to measure the time complexity of the Knuth-Morris-Pratt algorithm we can measure the computation of two failure functions, one for a pattern of length m and one for a pattern of length n. We conclude that the overall time complexity of the Knuth-Morris-Pratt algorithm is $O(m+n)$.

Note that the time complexity is $O(m+n)$ also if we measure the number of tests performed by the Knuth-Morris-Pratt algorithm, instead of the number of assignments to j. Indeed, for all values of j, we make an assignment to j after at most two tests, which are: (i) $j > 0$, and (ii) $p[j] \neq p[i]$. We do not have to count the test $p[j] = p[i]$ because if we know the value of the test $p[j] \neq p[i]$ we also know the value of the test $p[j] = p[i]$.

It is easy to see that the same time complexity of $O(m+n)$ for the Knuth-Morris-Pratt algorithm holds if we measure the sum of the number of the assignments to j and the number of tests.

9.1.2. Java Implementation of the Knuth-Morris-Pratt Algorithm.

Below we present a Java program which implements to Knuth-Morris-Pratt algorithm for pattern matching. It runs under the Java compiler 1.5.0-13 and Mac OS X. In this program, instead of constructing the list λ of positions, we have printed out the position of every occurrence of the pattern as soon as it has been computed.

The test case presented in the final comments of the program shows the values of the variables i and j during the execution of the Knuth-Morris-Pratt algorithm for the subject $a\,a\,b\,a\,c\,a\,a\,b\,a\,a\,b\,a\,a$ and the pattern $a\,a\,b\,a\,a$ which occurs at positions 5 and 8.

```
/**
 * ===============================================================----========
 *                    KNUTH-MORRIS-PRATT PATTERN MATCHER
 * Filename: "KMP.java"
 *
 * ===========================================================================
 */

public class KMP {

 private static void printar(int[] array, int size) {
   for (int k=0; k<size; k++) {System.out.print(array[k]+" ");}
   System.out.println();
  }

 /**
  * ---------------------------------------------------------------------
  *                         main
  * ---------------------------------------------------------------------
  */

 public static void main(String[] args) {
 boolean traceon = true;    // traceon: tracing variable

 String s, p;               // s: given subject
 int    sl,pl;              // p: pattern to search

 s = "aabacaabaabaa";
 p = "aabaa";

 sl = s.length();
 pl = p.length();
```

```
System.out.println("\nThe given subject string s of " + sl +
                   " elements is:\n " + s);
System.out.println("\nThe given pattern p of "+pl+" elements is:\n "+ p);

/**
 * -----------------------------------------------------------------------
 * Recall that indexing in Java begins with 0 (as in C++). Thus,
 *
 *        stp=abcab  length(stp)=5    stp.charAt(2) is c.
 * index:      01234
 *
 * lstp1=4
 * -----------------------------------------------------------------------
 */

 /**
  * ----------------------------------------------------------------------
  *                    computing the failure function pi
  * ----------------------------------------------------------------------
  */
int [] pi = new int [pl]; // the length of pi is the length of the pattern
int i, j;

pi[0]=0;
j=0;
for (i=1; i<pl; i=i+1) {                           // <<----------------------+
    while (j>0 && p.charAt(j)!=p.charAt(i)) {j=pi[j-1];};        // |
    if (p.charAt(j)==p.charAt(i)) {j=j+1;};                      // |
    pi[i]=j;                                                     // |
    }; // end of for                               // <<----------------------+

//--------------------------------------------------------------------------
System.out.print(
        "\nThe failure function is given by the following array pi" +
        "\nof " + pl +  " elements:\n ");
printar(pi,pl); System.out.println();
//--------------------------------------------------------------------------

/**
 * ----------------------------------------------------------------------
 *                    finding the occurrences of the pattern
 * ----------------------------------------------------------------------
 */

j=0;
for (i=0; i<sl; i=i+1) {                           // <<----------------------+
  while (j>0 && p.charAt(j)!=s.charAt(i)) {j=pi[j-1];};          // |
  if (p.charAt(j)==s.charAt(i)) {j=j+1;};                        // |
  if (traceon) {System.out.println(" i="+i+" j="+j);};  // tracing  // |
  if (j==pl) {                                                   // |
   System.out.println("The pattern occurs at position "+(i-pl+1)+"\n");// |
   j=pi[j-1];                                                    // |
   };                                                            // |
  }; // end of for                                // <<----------------------+
} // end of main
}

/**
```

```
*  input:        output:   (with traceon == true)
*  -----------------------------------------------------------------
*  javac KMP.java
*  java  KMP
*
*              The given subject string s of 13 elements is:
*                aabacaabaabaa
*
*              The given pattern p of 5 elements is:
*                aabaa
*
*              The failure function is given by the following array pi
*              of 5 elements:
*                0 1 0 1 2
*
*                i=0 j=1
*                i=1 j=2
*                i=2 j=3
*                i=3 j=4
*                i=4 j=0
*                i=5 j=1
*                i=6 j=2
*                i=7 j=3
*                i=8 j=4
*                i=9 j=5
*              The pattern occurs at position 5
*
*                i=10 j=3
*                i=11 j=4
*                i=12 j=5
*              The pattern occurs at position 8
*
*  -----------------------------------------------------------------
*/
```

9.2. String Matching in Prolog

The following Prolog program tests whether or not a pattern P (viewed as list of characters) occurs in a string S (also viewed as a list of characters). The pattern P occurs in S iff in S there exists a consecutive list of characters which is a substring of S and is equal to P.

In order to understand the way in which this program works it is enough to recall the usual definition of the *append* predicate, that is, $append(Xs, Ys, Zs)$ holds iff the string Zs is the concatenation of the strings Xs and Ys. For instance, we have that:

$append([2, 3], [4, 2], Zs)$ holds iff $Zs = [2, 3, 4, 2]$

$append(Xs, [4, 4], [4, 3, 4, 4])$ holds iff $Xs = [4, 3]$.

String Matching in Prolog: basic version.

1. $occur(P, S) \leftarrow append(I, R, S), append(L, P, I)$
2. $append([\,], Ys, Ys) \leftarrow$
3. $append([X|Xs], Ys, [X|Zs]) \leftarrow append(Xs, Ys, Zs)$

We have that $occur(P, S)$ holds iff the pattern P occurs in the string S. Indeed, clause 1 says that P occurs in S iff there exist three lists of characters I (short for *Intermediate*), R (short for *right*), and L (short for *left*) such that both $append(I, R, S)$ and $append(L, P, I)$ hold. We can depict this situation as in the following figure, where the list I is the concatenation of the lists L and P, and the list S is the concatenation of the lists I and R.

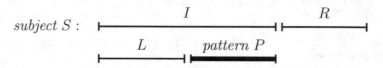

Note that, although the position of the atoms does not influence the logical meaning of a clause, it may influence its operational behaviour. In particular, due to the implementation of the *append* predicate in Prolog, the position of the atoms $append(I, R, S)$ and $append(L, P, I)$ in the body of clause 1 should not be interchanged because, otherwise, the computation may not terminate.

From the length of the list L we can get the position of the pattern P in the subject string S.

Then the various positions in which the pattern occurs in the subject, can be obtained by using the backtracking facility available in Prolog. This can done by using the *findall* predicate as indicated in the following program.

String Matching in Prolog: finding all occurrence positions.

1. $occur(P, S, N) \leftarrow append(I, R, S), append(L, P, I), length(L, N)$
2. $append([\,], Ys, Ys) \leftarrow$
3. $append([X|Xs], Ys, [X|Zs]) \leftarrow append(Xs, Ys, Zs)$
4. $length([\,], 0).$
5. $length([H|T], N1) \leftarrow length(T, N), N1$ is $N+1$

Recall that in Prolog $findall(N, Goal, Ns)$ returns a list Ns which represents the multiset of all instances of the variable N such that $Goal$ is satisfied. The variable N should appear within the clause only in the term $Goal$. By submitting the query:

$\leftarrow findall(N, occur([a\,a\,b\,a\,a], [a\,a\,b\,a\,c\,a\,a\,b\,a\,a\,b\,a\,a], N), Ns)$

we get the value $[5, 8]$ for the variable Ns (see also Figure 9.1.4 on page 287).

CHAPTER 10

Supplementary Topics

This last chapter is made out of two sections devoted to supplementary topics. In the first section we present, in particular, some Prolog programs for sorting and parsing strings, and in the second one we present some decidability and undecidability results concerning the $LL(k)$ and the $LR(k)$ grammars and languages.

10.1. Simple Prolog Programs and Parsing Sentences in Prolog

In this section we present a few simple Prolog programs for:
 (i) checking natural numbers,
 (ii) sorting strings, and
(iii) parsing strings.

Checking Natural Numbers.
The following program tests whether or not a given term X is a natural number in the set $\{0, s(0), s(s(0)), \ldots\}$. X is a natural number iff $nat(X)$. The following two clauses define the unary predicate $nat(X)$.

Natural Numbers

1. $nat(0) \leftarrow$
2. $nat(s(X)) \leftarrow nat(X)$

For instance, we have that the query $\leftarrow nat(s(s(s(0))))$ evaluates to true.

Sorting Strings.
The following program sorts a given list of natural numbers. Each natural number is an element of the set $\{0, 1, 2, \ldots\}$. This program is a very slow program because it constructs all possible permutations of the elements of the given list and then it outputs the permutation which is ordered. Since there are $n!$ distinct permutations of n distinct elements, this program has worst case time complexity of order $O(n!)$.

Recall that: (i) $2^n = O(n!)$ and (ii) $n! = O(n^n)$, while (iii) $n! \neq O(2^n)$ and (iv) $n^n \neq O(n!)$.

Permutation Sort

1. $sort(L1, L2) \leftarrow permutation(L1, L2),\ sorted(L2)$
2. $permutation([],[]) \leftarrow$
3. $permutation(L, [H|T]) \leftarrow append(U, [H|V], L),$ % place H in a position in W
        $append(U, V, W),$ % split W into U and V
        $permutation(W, T)$ % take a permutation W of T

> 4. $sorted(L) \leftarrow sorted1(0, L)$
> 5. $sorted1(N, [\,]) \leftarrow$
> 6. $sorted1(N, [H|T]) \leftarrow N \leq H,\ sorted1(H, T)$

For instance, we have that the query $\leftarrow sort([3, 2, 2, 4], L2)$ evaluates to true with the variable $L2$ bound to $[2, 2, 3, 4]$.

Now we present a different Prolog program for sorting a given list of natural numbers. This program is based on the Quicksort algorithm, and it is much faster than the previous program, because its worst case time complexity is of order $O(n^2)$, where n is the length of the list.

> Quicksort
> 1. $partition(H, [A|X], [A|Y], Z) \leftarrow A \leq H,\ partition(H, X, Y, Z)$
> 2. $partition(H, [A|X], Y, [A|Z]) \leftarrow A > H,\ partition(H, X, Y, Z)$
> 3. $partition(H, [\,], [\,], [\,]) \leftarrow$
> 4. $quicksort([\,], [\,]) \leftarrow$
> 5. $quicksort([H|T], S) \leftarrow partition(H, T, A, B),$
> $quicksort(A, A1),\ quicksort(B, B1),$
> $append(A1, [H|B1], S)$

Parsing Sentences.

The following programs show how to parse sentences generated by context-free grammars. We follow the approach described in [5, Chapter 9]. Here we will not present the general parsing methodology and the reader may refer to [5, Chapter 9] for more information on this topic.

Let us consider the context-free grammar G with axiom *sentence* and the following productions:

sentence	$\rightarrow$	*noun-phrase verb-phrase*
noun-phrase	$\rightarrow$	*determiner noun*
verb-phrase	$\rightarrow$	*verb noun-phrase*
verb-phrase	$\rightarrow$	*verb*
determiner	$\rightarrow$	*the*
noun	$\rightarrow$	*apple* | *man*
verb	$\rightarrow$	*eats* | *sings*

Here is a simple Prolog program for parsing strings of the language generated by that grammar.

Parsing Sentences. Program $P1$

1.1 $sentence(X) \leftarrow append(Y, Z, X), noun\_phrase(Y), verb\_phrase(Z)$
1.2 $noun\_phrase(X) \leftarrow append(Y, Z, X), determiner(Y), noun(Z)$
1.3 $verb\_phrase(X) \leftarrow append(Y, Z, X), verb(Y), noun\_phrase(Z)$
1.4 $verb\_phrase(X) \leftarrow verb(X)$
1.5 $determiner([the]) \leftarrow$
1.6 $noun([apple]) \leftarrow$
1.7 $noun([man]) \leftarrow$
1.8 $verb([eats]) \leftarrow$
1.9 $verb([sings]) \leftarrow$

If we want to parse, for instance, the string '*the man eats the apple*', we have to submit to the above Prolog program $P1$ the following query:

$$\leftarrow sentence([the, man, eats, the, apple])$$

By evaluating that query we get the empty clause, and the trace of that evaluation gives us the derivation tree of the given string '*the man eats the apple*'.

Here is an alternative Prolog program for parsing strings of the language generated by the grammar G given above. It runs faster than Program $P1$, because it avoids the use of *append* and uses, instead, the so called *difference lists* [**27**, page 283].

Parsing Sentences (Use of difference lists). Program $P2$

2.1 $sentence(S0, S) \leftarrow noun\_phrase(S0, S1), verb\_phrase(S1, S)$
2.2 $noun\_phrase(S0, S) \leftarrow determiner(S0, S1), noun(S1, S)$
2.3 $verb\_phrase(S0, S) \leftarrow verb(S0, S1), noun\_phrase(S1, S)$
2.4 $verb\_phrase(S0, S) \leftarrow verb(S0, S)$
2.5 $determiner([the|S], S) \leftarrow$
2.6 $noun([apple|S], S) \leftarrow$
2.7 $noun([man|S], S) \leftarrow$
2.8 $verb([eats|S], S) \leftarrow$
2.9 $verb([sings|S], S) \leftarrow$

For this program if we want to parse the string '*the man eats the apple*', we have to submit the following query:

$$\leftarrow sentence([the, man, eats, the, apple], [])$$

Now we present a third Prolog program for parsing strings of the language generated by the same context-free grammar G given above. This program uses the so called *definite clause grammars* (or DCG's) which, indeed, were introduced for making it easier the specification and the solution of parsing problems [**5**, Section 9.1]. Rules 3.1–3.9 below encode the rules of the given context-free grammar. We write each rule using the arrow '-->' to separate the left hand side from the right hand side, and we write a dot at the right end of each rule.

Parsing Sentences (Use of definite clause grammars). Program $P3$

3.1	*sentence*	$\texttt{-->}$	*noun-phrase, verb-phrase.*
3.2	*noun-phrase*	$\texttt{-->}$	*determiner, noun.*
3.3	*verb-phrase*	$\texttt{-->}$	*verb, noun-phrase.*
3.4	*verb-phrase*	$\texttt{-->}$	*verb.*
3.5	*determiner*	$\texttt{-->}$	*[the].*
3.6	*noun*	$\texttt{-->}$	*[apple].*
3.7	*noun*	$\texttt{-->}$	*[man].*
3.8	*verb*	$\texttt{-->}$	*[eats].*
3.9	*verb*	$\texttt{-->}$	*[sings].*

If we want to parse the string '*the man eats the apple*', we have to submit the following query:

$$\leftarrow sentence([the, man, eats, the, apple], [\,])$$

If we also want to construct the parse tree of the sentence being parsed, we need the following program which uses a definite clause grammar with arguments:

Parsing Sentences with Parse Trees (Use of definite clause grammars). Program $P4$

4.1	$sentence(st(NP, VP))$	$\texttt{-->}$	$noun\text{-}phrase(NP),\;\; verb\text{-}phrase(VP).$
4.2	$noun\text{-}phrase(np(D, N))$	$\texttt{-->}$	$determiner(D),\;\; noun(N).$
4.3	$verb\text{-}phrase(vp(V, NP))$	$\texttt{-->}$	$verb(V),\;\; noun\text{-}phrase(VP).$
4.4	$verb\text{-}phrase(vp(V))$	$\texttt{-->}$	$verb(V).$
4.5	$determiner(d(the))$	$\texttt{-->}$	$[the].$
4.6	$noun(n(apple))$	$\texttt{-->}$	$[apple].$
4.7	$noun(n(man))$	$\texttt{-->}$	$[man].$
4.8	$verb(v(eats))$	$\texttt{-->}$	$[eats].$
4.9	$verb(v(sings))$	$\texttt{-->}$	$[sings].$

If we want to parse the string '*the man eats the apple*' and we want to construct the parse tree of that string, we have to submit the following query:

$$\leftarrow sentence(X, [the, man, eats, the, apple], [\,])$$

and we get the following parse tree represented as a term bound to the variable X (see also Figure 10.1.1 on the next page):

$$X = st(np(d(the), n(man)), vp(v(eats), np(d(the), n(apple))))$$

□

10.2. Decidability Results for $LL(k)$ and $LR(k)$ Grammars and Languages

In this section we present some decidability and undecidability results about the $LL(k)$ and the $LR(k)$ grammars and languages (see also [**10**, Section 8.5]). Some

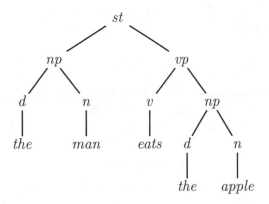

FIGURE 10.1.1. The parse tree of the string '*the man eats the apple*'.

other decidability and undecidability results concerning the context-free languages can be found in [21].

THEOREM 10.2.1. [**Undecidability of Equivalence of Context-Free and** $LL(k)$ **Grammars**] (i) It is undecidable whether or not given a context-free grammar G, there exist $k \geq 0$ and an $LL(k)$ grammar $G1$ such that $L(G) = L(G1)$ (see [22, Theorem 13] and [3, page 361]).

(ii) It is undecidable whether or not given a context-free grammar G and a number $k \geq 0$, there exists an $LL(k)$ grammar $G1$ such that $L(G) = L(G1)$ ([22, Theorem 13] and [3, page 361]).

Recall that we have the following decidability result which we stated in Theorem 4.1.5 on page 48): it is decidable whether or not given a context-free grammar G, there is an equivalent $LL(0)$ grammar.

This decidability result is consistent with Point (ii) of Theorem 10.2.1 above, where we have $k \geq 0$ (not $k > 0$), because an instance of the problem of Point (ii) is a pair $\langle G, k \rangle$, where G is a context-free grammar and k is any non-negative integer.

A set of problems, which does *not* include the problem of Point (ii), is the set $\{P_k \mid k \geq 0\}$, where for each $k \geq 0$, the set of instances of problem P_k is the set of the context-free grammars, and problem P_k is decidable if there exists an algorithm A_k such that for each given context-free grammar G, algorithm A_k tells us whether or not G has an equivalent $LL(k)$ grammar. In problem P_k the number k is *not* an input to the algorithm A_k. Thus, it may be the case that for some k, the problem P_k is decidable, while for some h, different from k, the problem P_h is undecidable.

In particular, the decidability result of Theorem 4.1.5 which we have recalled above, shows that problem P_0 is decidable. We have that, for any $k > 0$, problem P_k is undecidable (see [22, Theorem 13]).

THEOREM 10.2.2. [**Undecidability of Equivalence of Context-Free and** $LR(k)$ **Grammars**] (i) It is undecidable whether or not given a context-free grammar G, there exist $k \geq 0$ and an $LR(k)$ grammar $G1$ such that $L(G) = L(G1)$ (see [12] and [3, pages 397–399, Exercise 5.2.12]).

(ii) It is undecidable whether or not given a context-free grammar G and a number $k \geq 0$, there exists an $LR(k)$ grammar $G1$ such that $L(G) = L(G1)$ [**3**, pages 397–399, Exercise 5.2.12].

The undecidability result of Point (i) of the above Theorem 10.2.2 on the preceding page can be derived as follows. We have that:

(1) the class of the $LR(0)$ languages (which is the class of prefix-free, deterministic context-free languages) is contained in the class of the $LR(1)$ languages (which is the class of deterministic context-free languages), and thus

(2) $\{L \mid L$ is an $LR(k)$ language and $k \geq 0\} =$
$\{L \mid L$ is an $LR(k)$ language and $k > 0\} =$
$\{L \mid L$ is an $LR(1)$ language$\}$.

Hence, undecidability holds because, otherwise, it would have been decidable the problem of knowing whether or not a context-free grammar generates a deterministic context-free language.

The undecidability result of Point (ii) can be derived as follows. Since for any $k > 0$, the class of the $LR(k)$ languages is equal to the class of the $LR(1)$ languages, the problem of Point (ii) is undecidable when k can be any positive number, because otherwise the problem of testing whether or not a context-free grammar generates a deterministic context-free language would have been decidable. Now, obviously, if the problem of Point (ii) is undecidable when k can be any positive number, then it is undecidable also when k can be any non-negative number.

Note that it is also undecidable whether or not, given a context-free grammar G, there exists an $LR(0)$ grammar $G1$ such that $L(G)\,\$ = L(G1)$, with $\$ \notin V_T$. This undecidability result is a consequence of the fact that the undecidability of the problem, call it problem (A), of deciding whether or not, given a context-free grammar G_A, there exists an $LR(1)$ grammar $G1_A$ such that $L(G_A) = L(G1_A)$, can be reduced to the undecidability of the problem, call it problem (B), of deciding whether or not, given a context-free grammar G_B, there exists an $LR(0)$ grammar $G1_B$ such that $L(G_B)\,\$ = L(G1_B)$, with $\$ \notin V_T$.

This reduction is based on the total, computable function r that, given the grammar G_A with axiom S, which is the input to problem (A), constructs a grammar G_B with axiom S', which is the input to problem (B), by adding to G_A the production $S' \to S\,\$$, with $\$ \notin V_T$. Note that, by construction, $L(G_B)$ is a prefix-free language. Now, we get the undecidability of problem (B), because there is a positive answer to problem (A) with input grammar G_A iff there is a positive answer to problem (B) with input grammar $r(G_A)$. Indeed, it is well known that a language L is an $LR(1)$ language, that is, L is a deterministic context-free language, iff $L\$$ is an $LR(0)$ language, that is, $L\$$ is a prefix-free, deterministic context-free language.

THEOREM 10.2.3. [**Undecidability of Existence of k for $LL(k)$-Testing and $LR(k)$-Testing of Context-Free Grammars**] (i) It is undecidable whether or not given a context-free grammar G, there exists $k \geq 0$ such that G is an $LL(k)$ grammar (see [**22**, Theorem 11] and [**25**, page 399]).

(ii) It is undecidable whether or not given a context-free grammar G, there exists $k \geq 0$ such that G is an $LR(k)$ grammar [**25**, page 399].

We have, however, the following decidability results.

THEOREM 10.2.4. [**Decidability of Fixed-k $LL(k)$-Testing and Fixed-k $LR(k)$-Testing of Context-Free Grammars**] (i) It is decidable whether or not given $k \geq 0$ and a context-free grammar G, the grammar G is an $LL(k)$ grammar. (ii) It is decidable whether or not given $k \geq 0$ and a context-free grammar G, the grammar G is an $LR(k)$ grammar.

Obviously, also the *negation* of the two problems considered in this Theorem 10.2.4 are decidable.

Thus, we have that it is decidable whether or not given $k \geq 0$ and a context-free grammar G, the grammar G is *not* an $LL(k)$ grammar, and it is decidable whether or not given $k \geq 0$ and a context-free grammar G, the grammar G is *not* an $LR(k)$ grammar.

In [**25**, page 399] it is shown that these two *negated* problems are decidable in nondeterministic 1-exponential time when k is given in binary, that is, they are decidable in $O(2^{p(n)})$ time by a nondeterministic Turing Machine, where $p(n)$ is a polynomial on n, where n is the sum of the size of the input grammar G (that is, the total number of characters occurring in its productions) plus the size of k written in binary.

In Column 1 of Table 5.1 on page 148 we have shown the deterministic time complexity of testing whether or not a given context-free grammar is $LL(1)$ and also the deterministic time complexity of testing whether or not a given context-free grammar is $LR(1)$.

THEOREM 10.2.5. [**Decidability of Existence of k for $LL(k)$-Testing of $LR(h)$ Grammars**] It is decidable whether or not given $h \geq 0$ and an $LR(h)$ grammar G, there exists $k \geq 0$ such that G is an $LL(k)$ grammar [**22**, Theorem 12] and [**4**, page 690]. (In [**3**, page 397] it is incorrectly stated that the latter problem is undecidable.)

The following Facts 10.2.6 and 10.2.7 are a consequence of what has been shown in [**23**], that is, the decidability of the equivalence of two deterministic context-free grammars, because every $LL(k)$ or $LR(k)$ grammar generates a deterministic context-free language.

FACT 10.2.6. [**Decidability of Equivalence for $LL(k)$ Grammars**] For all $k \geq 0$, given any two $LL(k)$ grammars $G1$ and $G2$, it is decidable whether or not $L(G1) = L(G2)$ [**3**, page 362] (see also Fact 4.3.26 on page 80).

Note that if $G1$ is an $LL(k)$ grammar, for some $k \geq 0$, and $G2$ is an $LL(h)$ grammar, for some $h \geq 0$, we can consider both grammars $G1$ and $G2$ to be $LL(\max(k,h))$ grammars.

FACT 10.2.7. [**Decidability of Equivalence for $LR(k)$ Grammars**] For all $k \geq 0$, given any two $LR(k)$ grammars $G1$ and $G2$, it is decidable whether or not $L(G1) = L(G2)$ (see also Fact 5.8.16 on page 155).

As in the case of $LL(k)$ grammars, if $G1$ is an $LR(k)$ grammar, for some $k \geq 0$, and $G2$ is an $LR(h)$ grammar, for some $h \geq 0$, we can consider both grammars $G1$ and $G2$ to be $LR(\max(k,h))$ grammars.

We have also the following decidability result [26, 29] (see also [21]).

THEOREM 10.2.8. [**Decidability of Regularity of a Deterministic Context-Free Language**] It is decidable whether or not given $k \geq 0$ and an $LR(k)$ grammar G, the language $L(G)$ is regular, that is, it is decidable whether or not a deterministic context-free language is regular.

List of Algorithms and Programs

© Springer Nature Switzerland AG 2021
A. Pettorossi, *Techniques for Searching, Parsing, and Matching*, https://doi.org/10.1007/978-3-030-63189-5

Index

© Springer Nature Switzerland AG 2021
A. Pettorossi, *Techniques for Searching, Parsing, and Matching*, https://doi.org/10.1007/978-3-030-63189-5

Bibliography

[1] A. Aho, J. E. Hopcroft, and J. D. Ullman. *Design and Analysis of Computer Algorithms.* Addison-Wesley, 1974.

[2] A. Aho, R. Sethi, and J. D. Ullman. *Compilers: Principles, Techniques, and Tools.* Addison-Wesley, 1986.

[3] A. V. Aho and J. D. Ullman. *The Theory of Parsing, Translation and Compiling,* Volume 1. Prentice Hall, 1972.

[4] A. V. Aho and J. D. Ullman. *The Theory of Parsing, Translation and Compiling,* Volume 2. Prentice Hall, 1973.

[5] W. F. Clocksin and C. S. Mellish. *Programming in Prolog.* Springer-Verlag, New York, Second edition, 1984.

[6] E. W. Dijkstra. A Short Introduction to the Art of Programming. Technical Report, EWD 316, 1971.

[7] C. Donnelly and R. Stallman. Bison: The Yacc-compatible Parser Generator (Version 3.5). Technical report, Free Software Foundation, 51 Franklin Street, Boston, MA 02110-1301, USA, 7 December 2019. ISBN 1-882114-44-2.
`http://www.gnu.org/software/bison/manual/index.html`.

[8] J. B. Fraleigh. *A First Course in Abstract Algebra.* Addison-Wesley, 1977. Second Edition.

[9] M. A. Harrison. *Introduction to Formal Language Theory.* Addison-Wesley, 1978.

[10] J. E. Hopcroft and J. D. Ullman. *Introduction to Automata Theory, Languages and Computation.* Addison-Wesley, 1979.

[11] S. C. Johnson. *YACC: Yet another compiler-compiler. Unix Programmer's Manual,* Volume 2b. AT&T, 1979.

[12] D. E. Knuth. On the translation of languages from left to right. *Information and Control,* 8:607–639, 1965.

[13] D. E. Knuth. Semantics of context-free languages. *Mathematical Systems Theory,* 2:127–145, 1968. Correction: *Mathematical Systems Theory,* 5:95–96, 1971.

[14] D. E. Knuth, J. H. Morris, and V. R. Pratt. Fast pattern matching in strings. *SIAM Journal on Computing,* 6(2):323–350, 1977.

[15] M. E. Lesk and E. Schmidt. LEX – Lexical Analyzer Generator. In A. G. Hume and M. D. McIlroy, editors, *Unix Programmer's Manual.* Tenth Edition. Volume 2. AT&T Bell Laboratories, Murray Hill, NJ, 1990.

[16] C. H. Papadimitriou and K. Steiglitz. *Combinatorial Optimization: Algorithms and Complexity.* Prentice-Hall, 1982.

[17] L. C. Paulson. The foundation of a generic theorem prover. *J. Automated Reasoning,* 5:363–397, 1989.

© Springer Nature Switzerland AG 2021
A. Pettorossi, *Techniques for Searching, Parsing, and Matching,* https://doi.org/10.1007/978-3-030-63189-5

[18] V. Paxson, W. Estes, and J. Millaway. Lexical Analysis with Flex. Edition 2.5.37. Technical report, The Flex Project, 22 July 2012. Latest releases available from: `https://github.com/westes/flex/releases`.

[19] A. Pettorossi. *Programming in C++*. Aracne Editrice, 2001. ISBN 88-7999-323-7.

[20] A. Pettorossi. *Quaderni di Informatica. Parte I*. Aracne, Second edition, 2004.

[21] A. Pettorossi. *Automata Theory and Formal Languages*. Aracne Editrice, Fourth edition, 2013.

[22] D. J. Rosenkrantz and R. E. Stearns. Properties of deterministic top-down parsing. *Information and Control*, 17:226–256, 1970.

[23] G. Sénizergues. The equivalence problem for deterministic pushdown automata is decidable. In *Proceedings ICALP '97*, Lecture Notes in Computer Science 1256, pages 671–681, 1997.

[24] S. Sippu and E. Soisalon-Soininen. *Theory of Parsing: Languages and Parsing*, Volume 1. Springer-Verlag, 1988.

[25] S. Sippu and E. Soisalon-Soininen. *Theory of Parsing: LR(k) and LL(k) Parsing*, Volume 2. Springer-Verlag, 1990.

[26] R. E. Stearns. A regularity test for pushdown machines. *Information and Control*, 11:3, 323–340, 1967.

[27] L. S. Sterling and E. Shapiro. *The Art of Prolog*. The MIT Press, Cambridge, Massachusetts, 1994. Second Edition.

[28] L. G. Valiant. General context-free recognition in less than cubic time. *Journal of Computer and System Sciences*, 10:308–315, 1975.

[29] L. G. Valiant. Regularity and related problems for deterministic pushdown automata. *JACM*, 22(1):1–10, 1975.

Printed in the United States
by Baker & Taylor Publisher Services